IMAGES WITH IMPACT

Design and Use of Winning Trial Visuals

Kerri L. Ruttenberg

Cover design by Tahiti Spears/ABA Design.
Interior design by Betsy Kulak/ABA Design.

Printed in the United States of America.

21 20 19 18 17 5 4 3 2 1

ISBN: 978-1-63425-741-1

e-ISBN: 978-1-63425-742-8

Discounts are available for books ordered in bulk. Special consideration is given to state bars, CLE programs, and other bar-related organizations. Inquire at Book Publishing, ABA Publishing, American Bar Association, 321 N. Clark Street, Chicago, Illinois 60654-7598.

www.shopABA.org

For Harry

Contents

About the Author

Kerri Ruttenberg is a trial lawyer based in Washington, D.C., and a partner in a top-tier global law firm. With a local and national practice, Kerri has tried cases in state and federal courts around the country. Kerri centers her practice on white-collar and complex criminal defense and parallel civil enforcement actions. She has secured defense jury verdicts in cases involving a broad spectrum of allegations ranging from securities fraud, conspiracy and False Claims Act violations to kidnapping, grand larceny and first-degree murder. In addition, Kerri has represented clients in litigation, bench trials and arbitrations involving patent infringement, antitrust violations, theft of trade secrets and contract and fiduciary duty claims.

Kerri has consistently been selected to *Washington DC Super Lawyers* every year since 2013. Beyond her significant trial victories, Kerri also has a successful appellate practice, and has been selected to the *National Law Journal*'s "Appellate Hot List."

Based on nearly 20 years of trial experience and juror interviews, as well as her own study of graphic design and frequent work with designers, Kerri conducts seminars and a continuing legal education program on the design and use of visuals for effective communication. Lawyers, law students, professors and expert witnesses and consultants have attended Kerri's presentations, later implementing her strategies in jury and bench trials, significant motions, expert reports and even in the classroom.

When she's not practicing law, giving presentations on visual communication or reading books on graphic design, Kerri is an avid landscape and travel photographer. She has had a gallery showing in Maryland, and much of her photography is featured at an internationally-recognized healthcare institute based in Baltimore.

Kerri can be reached via LinkedIn or by email at kerri.ruttenberg@gmail.com.

Acknowledgments

One of my law partners recently asked me whether I was the sole author of this book, or whether I was working with a team of contributors. The answer, resoundingly, is both. This book—although authored by me—absolutely would not have been possible without the help, support, and contributions of many. And this section is where I get to thank them in print—not just over the phone, or in an email, or with a hug or a shipment of minicupcakes (though I'm told those were delicious!). So, that's what I'll do.

To begin, I must profusely thank the phenomenal graphic design teams at Barnes & Roberts, Chicago Winter, Core Legal Concepts, and RLM | TrialGraphix. I knew when I first thought about writing this book over five years ago that it wouldn't work without the involvement of professional designers, and ideally with multiple designers in order to showcase different styles and approaches. A book about graphics with no graphics would be pretty useless. But a book about graphics with sloppy, inadequate graphics would be both useless and embarrassing. Thanks to the contributions of the talented designers at these terrific firms, who have decades of experience in thousands of trials all over the country, we've put together a book I'm so proud of, and a book that will hopefully inform and inspire its readers for years to come. For that, I owe a huge debt of gratitude to Jason Barnes, Dan Winter, Kim Levine, and Guy Joubert, as well as their talented and creative teams of graphic designers.

This book also would not have happened without the selfless guidance, encouragement, mentoring, and infectious energy of my friend Adam Gropper, who was positive I'd publish this book before I'd even pitched it. His belief in the idea of this book (and in my ability to pull it off!) was steadfast, and for that I am eternally grateful.

Thank you to the senior trial lawyers, like my partner Hank Asbill, who have inspired me for years and who have recognized the importance of trial graphics long before most (and who trusted me with the freedom and creativity to turn our case themes into visual images). Thank you to the designers I've worked with so closely in trial who have graciously shared their expertise. And thank you to those who have supported my interest in and appreciation for this topic by inviting me to speak to groups of practicing lawyers, professors, and law students. There are too many to list them all, but a special thank-you to Joan Meier, Ellen Podgor, David Markus, and Norman Reimer for your continued and unwavering support.

I also want to express my gratitude to the many people at Jones Day who have supported and believed in this book. Thank you to Joe Altobelli, Greg Wing, Christine Panchur, and Julianna Kovach Zingale, all of whom helped me with some of my own graphic designs. Thank you to Michael Stork, Maria Monaghan, Katie Smithgall, and Jordan Patterson for your research assistance with the mini-treatise that became Chapter 24. And, especially, thank you to Steve Brogan, Greg Shumaker, Mike Shumaker, and Rob Ducatman for supporting the idea for this book from the outset. There are few words that can adequately express how proud I am to be a part of your team and how grateful I am for the opportunity.

Thank you to the American Bar Association, and especially Shannon Lessman, Bryan Kay, Marisa L'Heureux, Betsy Kulak, and Rick Paszkiet, for your help and guidance. Betsy, thank you for your patience, understanding, and creativity with the book's layout; you helped me turn a dream into reality, and I'm truly grateful. And Rick, thank you for believing in this book when it was just an idea from an enthusiastic lawyer who has never written a book in her life.

Finally, thank you to my family, and especially my husband Ed, for their ever-present support and encouragement, particularly when juggling this book and my law practice often meant very little sleep and nonexistent work-life balance. I love you all.

Introduction

How do you help jurors whose professional background in is music, medicine, or mechanics understand the nuances of section 10b of the Securities Exchange Act?

How do you convince a juror who is skeptical of lawyers to put his trust in you and believe your impassioned arguments?

How do you help a juror remember key evidence and case themes after days, weeks, or even months of trial in enough detail to vote your way and confidently argue your position in the jury room?

The consistent answer to these questions—according to jury consultants, psychologists, neurologists, and even jurors themselves—is to add a visual component to your case presentation.

But how is it done?

There are many, many books, articles, and even blogs on improving visual presentations. I have read many of them myself over the years, and I cite a number of them in this book. I keep design books on a shelf within easy reach, and I regularly consult them when I'm designing a new presentation. I have no doubt that these books have helped me increase the effectiveness of my own visuals, and thereby my communication.

But there's a conundrum. Presentation advice that makes perfect sense when addressing students, clients, investors, boards of directors, or conference attendees often doesn't translate to the trial setting. Likewise, design tips that work well in business meetings, or for commercial materials such as menus, pamphlets, or marketing brochures, don't take into account evidentiary rules, time limitations, and the overall tone of jury trials. Many presentation books, for instance, suggest using powerful photographs to appeal directly to the viewer's emotions. In a jury trial, that approach would likely violate evidentiary rules, and the visual would be excluded. The bottom line is that what works great for workshops and webinars (or board meetings, keynote speeches, sales pitches, etc.) is often counterproductive—and sometimes even affirmatively disallowed—in the unique setting of a jury trial.

So that's why I wrote this book. I wanted to create a resource for trial lawyers—and perhaps other presenters—that will help turn your trial themes into visual images that a jury is more likely to understand, believe, and remember. I also wanted to pass along some of the graphic design techniques I've learned through the years that will help you improve your own visuals. And, with a target audience of lawyers, I wanted to provide some strategic considerations for using visuals in court.

In that vein, this book is divided into four parts.

- **Part I:** I start this book with an explanation of why visual communication matters, particularly in the unique context of a jury trial, and why turning themes into pictures helps win cases. Studies on visual perception provide a fascinating look into human communication, and, for our purposes, they have a lot to tell us about how we can best reach our jurors.
- **Part II:** The second part of this book is about the most common tools for communicating visually with juries, from charts and graphs to maps and diagrams. I use many examples from my own trials, and I've created many more images just for this book. But I also wanted to present a range of design styles and approaches. Indeed, there's never just one "right" way to approach a particular theme. So, I worked with four fantastic graphic design firms, each with decades of experience creating visuals for thousands of jury trials. Multiple artists at each firm contributed images to this book, sometimes even illustrating the same concept. By providing a variety of stylistic approaches to communicating different substantive themes, my goal is to give you a jumping-off point to brainstorm your own case themes in a more visual way.
- **Part III:** In the third section of this book, I share some graphic design basics that will improve the look, feel, and effectiveness of your self-created visuals. This knowledge will also help you more accurately and efficiently communicate with graphic designers when you have them on your trial teams.
- **Part IV:** Finally, I set forth some strategic considerations, including how to spot misleading visuals. Knowing what to look for will help you avoid these problems when creating your own images and will help you exclude (or exploit) misleading visuals by your opponents. I also provide practical tips for creating visuals and using them in the courtroom, both in high- and low-tech presentations. And, in the last chapter, I'll review state and federal law on demonstrative evidence.

Before we begin, here are a few important notes about reading this book.

First, this book is not intended to teach you how to use PowerPoint, Keynote, or any other computer program. I do provide a few technology tips and tricks here and there that can do wonders for your slide design. But this book is really about the *substance* of your visuals and how you use them in court, not which button to press to create them. To that end, nearly every suggestion in this book applies just as much to visuals you show jurors on enlarged boards or flip charts as it applies to visuals created with computer software (which I'll often refer to as "slides," as that's the terminology typically associated with visuals displayed through computer software on a monitor or projection screen). Even if you're working with a graphic design team to physically create all of your visuals, this book will still arm you with valuable strategic, substantive, and design insight to more effectively and efficiently direct your team to create winning visuals.

Second, the benefits of visual communication, and the graphic design techniques that make our visuals more effective, aren't limited to the jury trial context. Most of the suggestions and examples in this book apply to visuals you might use in bench trials, hearings, or even written submissions like summary judgment motions or expert reports. Recognize the tremendous value of using visuals in those contexts, as well, modifying the content and tone as appropriate.

Finally, many images in this book were shown to juries during real trials, but I've changed all names, companies, and industries. Any photographs of people appearing in this book come from stock images and are not the real plaintiffs, defendants, or witnesses from the corresponding trials. Likewise, all names, companies, and disputes depicted in visuals created for this book are fictitious, and any similarities to real cases or people are purely coincidental.

I hope you enjoy reading this book as much as I enjoyed writing it. And now, onto the visuals!

PART I

Why We Should Use Visuals to Turn Themes into Pictures

At its core, this book is about helping you win trials with effective visual images. Each chapter builds to give you substantive ideas, design guidance, and practical and legal tips for improving your jury visuals. But before I dive into discussing the tools at our disposal, or graphic design techniques, or how courts view demonstrative evidence, it's important to understand why all this matters.

Many studies have been conducted over the years on the importance of visual perception and visual communication. The consistent takeaway is that using visuals makes a difference in how humans communicate and the effectiveness of that communication. And then there's the jury setting itself—it is like no other. And that matters, too. Appreciating how jury trials are fundamentally different from other communication settings is critical to the effective design of our trial visuals.

Collectively, that's the focus of Part I of this book. I'll address the key limitations on our jurors (and on ourselves) that impact how we design and use visuals in this unique setting. I'll also discuss the critical insights we glean from studies about the power of jury visuals and why using them can make a huge difference in our cases. Finally, I'll talk about what it means to turn case themes into pictures, creating visual memories for our jurors.

1

Why Visual Communication Matters

Effective communication with a jury is essential to winning a trial. But the contrived setting and constraining procedural rules impose unique and substantial challenges. How do we communicate unfamiliar, voluminous, and complex material to an audience that may not begin their jury service with the background to understand it? And, the challenge gets worse. As the complexity of the case increases, the jurors' interest, comprehension, and retention all decrease. This does not bode well for accomplishing our ultimate goal of persuading the jury to decide a case in our client's favor.

The central premise of this book is that everything we say to jurors, and everything we show them, should satisfy at least one of three basic goals: we must help jurors **understand**, **believe**, and **remember** our message.

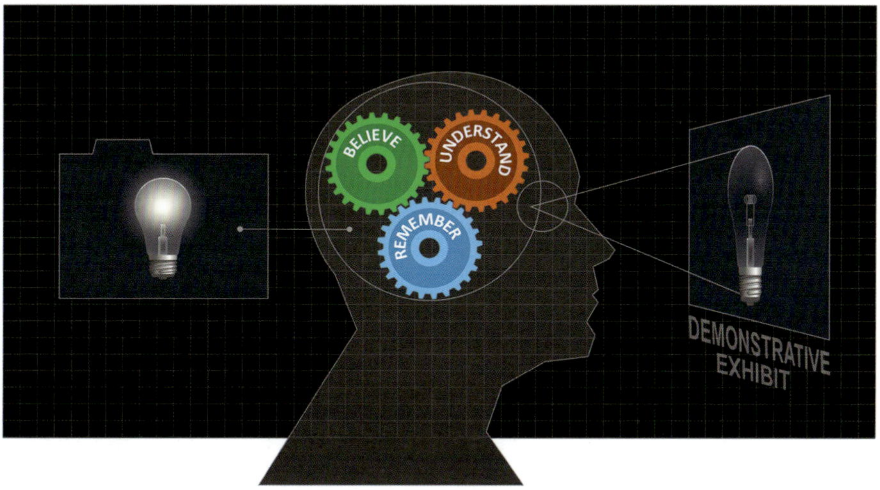

The importance of visual presentations for accomplishing these goals cannot be overstated. Many disciplines have long recognized the benefits of visuals for effective communication, from cognitive psychology and neurobiology to linguistics and the graphic arts. But the legal profession? Not so much. Most often, a lawyer's idea of a "visual" amounts to a text-based PowerPoint slide. And that's not surprising, given the nature of trial proceedings.

We give opening statements and closing arguments orally, maybe showing some text slides along the way. We elicit testimony from live witnesses through verbal questions and answers, sometimes for hours at a time. We read parts of documents into the record, either ourselves or through witnesses. Jurors are receiving all of this information primarily through auditory means, and it has very little visual impact. Sure, new witnesses take the stand, multiple lawyers are involved, and there's back-and-forth dialogue during direct and cross-examination. But very little of what's presented has visual interest beyond watching the participants speak and looking at the documents we introduce into evidence. Sometimes those documents are visually interesting. Most of the time they're not.

Certainly, some legal fields naturally are more conducive to explaining material with visual aids. But even then, the use of visuals—other than actual models or physical evidence—tends to be limited to pictures of direct evidence in the case, such as an image of the logo at issue in a trademark case, a photograph of a crime scene, or a patent diagram.

Visuals can do so much more. They're essential tools for increasing comprehension, credibility, and recall, and they involve simple techniques that are often overlooked or misapplied in the trial setting. Fortunately, there are ways to design and use visuals that will help jurors understand and remember critical facts and legal themes. They'll also increase our own credibility, including building the jurors' trust in us as their native guides through the case.

The key to increasing the effectiveness of jury communication is learning to turn case themes into visual images. This doesn't mean displaying irrelevant photos or recklessly bombarding jurors with imagery just to keep their attention—in fact, such tactics are often counterproductive for a variety of reasons that will be discussed throughout this book. Instead, identify the themes you want to communicate to your jurors, and think about how to translate them visually.

It's about taking a theme from this . . .

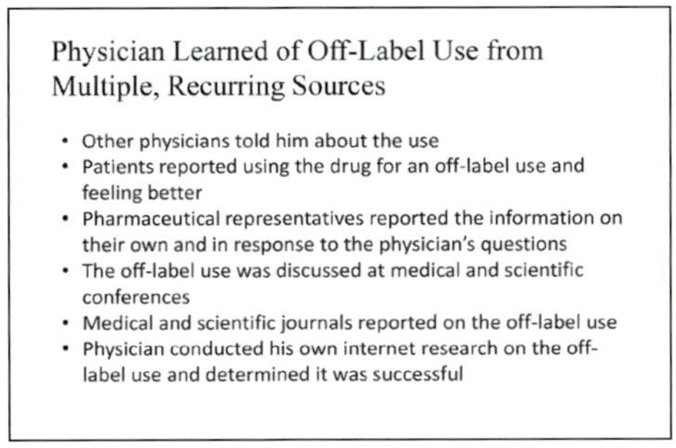

. . . to this.

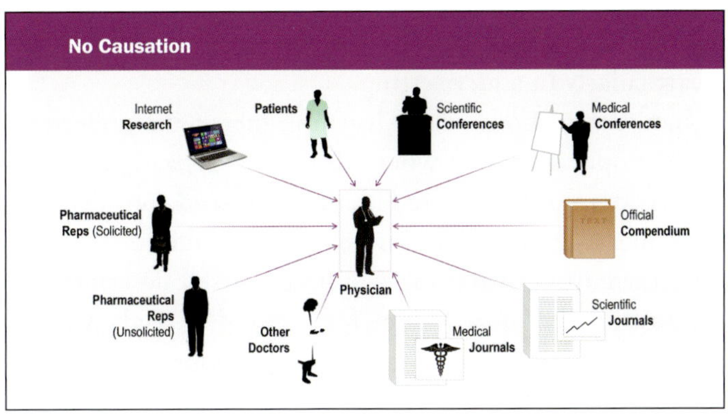

Design is about more than just making the slide look pretty; it's about enhancing the clarity of the message. When visuals are designed well and used effectively, they buttress our oral communication. I'll be sharing many design and presentation techniques with you and providing examples of how they can be successfully adapted to jury trials. The goal, of course, is effective communication in an extraordinarily unique environment.

Learning Styles

For years, those who studied learning styles explained that people generally learn through visual (seeing), auditory (hearing), or kinesthetic (feeling) modalities, and that individuals usually prefer one modality over the other two. Thus, the argument went, when presenting information to someone else, we should present it in the recipient's preferred modality, or learning style, which is how they will best learn the material. Under this approach, which became known as "meshing," if someone's an auditory learner, simply speaking to them should be sufficient. If the person is visual, add visuals to the presentation regardless of the subject matter. And if they're kinesthetic, try to involve the person in the presentation, getting them to participate and learn by doing. (That's not really an option in a jury trial beyond notetaking, but that's a separate issue.)

While all this makes some intuitive sense, more recent studies have raised questions about the validity of learning styles theory. In 2008, for example, the Association for Psychosocial Science brought together a group of psychologists and cognitive scientists to review and evaluate the prolific evidence of learning styles. Their conclusion? "Although the literature on learning styles is enormous, very few studies have even used an experimental methodology capable of testing the validity of learning styles applied to education. Moreover, of those that did use an appropriate method, several found results that flatly contradict the popular meshing hypothesis."[1] The problem, according to this evaluation, is that there's no proof that we can really measure which learning style is most effective for a specific individual. And, of course, there's not always a realistic way to modify how we're presenting information to match someone's learning style, particularly in a jury setting.

So, rather than worry about which learning method is preferred by individual jurors, or even the population as a whole (learning styles theory posits that visual learning is the most commonly preferred method), instead consider which style works best for presenting the substance of your message. Certain information naturally lends itself to a visual presentation. Anything you find yourself describing (locations, relationships, processes) can be great fodder for a visual at trial. And if there are key themes and theories you really want to make sure your jurors "get," think about turning those into visual images, as well. As the studies discussed below demonstrate, irrespective of learning styles theory, there's no doubt we can increase the effectiveness of our communication by incorporating visuals into our trial presentations.

Jurors' Challenges to Learning

Memory

Studies on jurors aren't plentiful, but what's out there is frightening. Jurors *immediately* forget as much as two-thirds of the facts we present to them.[2] That means two-thirds of what we tell jurors doesn't even make it into their short-term memory, much less their medium- or long-term memory for eventual consideration during deliberations. Add to this the challenge of remembering complex, unfamiliar information presented in an often boring setting (yes, I said it!), and juror recall plummets even further. Memory also degrades as people age—so jurisdictions that skew heavily toward older jury pools present an additional challenge for trial lawyers. While we don't need a degree in neurology to be effective trial lawyers, knowing a bit about human memory is helpful for understanding how certain visual designs—and how we use visuals in the courtroom—can be most effective with our jury.

There are actually several different types of memory. When we first perceive something, that perception is in our sensory memory. We perceive far more information than we could ever use or remember,[3] and most of this information goes no further. This is a good thing—we don't need to remember everything we see, touch, hear, smell, or taste, so instantly forgetting it helps us filter information and focus on what actually matters.

When we do pay attention to something we sense, that information passes into our short-term memory. It's only there for a matter of seconds, sometimes up to a minute, which is just long enough for us to act on the information.

To move information from short-term to medium- or long-term memory, we must consciously try to retain it. Thus, jurors must actively convert facts, case themes, and impressions into their medium- or long-term memory, or that information won't be there during deliberations.

The transfer of information from short-term to long-term memory is influenced by a variety of factors, including our motivation to remember it. How this occurs in the human brain is complex and (fortunately for us) is beyond the scope of this book. For present purposes, suffice it to say there are techniques that will help us enhance jurors' recall of key information. These include repeating key facts and themes, simplifying and controlling the flow of information presented, and—you guessed it—using visuals.

Fatigue

Then, of course, there's the ever-present problem of fatigue. As anyone who has tried more than a handful of cases knows, at some point in trial, at least one juror will nod off. What the jurors never hear stands no chance of being remembered. And even when a sleepy juror manages to keep himself awake—by clenching his teeth, squeezing his arm, or biting his tongue—his eyes might be open, but he sure isn't concentrating on the trial.

And that's just one sleeping juror. I remember reading about a study conducted in 1963 finding that sixty-six percent of jurors fall asleep during trial. I have no idea how accurate that statistic was in 1963, and I certainly don't know how accurate it is now. In fact, the current picture is likely worse, thanks to dramatic technological advances since then that have increased our expectation of receiving information immediately and in a readily digestible, often entertaining, format.

The problem of fatigue is magnified in the midafternoon hours, when our bodies naturally crave sleep. Just as conference attendees and students struggle to stay awake, so too do our jurors. John Medina, a developmental molecular biologist and the author of the fascinating book *Brain Rules*, explains the basic science behind this struggle.[4] He even cites studies demonstrating that affirmatively stopping what we're doing and taking a nap rather than pushing to stay awake will boost cognitive performance. Unfortunately, our jurors (like most of us) have no choice—they must fight through their fatigue and keep listening to our examinations and arguments. Some will lose this battle.

What's more, for some jurors, merely serving on a jury exacerbates an already sleep-deprived existence. Jurors who rely on coffee throughout the day to stay engaged are now trapped for hours at a time in a jury box without access to caffeine. They might work multiple jobs, or night shifts, or have young children at home, or they might be going through extraordinary personal, work, or family stress. Those folks are already exhausted. Now, they have to manage work, family, and other responsibilities in addition to their jury service. So aside from the ordinary biological and neurological limitations at work, some jurors might lose concentration or even fall asleep simply because of the toll jury service takes on their already-packed lives and schedules.

Regardless of the statistics or the reasons, from my own experience of trying cases lasting days, weeks, and even months, the simple fact is that many jurors have a hard time staying awake throughout the trial. This reality has significant implications for our trial presentation.

Inattention

Even when they're awake, there will most certainly be times when your jurors aren't paying attention. It might not be every juror, and it might not be all the time, but you can count on many jurors missing at least some of your evidence presentation and argument simply because their thoughts wander elsewhere.

That said, broad proclamations about limits on peoples' attention spans are meaningless, as our attention spans are context dependent. If something is boring, it shouldn't be surprising that we'll lose interest and stop paying attention rather quickly, perhaps within the first few minutes. On the other hand, if we're interested in or entertained by something, we'll pay close attention for the duration. Entertainment streaming services have gained immense popularity in recent years, in no small part because they allow us to "binge-watch" television programs, watching hours upon hours of a program in one setting. The practice is so common that the term "binge-watch" was added to the Oxford Dictionaries in 2014. When we're interested or entertained, our attention spans seem to know no bounds.

But the converse is also true. Medina puts it succinctly: "People don't pay attention to boring things." That's actually his Brain Rule Number 6. It might sound obvious, but there's substantial science to back it up, and its implications for trial are significant.

It shouldn't surprise anyone that jurors lose focus or doze off during a trial. Trials aren't Hollywood movies, and the process isn't designed to entertain. That's not to say entertaining things don't happen during trial; it's just that the process itself isn't designed for this purpose. We might spend thirty minutes digging into a single paragraph in a dense, complex contract. Our damages expert might discuss a regression

analysis for ten minutes (which will feel like an hour to our jurors). Even in criminal cases, jurors will quickly realize that forensic testimony in a real trial isn't quite as scintillating as it is on TV. Add to that the interruptions for bench conferences, recesses, an out-of-order witness, or a multitude of other issues that arise, and it's that much more difficult for our jurors to stay fully engaged—much less fully awake—for the duration of trial.

Jurors' ability to pay attention and concentrate is affected by all sorts of factors, including fatigue, interest, age, intellect, and drug usage.[5] Post-trial interviews of jurors, not surprisingly, reveal that the lawyers' most important arguments often were missed entirely by some jurors, who don't recall ever even *hearing* them.

We also know that the brain cannot pay attention to two things at once.[6] Yet at some point during trial, a juror's mind will wander. Instead of focusing on the testimony or argument we're presenting, he'll think about a difficult problem at work, or an argument he had with his significant other that morning, or how the plaintiff's lawyer reminds him of a former neighbor. Jurors' minds don't have to wander far—they could even start thinking about their own frustration or boredom with the trial. Whatever the topic, when their attention is diverted from what's happening in trial, they're missing our message.

The Consequences

Think about what all this means by the time you get to your closing argument. Most lawyers view their closing as an opportunity to summarize and highlight trial evidence the jury *already has seen* and *already understands*. In reality, particularly in lengthy and complex trials, many of the jurors will be hearing at least some of the facts we're "summarizing" *for the very first time*. What's more, we typically won't know how much evidence didn't register, which evidence didn't connect, or how many or which jurors didn't get it all.

Not surprisingly, then, "[e]xtensive research indicates that jurors make decisions using a very limited number of facts. Even in extremely complex cases with hundreds of facts presented, jurors will *selectively retain only three or four facts* which they perceive to be the most salient. . . . Simply put, the average juror cannot sort and process large amounts of factual data, but will minimize the complexity of the case, choose a few issues he or she understands or perceives to be most pertinent, and fit all other data into this framework."[7]

How Visuals Help

Fortunately, the research also suggests what we can do to help our jurors, and thereby, help ourselves and our clients. Studies consistently find improvements in recall, both

immediate and over time, when a visual component is added to the information presented.

One of the most often-cited studies on the topic was sponsored by 3M Corporation in 1986.[8] Researchers from the University of Minnesota and at 3M examined how the use of visuals affects the persuasiveness of a presentation. To be clear, the presentation in the 3M study wasn't a trial. It was a ten-minute videotaped presentation, shown to nine groups of college juniors, that attempted to persuade the audience to commit time and money to attending time-management seminars.[9] One group saw the presentation without visual support, and the remaining eight groups saw presentations with one of the types of visuals tested (color vs. black and white, the use of plain text vs. clip art and graphs, and (given the study's age) the use of 35mm slides vs. overhead transparencies).[10] The study found that, overall, presentations using visuals were "43% more persuasive."[11] In particular, the audience's attention, comprehension, yielding (the degree of agreement with the presenter's position), and retention were enhanced by the use of visuals.

In the years since the 3M study, some have questioned the robustness of its results. But subsequent studies on using visuals in presentations support the basic findings of the 3M study—that the use of visuals enhances audience comprehension and retention.[12] Boyll's study, for instance, found that people retained only 14 percent to 33 percent of information presented through purely auditory means, but 85 percent of that same information when it was also presented visually.[13] Similarly, Medina notes that after three days have passed, we remember only 10 percent of information presented verbally, but 65 percent of information presented both visually and verbally.[14] Hence, Medina's Brain Rule Number 9—"Vision trumps all other senses."[15]

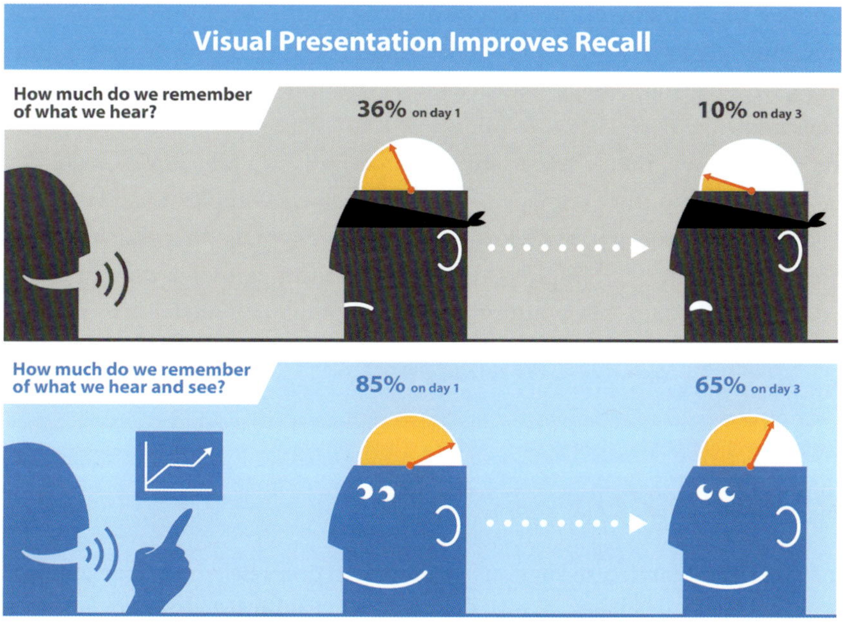

Researchers have known about this "pictorial superiority effect" for over one hundred years. As Medina explains, "the more visual the input becomes, the more likely it is to be recognized—and recalled."[16] And for our present purposes, that matters a lot.

Indeed, multiple studies conducted with mock jurors are consistent with the studies on presentations generally. For example, mock jury studies have found that visual displays can enhance jurors' attention and recall.[17] A 2011 study of 1,375 mock jurors found that the consistent use of visuals increased the jurors' ability to understand and remember the defendant's causation arguments when compared to the same presentation made without the use of visuals.[18] And, mock jurors who received information throughout trial by visual means (such as imagery and charts) had better recall of causation arguments and damages numbers, which were the variables tested.[19]

One mock jury study even found that visuals increase jurors' overall level of engagement, motivating them to decide a case more accurately.[20] This is particularly helpful in light of the reality that jurors, by definition, have no personal stake in the outcome of the case they're deciding—an issue that will be discussed further in the next chapter.

And as for those text-based PowerPoint slides, two unpublished mock jury studies underscore what biology, neurology, and psychology—as well as common sense and our own shared experience—have told us for years. Showing a bunch of words on a screen does not magically create an effective visual. In one study, the plaintiffs featured graphs on their PowerPoint slides to visually illustrate statistical evidence. Those slides were found to have increased the defendant's judged responsibility.[21] In the other study, text slides that merely summarized an expert's testimony had no effect on the jurors' judgments of guilt.[22] It really is true—just typing your message onto a slide, without more, doesn't suddenly turn your spoken message into a visual image.

So that's what the rest of this book is about. Think about your case visually, integrate those visuals into your trial presentation wherever you reasonably can, and design your visuals to maximize the clarity of your message.

2

Uniqueness of the Jury Setting

The jury trial setting is unique. There is simply no other presentation environment quite like it. To maximize the effectiveness of our communication in jury trials, it's important to appreciate the unique features of that setting and its audience and how we can directly address those characteristics through our visuals.

Certainly, most of the design and presentation techniques described in this book apply across a broad spectrum of settings. Whether we're speaking to clients, conference attendees, corporate directors, students, judges, or even our own colleagues, the effectiveness of our communication increases when we design and use visuals well.

When lawyers decide to use visuals in trial, they make a mistake when they fail to take account of the significant and fundamental differences between presenting to a jury and presenting to any other group. Some of those differences don't matter much, but many do. Appreciating those differences is the first step in creating effective visuals for trial.

Fortunately, this is not a daunting task. We already know we have to consider our audience. Just as a comedian might tell jokes differently in Boston than in Birmingham, so too might the trial lawyer modify the substance of a closing argument. We do this because we're already sensitized to the fact that jurors' backgrounds and biases might impact how our messages are received. That's partly why we're given basic information about our jurors before trial and why we elicit as much additional information as we can during voir dire. Age, life experience, socioeconomic background, education, occupation, family history, physical health, and many other factors not only impart biases to individual jurors, they also may impact the jurors' ability to comprehend the trial evidence and even how they'll interpret it. So, if we know none of our jurors has an engineering background and we're trying a patent case, we might adjust our visuals accordingly. And beyond the jurors' own substantive perspectives and biases, we also need to account for limitations inherent in the jury trial setting itself, both in our slide design and our overall presentation strategy.

To state the obvious, it's tough to overcome challenges if you don't first consider what those challenges are. What follows are key differences between presenting to a jury and presenting to other groups. These are the ones I keep in mind and try to address when I design visuals and decide how best to use them in trial. The first three are limitations on the jurors; the last three are limitations on us as presenters, which directly impact our communication. All of the design tips I'll provide in this book are intended to address these considerations so we can best advance our chief goals—helping the jurors understand, believe, and remember our message.

Personal Interest in the Outcome/Subject Matter

Having a personal stake in the information being presented will naturally increase the listener's motivation to absorb it. In most presentation settings, this gives us an immediate advantage. Clients, conference attendees, and students are inherently motivated to understand and remember the information we're presenting. That's not to say it's easy to speak to these groups—we might be presenting complex material, explaining nuanced strategy, or even delivering bad news. But clients are directly impacted by the outcome of their case. Conference attendees chose to attend the conference—perhaps even your break-out session—to learn what you have to tell them. (They might be trying to get their money's worth, to boot.) Students need to pass exams based on the material you're teaching them, and eventually they'll need to put that information into practice. Personal interest gives these audiences a strong motivation to understand and remember the information you're presenting.

In stark contrast, your jurors didn't choose to sit through your trial. At least a few affirmatively tried to get out of it and might even resent being there. And those who made it onto your jury were only qualified to serve if they were *disinterested* in your case. (Had you discovered otherwise during *voir dire*, that juror would have been stricken for cause.) Certainly, jurors might have a sense of civic duty, and they might develop an intellectual or even emotional interest in your case over the course of the trial. But the fact is, jurors generally begin their jury service with no particularized interest in the case they'll be deciding. The result is that we start in a hole when presenting to a jury—a disadvantage we don't face in most other settings.

Skepticism of the Presenter

Effectiveness with a jury requires credibility and trust. A carefully crafted closing argument with powerful language, strategic organization, and a dynamic delivery won't win the day if the jury doesn't believe the lawyer delivering it.

Unfortunately, we often start with a disadvantage. Many jurors have a natural skepticism of lawyers. They know we're advocates for our clients and that our necessary bias gives us a strong interest in the outcome of the case. They know we have an incentive to "spin" information in our clients' favor. When jurors view lawyers in that light, they can be skeptical of everything we do—including how we use exhibits and visuals. When we show part of an email, they might assume the rest of the email would be damaging to us. When we put text on the screen and don't give them time to read it, they get frustrated and assume we're pulling some sleight of hand. When our slide deck is full of confusing visuals and complicated text, they assume we're hiding something or at least that we're trying to distract from a weak message.

Fortunately, there are ways to both design and use visuals that can enhance our credibility and effectiveness as advocates. These techniques, which I'll discuss throughout this book, include using images of the actual trial exhibits and transcripts of testimony in our visuals, displaying exhibit numbers in our design, and even taking the time necessary to help jurors comprehend and absorb any data summaries or explanations we choose to show them.

Familiarity with Subject Matter

Another significant difference between presenting to jurors and other audiences—clients, for example—is their level of familiarity with the subject matter of the presentation. Here, that means the case facts and applicable law. Clients often already are familiar, if not experts, with the case facts or at least with the relevant industry and its players. Clients might even have some familiarity with the law, thanks to legal or compliance training, or even through working with counsel during the course of the case. In fact, clients typically educate their lawyers just as much as lawyers educate their clients, particularly in the beginning of the representation.

Jurors, on the other hand, might have no background with the client's industry or the relevant law. If they do, their understanding might be materially wrong. And, aside from pre-trial publicity, jurors likely will have no familiarity with the case facts.

So, in a complicated case, or one involving a likely unfamiliar industry, we'll need to help jurors understand and remember complex material in an intuitive way. Visuals can be invaluable tools for this effort.

Inability to Study Presentation or Interact with Presenter

Presentation and design gurus Nancy Duarte and Garr Reynolds have each written some terrific books in their fields.[1] They both address the topic of text-heavy visuals. Reynolds calls them "slideuments"—slides that are really just documents—and he advises that slides with a lot of text are better distributed to the audience as a handout. Duarte agrees. In her view, slides with over seventy-five words are really documents. She suggests reducing the amount of text on the slide or, alternatively, hosting a meeting instead of a presentation and circulating the document in advance or allowing the audience to read it at the start of the meeting.

This is all excellent advice, and I often follow it when I give presentations to colleagues, law students, and continuing legal education (CLE) attendees. But here, again, we have another significant difference when presenting in a jury trial. In many jurisdictions, visuals we create that are purely illustrative exhibits—such as our closing argument slides—are not admissible into evidence, which means the jury won't get a copy. Unlike the handouts we give seminar attendees, students, and even judges, our jurors don't have the luxury of reading our materials at their leisure, refreshing their memories, and studying the detail we've provided.

What's more, audiences in typical presentation settings *know* that they'll get hard copies of our slides. (They might even have the slides in front of them while we're speaking.) That knowledge, alone, can make a big difference. If text appears on a slide and we don't directly address it during the presentation, they know they don't have to struggle to read it immediately. This reduces their frustration if we move through slides too quickly for them to fully comprehend the information. (Although I wouldn't recommend such an approach—if you include a slide in your presentation, presumably you want the audience to read it. More on that later.)

And, unlike many other presentation settings, trials won't become interactive conversations, and we won't have a free-flowing question and answer session after closing arguments, even in those jurisdictions that allow jurors to ask questions. We certainly won't have "office hours" or the opportunity for one-on-one discussion after our closing argument as we might in other settings. Without this interaction, we won't get timely, usable feedback on whether we need to provide more information, clarify a point, or remind someone of something we said.

So, we've got to make it easy on our jurors by accounting for these limitations. We have to control the order and pace of the information we provide using graphic design and presentation techniques. We'll increase the likelihood that jurors will understand and remember our message, and we'll gain credibility and build trust along the way.

Control over Presentation Order and Flow

When we plan presentations, we try to order information in a way that makes sense based on the substance of our communication. We might use a simple chronology, or perhaps we'll present information categorically. Whatever order we choose, *we choose it and we control it.*

But we don't always have this luxury in a trial setting. Oh, we try. In opening statements, we give jurors a framework for the case. We endeavor to do the same with our evidence presentation, carefully planning our witness order and structuring our examination outlines. And then, it all flies out the window.

A witness examination you thought would take an hour takes all morning; a juror has an emergency and has to leave early; the court has an unexpected matter on its docket and adjourns the case for the day; the next witness you planned to call missed his flight; the court takes testimony out of order to accommodate a witness's travel schedule; or any one of a million other things happens and causes a shift in the schedule—and your carefully crafted plan goes up in smoke.

Moreover, testimony and evidence on a particular topic or subtopic often is spread across multiple witnesses, who might not testify sequentially. And those witnesses will testify about other topics, too (e.g., their own backgrounds, their relationships with other witnesses, their role within the company, their role in the incident at issue in the trial, their opportunity to observe what they witnessed, etc.). The result is that evidence on a particular topic might be separated by days or even weeks.

Even when our presentation is logical and complete, it is rarely uninterrupted. Objections, bench conferences, and "brief recesses" all detract from the smooth flow of a trial presentation, which makes holding or regaining jurors' interest that much more challenging. Hopefully, by the end of trial we've successfully introduced the evidence we need, but our jurors might have strained to follow it. Some will not have succeeded.

In all, this can make our evidence presentations confusing and overwhelming—jurors have to work harder to understand the evidence and to put interrupted evidentiary points into a coherent, linear story. We must consider and address all of these challenges to our presentation order and flow when we design and use visuals. Creating demonstratives that are clear and visually memorable, and controlling the flow of information along the way, will help jurors understand and remember our message despite these inevitable challenges.

Time Limitations and Detail

The goal in a presentation to clients is often to show detail. Doing so lets us fully educate our clients so they can make informed decisions, and it demonstrates our own due diligence. For significant presentations by outside counsel, clients might set aside a full day or continue the discussion if there's more to cover. If we omit detail, clients can ask follow-up questions.

The goals and time limitations in trial can be dramatically different. Rather than presenting detail, our opening statements and closing arguments are designed to summarize the detail we will present (or have been presenting) over the course of a trial. And when we do provide detail through testimony and other evidence, it doesn't always come in as smoothly as we'd like. Finally, the judge may set strict time limitations on the trial as a whole, or even just for our openings and closings. Together, these challenges only heighten the importance of designing and using visuals strategically, helping jurors to process whatever detail we are able to provide.

Rehearsal/Preparation Time

Many presentation books rightly advise presenters to rehearse. This makes good sense. There really is no substitute for preparation, and rehearsing your presentation is part of that preparation. But trials aren't static events, with a group of actors working cooperatively to deliver scripted lines. Trials are adversarial, strategic, and unpredictable. They're governed by a set of rules that judges have tremendous discretion to interpret—often on the fly after an objection—and not every judge interprets them the same way. This, of course, adds to the unpredictability of the trial.

Some aspects of our trials are easier to plan than others. Opening statements and direct examinations are generally more predictable than cross-examination and closing. But even then, unless you're the first party to deliver your opening, you might choose to respond immediately to something your opponent said, going "off-script" even in your opening statement. And any seasoned trial lawyer knows that even direct examinations can run off the rails in a heartbeat, with witnesses you've worked with for months getting confused or failing to remember details under the pressure of trial, or even giving answers you've never heard before. Cross-examinations, of course, can be even less predictable. We can moot how we think they might go and have our impeachment documents at the ready, but "rehearsing," well, that's not a luxury we'll often have.

And then there's closing (or rebuttal closing) argument. Done right, closings incorporate evidence that might have come into the trial the day—or even just minutes—before they're delivered. You'll also likely change the substance and order of your closing to respond to your opponent. You might not have planned to address a particular issue at all, but your opponent raised it and struck a few blows, and you have no choice but to respond. Or perhaps you planned to discuss a particular topic well into your closing argument, but your opponent ended strong on that issue and you want to address it immediately. You'll also need to read your audience—the jury—to see if you need to make any adjustments. If you get the sense jurors aren't following your argument, or they clearly get your point and you're starting to bore them, or if you get the sense they just aren't buying a particular theme, you might need to respond right away to that real-time feedback, adjusting your closing argument while you're giving it.

For the most part, these strategic adjustments to your evidence presentation and jury arguments take skill, experience, and judgment, and cannot be "rehearsed." You may be creating or editing slides the night before or the morning of your closing argument. You might drop or re-order slides while you're giving your closing. You might even need to change the substance of a slide based on a last-minute ruling by the judge. I've experienced all of these issues and more in my own trials. Trials are dynamic, and effective trial lawyers make strategic adjustments. That includes when, whether, and how we use our visuals.

Despite all this—disinterested, skeptical jurors who lack familiarity with the subject matter and who must endure a disjointed and sometimes boring presentation—this is the typical style of slide deck I see lawyers use in court:

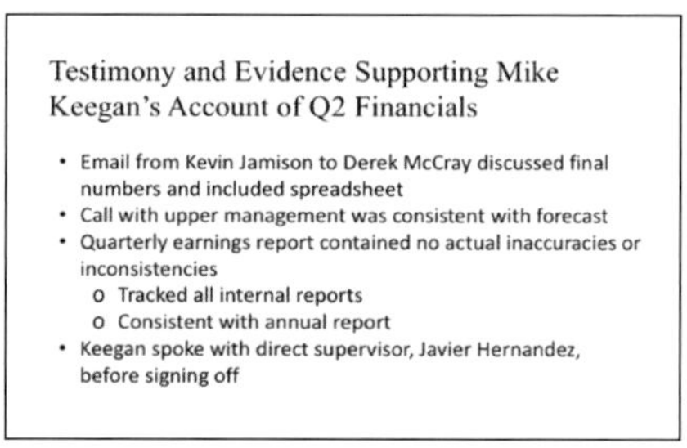

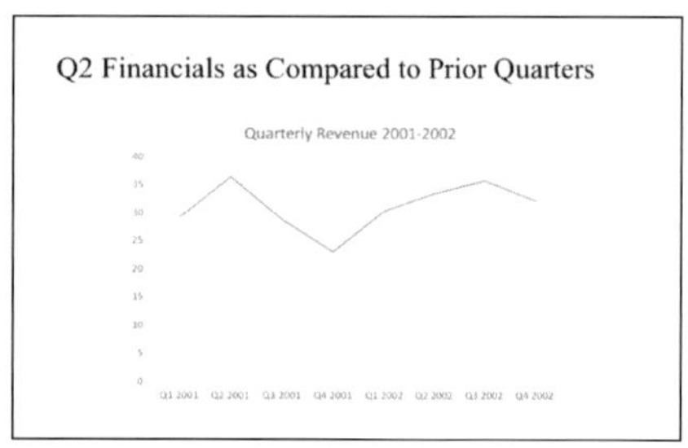

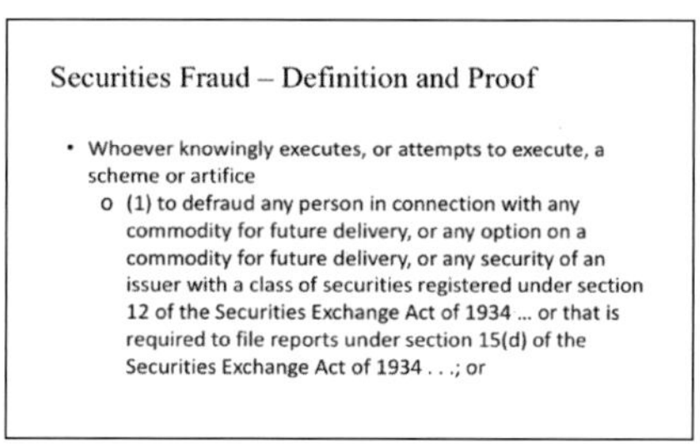

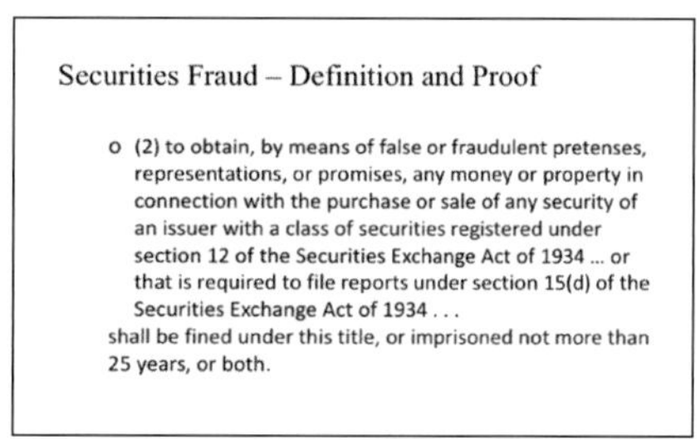

Or sometimes I'll see this:

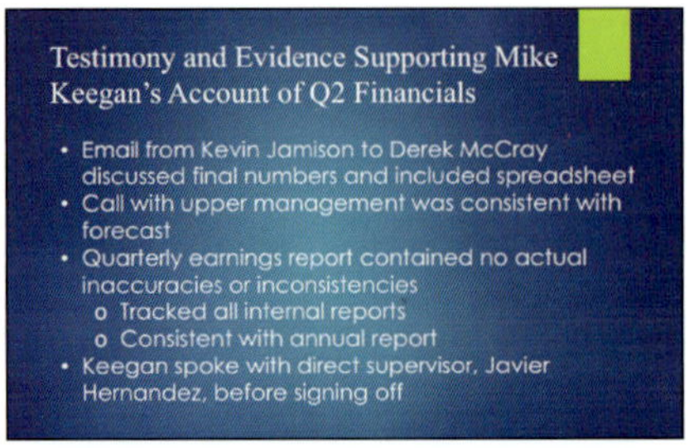

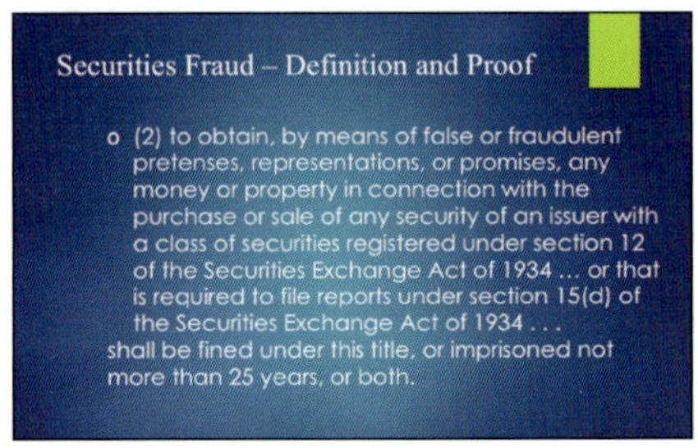

Or maybe this:

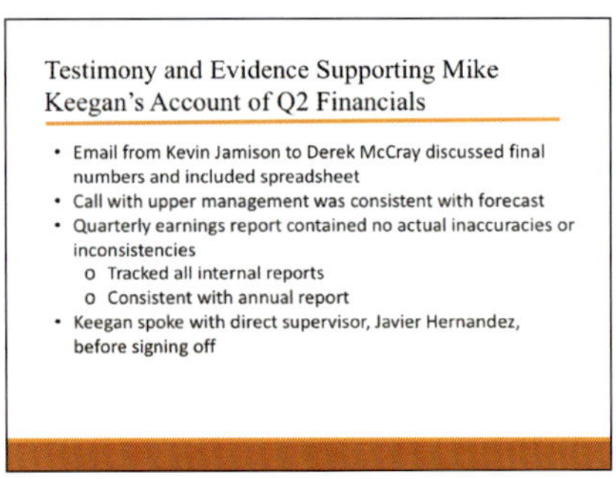

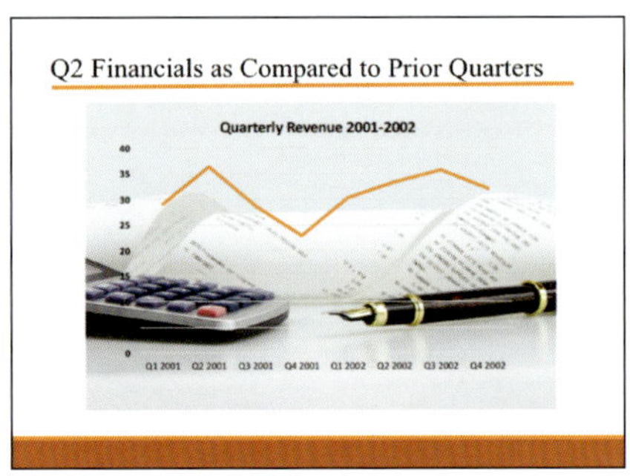

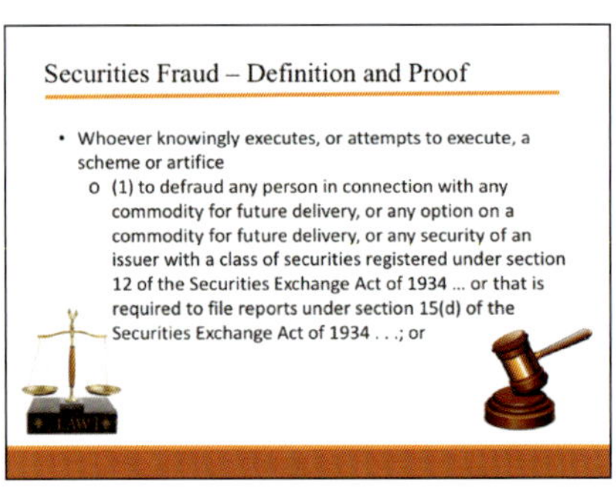

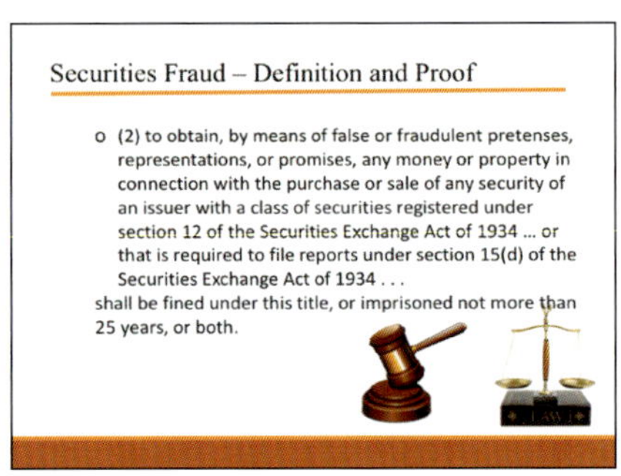

A bunch of bulleted text won't enhance understanding in the least and certainly won't create a useful visual memory. Nor does it do anything to enhance our jurors' trust in us as messengers. Remember, we start in a hole. Consider the jurors' limitations—those personal to each juror and those imposed upon them by the contrived setting—and design and use visuals to address those limitations.

Keep in mind, of course, that, although some characteristics of jury trials are consistent wherever we practice, others differ from jurisdiction to jurisdiction or even from judge to judge. I design and use visuals differently depending on a host of factors, such as whether the jurors will be permitted to take notes, whether they'll have written copies of jury instructions during deliberations, what technology will be available in the courtroom, and whether the judge will impose time limitations on witness examinations or argument.

The point is, your efforts are worth it. And they're likely to be more far-reaching than you realize, as you'll arm jurors with the tools they need to explain their position to other jurors during deliberations. The same visuals that help one juror understand and adopt your position—complete with relevant images, clear diagrams, and organized design—can also help that juror advocate for your point of view when it really matters in the jury room. When jurors are confident in their own understanding of the case facts and legal issues, they are empowered to articulate their (i.e., your) position, and continue engaging when they encounter opposing views.

In the end, jurors want to be fully informed, and they want to make the right decision. Our visuals should help jurors understand the unfamiliar, keep them engaged, and create visual memories throughout the trial.

3

Turning Themes into Pictures

Too often, lawyers use visuals as a crutch. Despite demonstratives' immense power to help jurors understand our message, we use slides as cheat sheets to help us keep our place in an argument, or to make sure we've covered all the points we want to make in opening, closing, or with a witness. When we do that, we're not really using visuals to help the jury. We're using them to help ourselves.

Intellectually, most lawyers recognize that effectively using visuals means more than just typing the words they intend to speak onto a slide. Still, their best effort at creating visuals is to shorten full sentences to incomplete ones and type them next to bullet points (or arrows or flowers or stars or whatever else strikes their fancy at that moment).

But the incomplete sentences are still too long. The type they're written in is too small. There's too much text on a single slide. And other than an image of a document (itself just text that was admitted into evidence), or maybe a random piece of clipart, that's the whole presentation. There's nothing visual or even visually memorable about it. The slides have added no value, and in fact, they likely have detracted from the communication.

As we saw in Chapter 1, study after study has demonstrated that we remember visual images more than we remember text or the spoken word, and that visuals help jurors understand and remember complex material. The point of using visuals in the courtroom is to effectively capitalize on these realities.

The Beauty of Visual Memories

"Visual memory" is likely a term of art in neuroscience and other such disciplines. But I'm using the term quite literally—creating a memory of what something looks like. We create visual memories naturally, and we use them constantly. They're what allow us to look for particular language in a court opinion, statute, or contract that we've read before without having to reread the entire document to find it. Instead, we remember the visual image of where that language is located on the page (top, bottom, left side), or we remember the image of indented text, or the image of a diagram next to the text we're looking for. Sometimes the memory is of our own notes on the page, or where we put an asterisk next to a key term and highlighted it. When we have a visual memory of the page containing the text, we're able to quickly flip through the document to look for that image rather than having to reread the text in its entirety.

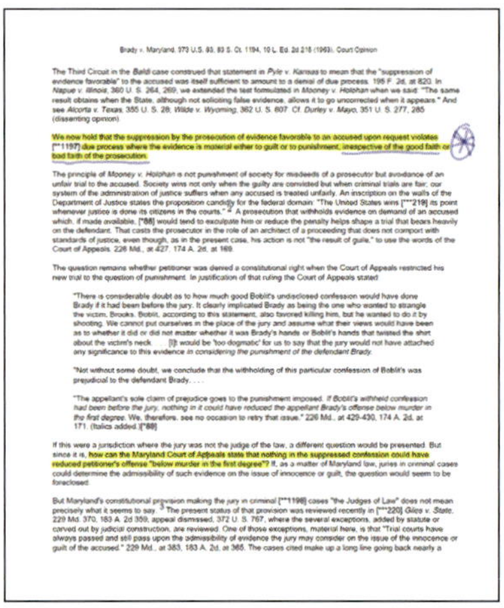

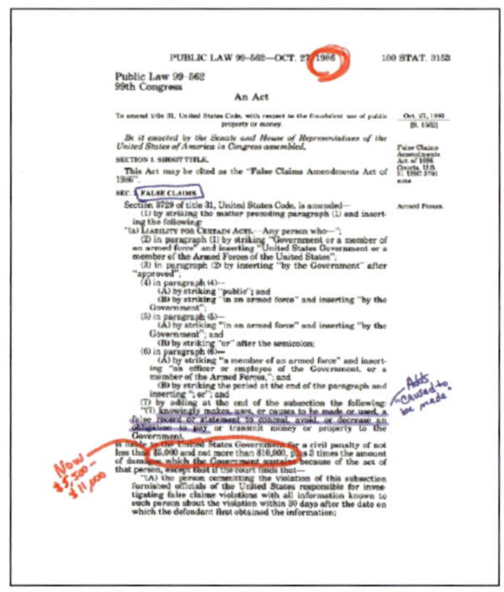

We create visual memories for ourselves without realizing it all the time. You scramble for a piece of paper to jot down some notes when a client calls. In the midst of a longer discussion, she passes along a few names of potential witnesses, and then rattles off their phone numbers. You finish the call, get distracted with something else, and forget to transfer the hastily written notes to a more permanent file. A few days later, you need to find that piece of paper amongst many others on your desk. Fortunately, you have a visual memory of the notes. The paper was yellow, not white. It was torn in the upper left corner. You wrote in blue ink. There's a doodle in the upper right. You can picture the arrows you drew connecting names and phone numbers.

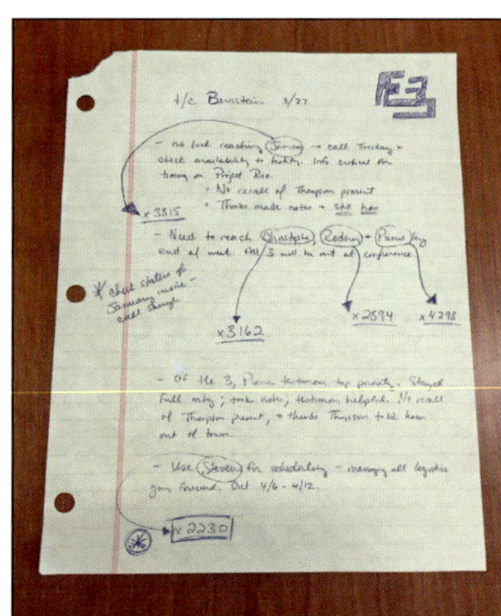

You might not remember the substance of a single thing on the page—not a name, not a number, maybe not even what you doodled. But you'll know it when you see it. You don't have to look at every piece of paper on your desk, and you certainly don't have to read them.

Ultimately, we should be trying to create relevant visual memories for our jurors that reflect our case themes, key facts, and concepts. If we're successful, then even if jurors don't remember the details on the slide, they'll have a visual memory of the theme.

Creating Visual Memories for Jurors

Creating visual memories for our jurors in the trial context can require a bit more forethought. Typically, trials are a mix of auditory testimony and documentary exhibits with little visual interest. We do our best to put the pieces together for the jury, but our methods often do nothing to create or stimulate visual memories. We can make our case more understandable, believable, and memorable by turning the key themes, or components of themes, into visual images.

Well before trial begins, we know most of the key themes and facts that we likely will want to display on a visual. Ideally, we'll create visuals for those themes in advance.

But other themes and facts deserving (or needing) visual emphasis won't reveal themselves until we're in the midst of trial. Be on the lookout for these. Was there a particularly boring, but important, part of the trial that you think jurors might have tuned out? Was one witness particularly confusing? Did a witness say something surprising? Were jurors especially attentive during someone's testimony? Did an opposing expert muddy up the real issues? Was an analogy used repeatedly, or at least memorably, that you could adopt or that you need to distinguish? Is there substantial agreement between the parties such that you can narrow down the areas of disagreement for your jurors in a helpful, effective way?

Developments like these are great fodder for visuals; keep an eye out for them and stay flexible. You might need to edit or redesign planned visuals to account for what actually happens in court, or you might need to create new visuals to address new issues.

Helping Visuals Become Memories

Just like everything else we perceive, visual memory can be fleeting. As discussed in the last chapter, our brains (and thus our jurors' brains) must process and encode the information or it will not make its way into our long-term memory. In trial, it might not be enough to simply display the visual on screen and hope that the jurors affirmatively process the information. We need to help ensure that this processing takes place.

For instance, we can create or build our visuals in front of the jurors, walk them through the information directly, and make sure the visual is the focal point of our communication when we display it. And by giving jurors *time* to process the information, we increase the chance that they will actually do so.

We can also reinforce a visual's key message by explaining how it fits into our broader case themes. This helps jurors organize the information as part of the larger case structure. Explaining the visual's significance also helps them process its message accurately and in the way we intended, which is essential when jurors recall the information during deliberations.

Common Visual Tools

There are a number of standard tools at our disposal for depicting information visually. Select the tool that will most effectively convey your core message. Of course, you'll first need to identify what that core message is.

Ask yourself, "What's the point?" What do you really want the jury to understand and remember? You might be conveying an overall theme, such as the defendant had/lacked a motive; people should take responsibility for their own actions; management was only concerned with the bottom line; the plaintiff wants to have his cake and eat it, too. Or, you might need a visual that addresses one of the basic questions inherent in every trial—who, what, when, where, why, and how. With thematic visuals—whether overall themes or discrete subthemes—try to limit your slides to conveying one point or concept. When lawyers rely on slides to do too much at once, the message is often lost and the visual detracts more than it helps.

Decide on the key takeaway you want to convey to your jurors for a particular visual. Then select the tool that most effectively conveys that key point. I'll discuss many of these often-used visual tools in more detail in Part II of this book, but for now, here is an overview of the most common tools available and when to consider using them.

Charts

Charts typically divide information categorically. They help us organize information to identify patterns, relationships, and hierarchies. They often address questions such as "how much" or "compared to what"—key questions in many trials, particularly those involving data. Indeed, Edward Tufte, a professor emeritus at Yale University who is known in the design world as the father of modern informational graphics, emphasizes in his writings that "[a]t the heart of quantitative reasoning is a single question: *Compared to what?*"[1] He urges designs that "visually enforc[e] comparisons of changes, of the differences among objects, of the scope of alternatives."[2] Answering these questions will be critical for many of our visuals, and displays of data are at the top of the list.

Tables

Charts with columns and rows—whether drawn or implied—have become nearly ubiquitous for organizing, dividing, and comparing information.

Because their structure is already familiar, tables allow us to organize information without having to spend valuable trial time (or use valuable space on the slide) explaining the design. But think about data as more than just a collection of numbers to exhibit on the screen. Displaying an Excel spreadsheet (itself a table) won't help the jury's understanding or aid recall any more than a series of text-based slides with bullet points.

	No ATM fee	No foreign transaction fee	No monthly account fee	No minimum balance	Earn points or cash back
First Bank	X	X	X	X	X
National Trust	X			X	X
Regional Bank and Credit			X	X	
Savings Bank	X	X	X		
Northeast Bank		X	X	X	
Midwest Savings and Loan		X		X	X

For example, in a product liability case stemming from alleged brake failure in an automobile accident, you might have helpful crash test data comparing the number of total brake tests with the number of times the brakes failed:

BRAKE TESTS: MODEL PDX1234

Test Series	ABS Active?	Road Conditions	Speed (mph)	Reaction Time (sec)	Ft/Sec	Avg. Reaction Distance (ft)	Avg. Braking Distance (ft)	Avg. Total Braking Distance (ft)	Federal Standard (ft)	Number of Brakes Tested	% of Brakes Within Federal Standard
1	Yes	Dry	30	0.75	44.00	33.0	57.0	90.0	100.0	200	100
2	Yes	Dry	35	0.75	51.33	38.5	74.0	112.5	125.0	200	100
3	Yes	Dry	40	0.75	58.67	44.0	98.0	142.0	150.0	200	100
4	Yes	Dry	45	0.75	66.00	49.5	121.0	170.5	185.0	200	100
5	Yes	Dry	50	0.75	73.33	55.0	150.0	205.0	225.0	200	100
6	Yes	Dry	55	0.75	80.67	60.5	181.0	241.5	260.0	200	99
7	Yes	Dry	60	0.75	88.00	66.0	216.0	282.0	300.0	200	98
8	Yes	Wet	30	0.75	49.33	37.0	65.0	102.0	110.0	200	100
9	Yes	Wet	35	0.75	56.67	42.5	82.0	124.5	135.0	200	100
10	Yes	Wet	40	0.75	64.00	48.0	106.0	154.0	160.0	200	96
11	Yes	Wet	45	0.75	71.33	53.5	129.0	182.5	195.0	200	96
12	Yes	Wet	50	0.75	78.67	59.0	158.0	217.0	235.0	200	97
13	Yes	Wet	55	0.75	86.00	64.5	189.0	253.5	270.0	200	96
14	Yes	Wet	60	0.75	93.33	70.0	224.0	294.0	310.0	200	97
15	No	Dry	30	0.75	52.00	39.0	69.0	108.0	120.0	200	100
16	No	Dry	35	0.75	59.33	44.5	86.0	130.5	145.0	200	100
17	No	Dry	40	0.75	66.67	50.0	110.0	160.0	170.0	200	100
18	No	Dry	45	0.75	74.00	55.5	133.0	188.5	205.0	200	100
19	No	Dry	50	0.75	81.33	61.0	162.0	223.0	245.0	200	99
20	No	Dry	55	0.75	88.67	66.5	193.0	259.5	280.0	200	97
21	No	Dry	60	0.75	96.00	72.0	228.0	300.0	320.0	200	98
22	No	Wet	30	0.75	62.67	47.0	85.0	132.0	135.0	200	100
23	No	Wet	35	0.75	70.00	52.5	102.0	154.5	155.0	200	100
24	No	Wet	40	0.75	77.33	58.0	126.0	184.0	185.0	200	94
25	No	Wet	45	0.75	84.67	63.5	149.0	212.5	215.0	200	100
26	No	Wet	50	0.75	92.00	69.0	178.0	247.0	255.0	200	100
27	No	Wet	55	0.75	99.33	74.5	209.0	283.5	290.0	200	97
28	No	Wet	60	0.75	106.67	80.0	244.0	324.0	330.0	200	95
										5600	98.53571429

The spreadsheet certainly captures the data, but it has no visual impact and is not immediately perceived or memorable. Moreover, by including *all* of the data, the visual fails to focus on the key point—here, that the brake failures constituted a very small percentage of the total brake test failures compared to the total. The detailed data might be essential to admit into evidence, but it is not essential to the visual. Even a basic bar or pie graph would be an improvement for conveying the theme.

But by adding relevant visual interest to the graphs and using strategically placed color and text to emphasize the key points, we can make the data display more engaging, memorable, and clear. Here are two possible design options:

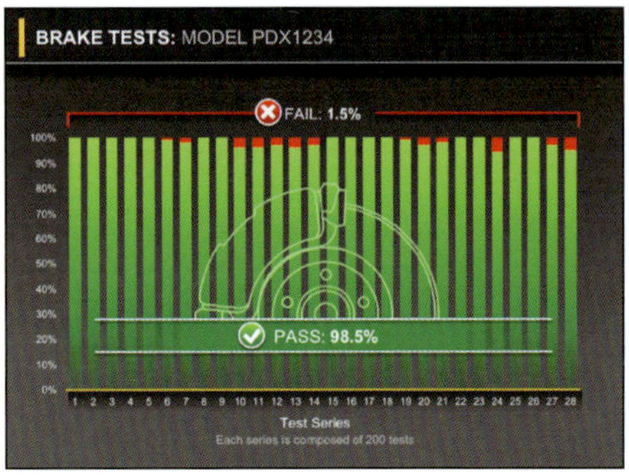

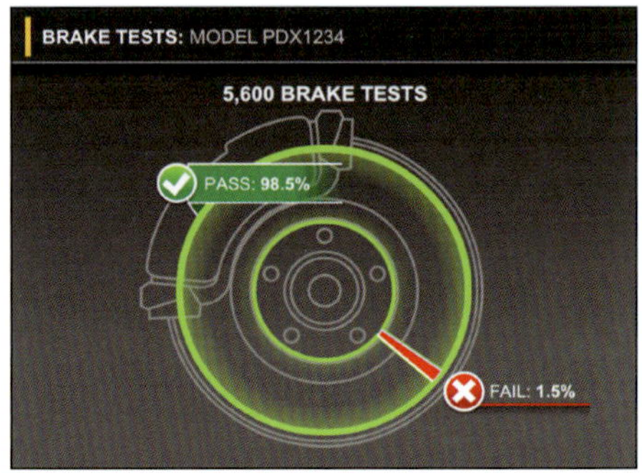

As with any of the examples in this book, there are many, many ways to design these slides. An image of a crashed car or a crash test dummy would also be relevant to the theme and stand out for the jurors. Just be careful that your images don't fight with the data (the real message of the visual). Don't compromise readability just for the sake of graphics. We advance our communication goals by designing the graphs and the images to work together.

Flowcharts

Flowcharts categorize information by separating what comes next from what came before. You might use a flowchart to show a chronology, such as an order of events. You might depict a process, showing which step comes before another. Or you might walk jurors through the steps in a line of reasoning, such as identifying the elements of a claim to suggest what questions must be answered and in what order.

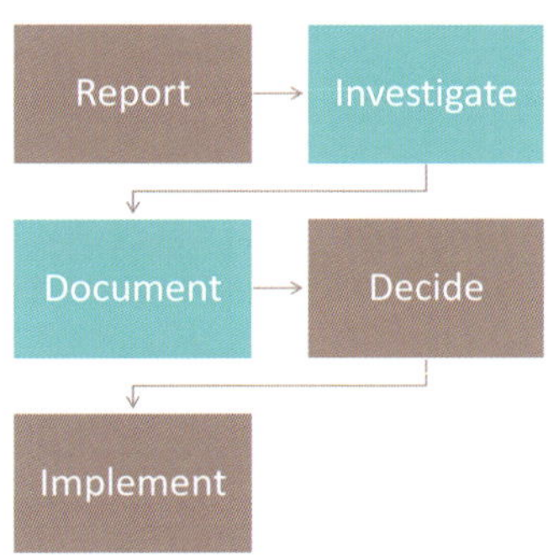

Whatever you're depicting, consider using a flowchart when the order of your information matters and when the question you need to answer is "how" or "when" something occurred or should occur.

Organizational Charts

Organizational charts are exceptionally useful for depicting hierarchies and relationships. As with tables, the meaning and structure of an organizational chart is well known, which allows jurors to perceive the underlying message quickly.

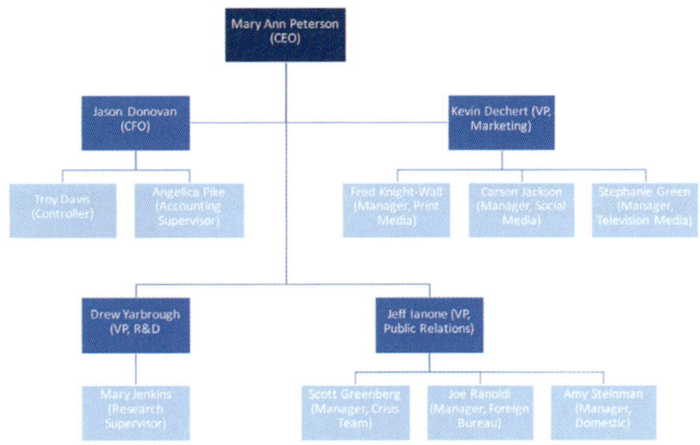

Graphs

Graphs are visual depictions of data. There are many types of graphs, and they each serve a particular function. When designed well, their message is understood almost immediately. Often, the same data can be effectively conveyed through multiple types of graphs, but each has its own advantages and limitations.

We can plot individual data points on a line graph to show trends and correlations.

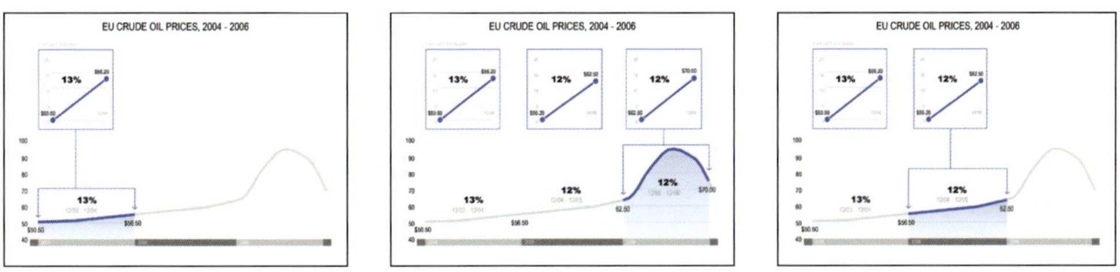

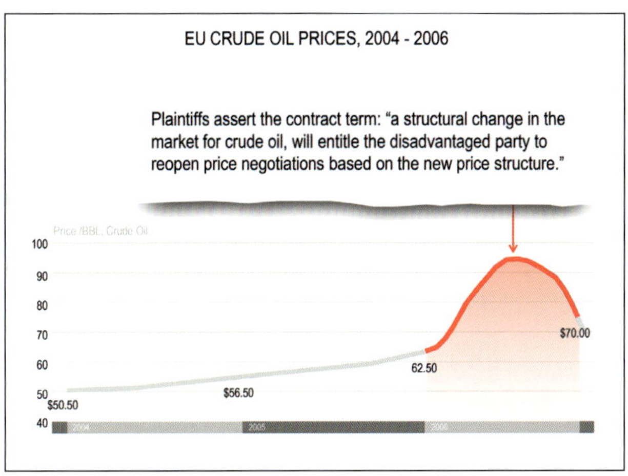

Bar or pie graphs can quickly show comparisons between sets of data for different variables. Like charts, they're also useful for answering the questions "how much" and "compared to what."

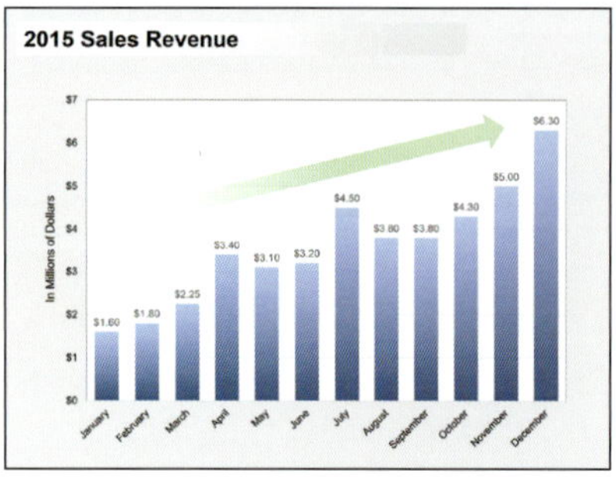

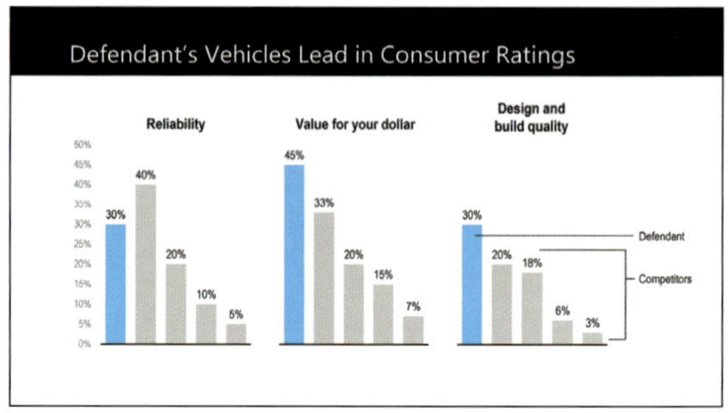

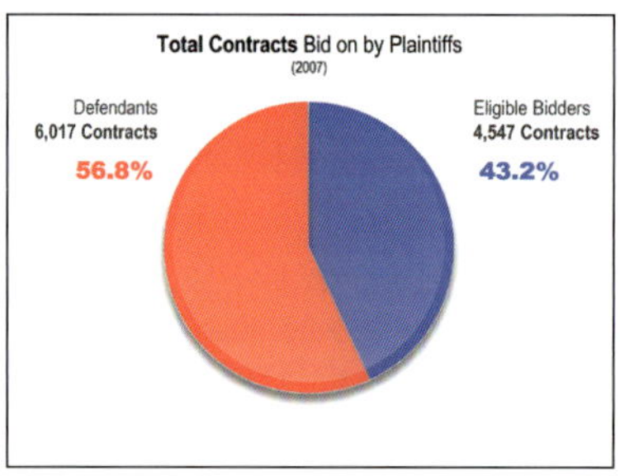

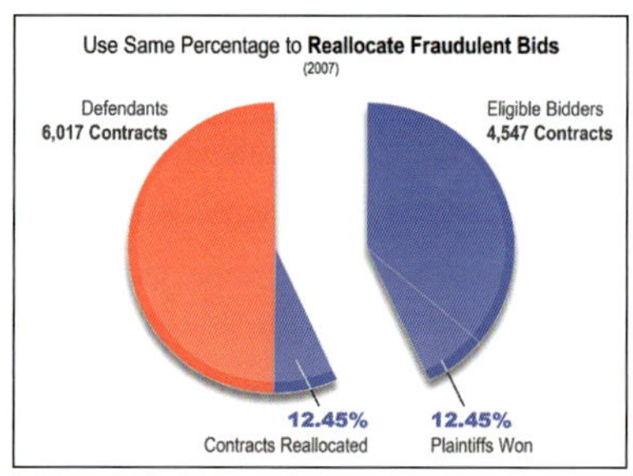

Timelines

Arguably a type of flowchart, a timeline is an extremely effective tool for depicting information chronologically. Where flowcharts typically depict an order of processes or reasoning, timelines depict an order of events.

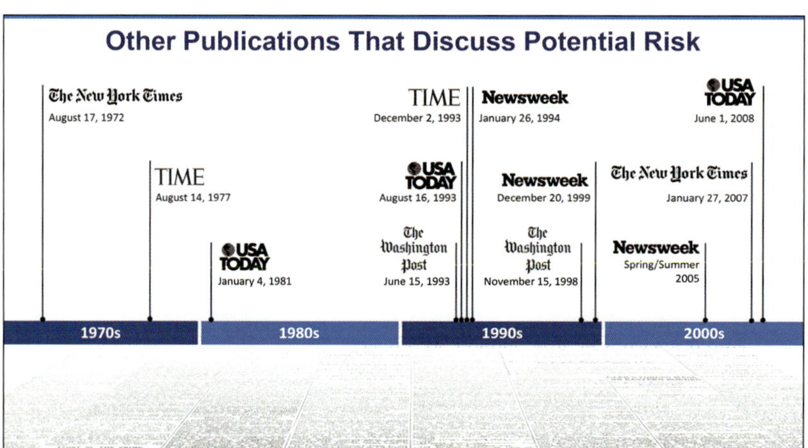

Timelines address "when" and "in what order" questions. When were corrections made? When were witnesses aware of key information, and who acted first? When did communications occur? Plotting the relevant events along a time continuum paints a visual picture of their order. But as with everything else, think outside the box. As I'll discuss later in this book, I've also used timelines to put information into context when my primary theme wasn't chronological.

The challenge with timelines is resisting the urge to include so many events and so much detail that jurors lose the forest for the trees. The point is to create a visual image that's memorable and turns your theme into a picture. So, using pictorial symbols on a timeline instead of text can be more memorable for jurors than a collection of dates and words. If your timeline is nothing more than a detailed description of events listed in order, you'll have missed a valuable opportunity for visual communication.

Maps

Maps, rather obviously, are great for showing location and proximity. When designed properly, they quickly and clearly answer the question "where?" Where did events take place? Where was a witness standing when he saw/heard key information? Where are businesses located?

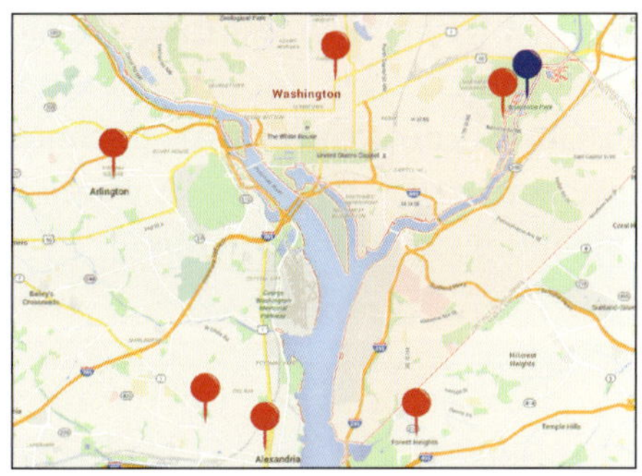

Maps are easy to prepare in advance and use repeatedly throughout trial during witness examinations. Witnesses can describe relevant details about what's depicted on the map, place themselves or others in precise locations, and even explain differences between the map image and what the same area looked like at a different time.

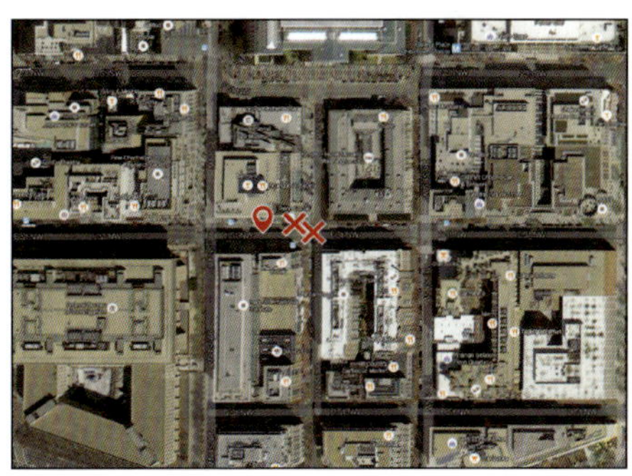

Whether the area you're mapping is large or small and whether the information you're conveying is simple or complex, a map devoid of extraneous clutter can leave a lasting impression and create useful visual memories for your jurors.

Photographs

Photographs are the very definition of visuals. We use them often in trial, most typically when it's impractical to introduce physical evidence. In criminal cases, photos of crime scenes, injuries, autopsies, suspects, and stolen property are routinely introduced into evidence. In civil cases, we use comparison photographs in patent, trademark, and copyright cases; photographs of injuries in medical malpractice and wrongful death cases; and even photos of deconstructed products in product liability cases.

But given their visual impact, think creatively when it comes to using photographs. In addition to using photos of physical evidence, think about using them to convey your core trial messages. When used effectively, photographs can depict an entire theme simply and immediately.

Advertising campaigns for all sorts of businesses, services, and products are based on this single premise. We see these photographs every day in ads for vacation travel, fitness clubs, pharmaceuticals, and even services such as tax preparation or in-home security. Rather than featuring a photograph of the literal product or service for sale—a pill or a tax form, for instance—advertisers often use a more powerful photo that instantly depicts their theme or concept. Often, they only need one or two words to give context to the photo. A travel agency marketing vacations to busy executives might use something like this:

Think about how you can use photographs to visually communicate your message. You'll need to be careful, of course. The same benefit we get from a photo that aids juror recall—its potential emotional impact—can lead to the photo's exclusion under Federal Rule of Evidence 403 and its state equivalents for being unfairly prejudicial. Ultimately, though, relevant photos are great tools that hit on all cylinders for jury communication. They aid jurors' understanding, help them remember what we're depicting, and can boost our credibility.

Graphics

Some of the most effective visuals I've used with juries have been out-of-the box graphics designed specifically to convey a particular case theme. I showed you one such graphic in Chapter 1 depicting the various sources of information about a drug that impacted a doctor's decision to prescribe the drug for an off-label use.

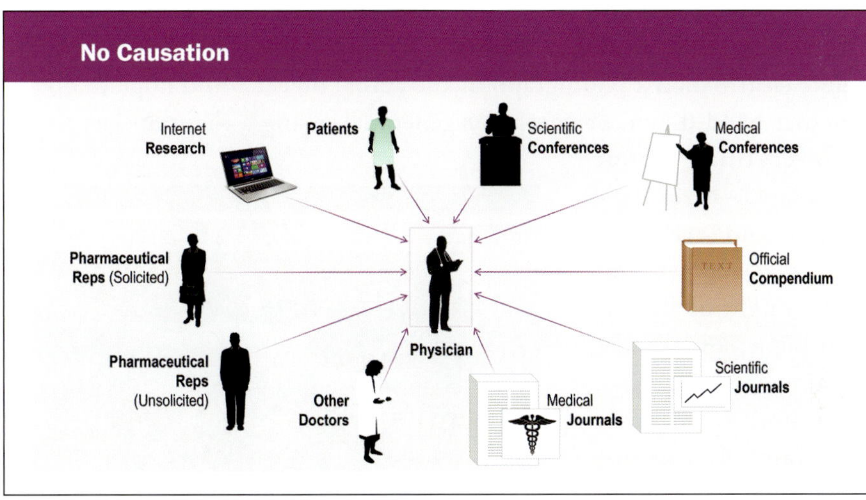

Graphics work exceptionally well for turning themes into images. While charts and graphs are tough to beat for visually depicting data and comparisons, graphics are my go-to for depicting themes and concepts.

Diagrams

Diagrams, also called illustrations or drawings, can help us visually depict something that's otherwise difficult to express with words and that may not be conducive to a photograph or data display. For instance, we might use a diagram to depict layers in an object that would be impossible to show in a photograph, or something that would otherwise be too large, too small, or difficult to control.

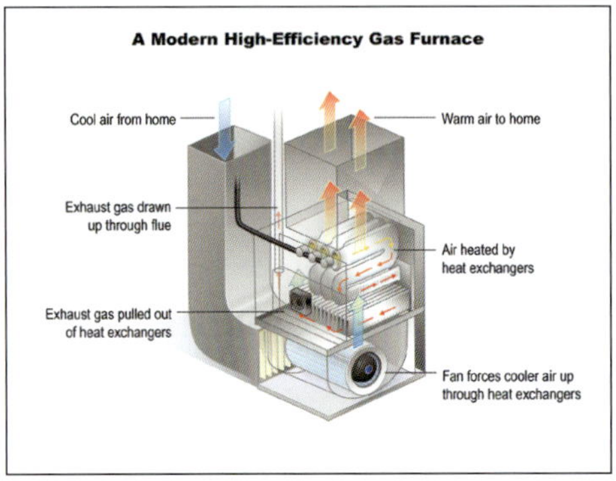

Diagrams also help us simplify our information presentation. That doesn't mean we won't (or can't) use complex diagrams. In fact, complexity might be the very theme we're conveying. But even when we're striving to show complexity, we can design diagrams to communicate complex facts and concepts more clearly than a photograph or the actual object could hope to do.

Whether hand-drawn or computer-generated, using a diagram lets us control almost everything about what's depicted—sizes, colors, labels, and even the point of view and level of detail. We might be depicting an airplane, a molecule, or anything in between—there's no limit to what we can diagram. Locations, processes, injuries, and even scientific concepts can all be illustrated.

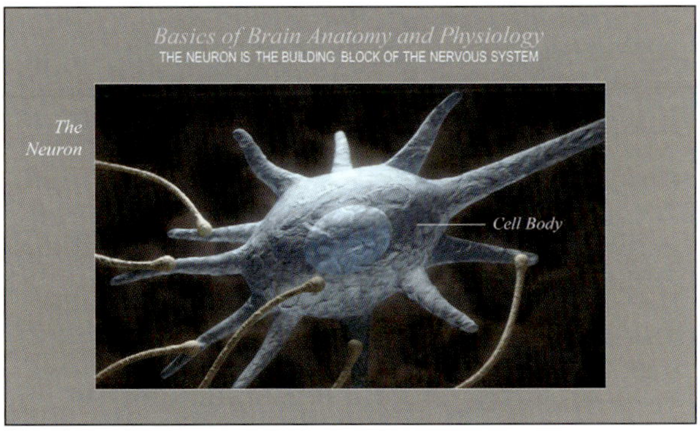

The point of this book is not to suggest that lawyers should add pictures of flowers or sunsets to their slides just for the sake of showing the jury visual images or that everything should be presented in a colorful bar graph. Robin Williams, author of *The Non-Designer's Presentation Book*, puts it well: "If your content is boring and your type is boring, some random graphic is not going to make it better. If you're using a default template with small black type on a large white background, indiscriminate clip art in the corners is not going to fix it."[3] She's right:

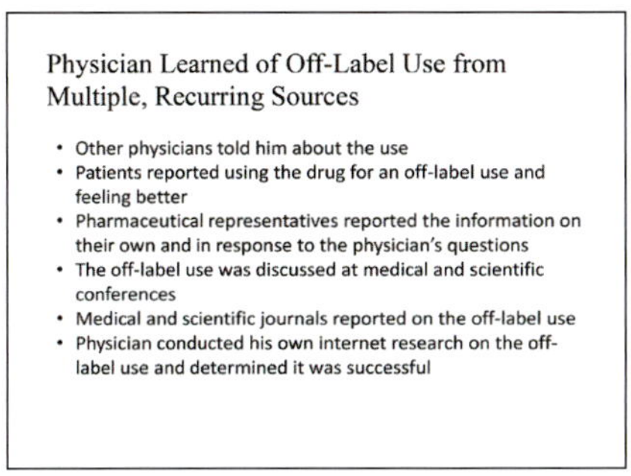

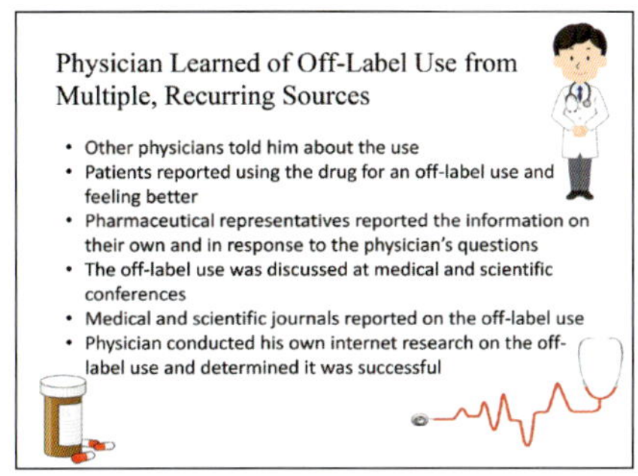

Because any one idea can be depicted in a variety of ways, it is wise to consider each visual not only by itself, but in the context of the presentation as a whole. If your presentation has nothing but text builds, the visual impact of each build is reduced. If you're using line graph after line graph, think about presenting data in a different way for a particular theme. The rest of this book will provide suggestions for creatively and strategically designing and using visuals to help your jurors understand, believe, and remember your message.

PART II

Tools for Visual Communication

Now that we've discussed why visual communication matters, let's talk in more detail about the tools we can use to create visual memories for our jurors. The techniques discussed in this section are by no means the limit of what's at our disposal. In fact, with some creativity and case facts to support it, the options for communicating visually with our jury really are limited only by our imagination. What I'll discuss here are the most common tools we use in jury trials, which can be applied to an extraordinarily broad array of cases and legal fields (and beyond!).

d to his death. I, too,
red the sweep-
Sandoval called
them a relative.
apartment. She
never intervene
beating or the
held against h
He has
welcomed with
cozied up to.
the
age, to grovel at
offer riches to the
kiss his ... champi
Kobe worked the
like a borrowed ox

4

Using Basic Text

Words are powerful. They convey feeling, express ideas, and explain complexities. Words even evoke visual imagery. In the legal profession, words are the building blocks of everything we do. We use words to create laws, form companies, and defend the accused. Words let us communicate with our clients, negotiate contracts, and close deals. And, we use words to persuade judges and juries.

Let's face it—we won't be delivering closing arguments through interpretive dance. We'll be using words.

In the world of graphic design, the words on the page are known as text. Given its importance, text will be the most frequently used tool in our communication arsenal. And there's the rub. When spoken, words are merely auditory. We don't suddenly create an effective visual just by slapping them on a screen. The key is to translate our facts and themes into understandable visual images and effectively control the flow of information to our jurors.

When I speak to groups about effective visuals, I often ask them to describe a typical slide presentation they've seen or given themselves. Usually, they describe a long series of text-heavy slides, typically on a monotone background, with the occasional bullet point or dash to signify a new thought. Occasionally, someone will describe a presentation with busy and colorful backgrounds, maybe even featuring random clip art to fill any spot not taken up with text. And, of course, there's the in-between—slides that clearly had a graphic design influence and so are arguably less offensive to the eye but still do not reflect the use of text in a way that enhances visual communication.

Throughout this book, I'll be discussing both substantive and stylistic techniques for working with text. I'll also suggest eliminating or greatly reducing the amount of text used wherever possible. But often, basic text is a perfectly effective way to express an idea.

For example, I represented an executive at a large company who was accused of backdating documents and taking other fraudulent steps to artificially inflate the quarterly earnings of a business partner. The contract at issue—which the government alleged motivated the executive to commit fraud—was worth $3 million over the course of three years. According to the government, the client's fraud was designed to help his company's bottom line.

Now, in a vacuum, $3 million is a tremendous amount of money. But *in context*, that amount of money would not have motivated this law-abiding, responsible executive to commit a felony and risk his career, reputation, family, and freedom. Indeed, to the company, a $3 million contract was negligible at best. At the time this "fraud" supposedly was taking place, the company was making $100 million *every day*. A $3 million contract—over the course of three years—was barely a drop in the bucket.

So, the question was how to put the $3 million contract into context. There are a lot of ways to do this, but one perfectly viable option—particularly where the information is simple and the numbers speak for themselves—is a basic text slide. And that's what we used with the jury:

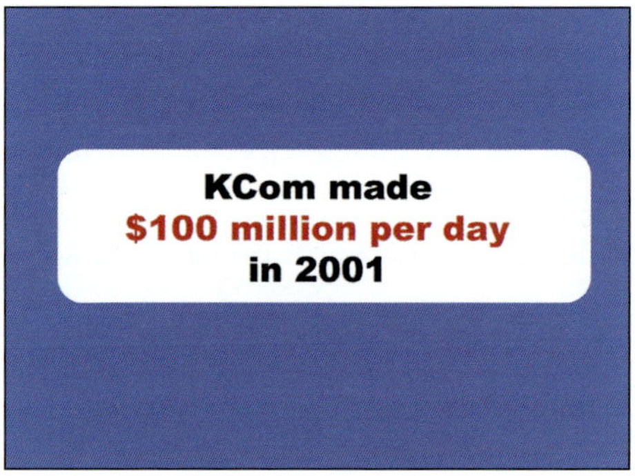

This slide served as a jumping-off point in the closing argument to explain why the company didn't depend on this single contract, thus undermining the government's argument that our client's motive was, in part, to help his company's bottom line. Any juror taking notes could easily copy down this simple text. And even if jurors didn't write it down, the message was powerful enough—and was presented clearly enough—that it stood a strong chance of being remembered. Certainly, we could have chosen to show the size of the contract at issue in comparison to the company's daily earnings, in which case a more graphic representation would have been better. (I'll show examples of this in later chapters.) The point, though, is that when basic text will do, it's simply a matter of eliminating extraneous detail and making the text legible.

Indeed, the problem with jury visuals is not the mere use of text—the problem is how that text is often presented. Usually, if you choose to place text on a slide, you want the jury to be able to read it. The size of the text obviously will impact its legibility, but so will other design choices. Your choice of background, color, and font, and even your line, word, and letter spacing, can contribute to how easily the jury can read your message. In a later chapter, I'll address typography considerations in more detail, but here are some basic principles to keep in mind when using simple text slides. While all of these principles are rather obvious, few are routinely followed.

Text over Busy Backgrounds

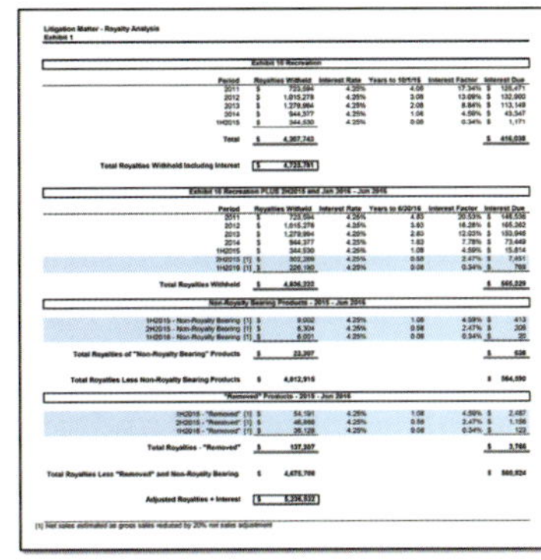

Sometimes, an important trial exhibit is visually memorable. When that's the case, I often like to keep the exhibit on the screen when I'm discussing it, even if I add text to the slide, as it helps create a visual memory of the document—and my theme—for the jurors.

Not surprisingly, however, text over a busy background can be tough to read. Likewise, if the background changes color, text that was perfectly readable on one part of the slide might be invisible somewhere else.

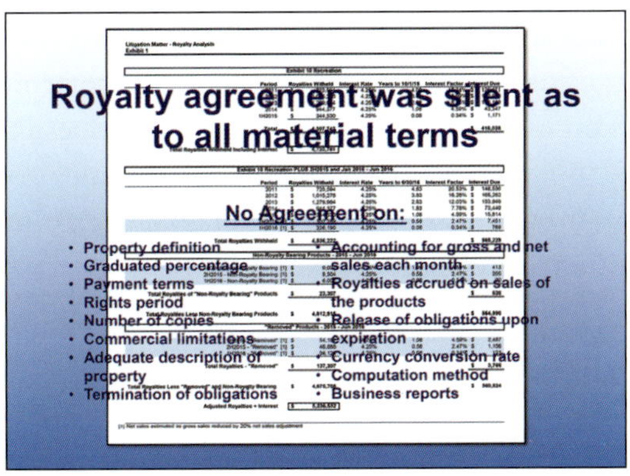

To address this issue, one simple solution is to introduce a block of color between the text and the background.

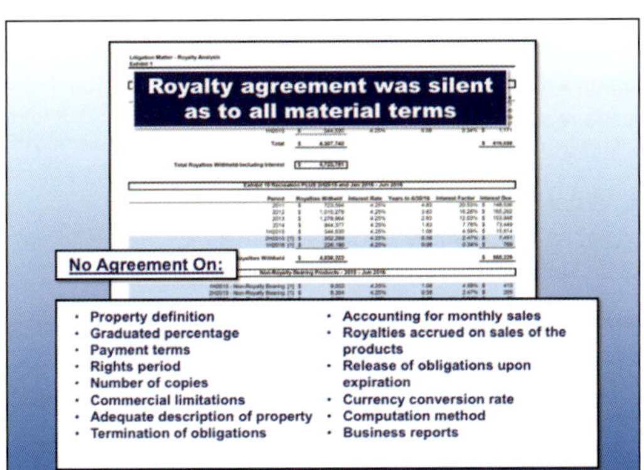

I'll share some additional ideas for making text legible over busy backgrounds in Chapter 20. For now, just keep in mind that busy backgrounds have their place, and when you use them, pay close attention to the legibility of any text you place in the foreground. Then, be consistent and use a similar technique throughout the presentation so everything looks purposeful and unified.

Eliminate Extraneous Text

Over the years, I've heard various proclamations about how much text you're "allowed" to put on a slide. I've even read articles advising (commanding?) a specific word limit. Presumably, such rules are intended to apply to the text we create ourselves—we certainly wouldn't refrain from showing the jury an important case document, a jury instruction, or a statute simply because it had more than the advised "maximum" number of words. But even as applied to the text we create, hard and fast rules are pretty silly. In fact, as I'll discuss in a chapter on volume builds, sometimes using a good deal of text—if presented the right way—can serve a valuable purpose.

In the ordinary course, however, I certainly agree with the view that we should minimize the amount of text on our slides. This means shortening our sentences and using fewer sentences on each slide wherever possible. It doesn't cost more money or take more time to use more slides if the amount of substance you're presenting is the same. Think about it—it takes just as long to explain three points on three slides as it does to explain those same three points on one slide.

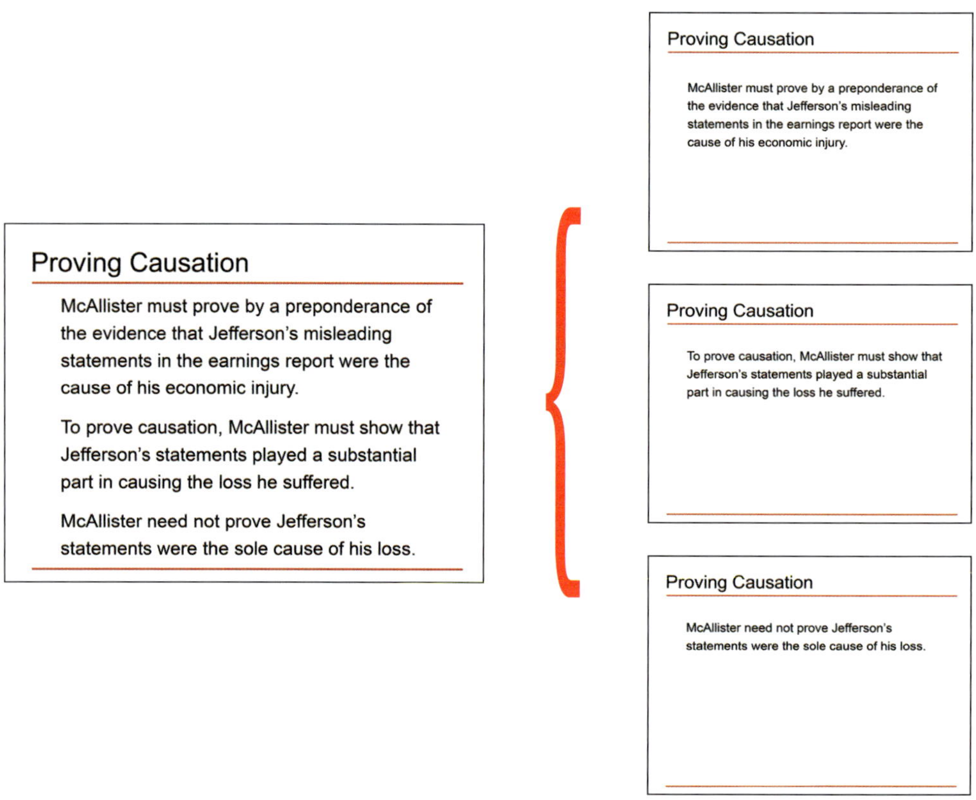

Yet it seems presenters feel a tremendous internal pressure to fit as much information as possible on a single slide. Perhaps they think it shortens the presentation. (It doesn't.) Or maybe they think it demonstrates their efficiency. (It doesn't do that, either.) There certainly are times when space is at a premium, such as when your only reasonable display option is an enlarged foam board. Still, my solution would not be to put a ton of tiny text onto a foam board simply to fit everything in. That strategy doesn't work in most circumstances and in fact can be quite counterproductive. With a text-heavy visual, if you talk about something else or paraphrase, you fight with the slide. Jurors have to choose whether to comprehend the written text or comprehend your spoken message. They can't do both.

What's more, keeping text to a minimum actually encourages jurors to take notes. Jurors are overwhelmed when they see a lot of text. Most likely, they won't bother to write any of it. If they do try to copy down some of the tome you've presented on screen, they won't be listening to you speak. Remember, the brain can't multitask when it comes to paying attention. It takes some of the jurors' concentration to decide what to write, particularly when they're also trying to read and comprehend the text in the first instance. They can't do that and simultaneously pay attention to whatever you're saying.

So make it easy on them. The whole idea of using visuals is to bolster your oral communication; the visuals shouldn't replace you altogether, or even compete with you. Give jurors only what they need, and present the information in a manageable way. When done right, note-taking jurors are aided by your efficient and effective use of text.

And this goes for all of the text you include on a slide, not just text next to bullet points in the body of the visual. Eliminate the extraneous everywhere. Does the case number really need to be on your trial slides? Do the axes in your graphs need so many words? Does your map depicting how far apart competitors are in the same county really need to label rivers, mountains and state borders? Do your text lists need to be in complete sentences? When the answer is no, get rid of the unnecessary words.

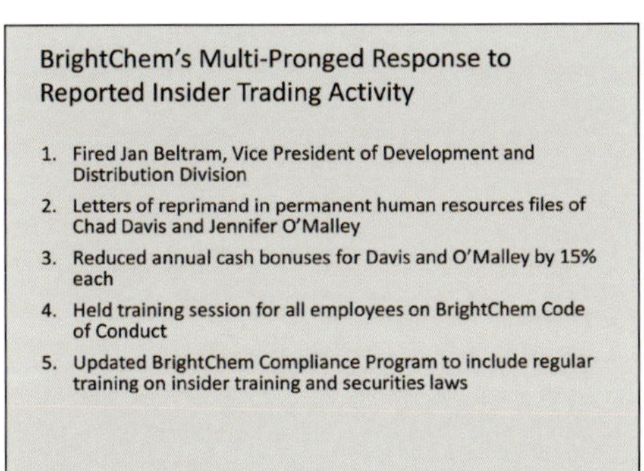

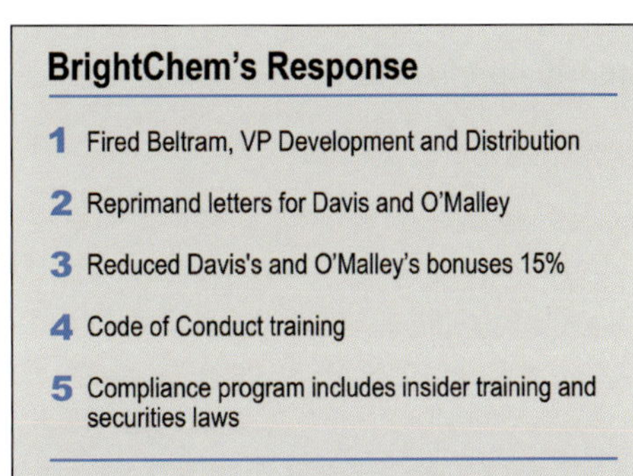

In addition to overwhelming the jury, too much text on a slide can decrease its readability. Moreover, to fit a lot of words into a finite space, we reduce their size. When we shrink the text, it's harder to read. Eliminating excess text opens up your design options. You can enlarge exhibits, fill the screen with relevant images or charts, or just use larger text. You'll keep the jury more interested, present with greater clarity, and increase the likelihood that the jurors will remember your message.

Write Enough to Make Sense Later

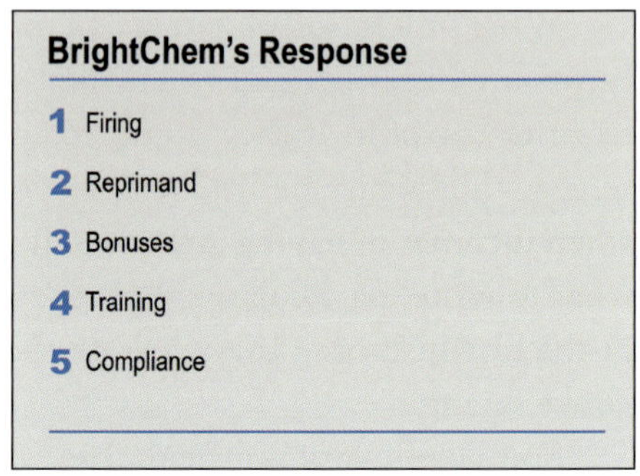

Of course, the text should be clear enough that if jurors copy it down exactly, they will understand their own notes when it's time to deliberate.

If just writing a word or two—"causation" or "Richard Jones" or "telephone call"—is likely insufficient to trigger the jury's memory of a key evidentiary point, then use more (or different) words. You've accomplished nothing if jurors take diligent notes but have no idea what the notes mean days, weeks, or months later when they're deciding your case. Similarly, make sure you don't sacrifice truth or accuracy for a shorter slide. We wouldn't do that in a written brief; don't do it in your visuals.

Bullet Points

"Bullet points," which often take the form of little circles to the left of each new text idea, have become the disdain of presentation designers and audiences alike. Some designers will tell you in no uncertain terms that you should never use bullet points.

But what does that really mean? Are designers and presentation gurus just vehemently opposed to little circles?

Is this . . .

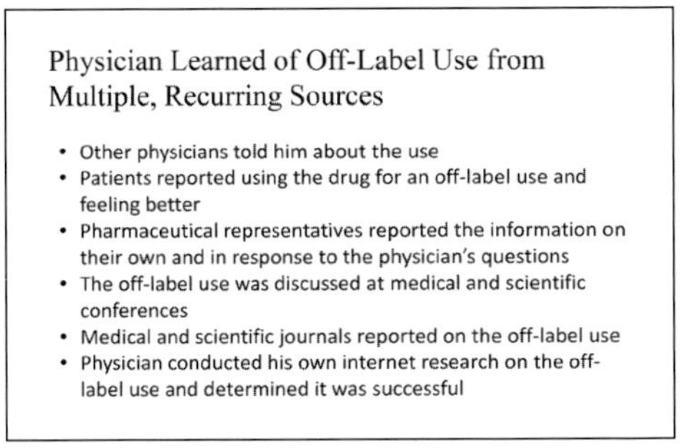

. . . really so much worse than this?

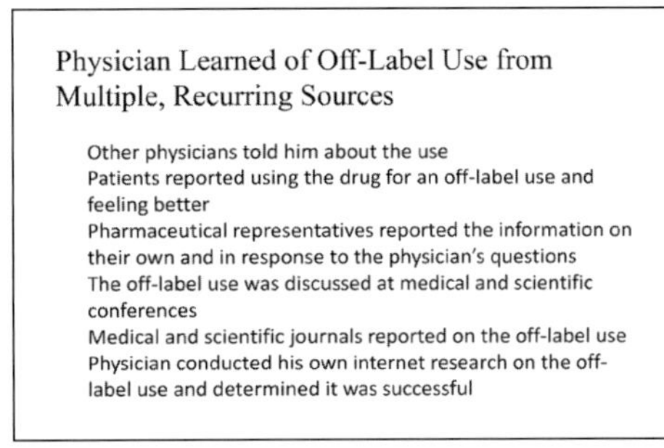

Of course not. The little circles alone aren't the problem. The problem is what those circles enable and encourage.

Ninety-nine times out of a hundred, when people are designing slides with bullet points, they're pairing the bullets with text. Most people agree that the slide above *without* bullet points is too text-heavy and overwhelming. But when the identical text is sitting next to a circle at the beginning of each sentence, suddenly most presenters are satisfied enough with the slide that they'll use it in their own presentations. It's as though the bullets are magic beans that transform what is essentially just a document typed onto a slide (Garr Reynolds's "slideuments") into an effective visual.

It's hard to fault folks for thinking that using bulleted text is the "right" or "necessary" way to give a professional presentation. After all, this message is reinforced constantly when we watch others' presentations, and many presentation software templates *default* to text-heavy slides with bullet points. Sure, the templates differ in color scheme, and corporate logos appear in different positions on the slides, but most of these templates immediately begin each presentation with the expectation of bullet-pointed text appearing in slide after slide.

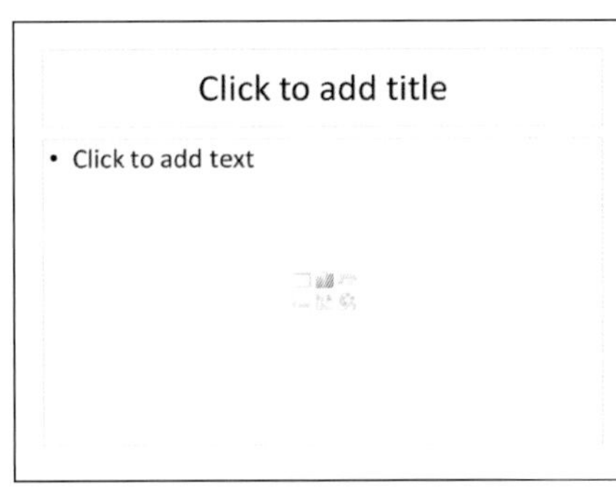

With a large message to "Click to add text" and a bullet point eagerly awaiting your typing, the templates not-so-subtly suggest to the nondesigner to "Put text here!" So we do. Then we hit the return key, and lo and behold, *another* bullet point appears, along with a cursor blinking in anticipation.

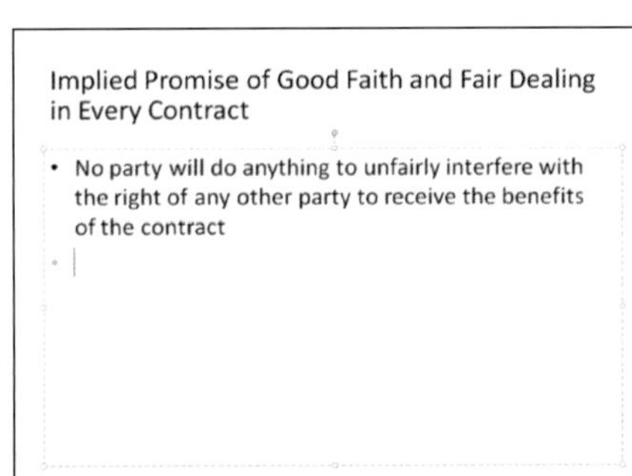

The implicit message: "You have room for more text! Put more text here!"

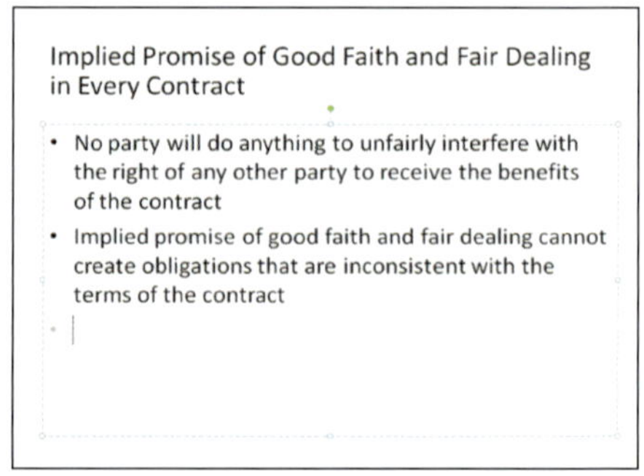

The process repeats, with more bullets begging us for more text. And then we get to the bottom of the slide, and we don't have room for the additional text that we need to complete our thought.

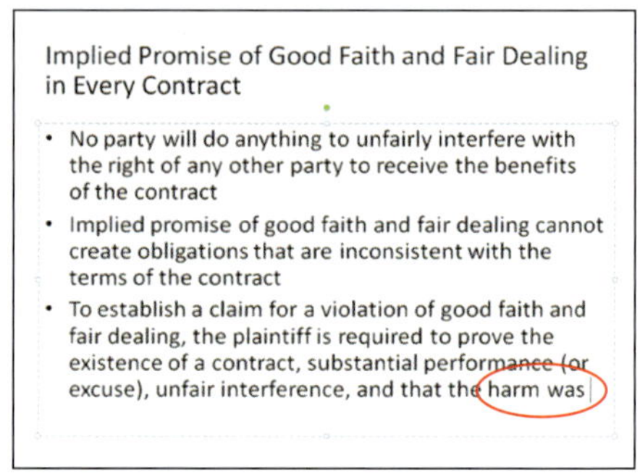

So, we solve that apparent problem by creating a new one—we reduce the size of the text. And wouldn't you know it, now we can "Fit more text here!"

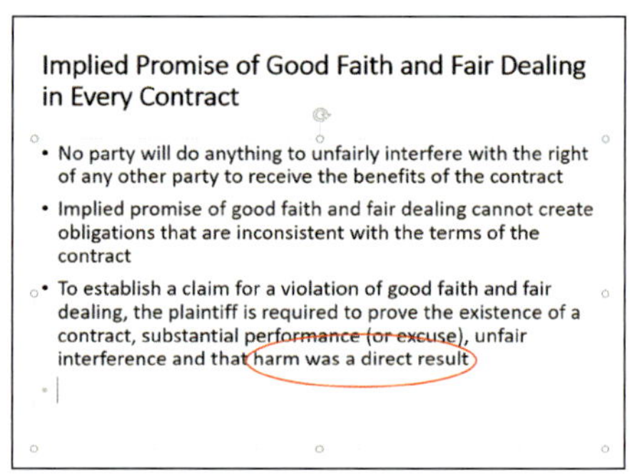

And that's the problem with bullet points. They encourage and enable text-heavy presentations that do nothing to enhance the viewer's understanding or recall of our message. Think about bullet points just as you would any other graphic element on a slide. If you can articulate a relevant design or substantive reason for their use, they can add value to a visual. But don't fill the slide with them just because you can.

Generally, I'm in favor of resisting the bullet-point temptation. When we type text next to bullet points, we're really just listing information. The bullet is there to help us immediately perceive that there are separate thoughts on the page. But we can accomplish that goal with appropriate line spacing; we don't need the little circles.

Use Visual Design to Emphasize Separate Points

Sometimes, the point we want to emphasize is the fact of the list itself even more than the substantive entries. When that's the case, there are much more effective and visually interesting ways to depict this theme than just typing a text list—whether or not the text is next to bullet points.

Let's say an important theme in your case is that your client's company took five steps in response to learning of employees engaging in insider trading. I showed you the typical slide used to convey this theme.

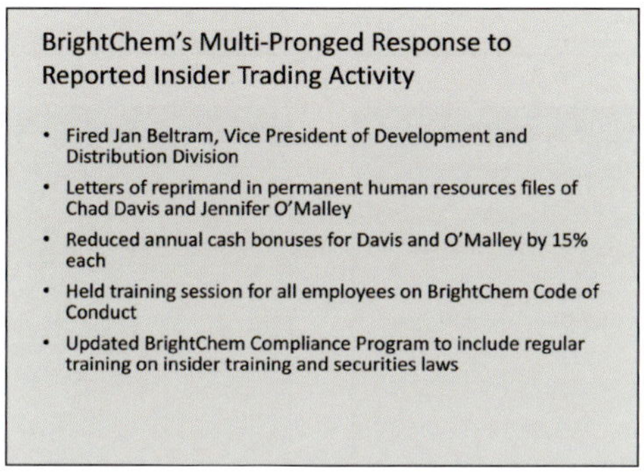

The bullet points enumerate the thoughts, and relatively quickly the jurors can see there were five separate steps. Some lawyers will even think to use numbers as their "bullets" rather than circles or other symbols:

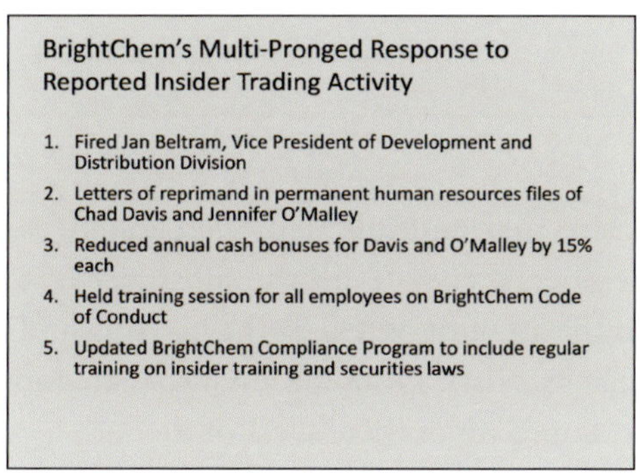

But if the point is that five steps were taken and that's what you want the jury to remember, then consider abandoning the traditional "list" approach altogether. The idea is to create a visual image of the theme, and neither of the above slides will enhance the jurors' recall of this theme in a slide deck full of text slides with multiple bullet points. Instead, consider emphasizing what really matters—here, that five steps were taken.

These slides emphasize that multiple steps were taken, as that is the main point I want the jury to remember. If they recall the substance of each step, all the better. You'll see I also reduced the amount of text in the heading and the body of the slide as compared to the previous text lists. Note-taking jurors are more likely to jot it down, and I can make the text larger when there's less of it.

If you find yourself stuck for a visual way to convey a theme, you can get ideas from a simple Internet search, or even by searching one of the many stock image websites available (I'll discuss this a bit more in later chapters). In this example, searching for "five steps" can yield some creative solutions. Just be careful with the tone of the slide, and make sure the design isn't so complicated or ornate that it fights with or obscures the message.

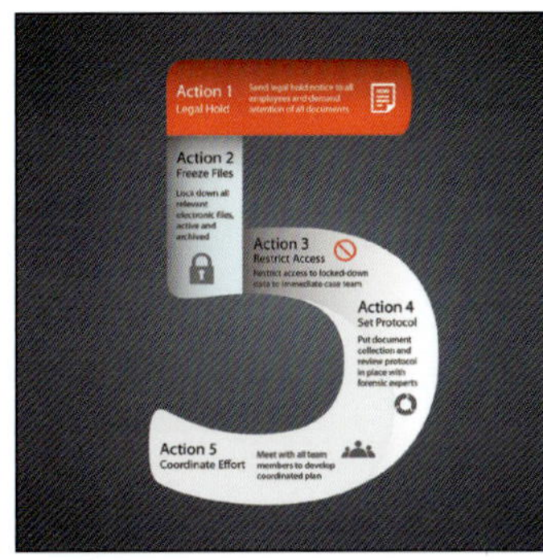

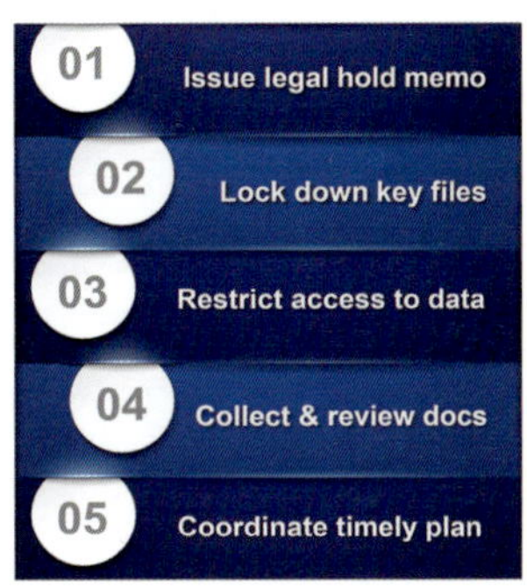

Font Choice

Select a legible, tone-appropriate font, especially if you're using a lot of text. A few words in a tough-to-read font might still be legible (though I'm not sure why you'd want to do that in any event). But the more text you have, the more likely the extra ornamentation on the letters will result in a legibility problem.

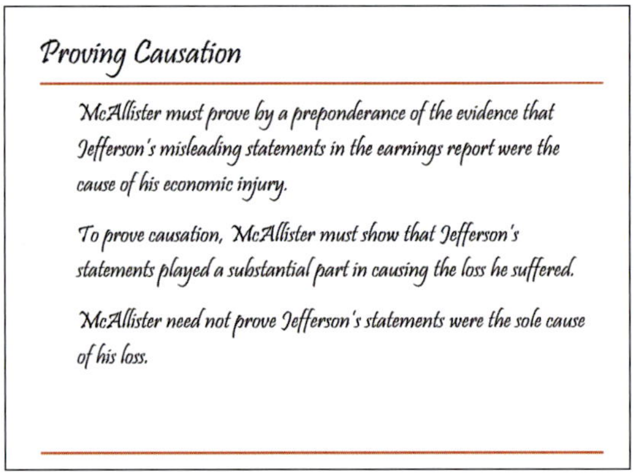

Capitalization

Think twice about using all capital letters. If you're using all caps because that's how your client writes its name—e.g., MGM, IKEA, or CNN—that's one thing. But if you're relying on capital letters to set your heading apart from your text, think again. First, there are many other ways to set your heading apart, and we'll cover a lot of them in this book. More important for present purposes, though, is that writing in all caps is harder to read than initial caps, and it takes up more space. Switching to initial caps is more readable and allows you to say the same thing in a larger size.

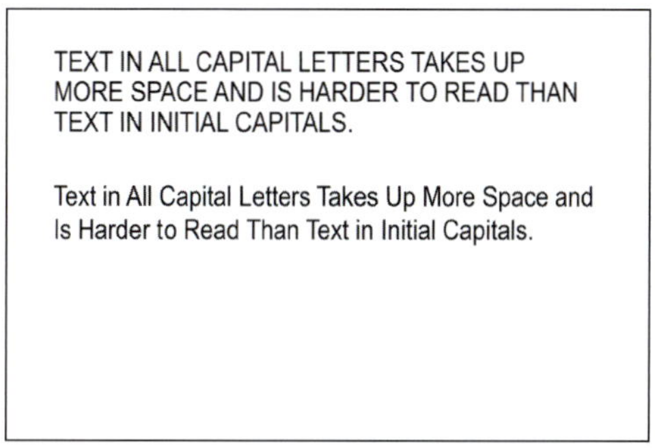

If you can reduce the amount of text in the heading altogether, even better. As designers like to remind us, and in contrast to the approach many lawyers take in written briefs, "it's a headline, not a sentence."

Proofreading

Finally, make sure you proofread your slides, both substantively and stylistically. Jurors notice errors in grammar, spelling, and design. When they do, they're distracted from your message. They start thinking about the mistake and miss whatever you're saying or showing them. And if you have more than one error, it looks unprofessional and risks sending the message that you don't care.

Visuals shouldn't be a crutch to type your whole closing argument (or most of it) onto slides. But when you do use text—and you will—make sure jurors can see it and have time to comprehend it, and that it's not so overwhelming that they'll never write it down. Make your text contrast with the background so it's legible, and give jurors a mental break to read it or read it to them. Unleash the power of your words.

5

VOLUME BUILDS

Presentations filled with text-heavy slides are overwhelming visually and underwhelming substantively, whether surrounded by colorful swirls and clip art or placed on a simple monotone background. The same is true for slide decks filled with graphics, arrows, or bubbles. Everything on the slide takes concentration to sort through and comprehend. Clutter risks distracting the viewer and undermining efforts at effective communication.

But an *individual* text or graphic-heavy slide—well-designed and deliberately presented—can be extraordinarily effective for conveying certain trial themes. Indeed, sometimes the very message we're trying to depict is the volume itself—"a lot" of something. You might be showing steps taken to respond to accusations of wrongdoing; compliance efforts; performance problems (or kudos); repeated warnings or opportunities for mitigation; a growing presence in a market or industry—it all can be depicted effectively with a volume build.

In fact, volume builds can even be effective for showing what's *not* there. Whenever you have to prove a negative—e.g., that your client had no motive to do what he's accused of—consider what you would expect to see if the accusation were true. If you come up with a list of what's "missing," you have a potential volume build. For instance, to prove a lack of motive, you might list all the circumstances that would logically lead to a motive for your client but that are missing in your opponent's evidence. No stock options, no chance of promotion, no personal crisis, no soured relationship, etc.—all of these missing pieces could be depicted visually, even using images instead of text, and presented through a volume build.

The key to effectively presenting a busy visual lies in controlling the flow of information. When jurors feel rushed or overwhelmed, they become frustrated. They will direct that frustration at the presenter. They'll either lose interest and ignore the slide entirely, they'll struggle through it (increasing their frustration), or they'll read ahead.

When jurors read ahead, they're missing whatever we're saying at the same time, and either the written text or our spoken words (or both) won't be comprehended. The reality is, we read faster than we speak. Both John Medina and Edward Tufte point out that the average PowerPoint slide contains forty words, and the average viewer reads that slide in five to eight seconds.[1] But it will take us longer than eight seconds to read the slide aloud. And, we might have more than five seconds' worth of spoken material we want to cover about *each point* we've included on a slide. So while we're expanding upon the thought in the first text point, jurors are already reading our second, third, fourth, and fifth points, and missing our explanation of previous points.

Gradually building the slides before the jurors' eyes mitigates these concerns. You'll give jurors time to comprehend each new element, while you're still purposefully depicting volume in a visual way. The volume itself becomes the visual memory for the jury.

Creating the Builds

When I design a busy slide that I know I'll want to build in front of the jury, I start at the end. I design the final slide first—the text or graphic-heavy visual I want the jury to remember during their deliberations.

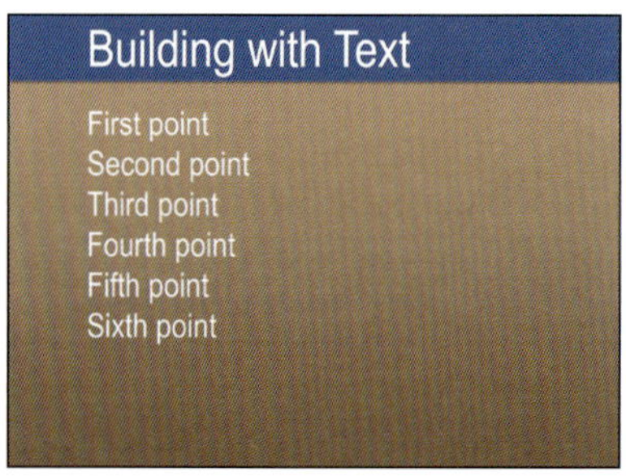

Then I systematically remove information to create the earlier part of the build.

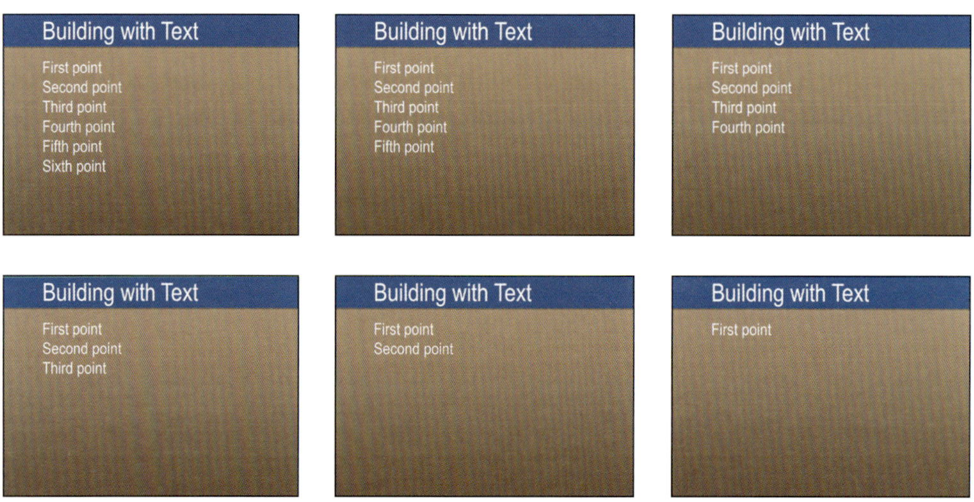

When I present the slides to the jury, I of course do so in the reverse order, adding one new piece of information at a time. I finish discussing that point before I reveal the next piece of the build. I control what the jurors see, when they see it, and how much time they have to absorb it. When it's time to reveal the next point in the build, I leave the prior point on screen to emphasize the increasing volume.

Sometimes I'll leave the prior point up as is, with each new point emphasized just as much as the last:

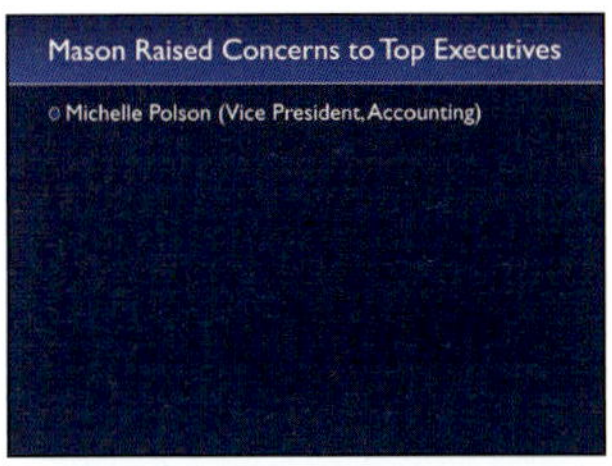

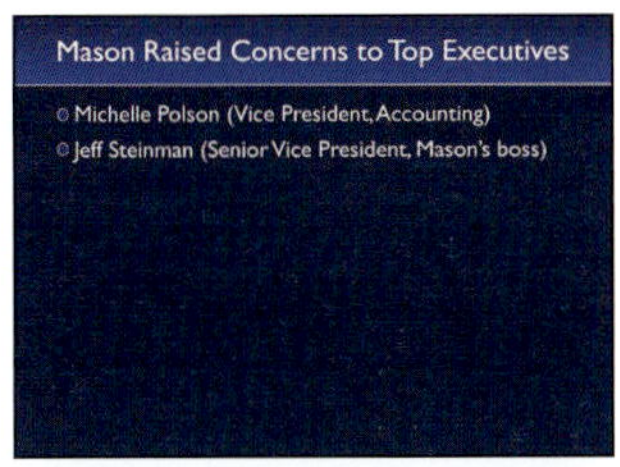

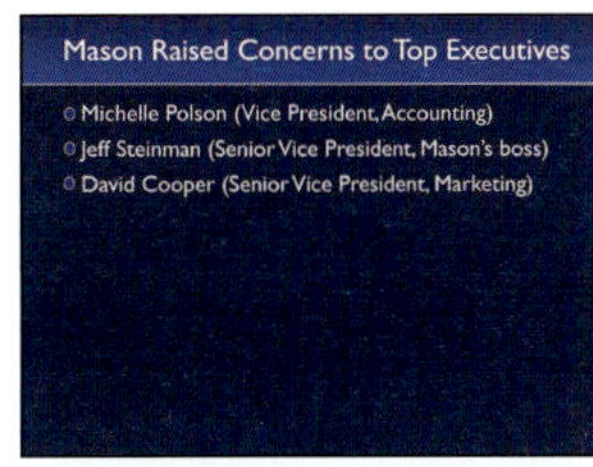

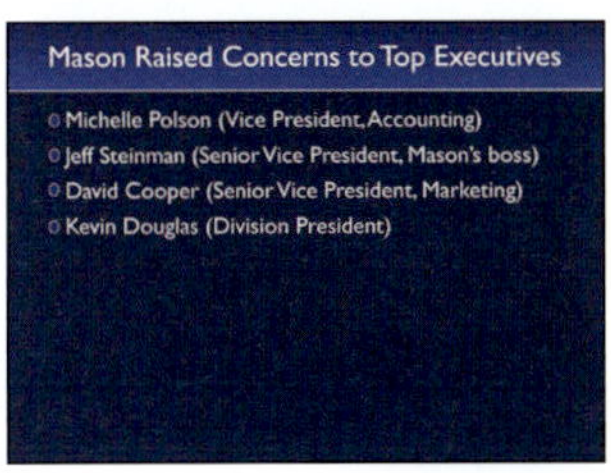

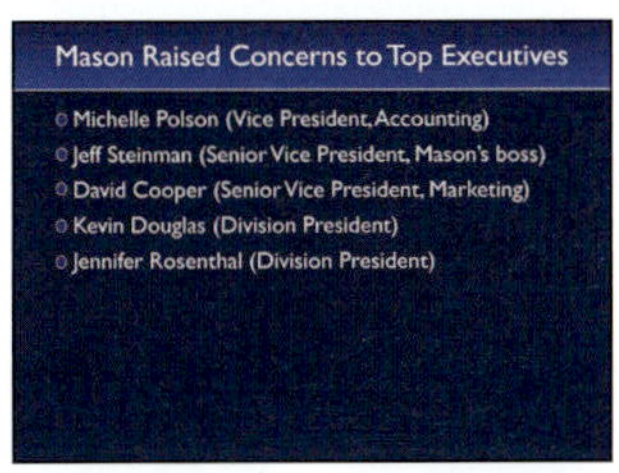

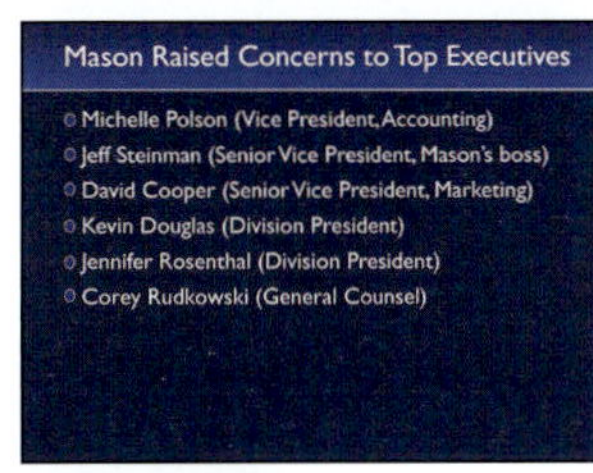

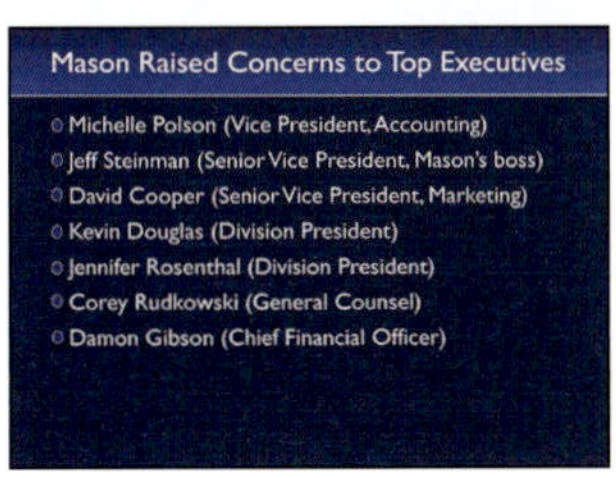

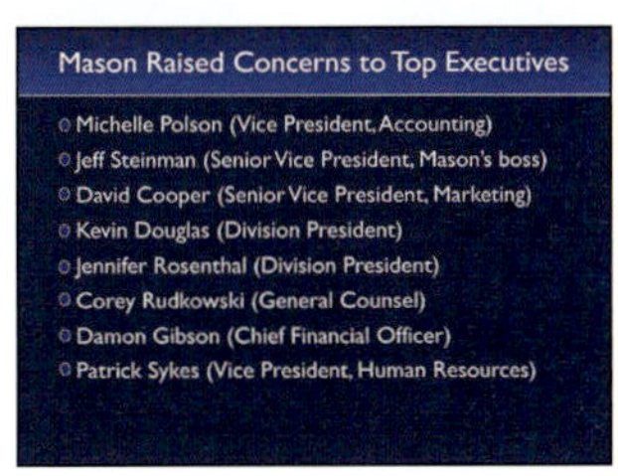

Other times, I'll gray out the points I've finished discussing so they're no longer commanding attention. This helps signal to the jurors that I'm moving to the next point. It's easy to do. Simply select each element you've already covered and change its color so it contrasts less with the background or less with the next element you bring up on the slide, and you'll fade the information you've already discussed into the background.

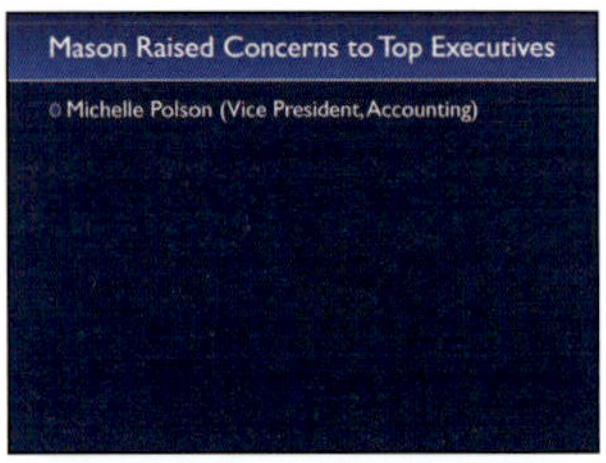

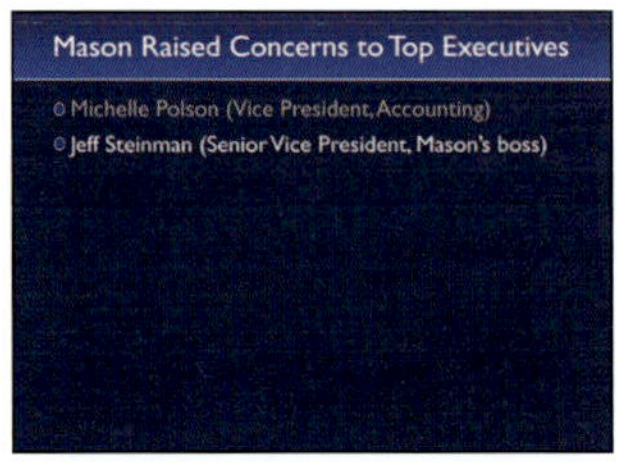

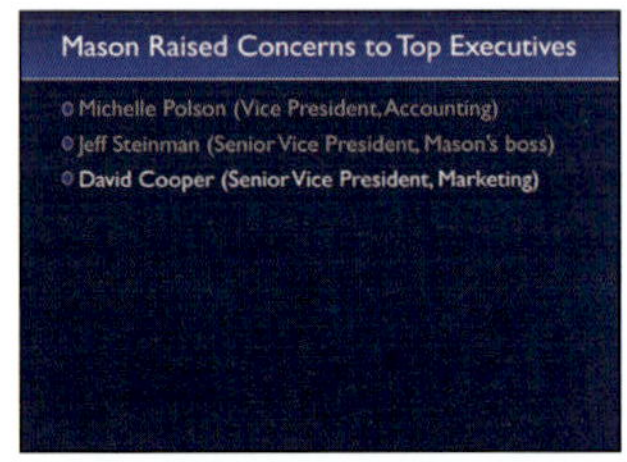

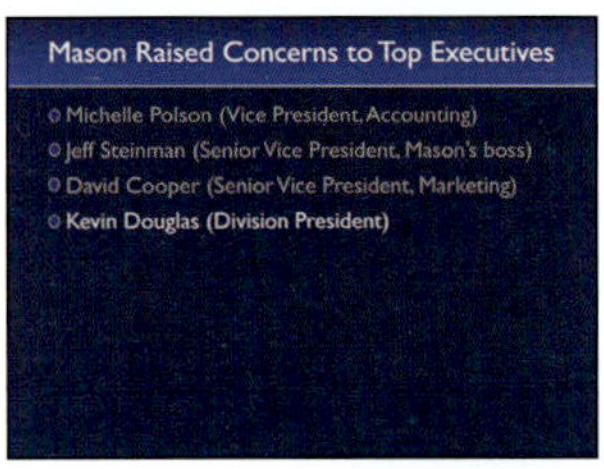

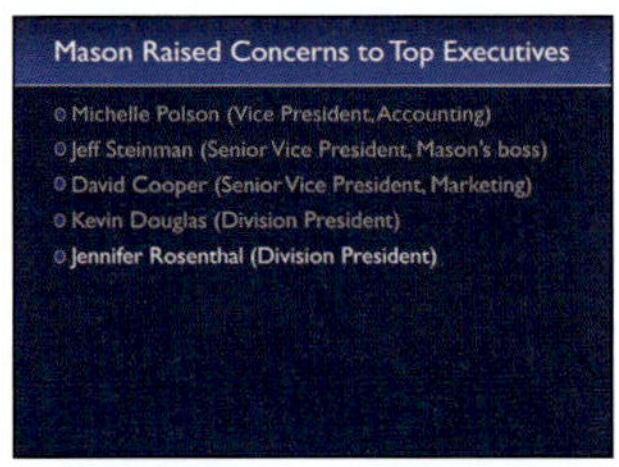

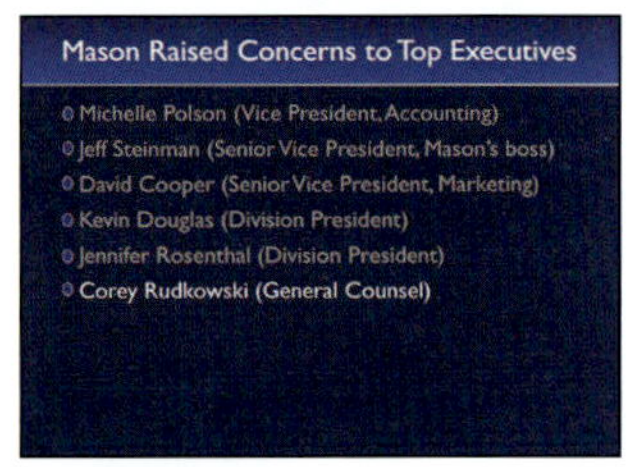

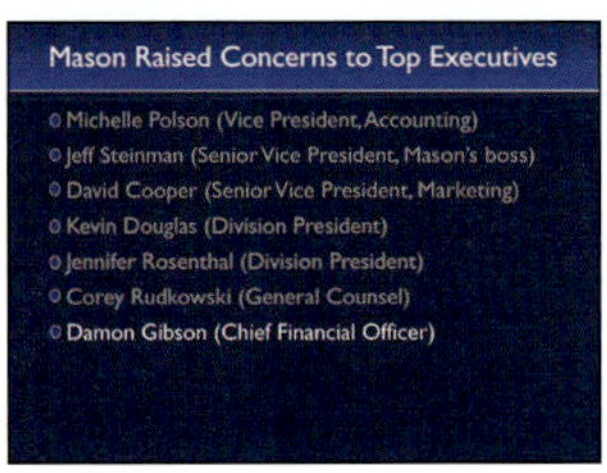

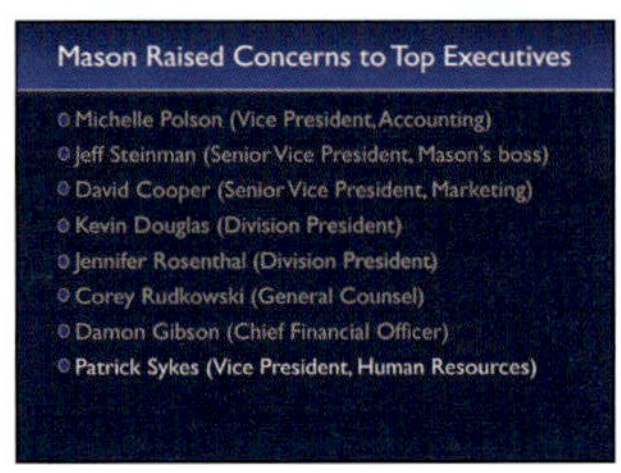

If there's not enough space to leave everything on the slide in the size you create it, you can shrink or move each element aside as you display a new point. Each of these techniques allows us to build volume gradually, giving the jurors time to read and comprehend it.

There's no one right way to create these builds. I'm sure the designers I work with have other techniques. But when I'm designing my own visuals, this is how I create builds. It works well for me, it's easy, and it effectively gives me the control I need over how the information is presented.

A note of caution—when creating slide builds, make sure identical elements that carry from one slide to the next actually remain identical. The viewer will notice changes. If text, bullet points, lines, graphics or any other elements shift from one slide to the next, even slightly, jurors will be distracted. At minimum, it looks unprofessional, like a typo in the midst of your text. When errors such as this occur, usually it's because an edit was made to one slide in the build but not carried onto all other slides in exactly the same way. For example, if you adjust the location of a text box just a little on one slide but you don't make the same adjustment on the other slides, then that text box will "jump" into and out of position as you advance the slides. Proofread your slide builds just like you proofread for substantive typos to avoid these distractions.

Building with Text

One widely recognizable example of depicting volume with text is the Vietnam Veterans Memorial in Washington, D.C. The Memorial Wall is actually two long, black, reflective walls that form an angle where they meet. The walls are etched with the names of over 58,000 military service members in simple, identical typeface, spaced evenly in horizontal rows. Edward Tufte discusses the Memorial in his book *Envisioning Information*, calling it a "micro/macro" design. Each name on the wall is meaningful on its own, but the names as a collective have a separate impact on the viewer.

Similarly, the complimentary micro/macro importance of information is often critical in a trial. The pieces matter individually, but considered together they take on another meaning. For instance, I tried a case where my client was accused of conspiring with others to commit securities fraud. An important defense theme was that my client's conduct was wholly inconsistent with being a member of a criminal conspiracy. As one example, he suspected other employees of engaging in improper activity, but rather than joining or assisting them, he *reported* their activity to his superiors. Individually, each person he reported to was important, as each one was very senior in the company. But taken together, the list took on another meaning, emphasizing his great efforts to report his suspicions. The client didn't just report his concerns to one or two people. He told *eight* of his bosses.

During closing argument, we wanted to remind the jurors of this theme. We could have displayed a succinct statement on a simple text slide:

But because the power of the theme was the *volume* of people he told, we instead made volume the visual, as you've seen in the builds above.

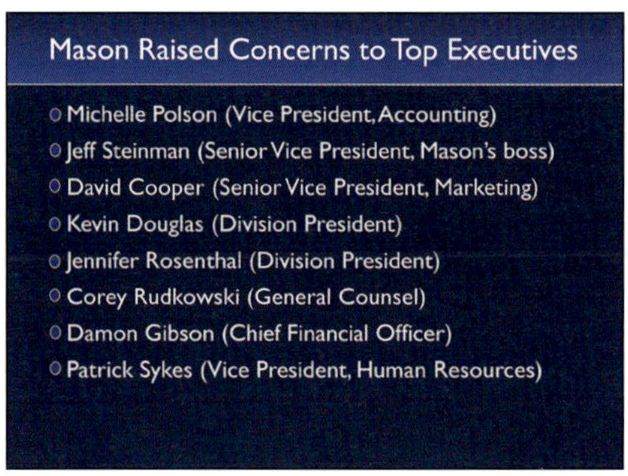

Just like the Vietnam Veterans Memorial, the individual and collective worked together. The list was presented one name at a time, and the jurors watched it build. Each name and title spoke to that individual's seniority, and the collective list conveyed the volume of people the client told. (And if all of these executives had testified in trial, using photos of each witness would add visual interest, remind the jurors of who was who, and create an even stronger visual memory of the theme.)

How you arrange the text on your slide can also convey substantive meaning. In this same case, undisputed evidence showed that our client asked to be taken off of the account at issue. This was additional conduct inconsistent with being in a conspiracy to manipulate that very account. And he didn't ask just once. He asked three times. In the context of this case, three was "a lot" of times. Similarly, the testimony showed he went to "a lot" of effort each time. So, using a volume build, we created a visual image of the client's repeated, onerous efforts.

We created a three-column design and began with the first of the client's three requests on the left side of the slide. The three columns immediately signaled that there was more to come. To further emphasize this point, the heading itself notes that this is the *first* attempt. Building the text as we went, we walked the jury through each point. We reminded the jurors of the testimony they'd heard during trial (and educated those who might have lost focus). We balanced using the minimum amount of text to convey the message with the goal of visually depicting volume. Thus, there was a purpose to the text-heavy nature of the slide.

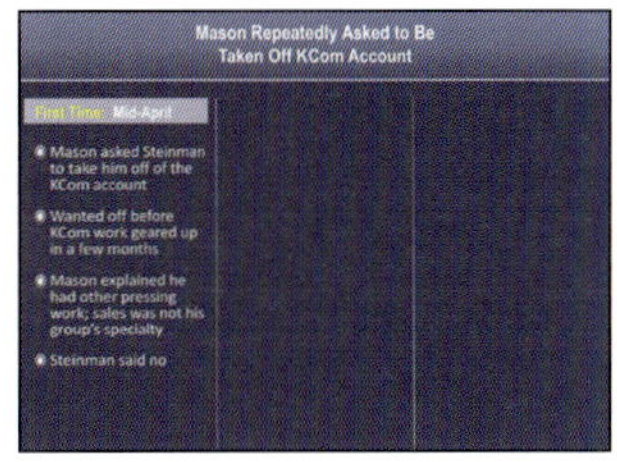

When it was time to add the second column, we left the text in the first column on the screen, but reduced its contrast with the background. The text on the left is now unreadable, but because we took the time to walk jurors through it, they'd already read it and didn't need to do so again. That text became a graphic element reminding the jurors visually that the client tried three times to remove himself from this account.

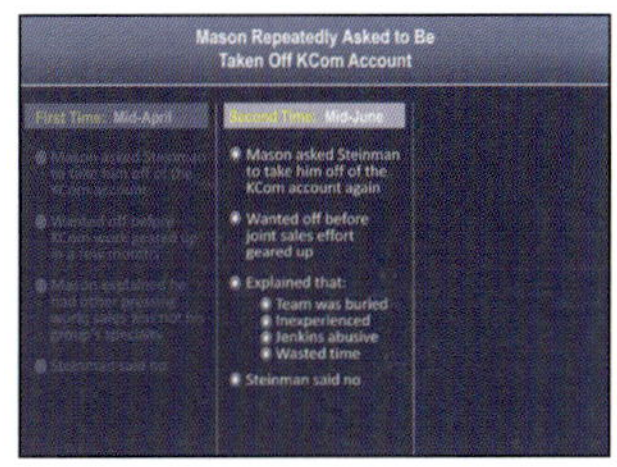

We used the same approach when we added the third column, building each text point to control the pace at which jurors received the information.

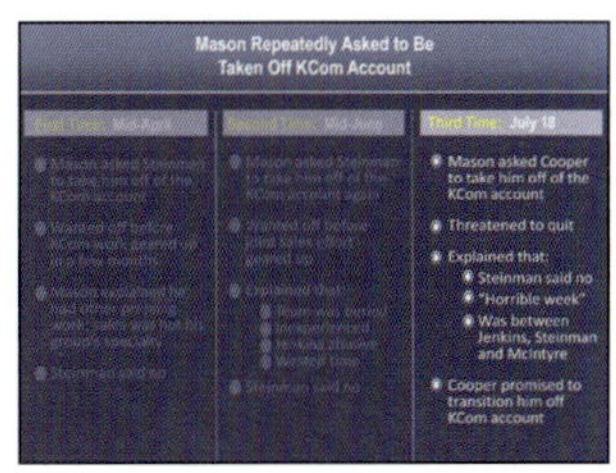

By the end of the build, the slide was purposefully full. The slides built to a visual representation of our client's significant efforts to get off of this account, reinforcing the volume of his efforts along the way. It didn't matter whether the jurors remembered the details of each try. If all the jurors remembered was that the client tried to get off the account, we'd made our point. If they remembered he tried repeatedly, even better. And if they remembered he did "a lot" each time, we'd hit a home run.

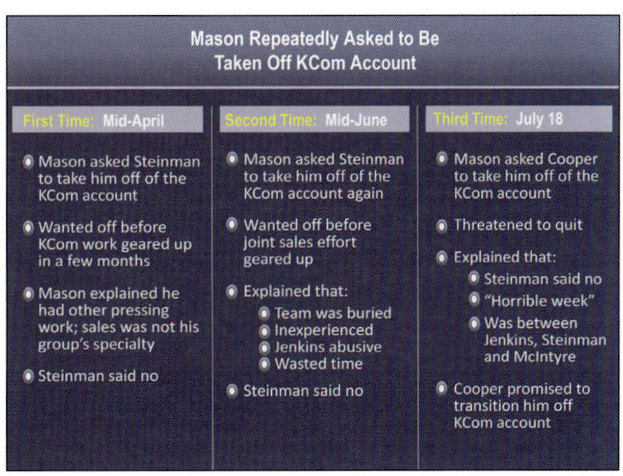

Of course, there were many ways we could have designed a visual to depict the extent of the client's efforts.

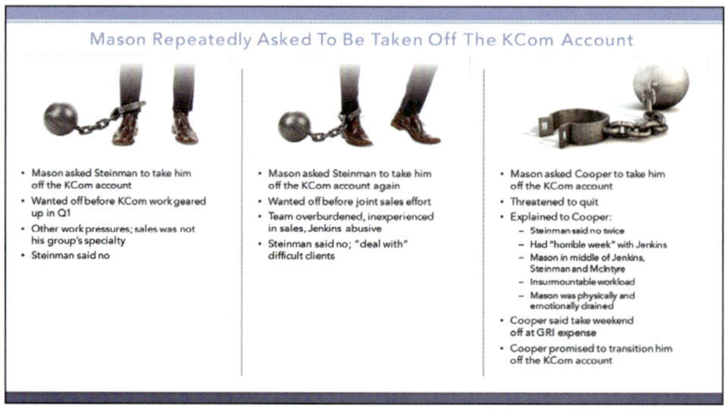

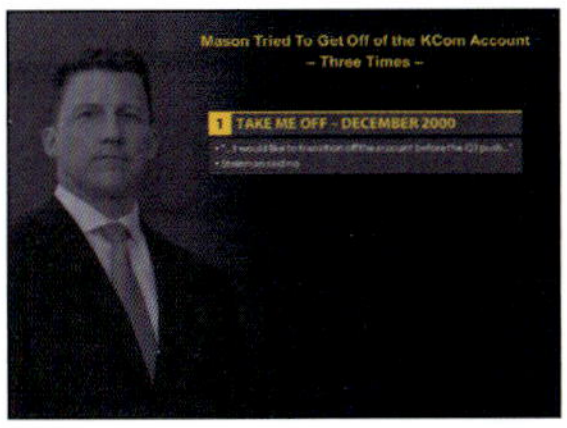

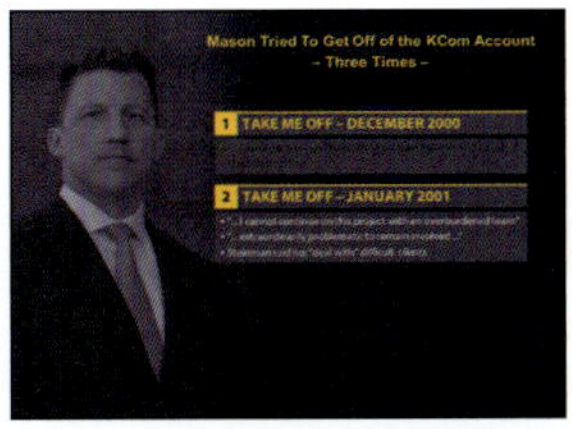

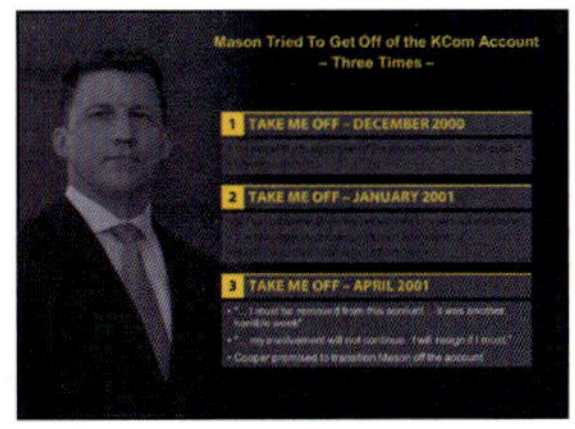

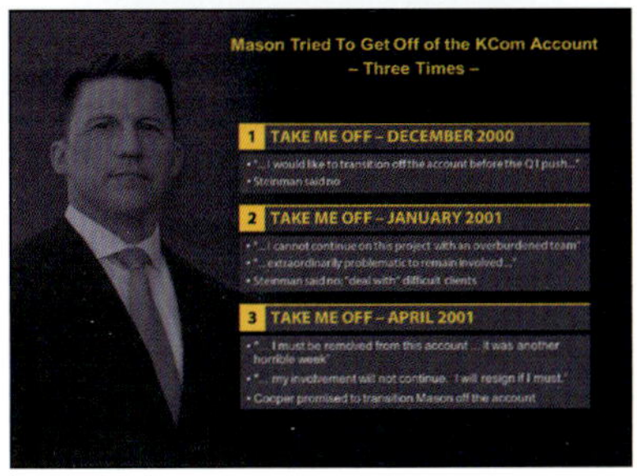

Whatever design you choose for a particular theme, you won't be designing your slides in a vacuum. Consider the other slides in your presentation, and use complementary designs so the presentation as a whole looks and feels cohesive.

Synthesizing Testimony and Evidence

Condensing large amounts of information into a digestible summary is nothing new to most trial lawyers. There are even federal and state evidentiary rules governing how to do it.[2] But the utility of synthesizing evidence isn't limited to numerical data or even "voluminous" data, and the display options aren't limited to the summary charts addressed in the rules. I regularly use visuals to synthesize testimony or other evidence on the same theme, building it in front of the jury.

In a case I tried under the False Claims Act, one allegation related to a dense contract that was about three inches thick. Many witnesses on both sides testified about the unique and onerous requirements of this contract. Even if the jury didn't remember each requirement, I wanted them to remember this basic theme.

I synthesized the information using a volume build. Each successive slide displayed another onerous requirement, along with the actual page of the contract with the relevant language enlarged and highlighted. I put the exhibit number on the slide, and, because the contract was so large, I also included the page number for that requirement. One by one, I walked through each requirement, reading the key text and the page number out loud. Next to the image, I used as little text as possible to summarize each requirement. Note-taking jurors were more likely to jot down my quick summaries than the lengthy contract language I'd highlighted.

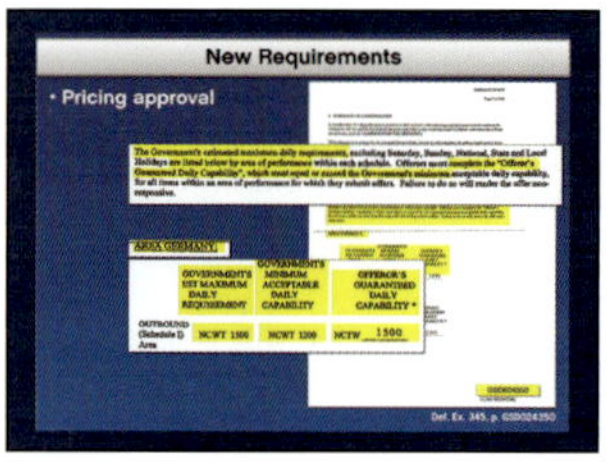

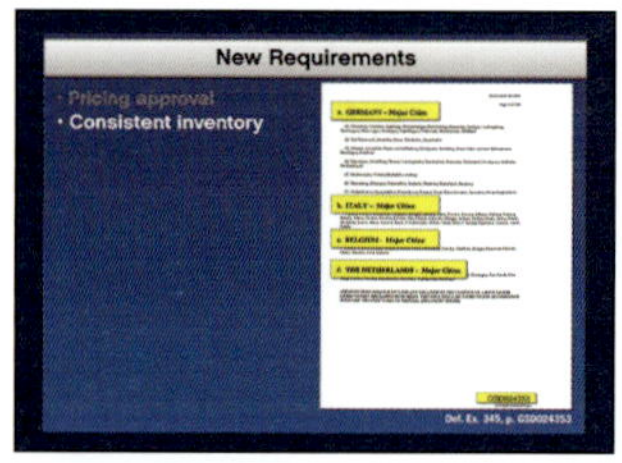

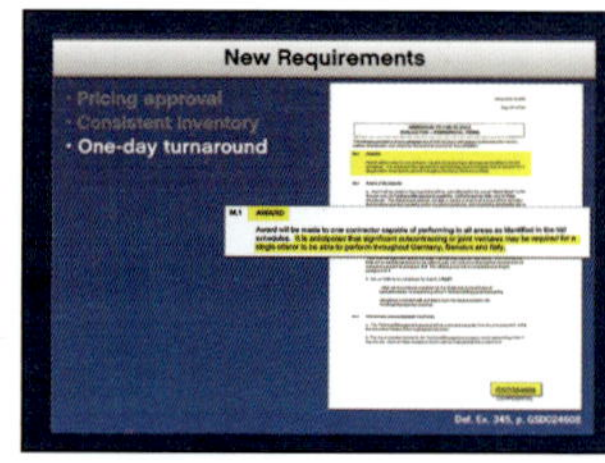

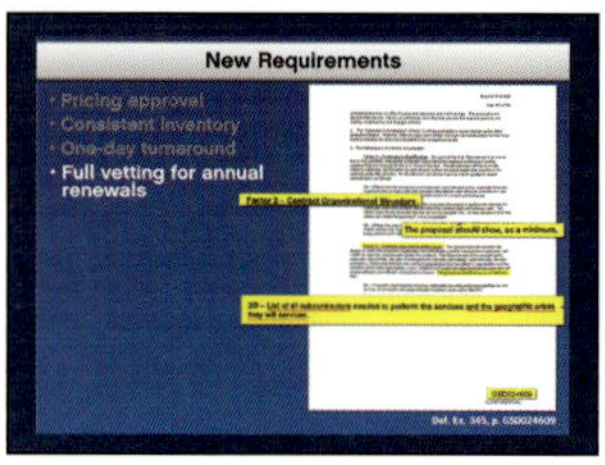

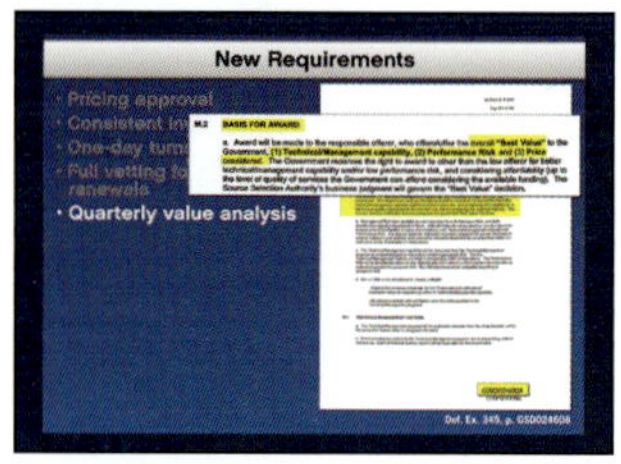

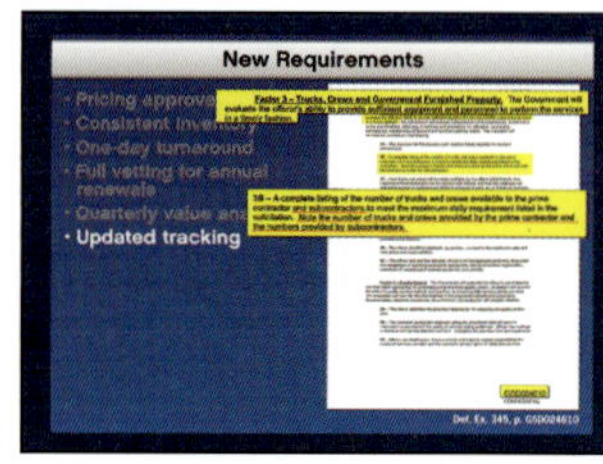

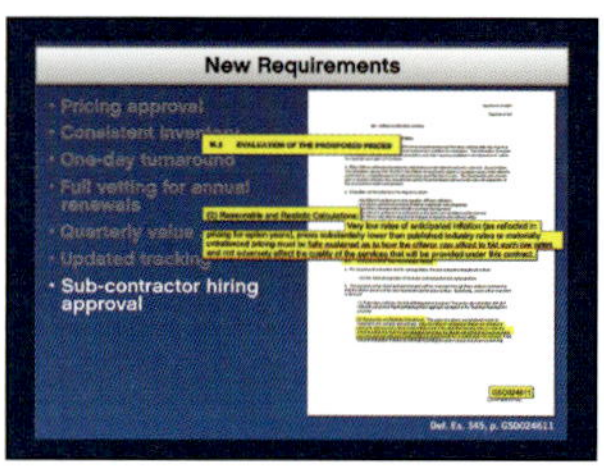

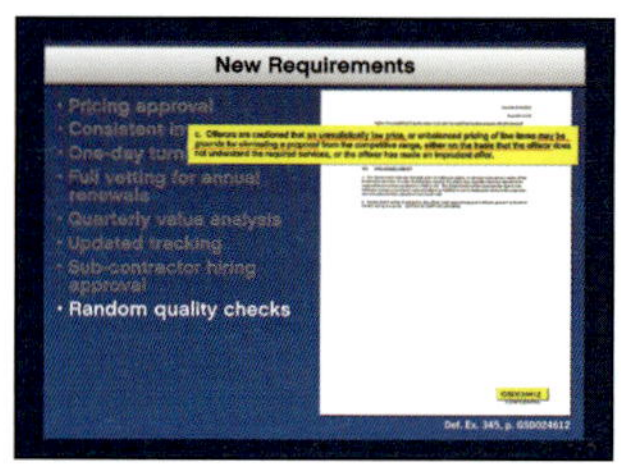

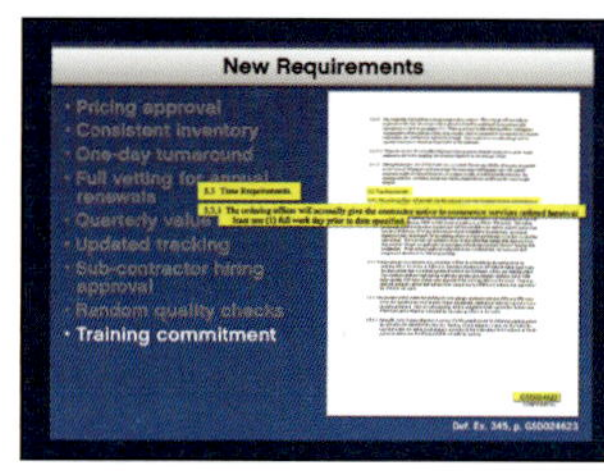

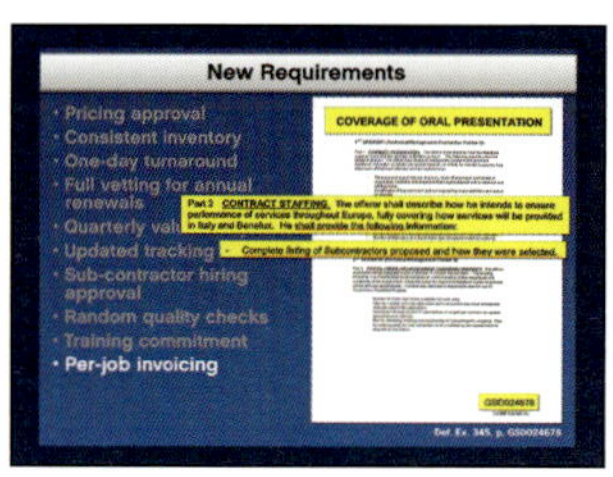

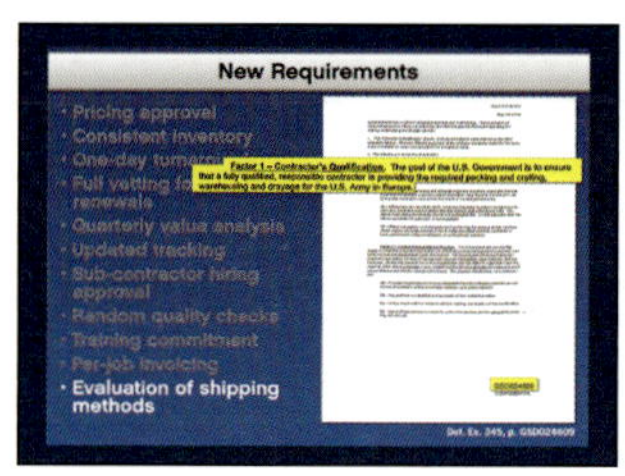

As I moved from slide to slide, I left up the prior points, but grayed them out to signal I was moving to the next requirement. Leaving the prior requirements up allowed the jurors to take notes at their own pace, and visually reinforced my theme that there were *a lot* of these onerous requirements.

Finally, the last slide was the complete list of requirements, which I had just proven in the prior slides with actual text from the contract.

I use the same approach to visually summarize all testimony on the same theme. I could certainly just tell the jurors in closing that ten witnesses all said the same thing. I could even paraphrase the testimony. But I have more credibility if I show them the actual transcript testimony from these witnesses, especially if it's been days or even weeks since the jury heard from them.

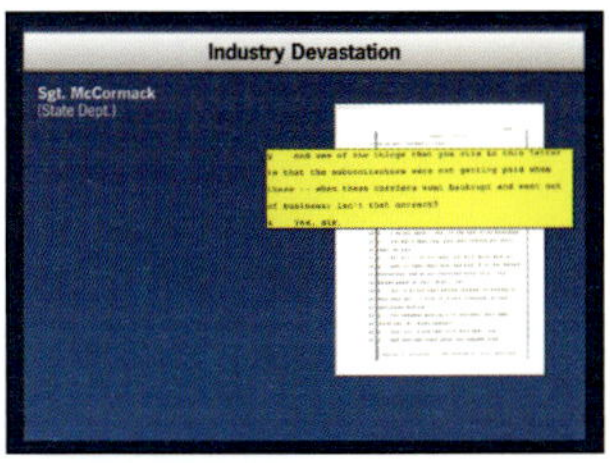

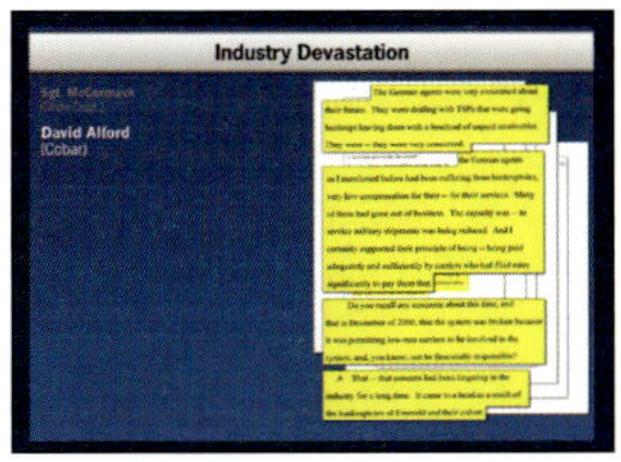

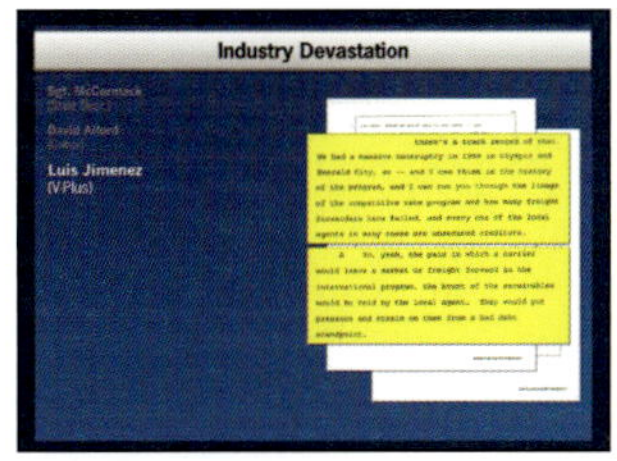

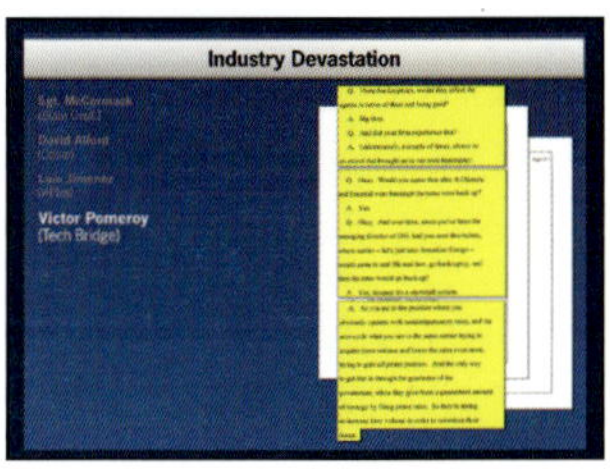

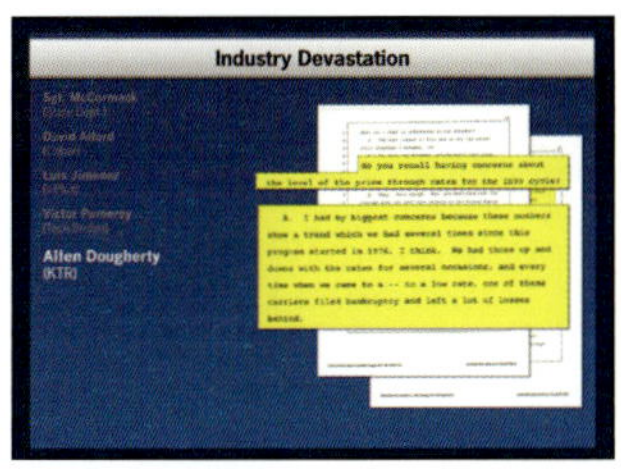

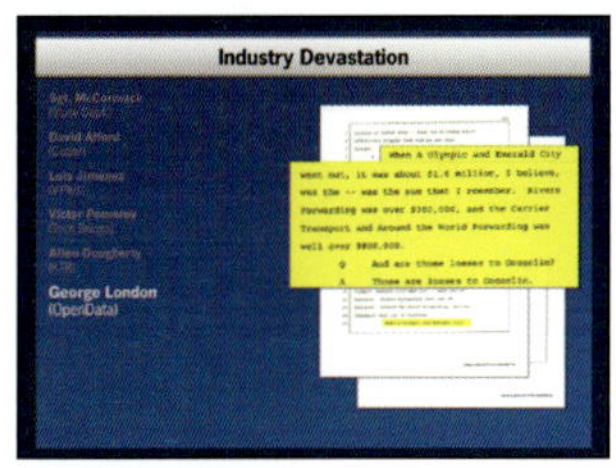

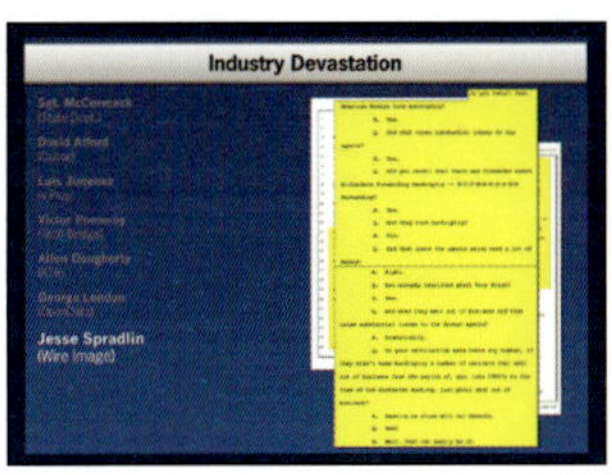

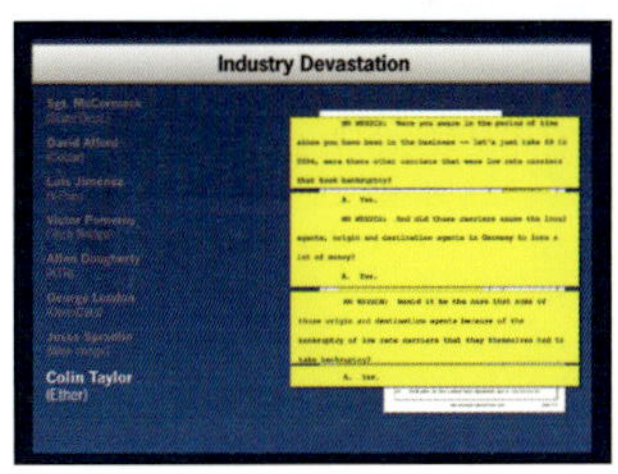

In this example, many witnesses had testified in support of a key theme, including several witnesses called by my opponent. I started with a simple heading the jurors could quickly write down in their notes. One by one, I displayed the transcript page with each witness's testimony, enlarging the relevant text. I listed the name of each witness next to the transcript and kept the names on the slide as I moved to the next witness and corresponding transcript page. My own text—the heading and names—is the information I'd most expect jurors to write down in their notepads, so I kept it short. By showing the relevant transcript excerpts along the way, I re-established each witness's testimony and strengthened my own credibility.

Building with Graphics

Just as the Vietnam Veterans Memorial embodies the individual/collective power of text, the mural at the Korean War Veterans Memorial does the same with graphics. The mural featured in this memorial uses no text at all, but rather features over 2,500 images sandblasted into a black granite background.

Each image is powerful on its own, depicting a person, a scene, or equipment associated with the Korean War. When the images are viewed collectively, the mural has a separate power and impact, telling a more fulsome story of the war. What's more, the arrangement of the etchings was designed to create the appearance of Korean mountain ranges, an effect that can only be seen and appreciated when the etchings are viewed collectively.

We can use this approach in trial to visually convey volume-based themes.

Consider, for example, an insider trading case. A key case theme rests on frequent calls and emails back and forth between two witnesses just before a purchase of stock, versus one-sided communication after the stock purchase. Certainly, the contacts could be listed on a text-based slide.

Martin (Tipper) Ceased All Communications with Aaron (Tippee) After May 21 Stock Purchase

May 1 (10:02 a.m.) – Aaron calls Martin
May 2 (11:57 a.m.) – Aaron calls Martin
May 2 (12:08 p.m.) – Martin calls Aaron
May 3 (11:30 a.m.) – Martin emails Aaron
May 4 (10:18 a.m.) – Aaron emails Martin
May 5 (9:25 a.m.) – Martin emails Aaron
May 5 (3:26 p.m.) – Aaron emails Martin
May 6 (3:45 p.m.) – Martin emails Aaron
May 7 (1:17 p.m.) – Aaron calls Martin
May 8 (9:25 a.m.) – Martin calls Aaron
May 9 (8:45 a.m.) – Aaron emails Martin
May 9 (1:03 p.m.) – Martin emails Aaron
May 10 (9:00 a.m.) – Aaron calls Martin
May 11 (10:06 a.m.) – Martin emails Aaron
May 11 (4:45 p.m.) – Aaron emails Martin
May 12 (9:05 p.m.) – Martin calls Aaron
May 14 (12:07 p.m.) – Martin calls Aaron
May 14 (12:09 p.m.) – Aaron calls Martin
May 15 (11:35 a.m.) – Martin emails Aaron
May 15 (2:24 p.m.) – Aaron emails Martin
May 16 (12:02 p.m.) – Martin calls Aaron
May 16 (3:45 p.m.) – Aaron calls Martin
May 18 (11:41 a.m.) – Martin emails Aaron
May 18 (5:30 p.m.) – Aaron calls Martin
May 20 (12:02 p.m.) – Martin calls Aaron
May 20 (12:03 p.m.) – Aaron calls Martin
May 21 – Aaron purchases stock
May 22 (8:27 a.m.) – Aaron emails Martin
May 23 (2:28 p.m.) – Aaron emails Martin
May 24 (10:05 a.m.) – Aaron calls Martin
May 25 (8:49 p.m.) – Aaron calls Martin
May 26 (7:36 p.m.) – Aaron emails Martin
May 28 (10:20 a.m.) – Aaron emails Martin
May 29 (9:45 p.m.) – Aaron emails Martin
May 30 (10:07 p.m.) – Aaron calls Martin

But using basic graphics in place of text can bring this trial theme to life in a much more visual way. Here, simple circles represent each call or email, and the color coding shows who initiated it. Just a few words—whether spoken orally or appearing on the slide—provide the necessary context.

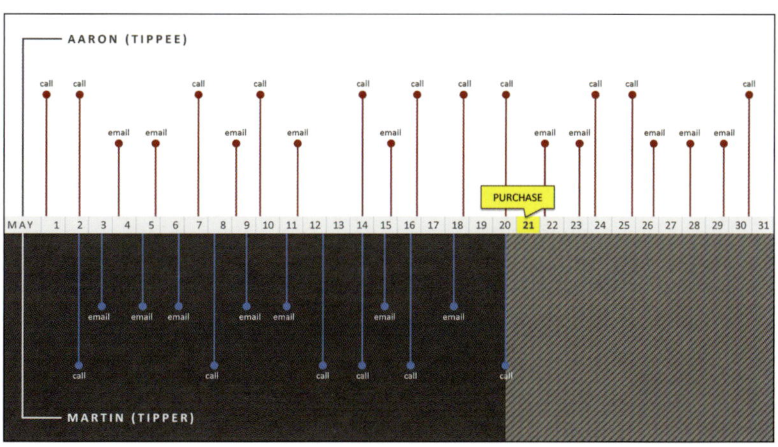

Or, instead of using small dots of color, meaningful symbols could represent each communication:

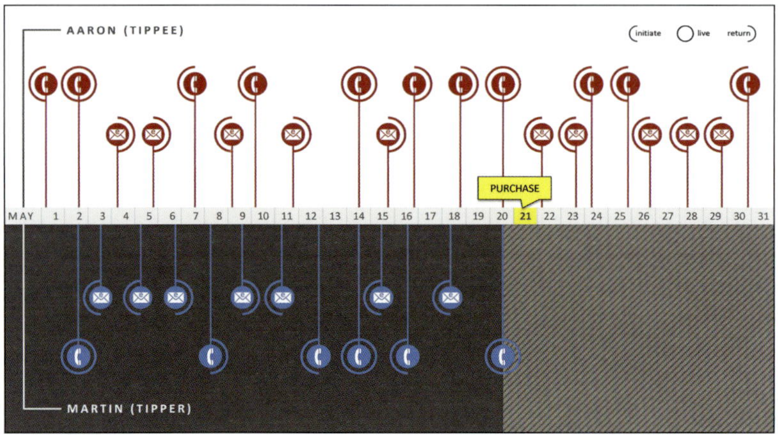

The symbols are visual and have familiar meaning, so are instantly comprehended. They also take up less space on the slide than typing "phone call" and "email" repeatedly, resulting in a calmer design.

Another option for this theme, since there are only two witnesses at issue, would be using their photographs to depict which witness initiated each contact.

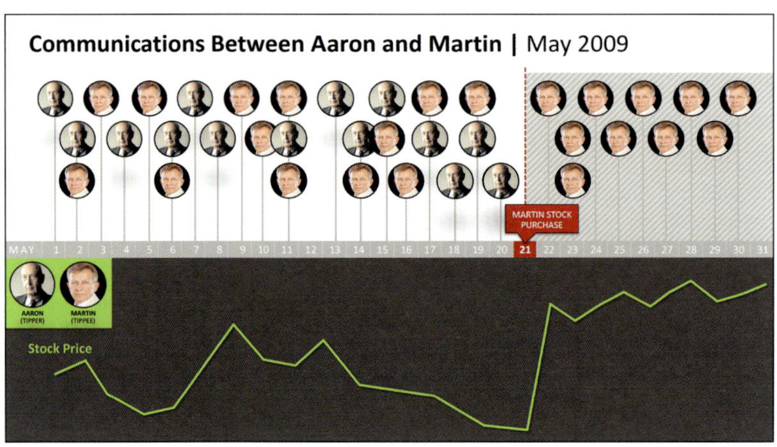

In this design, a stock chart below the timeline adds visual emphasis to the drop in the stock's price on the date of the tippee's purchase, followed by an immediate and dramatic price increase. But now, all the time entries appear together above the timeline. This design works because of the contrast between the two photographs. It is immediately apparent that the communication went both ways before the purchase and one way after the purchase. (Here, realizing what he had done, the tipper is avoiding the tippee's repeated calls for more information.)

Which design works best might depend on other circumstances in the case. In a long trial with a lot of witnesses, photographs might help remind jurors which two witnesses you're talking about. If you aren't concerned about jurors recalling specific witnesses (either because they'll obviously remember or because it doesn't matter), then simpler might be better. Solid circles (or squares or diamonds or whatever) of clearly contrasting colors would work just fine. Or, if it mattered in the case that the communication was by phone (for example, if other testimony suggested the witnesses were deliberate about not putting problematic communication in writing and you want to emphasize the phone calls), then using telephone symbols or images might create the most effective visual memory.

When we build volume with repeated symbols, we can move through the slides faster than we can with text-based slides. Each new slide adds another already-defined symbol, which in the first instance is either immediately recognizable (such as an image of a phone), or can be explained very quickly—e.g., a blue dot represents John Smith, or product sales, or instances of illness.

Advertisers use this technique all the time. Consider, for example, cellular phone service providers depicting the many places they offer coverage. They'll start with an empty map of the United States—itself an immediately recognizable symbol. Then they build the visual before our eyes, adding dots of a single color to symbolize their coverage. The dots quickly blend together and nearly cover the map. Today, these coverage maps are so ubiquitous that the need to build them has essentially evaporated. Instead, providers need only show the final, busy coverage map. Viewers instantly perceive the collective (macro) meaning—a lot of coverage—and they can easily look for the individual (micro) meaning by focusing on their own state to assess coverage where it matters to them.

Building Charts and Graphs

At bottom, a build is nothing more than a presentation technique for showing complexity or volume in a controlled manner, even if volume isn't the target theme you're depicting. Consider using some form of build even with charts and graphs, which often lend themselves to busy visuals. Building every detail from the ground up before the jury isn't always feasible (or desirable), but even a partial build can go a long way toward aiding the jury's understanding. Whenever the visual reasonably can be presented sequentially, I consider a build. A flowchart is a natural example.

When we use flowcharts, we're trying to illustrate the stages of a process. While it might not be feasible to build the individual elements of each step, it can work well to reveal each already-created step one at a time.

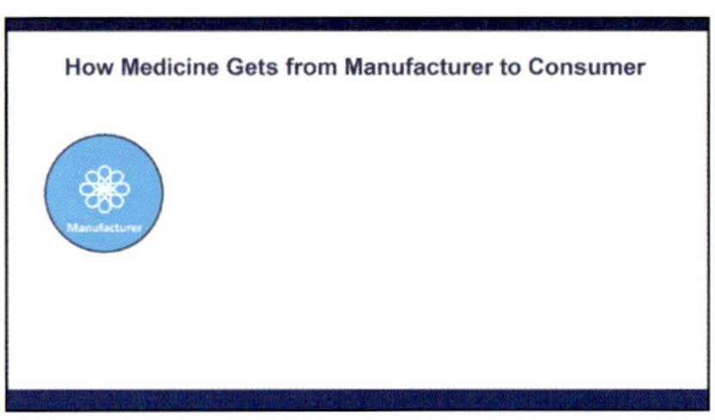

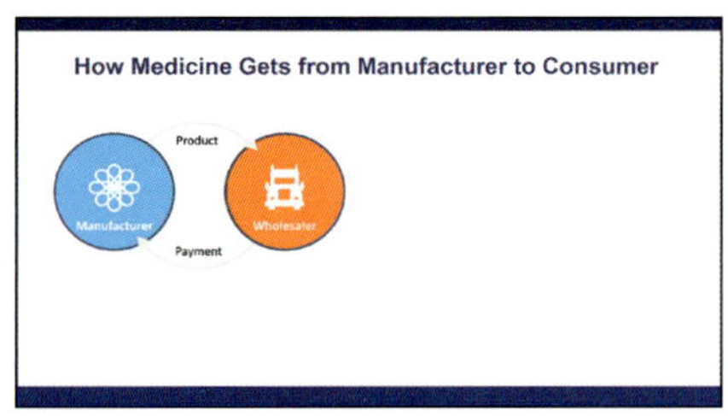

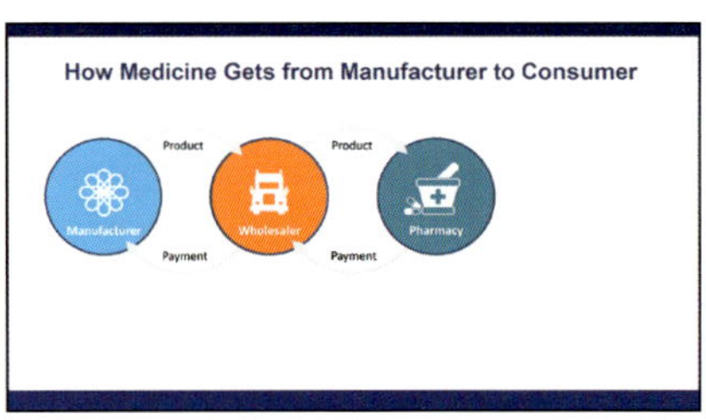

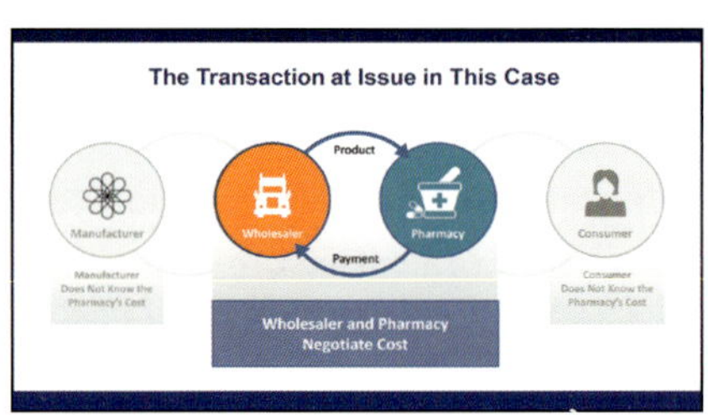

Occasionally, I use a build approach with line graphs (e.g., where I'm depicting several lines on the same graph), bar graphs, and even charts. It's not always necessary, but it's a useful technique to consider when the visual might otherwise be overwhelming.

Finally, just because we're depicting volume does not mean that irrelevant clutter is suddenly acceptable on the slide. Bells and whistles can't substitute for substance, which should convey volume in its own right. Tufte refers to the extra clutter on our visuals as "chartjunk." Filling your visuals with chartjunk won't create the illusion of substantive volume if there really is none. In fact, you might lose credibility with the jury just for trying such a stunt. Instead, just as you should with any other slide, keep text and other elements on volume builds limited to what's necessary for conveying your message.

6

Charts and Graphs

Charts and graphs are visual depictions of data. They help jurors understand information that might not readily lend itself to a verbal description in a trial setting. With charts and graphs, we can organize and compare information, dividing it into bite-size pieces. Tables, flowcharts, line and bar graphs, organizational charts, and pie charts all help identify patterns, highlight comparisons, and visualize relationships. Charts and graphs also let us depict trends and condense large data sets into manageable visual images.

Choosing which chart or graph to use can be a challenge. There are many different types, and each one has many design possibilities. So, just as with any other slide, the first question I ask when considering a chart or graph is "what's the point?" What do I want the jurors to understand and take with them to the jury room? The answer might not require a chart or graph at all. If you're really focused on a single statistic (e.g., a company's year-end 2012 revenue), then a simpler design such as a basic text slide might effectively convey the point.

If, however, your real point is for the jury to compare two or more pieces of data, such as 2012 revenue compared to the years before and after, then a chart or graph can help jurors visualize the theme. Below are some of the most common charts and graphs that work well in a jury setting. I'll discuss them individually, and then I'll provide some basic design tips that apply across the board when using these data displays. Keep in mind that there's rarely just one way to depict a particular theme. But by focusing on your key point, you can quickly narrow the universe of effective charts and graphs.

Common Charts and Graphs

Flowcharts

Flowcharts divide the parts of a process into discrete segments and present them in sequential order. Most often, flowcharts walk through a chronological, procedural,

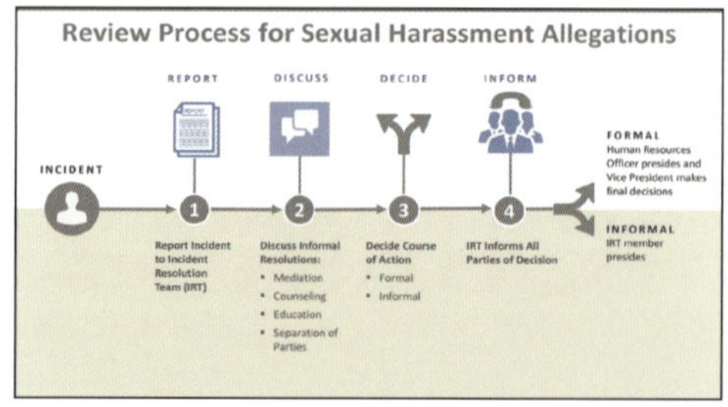

or analytical sequence. When you want to visually answer a "how" or "when" question, consider using a flowchart. You might depict a series of events, creating an illustrated chronology akin to a timeline. You might create a procedural flow, showing which step comes before another. Or you might walk jurors through the steps in a line of reasoning, such as identifying the elements of a claim to suggest what must be proven and in what order.

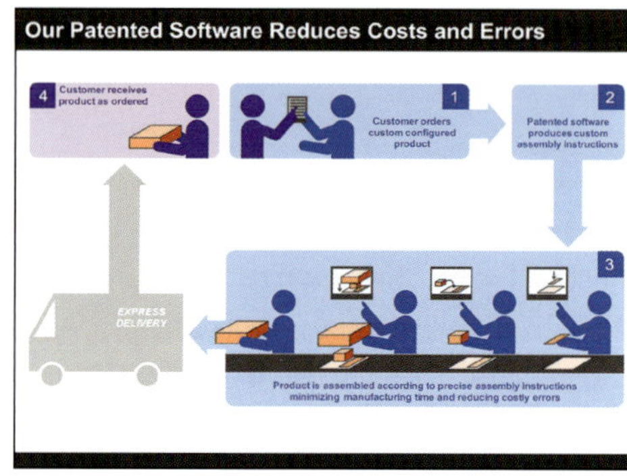

Be careful not to let the form of the flowchart overtake its function. Sometimes I see people get so focused on fitting all the steps on a single slide that the substantive logic disappears entirely. Instead, a convoluted system of boxes, arrows, and labels attempts to lead us through the design, which is otherwise not organized in any recognizable fashion.

We should always be cognizant of how many times our eyes have to bounce around on a slide to take everything in. Many of the graphic design techniques we'll discuss in this book are intended to organize the slide and minimize this phenomenon. With a flowchart, the need for organization is critical; without a clear design flow, the entire purpose of the chart is undermined. Don't let the design dictate or overshadow the content.

Organizational Charts

Organizational charts depict hierarchies and relationships.

In Chapter 5, I showed you this text build depicting my client's reports of suspected wrongdoing to "a lot" of senior executives within his company.

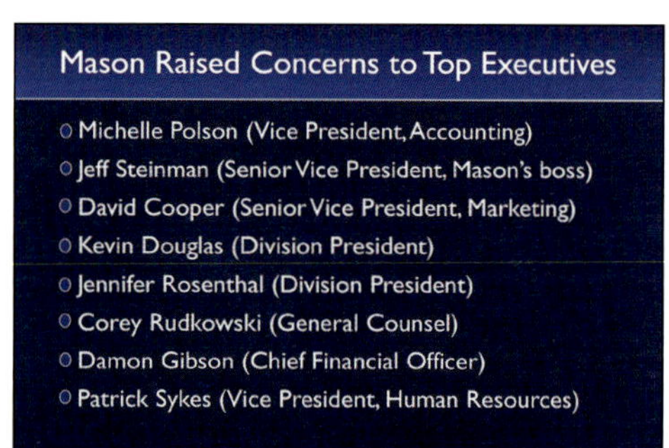

I included the executives' titles on the slide, but the list did nothing to communicate the corporate relationships between these people and my client. The real power in this "seniority" theme was in the comparison. My client reported concerns to executives who were, compared to him, much more senior in the company. A simple organizational chart made this clear immediately.

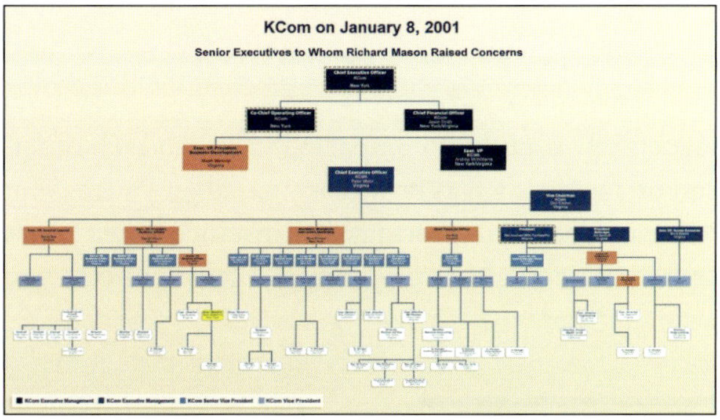

My client is in the yellow box, and the red boxes are the executives he reported concerns to. Because organizational charts are themselves familiar symbols, showing the full chart all at once worked just fine. Jurors immediately understood its structure. The individual names were purposely too small to read, so they were not distracting. By enlarging the yellow box to reveal the client's name, then enlarging a few of the red boxes to reveal the names of the senior executives (with whom the jurors already were familiar), we were able to "prove" the hierarchy and lend credibility to the theme.

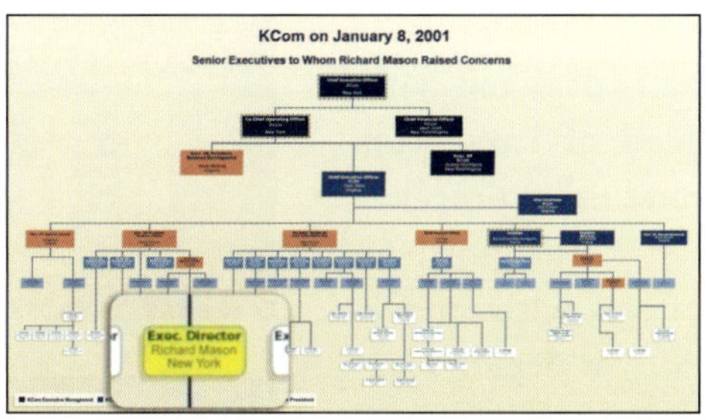

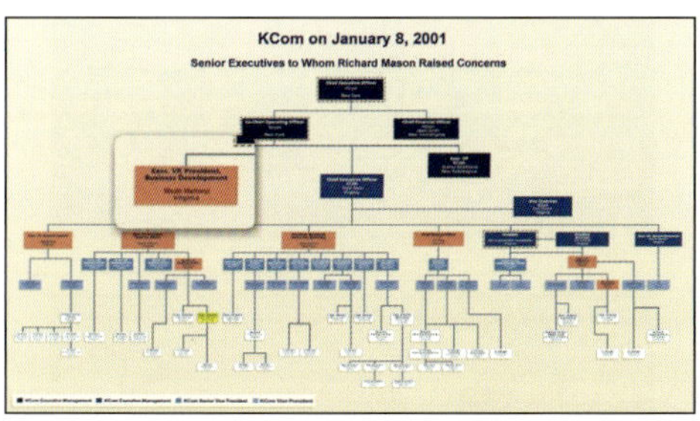

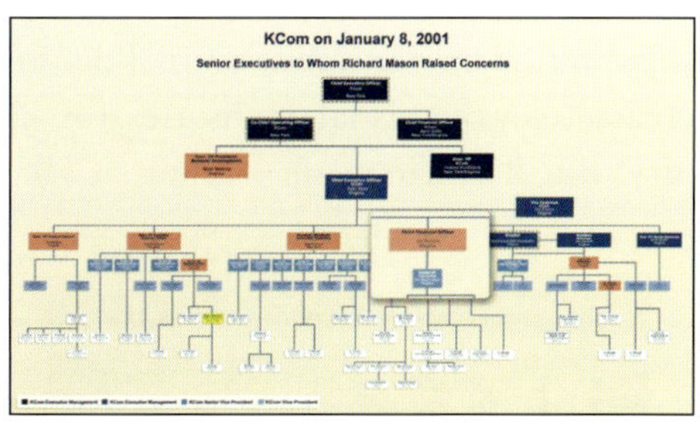

In this instance, the visual memory was the volume—the collective. *A lot* of red boxes appeared high above the yellow. If that's all the jurors remembered, we succeeded in communicating the theme.

Bar Graphs

Bar graphs are particularly useful for comparing values to each other. The design you choose will depend on factors such as how many variables you're comparing, and how legible your labels are in a particular format. For instance, when labels are too long for a vertical bar graph, a horizontal bar graph might communicate your message more effectively.

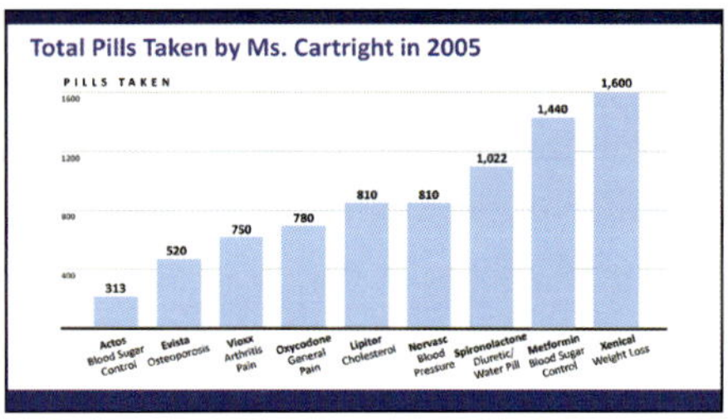

VS.

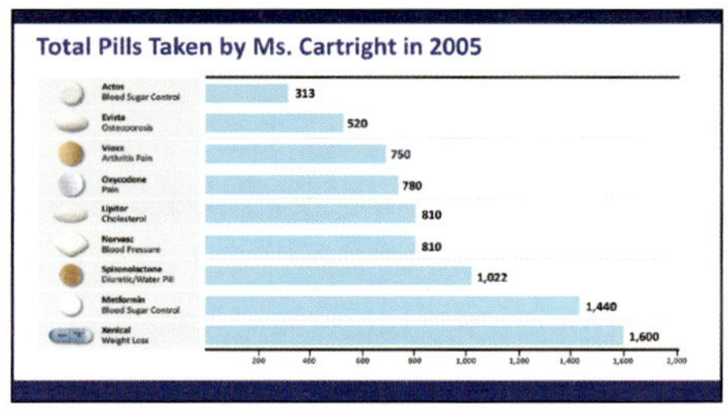

Picture Graphs

In a picture graph, data is depicted with relevant pictures instead of bars. You might compare crime rates using unrolled crime scene tape or a stack of guns, or show environmental effects with smoke stacks of varying heights, or depict accident statistics with stacks of crushed cars.

Used sparingly, picture graphs will stand out from the rest of your slides and create relevant visual memories for the jury. But if you're using a graph at all, it

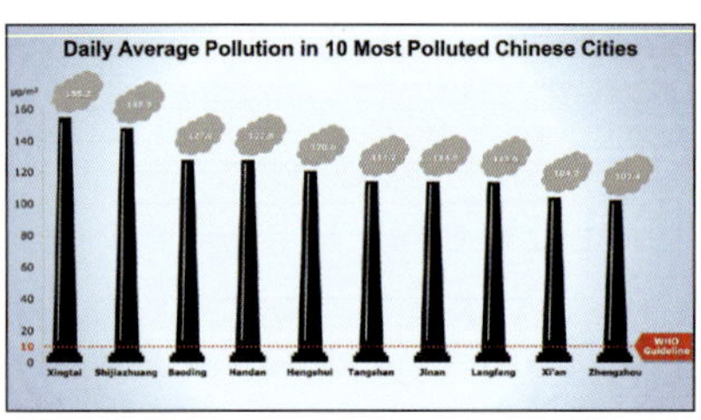

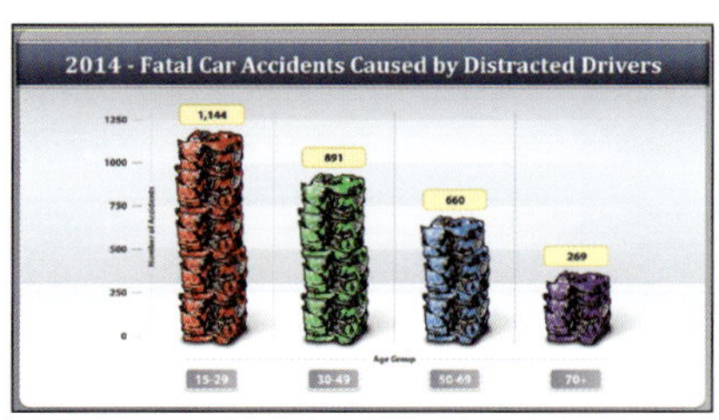

should be because the data is important enough to display visually and to take up some of your trial time. It may be best, then, to let the data speak for itself.

If you do use pictures in your graphs, make sure your photos don't obscure or misrepresent the data.

Where that's a risk, use a simple bar graph and if you think some other graphic image will help communicate your message, make it secondary to the data. Either relegate the picture to the background, or make sure the data is crystal clear despite the picture.

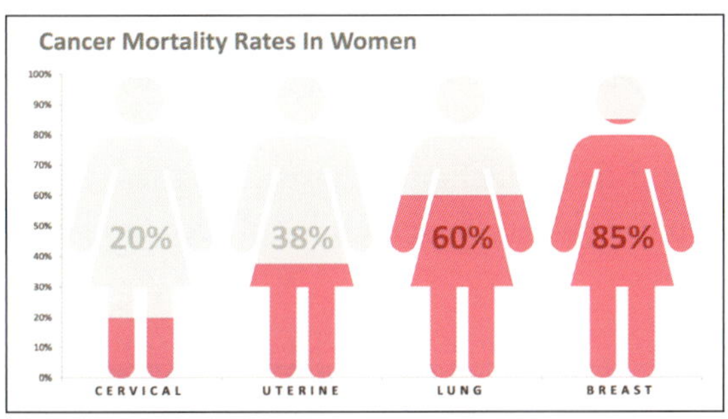

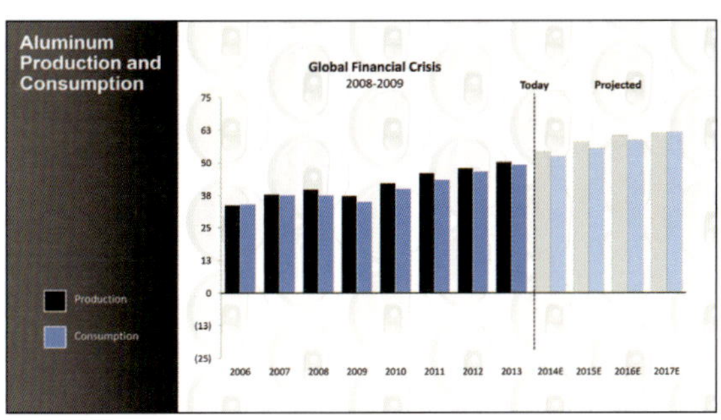

Pie Charts

Pie charts depict composition—the parts that make up the whole.

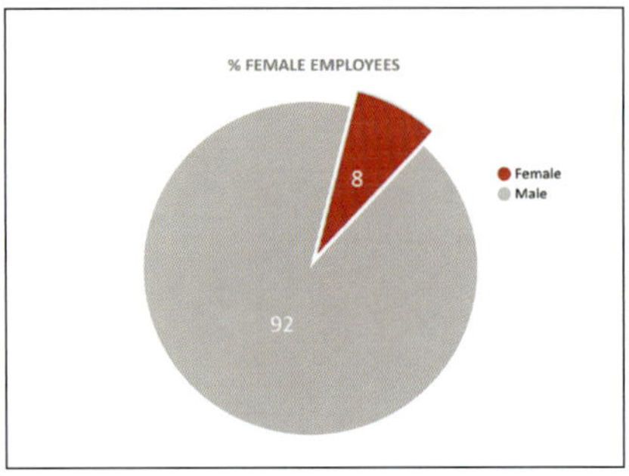

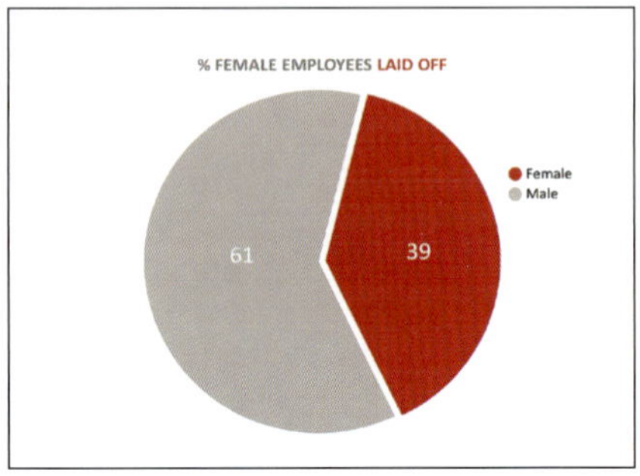

Graphic and information designers seem to have mixed views about pie charts. Some rely on them with frequency; others view pie charts as barely a step above sorcery. The root of their disagreement is the belief that we are less able to discern size differences in circles or pie shapes than in squares or rectangles, the shapes we use in bar graphs. And, indeed, a stacked bar graph can accomplish the same thing as a pie chart, simultaneously depicting composition and comparison. So, one might ask, why do you need a pie chart at all?

While I don't align passionately on one side of this debate or the other, I do tend to limit my use of pie charts to situations where I'm not concerned about precision in the data comparison. I'll consider a pie chart when there are only a few, easily distinguishable slices of pie, or when there are a lot of slices and differentiating between them isn't my key point.

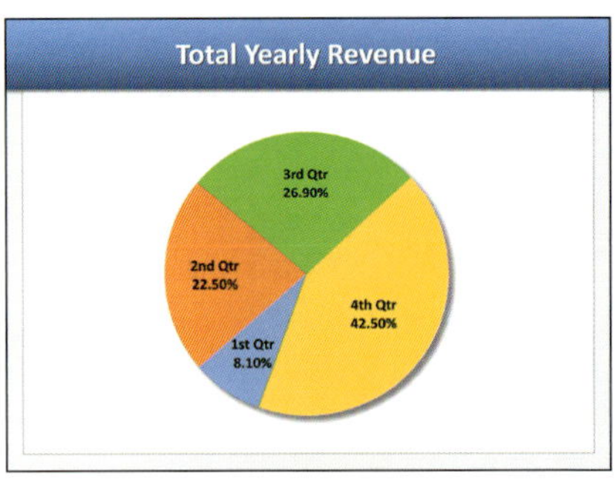

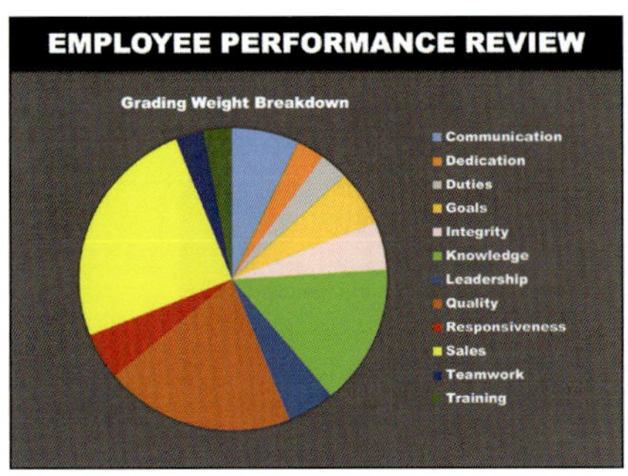

In the example on the left above, the four pieces of pie are substantially different from each other, so comparing them is easy and immediate.

In the example on the right, the viewer has no realistic hope of accurately comparing the pie pieces, but the chart effectively conveys that there are a significant number of components with limited variation among them. If the specific difference between the slices mattered, I'd use a different tool.

For example, depicting the performance review factors on a bar graph arranged in ascending or descending order would make it easier to compare their relative size, which equates to their weight, and therefore their importance.

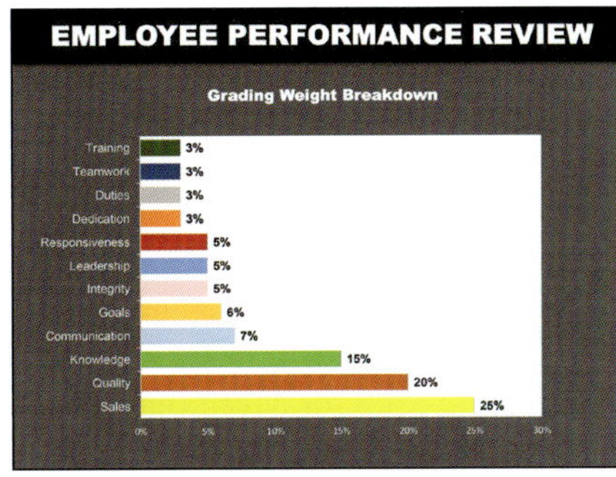

Another area in which pie charts can be useful is when you want to depict something that's a percentage of the total, but the rest of the composition doesn't matter. For example, you might want to show the percentage of market share one company has, but you aren't quite as concerned with the individual market shares of the other participants. A pie chart would instantly depict this compositional data.

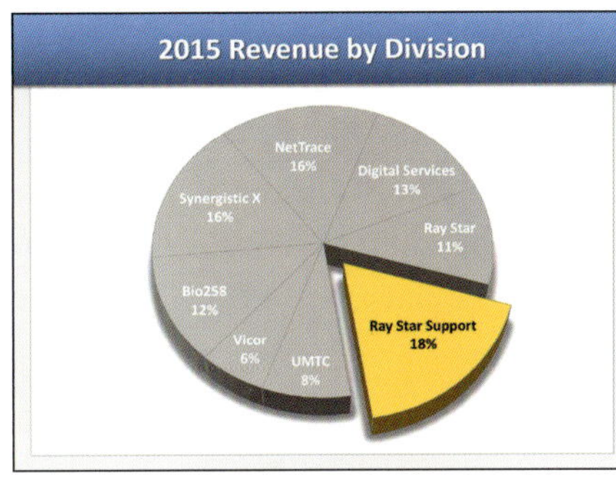

Venn Diagrams

Like pie charts, the Venn diagram can be a useful visual tool for depicting composition and comparison.

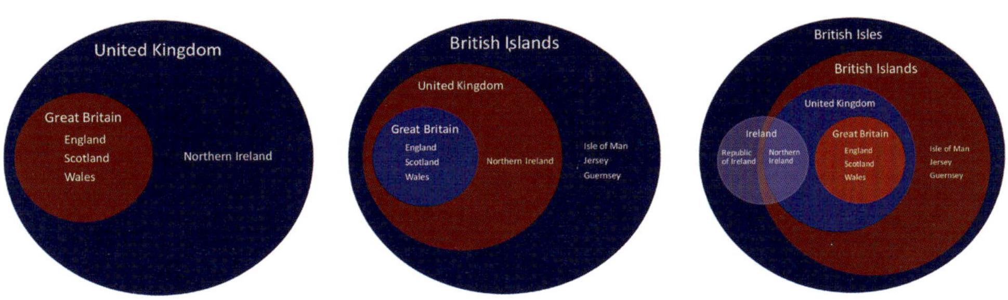

We typically think of them as two overlapping circles, but we're not limited to two points of comparison (or even to using circles). Whatever your design, just make sure the content is clear.

Line Graphs

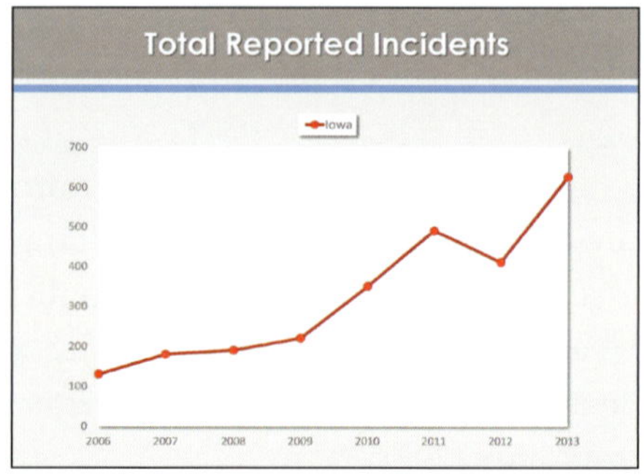

Line graphs are effective for depicting trends and patterns, particularly along a time continuum. In this hypothetical example, a product liability case involving a pesticide sold to farmers in the Midwest, a single line depicts total reported instances of sickness in Iowa from 2006 to 2013.

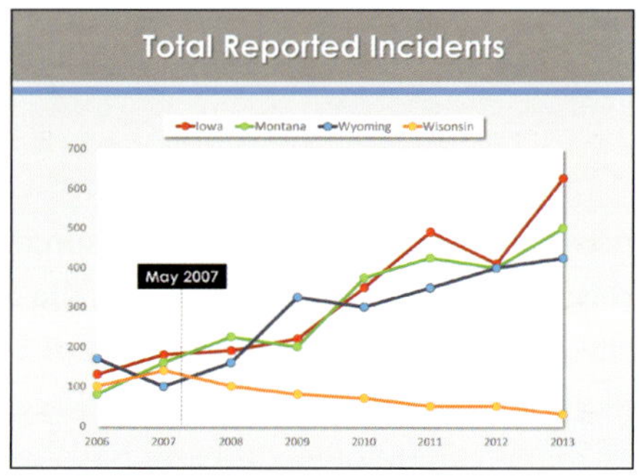

Adding lines for Montana, Wyoming, and Wisconsin, the lines now show both trends and comparisons. The pesticide was banned in Wisconsin in May 2007, which is depicted on the graph. The lines thus compare the pattern of sicknesses in each of the four states to each other, and also compare the trend in Wisconsin against the ban, thus revealing its potential impact.

Distribution Charts

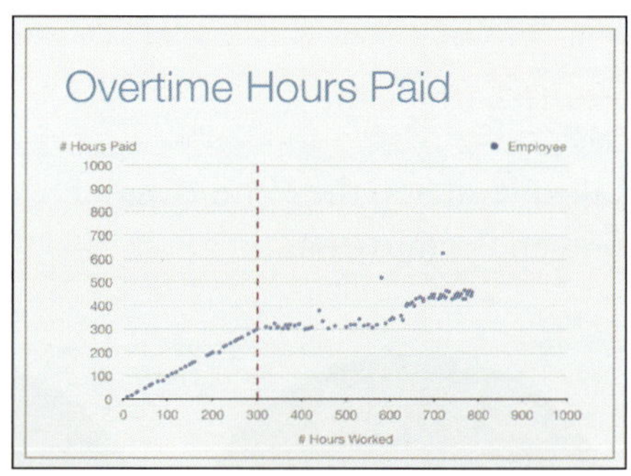

Sometimes, the point you're trying to convey is that something is an outlier; different from the rest. By a lot. A common chart used to depict the distribution of data is the scatter plot.

In this example, a scatter plot effectively depicts a company's pattern of paying (or in this case, not paying) employees for overtime work. When employees work up to 300 hours of overtime, they are paid per hour. But as they exceed 300 hours, even by a lot, the company generally stops paying for that overtime—a trend instantly apparent on the chart. What's more, by plotting each employee's overtime payment and not just using an average (which we might do on a line graph), we can also immediately discern that there are multiple outliers to this trend.

Chart and Graph Design Tips

Regardless of the type of chart or graph you're using, treat it in the same manner you would treat a text slide: walk jurors through complexity, and eliminate extraneous information. Your goal is not, in a vacuum, to create a "simple" chart or graph; it's to create a chart or graph that will effectively communicate the underlying data as clearly as possible. Sometimes that data will be quite complex. And sometimes the complexity of the data is an important theme in your case. So don't blindly aim for "simplifying data." Aim for simplifying the data presentation.

Benefits of Commonality

To that end, keep in mind that a significant benefit of commonly used charts and graphs is their very commonality. Their meaning and structure is well known, which allows jurors to perceive their underlying message quickly. Jurors don't have to spend time figuring out what all those boxes and lines are on a well-designed organizational chart; they already know. They don't have to fight an overwhelming sense of confusion when they see a well-designed set of color-coded bars shooting up from a horizontal line. They instantly recognize it's a bar chart, and they generally know how to read it.

Eliminate the Extraneous

As I've said previously, every element on your slide takes some of your jurors' attention to comprehend. This is as true of charts and graphs as it is of text slides. Every word and every number should be there for a reason. Every color change, graph label, and grid line should be included purposefully and should be minimized to reduce distractions. As Edward Tufte emphasizes throughout his writings, poor data or poor data design cannot be salvaged with ornamentation.[1] Eliminating extraneous information simplifies your design.

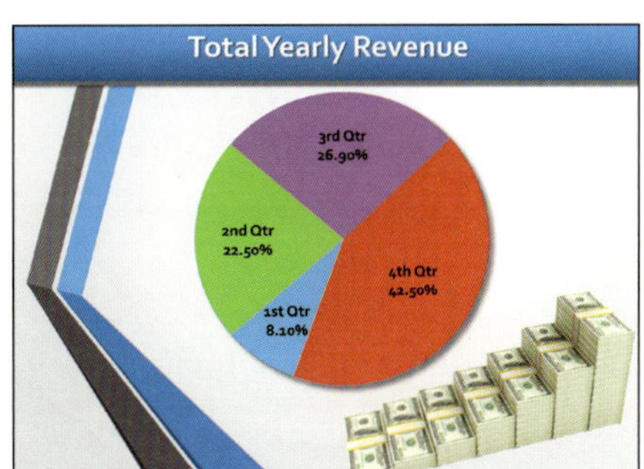

Randomly placed swirls or clip art are obvious examples of extraneous ornamentation.

But consider the rest of what's on your slide, too. Can you articulate a reason for every element? If not, get rid of it. And if less-important information has the same visual emphasis as key information, minimize (or cut) the unimportant to focus the viewer on the important.

Use Color Strategically

Does every bar in your bar graph really need to be a different color?

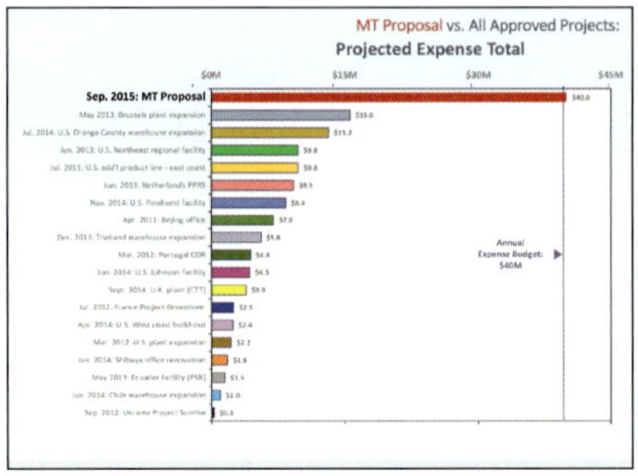

Color contrast is useful for directing the eye. But if everything is a different color, you're not actually emphasizing anything. Go back to the key question—what's your point? That's the bar to emphasize. If your bar or pie graph has a lot of bars or slices, you can even consider using various tints of the same color if the other information is secondary, with the key information the most vibrant by several levels. Or, you can use the same shade of gray for all but the primary piece of information, which can be in a distinct hue. The idea is to use color and other design elements to emphasize your primary point and relegate secondary information to a lower level of emphasis in the visual's hierarchy.

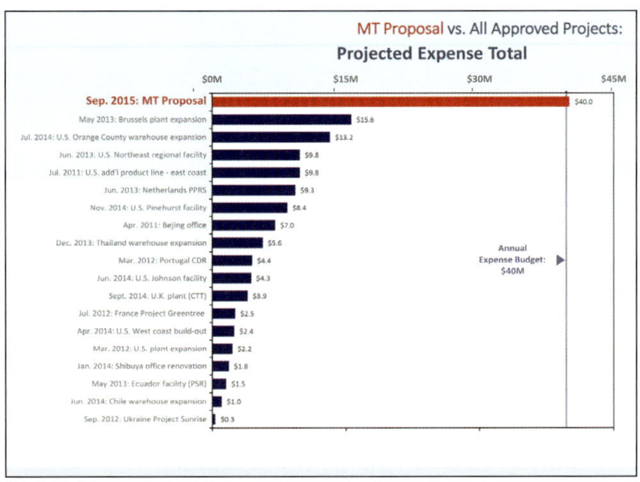

The design to the right immediately draws the viewer's eye to the key data, emphasizing its importance and creating a visual memory of the comparison. The ornamentation is limited. Since I've labeled the bar lengths, I didn't also need to label the scale at precisely the right intervals. I also didn't need grid lines running across or down the graph at every fifth or tenth or twentieth interval. All that really mattered was the comparison between the key project and the other projects on the graph. A single vertical line shows the total expense budget, an important data comparator for all of the projects. Showing lots of other dollar amounts along the axes would be irrelevant to my message. So they aren't there.

Embrace Empty Space

Keeping some space between bars or groupings can help make it easier to read the data displays in your charts and graphs.

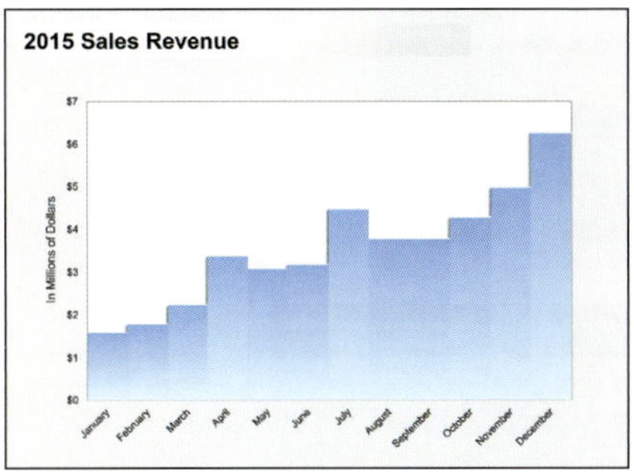

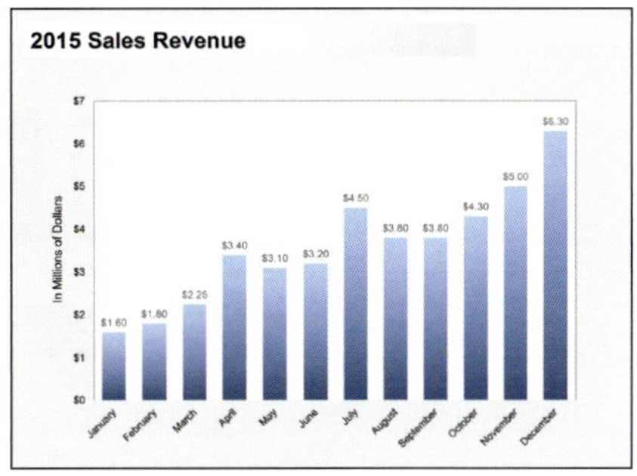

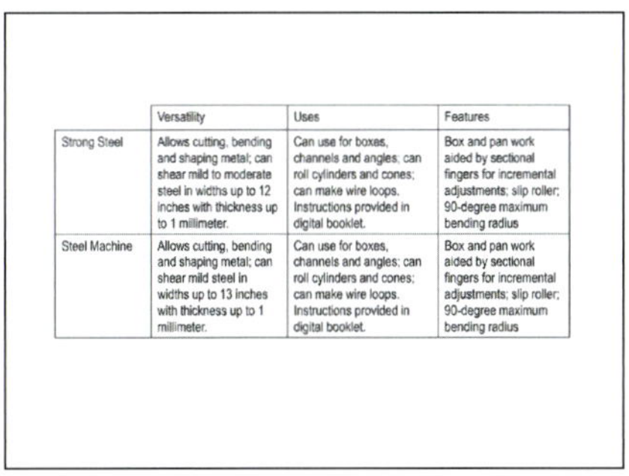

	Versatility	Uses	Features
Strong Steel	Allows cutting, bending and shaping metal; can shear mild to moderate steel in widths up to 12 inches with thickness up to 1 millimeter.	Can use for boxes, channels and angles; can roll cylinders and cones; can make wire loops. Instructions provided in digital booklet.	Box and pan work aided by sectional fingers for incremental adjustments; slip roller; 90-degree maximum bending radius
Steel Machine	Allows cutting, bending and shaping metal; can shear mild steel in widths up to 13 inches with thickness up to 1 millimeter.	Can use for boxes, channels and angles; can roll cylinders and cones; can make wire loops. Instructions provided in digital booklet.	Box and pan work aided by sectional fingers for incremental adjustments; slip roller; 90-degree maximum bending radius

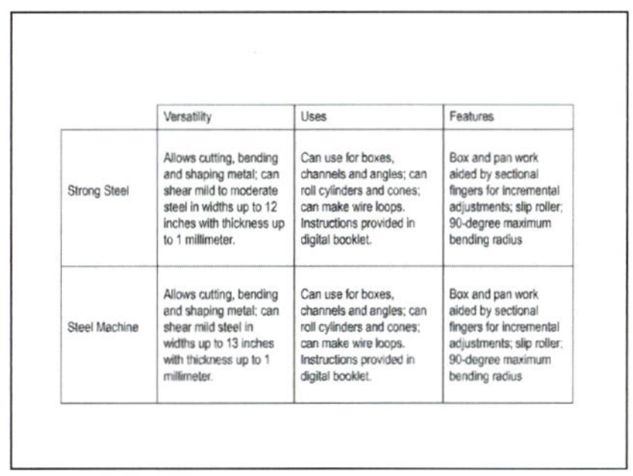

	Versatility	Uses	Features
Strong Steel	Allows cutting, bending and shaping metal; can shear mild to moderate steel in widths up to 12 inches with thickness up to 1 millimeter.	Can use for boxes, channels and angles; can roll cylinders and cones; can make wire loops. Instructions provided in digital booklet.	Box and pan work aided by sectional fingers for incremental adjustments; slip roller; 90-degree maximum bending radius
Steel Machine	Allows cutting, bending and shaping metal; can shear mild steel in widths up to 13 inches with thickness up to 1 millimeter.	Can use for boxes, channels and angles; can roll cylinders and cones; can make wire loops. Instructions provided in digital booklet.	Box and pan work aided by sectional fingers for incremental adjustments; slip roller; 90-degree maximum bending radius

The same is true of the area surrounding your chart or graph. Don't give in to the temptation of filling space just because it's there. Empty space helps keep the slide from feeling too overwhelming. It's an essential part of using graphic design to clearly and calmly depict complex data.

Avoid a Separate "Key" Where Possible

A key isn't so bad when the viewer has time to study the graph at his or her own pace. But in a jury trial, the less work jurors have to do to figure out a data display, the better. Try not to make them cross-reference information to understand it. Where possible, I like to include labels directly on, above, or next to their corresponding bars, lines, or slices of pie.

When cross-referencing is required, make it simple, intuitive, and organized. I designed the chart on the following page based on the structure of a real chart used in an advertisement. I used cell phones for this example, but it applies any time you'd want to make a comparison between features or characteristics—e.g., characteristics of an object in an intellectual property or product liability case; observations of eyewitnesses in a criminal case; or performance objectives in an employment case. The real advertisement had a good deal more ornamentation than I've included here, which further contributed to the confusing nature of the visual.

	Color Display	HD Display	Forward-Facing Camera	Rear-Facing Camera	Bluetooth	Fingerprint Recognition	Electronic Wallet
NSR600C	o		o	o	o		
LH160	o	o		o	o		o
PH1600	o	o	o	o		o	o
PH320X	o	o			o	o	o
TBY1452	o		o		o	o	

The product images are labeled A, B, C, D, and E, but they aren't lined up in order. Adding to the confusion, the labels and descriptions don't appear in the same place for all five products, and item A's larger size gives it additional, but unexplained, emphasis.

And then there's the "corresponding" chart below the phone images. Rather than using the A–E labels, the chart lists the products by product number. Thus, the A–E letters are wholly irrelevant, and instead the reader must work to figure out which picture goes with which product in the chart. What's more, the product models are not simple words, but rather are combinations of confusing and similar-looking numbers and letters that the viewer must match to the images. When the viewer does start matching the rows to the products—surprise!—he finds that that products are listed in a different order in the chart than in the images. Again, there's nothing in the chart to indicate why that's a sensible approach. (It is not.) And if there's a reason why product A's picture is set off from the rest—perhaps it's your client's product or the product that caused an injury—that emphasis is not carried through to the chart.

If we fix these design flaws, we might get something like this:

	Color Display	HD Display	Forward-Facing Camera	Rear-Facing Camera	Bluetooth	Fingerprint Recognition	Electronic Wallet
NSR600C	✓		✓	✓	✓		
LH160	✓	✓		✓	✓		✓
PH1600	✓	✓	✓	✓		✓	✓
PH320X	✓	✓			✓	✓	✓
TBY1452	✓		✓		✓	✓	

Notice that incorporating the product images directly into the chart eliminates the need for a key altogether. The visual is now intuitive, and reading and understanding its substance is effortless.

One Concept per Slide

Sometimes, you'll want to use two data displays to illustrate related points—perhaps a bar graph to compare revenue in one month to revenue in all other months of the same year and a line graph to show the revenue trend over five years. Both displays might be highly relevant to your case, but there's no reason you need to display them on the same slide.

Use a separate slide for each data depiction. Individually, each graph will be larger and more readable, and the visual as a whole will be less overwhelming.

Minimize (or Hide) the Grid/Table and Similar Distractions

Grids help us plot data points in the first instance, but it's usually not necessary to display them once the graph is complete. Yet, many nondesigners create bar graphs, line graphs, and tables that prominently feature the grid, or at least horizontal lines, running through their visual.

Consider removing these lines entirely. If you do use them, then minimize their emphasis so they're not competing with the data.

Particularly with tables, the dividing lines have no substantive value at all. They're there to help organize the text or data within the cells—the real substance on the slide. But thick, dark lines all over the chart are distracting and unnecessary. If you minimize their prominence or get rid of them altogether, you'll have a much less overwhelming design.

	Number of cars involved	Color of defendant's car	Races of individuals involved	Number of people with guns	Length of time of shooting	Number of shots heard
Keeney	2	Blue	Thinks one black, one white	2	1 minute	4
Smith	2	Blue-grey	One black, one Hispanic	1	10 seconds	3
Rogers	3	Green	Two Hispanic, one black	3	30 seconds	4
Martin	2	Silver	One black, other ???	2	2 minutes	6
O'Hara	3	Blue	All three black	1	1 to 2 minutes	3
Peabody	4	???	Two Hispanic, one possibly white, third???	2	45 seconds	5

	# Cars	Def's car	Races	# Guns	Time	# Shots
Keeney	2	Blue	1 black, 1 white	2	1 min.	4
Smith	2	Blue-grey	1 black, 1 Hispanic	1	10 sec.	3
Rogers	3	Green	2 Hispanic, 1 black	3	30 sec.	4
Martin	2	Silver	One black, other ???	2	2 min.	6
O'Hara	3	Blue	All three black	1	1 to 2 min.	3
Peabody	4	???	Two Hispanic, one possibly white, third???	2	45 sec.	5

	# Cars	Def's car	Races	# Guns	Time	# Shots
Keeney	2	Blue	1 black, 1 white	2	1 min.	4
Smith	2	Blue-grey	1 black, 1 Hispanic	1	10 sec.	3
Rogers	3	Green	2 Hispanic, 1 black	3	30 sec.	4
Martin	2	Silver	1 black, 1 other?	2	2 min.	6
O'Hara	3	Blue	3 black	1	1 to 2 min.	3
Peabody	4	???	2 Hispanic, 1 white?	2	45 sec.	5

Finally, do you really need boxes around the information you're displaying?

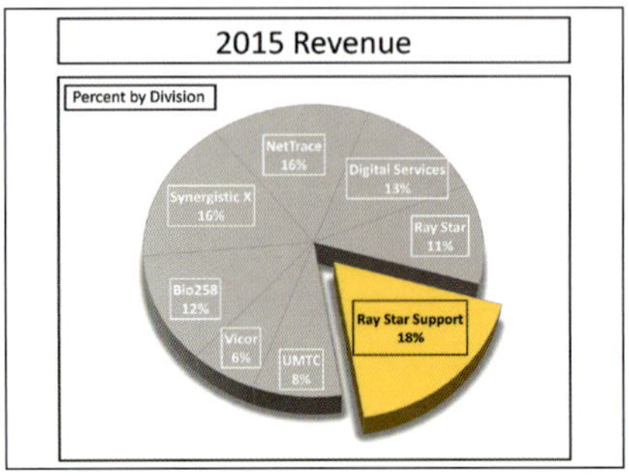

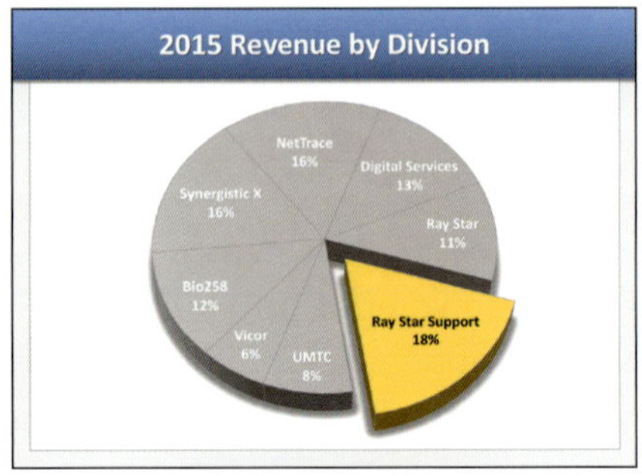

Any time you enclose something in a border—whether it's text, data, or a graphic image—you activate the empty space around the information, creating more distracting shapes and images. As you can see in the slide above on the left, the space between the text and its borders and the shapes created between multiple borders only serve to distract from the substance of the message. Rather than aiding clarity and organization, they have the opposite effect. Removing the unnecessary boxes keeps your focus on the content of the message, not the design of the display.

Minimize Axis Labels, Headings, and Other Text

I'm continually amazed at how much stuff people put on their slides, especially when the substance of the slide is complicated all on its own. As you look over your slide design, ask yourself if there's information you simply don't need but perhaps have included out of habit. Do you need all those words in your heading? Do you need a heading at all? (After all, you're explaining the slide to the jury while you're displaying it.) Usually, headings are quite useful. They let us frame the visual the way we want jurors to view and remember it. They remind jurors (whose minds may have wandered) of the topic we're discussing on the slide, providing important and consistent context. And if jurors write headings in their notes (which they're more likely to do if the headings are short), those jurors will have a written roadmap to our case themes and key facts when it comes time to deliberate. But that doesn't mean headings are mandatory for every visual. Eliminating a heading where the substance is obvious can make room to enlarge other key elements on the slide or add a relevant graphic that will aid juror memory much more than a long textual heading.

What about the axis labels on your charts and graphs? Do you need them all? Can you shorten them? The top and bottom of the *x* and *y* axes are usually important, but do you need every tenth value in between? Can you just include key values?

Whatever you do decide to include, use as little text to describe the values as possible. If you find yourself displaying text diagonally or vertically solely to fit it in, it's time to consider an alternative description or even another slide design.

On occasion, I've even used the labels along the *x* and *y* axes not as interval placeholders, but as the key data itself. Their spacing along the axes then conveys substantive meaning.

Sometimes, I eliminate the numerical values along the axes altogether and simply put the data in or above the bar or plot point.

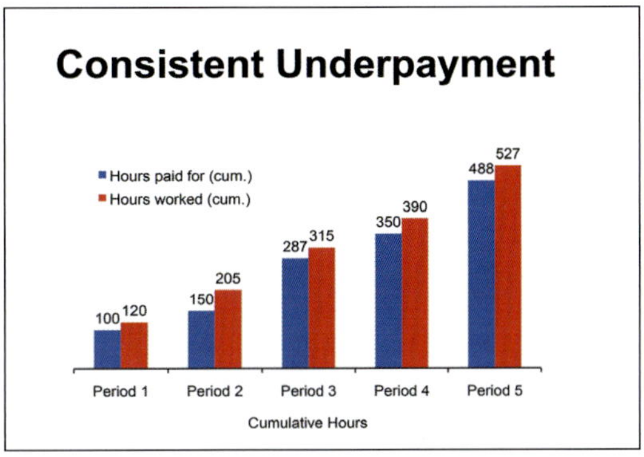

The desirability of reducing text applies to everything on your slide, from the column and row headings in your table to the information contained within the cells. Can you replace "Yes" and "No" with check marks or x's? Can you replace the words "telephone call" with a simple image of a phone? Can you replace names of people or products with their photos? Using alternatives to text—meaningful, clear, and helpful alternatives—adds to the communicative power of the visual.

The point of using charts and graphs with jurors is to help them visualize data and information. When we use these tools, it's usually because we want jurors to remember *the theme* of the data—the trend, comparison, or relationship—rather than every separate data point. Charts and graphs can be extraordinarily effective for helping jurors understand and remember data-oriented case themes.

1996
1998
1998
1999
2000

7

Timelines

Creative storytelling with timelines can be fun. In his independent film *Memento,* Christopher Nolan tells the story of Leonard Shelby. Leonard lost his ability to create long-term memories when he was attacked by the two men who killed his wife. He tries to find his wife's killers, but every conversation he has, every clue he discovers, and every lesson he learns disappears within a precious few minutes. To compensate, Leonard takes Polaroid pictures, writes himself notes, and even tattoos important information onto his body. The premise itself is unique enough, but Nolan goes a step further and tells the story through two alternating timelines. One is linear and traditional. The other is a reverse chronology—the story moves forward in small pieces, and the next vignette takes place before that one, ending where the prior one began. The unusual chronology is interesting, suspenseful, and memorable.

Fantastic movie device.

Terrible closing argument strategy.

Because we experience time linearly, we best understand the telling of events that way, too. So, using a traditional timeline with a jury is a logical, natural way to visually depict key events in our case and how they relate to each other. Of course, chronological order isn't the only way to effectively tell your trial story. Sometimes a presentation organized by event category, witness, or claim will be more effective, and even more interesting and engaging. But when timing matters and order is relevant, leave the complicated, nonlinear timing devices to Hollywood.

Most of us instinctively know what a timeline is and how it's used. Usually, our time entries run from left to right, with earlier events on the left and later ones on the right.

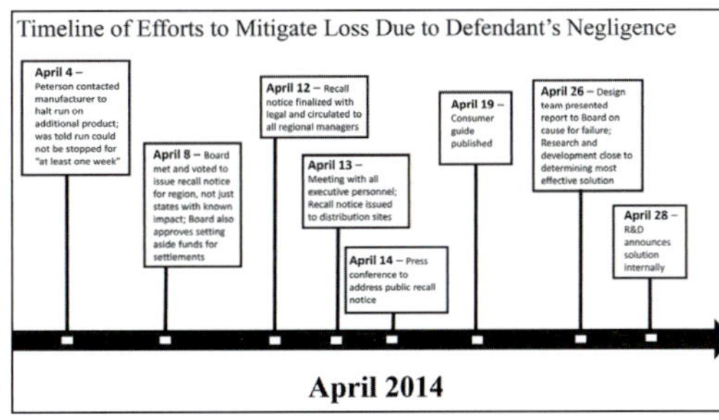

Sometimes we get "fancy," using a vertical line and putting earlier entries up top and later entries at the bottom (or vice versa).

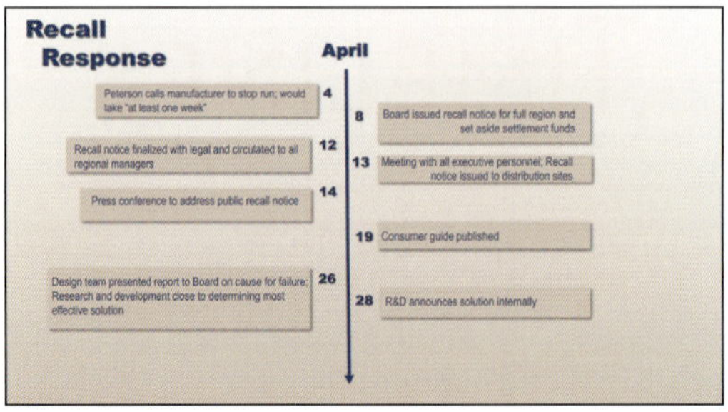

This timeline and the one on the prior page—typical of what I see lawyers use in trial—are really just text typed in chronological order next to a line. Nothing is particularly visual or visually memorable. We can do better.

Although text will often be an important component of our timelines, there are plenty of ways to add subtle, relevant visual interest. Doing so helps turn the theme into a picture, which in turn helps jurors remember the theme. Don't be afraid to use color, shape, and other design techniques to accomplish this goal. In the end, although each entry is important (or it wouldn't be on the slide), the jurors likely won't remember every detail. If you've turned the theme into a picture—if it creates a visual memory—then even if jurors forget the details they'll remember the theme.

Single Timelines

Here's a simple example. In a criminal conspiracy case, I wanted to show that my client's involvement with the three wrongdoers (who had already pled guilty) ended before the fraud occurred. I used a timeline to walk jurors through key events, demonstrating that every event involving my client took place before the other individuals' fraudulent plan was ever hatched. As the illegal scheme progressed, my client was nowhere to be seen.

To emphasize the dividing line, I used a blue background behind text describing my client's conduct and a red background to describe the fraud. The heading encapsulates the theme—the "real fraud" not involving my client—and rather than center it above the full timeline, it is centered above the section of the timeline it described.

When I presented the timeline to the jury, I built it the using the techniques described in Chapter 5. I brought up each event and its text large enough for the jurors to read. When I finished discussing one event, I reduced its size so it remained on the timeline but didn't distract from the next event.

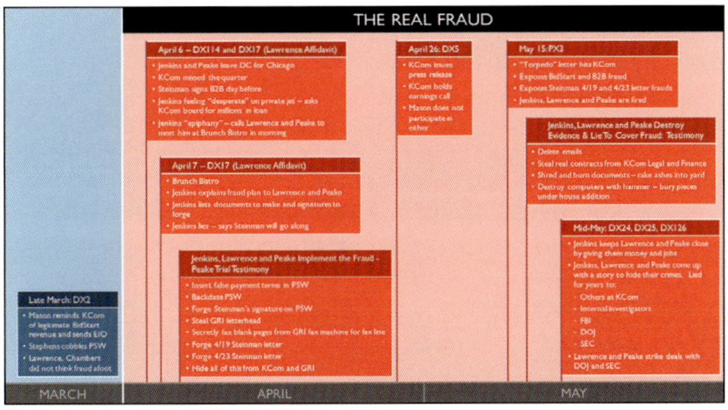

By the end of the build, I'd visually depicted a clear delineation between my client's actions and those of the other three executives, demonstrating the lack of overlap. But even if the jurors forgot the detail, they had a visual memory of the final image, with no overlap between the blue and red.

Parallel Timelines

Sometimes, the question is "What else was going on at the same time?" When that's the case, consider using what I call a "parallel timeline." You don't literally need two lines, but you can visually separate distinct categories of events occurring during the same time period. This approach compares the events and puts them in context with one another while still depicting their individual chronologies. You're essentially organizing the slide around these event categories.

For example, you might want to depict a chronology of fraudulent conduct and compare it to a parallel chronology of the defendant's increasing home and work stress. Or maybe you want to show time spent by an employee on different projects. Or perhaps you want to simultaneously depict the activities of two or more witnesses over the same time period. With a parallel timeline, each separate chronology is maintained, and the comparison is quick and intuitive.

I created a parallel timeline for a recent case where three event categories were at issue. A key factual question was whether a company was poised to enter the market with a new technology. Although there were some company emails suggesting excitement about the new technology, there was much more evidence showing a lack of executive and board approval and significant financial and technological barriers to entry. So, using a single line across the middle of the slide, I used spacing and color contrast to signify the three parallel chronologies at issue: financial, technological, and approval challenges. (I also relied on a graphic design firm to turn my rough drawings into a professional, trial-ready visual.)

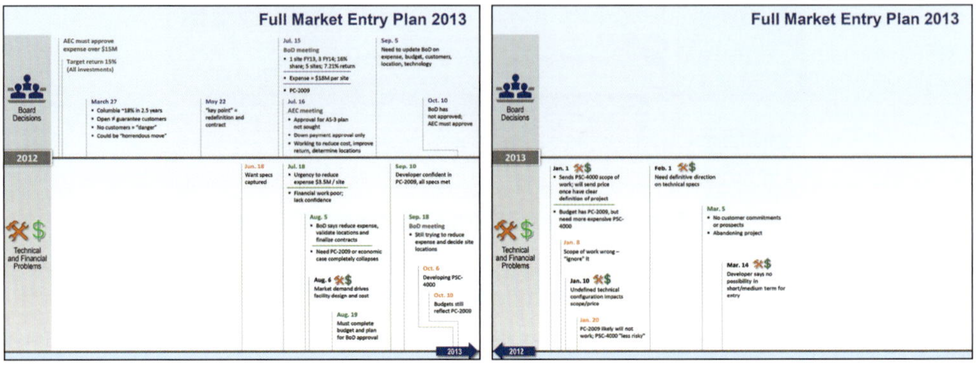

We divided the timeline into two slides simply due to space limitations. There were enough entries over a long-enough period of time so that displaying all of this information on a single slide would have been too busy, and the text would have been too small to read. Using two slides opened up our design options, and toggling between the slides was easy with the right and left arrow keys on our keyboard. When we did switch between images, they appeared to slide into place from left to right or right to left, depending on which direction we were moving, giving the illusion that the two slides were one continuous timeline (which, substantively, they were).

Above the timeline, we plotted board and executive concerns about market entry. These concerns were memorialized in emails, strategy presentations, internal memos, and meeting minutes. Below the line, we tracked the challenges with the new technology, which simply wasn't working. We also depicted the growing financial challenges—namely, that efforts to reduce the project's capital cost (required by the board for approval) were failing, and cost estimates were actually increasing. Color-coding signified the three event categories, and when one event implicated two categories—as multiple events did in 2013—color-coded symbols helped indicate the overlap. In the end, the collective—the busy timeline with lots of events on three parallel tracks—became a visual representation of the theme: the many problems, failures, and, ultimately, barriers to market entry.

One particular type of parallel timeline, I would argue, is the Gantt chart, named for its designer, engineer Henry Laurence Gantt. Developed in the 1920s, the Gantt chart features horizontal bars where the increments of time are measured along the top and bottom. The design allows us to compare both time and context over multiple variables.

For example, say you want to show when various employees worked in a particular division and then compare that to when illegal activity was allegedly taking place. First, you could use a horizontal bar to represent the time period for each person's employment.

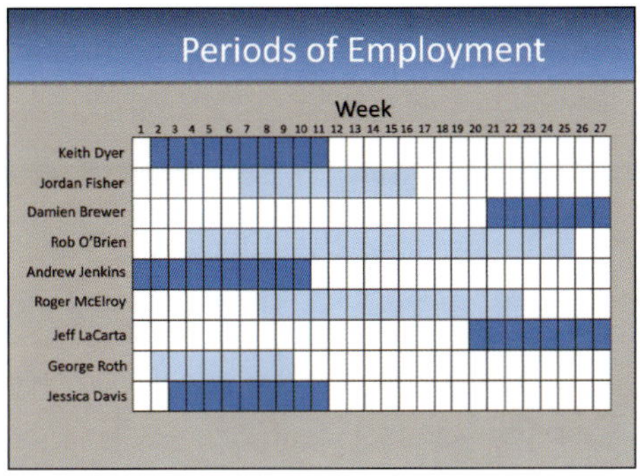

Then you could overlay that with the period of illegal activity. You'll immediately see who overlapped and who didn't, and for how long.

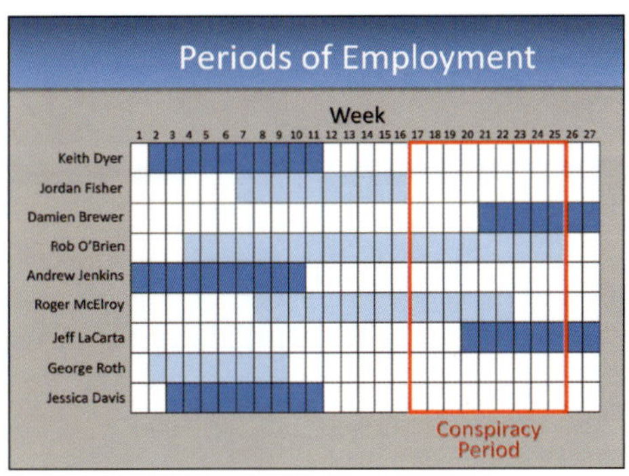

The same can be accomplished with a basic parallel timeline that plots the starting and ending dates for each person's employment, but spotting the theme won't be as immediate as it is with the Gantt chart. Consider using parallel timelines when both time and context matter. You can use parallel timelines to convert a myriad of case themes into visual images: cause and effect (causal events on one side of the line, effects on the other); mitigation vs. aggravation; speculation vs. reality; inconsistent communication (what the defendant said to one witness vs. another); or good faith (knowledge above the line, actions below it).

Proof Timelines

One of my favorite techniques with timelines is to use images of trial evidence to prove each point as it builds. The fraud timeline set forth earlier in this chapter was just that—as each time entry appeared on screen, the related exhibits or testimonial proof appeared below it.

There are, of course, many design options for this approach. Instead of having the exhibit appear below or next to the text, the whole timeline could shrink into a corner, fade into the background, or otherwise be de-emphasized as each specific time entry and its proof appears large and emphasized on the screen.

Timelines for Context

Even when chronology is not itself your trial theme, timelines can help put facts into context. For instance, in one case my client was accused of unlawfully refusing to sell his services to a customer. The plaintiff alleged that the refusal to sell stemmed from an improper motive, and that it constituted an illegal boycott in violation of antitrust law.

But the facts showed otherwise. The customer owed my client millions of dollars for past services, the debt was growing as my client sold him more services, and my client's repeated efforts to collect on the debt were unsuccessful. The government argued that this debt was just a pretext for the client's unlawful motives in refusing to sell. My position, of course, was that my client's motive was proper, and his refusal to sell was lawful.

In the closing argument, I wanted to emphasize my client's lawful motivation for refusing to sell services. There was nothing particularly chronological about the theme. It really just boiled down to a dispute about my client's true motive. I could have put the dollar amount of the debt on the screen and simply argued the point. But I believed that putting the refusal to sell in context—showing its relationship to the debt—would be the best way to get my client's reasonable and lawful motivation across to the jury.

So, I used a timeline. I depicted the debt's growth chronologically, proving it with invoices and emails evidencing both the debt and my client's efforts to collect. At the end of the build, I plotted my client's refusal to sell along the same timeline, showing that it fell between several efforts to collect.

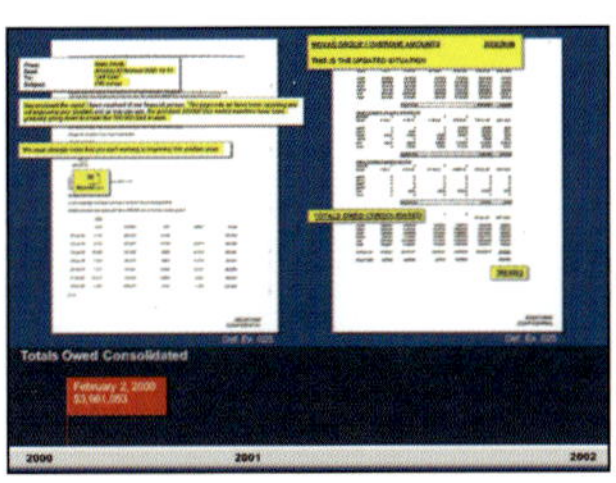

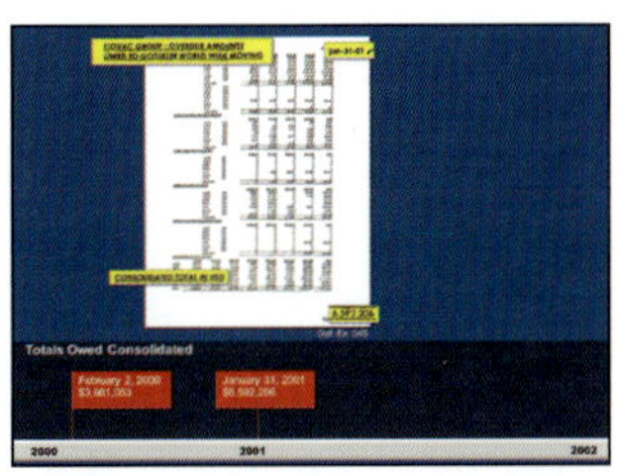

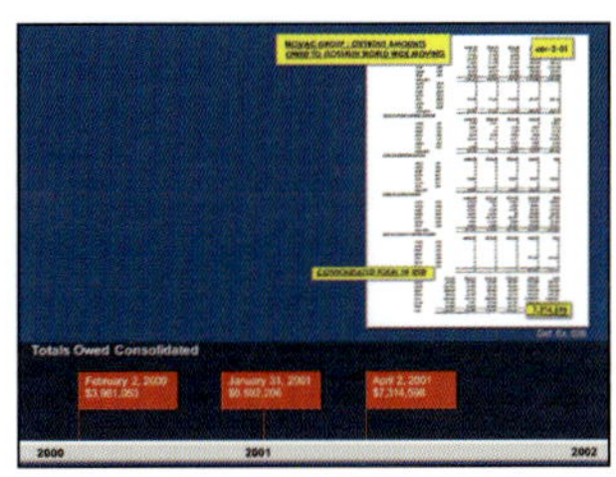

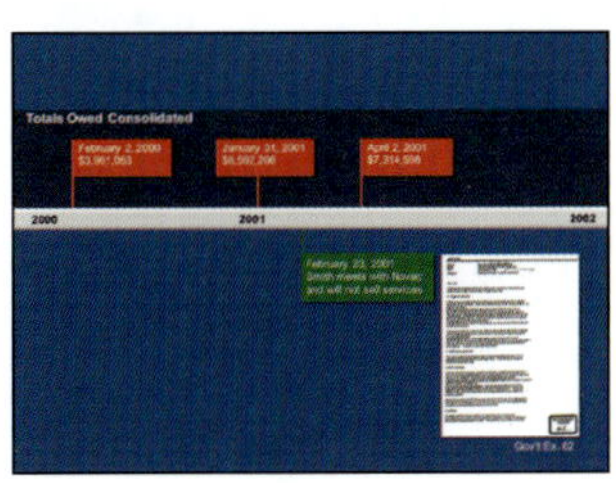

The debt was real and significant ($7 million was a lot of money in this client's industry), and the refusal to sell was now visually placed into context. As I built the timeline with evidence admitted during trial, I added to my credibility. What's more, the timeline stood out visually from other slides I used in closing. It didn't much matter whether the jurors remembered the specific amount of the debt or even which document proved each point. I'd created a memorable visual of my general theme. My client had a lawful, justifiable motive in refusing to sell further services to this customer. The jury rejected the plaintiff's effort to dismiss the debt as a pretext and found my client not liable for the alleged antitrust violation.

Interactive Timelines

An interactive timeline is just a regular timeline—however you've designed it—where some number of entries are hyperlinked to do something when you click on them. In the trial context, clicking on the entry will typically bring up that entry's proof, whether it's a documentary exhibit, deposition video, surveillance footage, photograph, or anything else. This approach allows tremendous flexibility during witness examinations and time-sensitive arguments. You can make judgment calls about which entries to "prove," and in what order.

The market entry timeline I showed you (under "Parallel Timelines") was actually interactive. We could click on any entry to bring up its evidentiary proof.

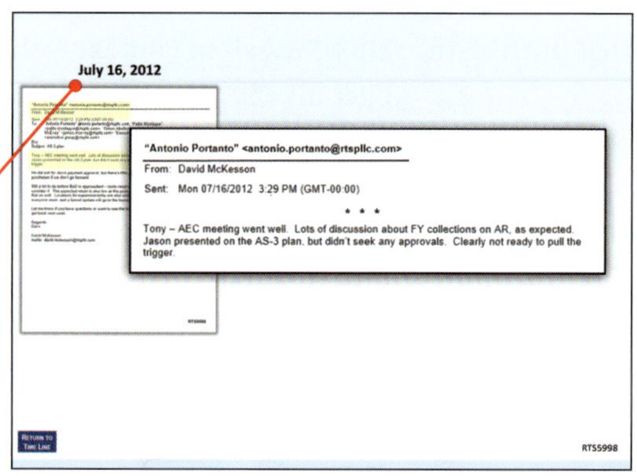

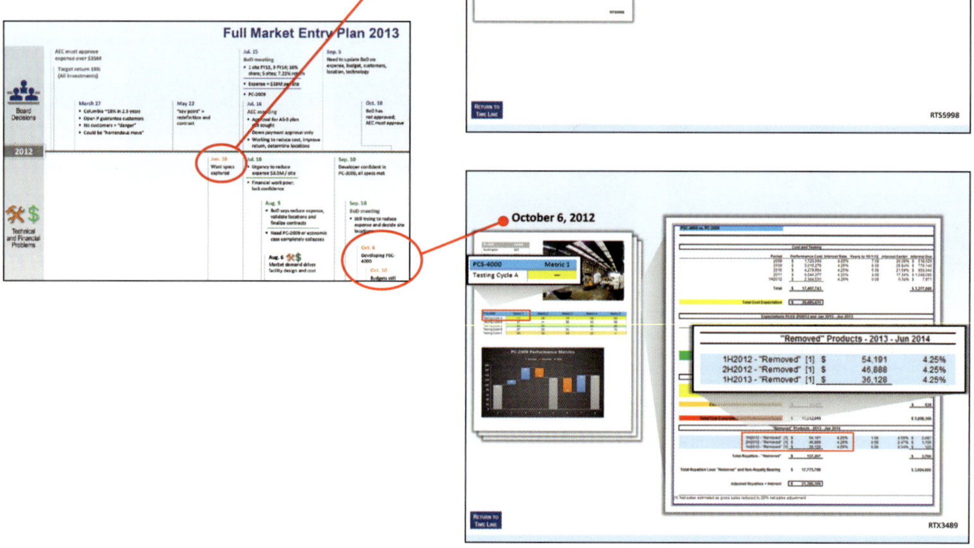

On the timeline itself, I used the fewest number of words I could to reasonably describe each event. The underlying proof emerged on screen simply by clicking the event text. The proof document disappeared by clicking on "return to timeline" at the bottom of the slide.

Interactive timelines are usually easy to create in advance of trial. It's no secret which events in your case are key, so selecting the timeline entries is generally straightforward. But during trial, some of those events might be less contested than others. Perhaps evidence came in better than you expected, and you don't need to spend as much time arguing that issue in your closing. If you had created a static set of closing slides in advance, you might have far too much detail on an issue that was essentially put to bed in trial. An interactive timeline gives you the flexibility to spend your trial time where it counts, while still showing the jury a complete timeline featuring all of the key events.

Timelines to Depict Trends

We discussed line graphs as a great way to depict data trends over time. But sometimes a timeline can work just as well and add more visual interest, particularly if you've got other line graphs in your presentation and you want a specific trend to stand out. And, if you want to depict other events occurring contemporaneously, the timeline will work better than a line graph in most situations.

Minimize Text and Ornamentation

As with all the other communication tools we've discussed, minimize the amount of text and unnecessary ornamentation in your timelines. Does there need to be a label for every month? Is it necessary to spell out "January" or can you abbreviate? Can you shorten your event descriptions? With some creativity, you might be able to eliminate most (if not all) of the text from your timeline by replacing event descriptions with images or symbols.

And, just as minimizing grid lines or axis marks can improve your graphs, minimizing the emphasis on unnecessary graphic elements can improve your timelines.

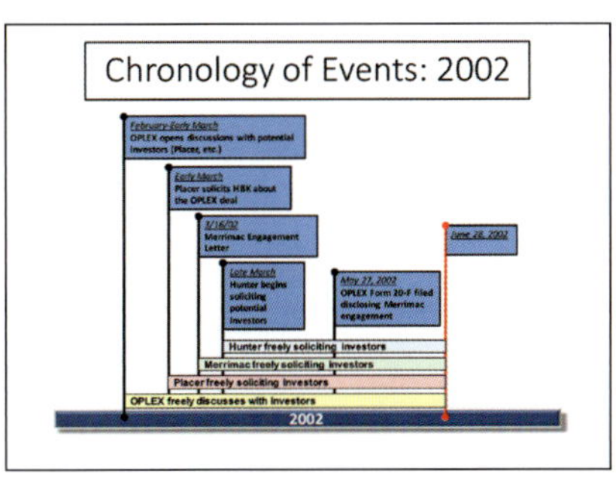

VS.

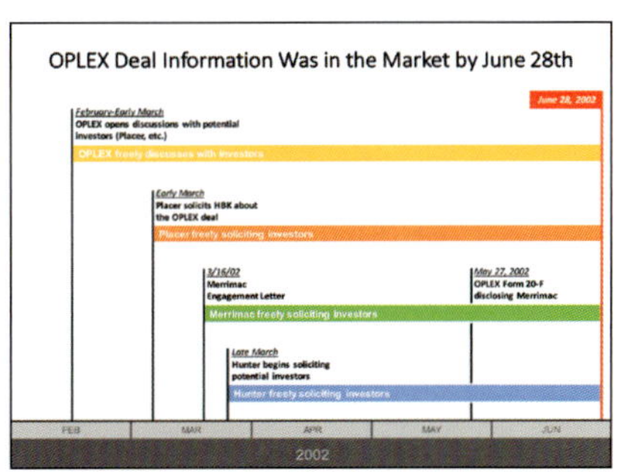

Minimizing ornamentation is also important for your overall timeline layout. Be careful about getting too cute with timeline design. It's certainly possible to design effective timelines that are vertical, diagonal, or even winding. But if the design is so "creative" that its structure is hard to follow and the information is difficult to perceive, we defeat the purpose of the visual.

In this example, the event markers are in order of depth (size in this two-dimensional graphic). But by using a winding road, the markers—themselves overly prominent—are out of order when viewed from left to right. And since that's how we're used to reading timelines, there's a confusing dissonance in the slide. The orange event, for instance, is the first event in the series, but it's the last event in a left-to-right ordering. And the yellow event is the last to occur and would ordinarily be the farthest right, but it's the second from the left—the spot usually reserved for the second event in time.

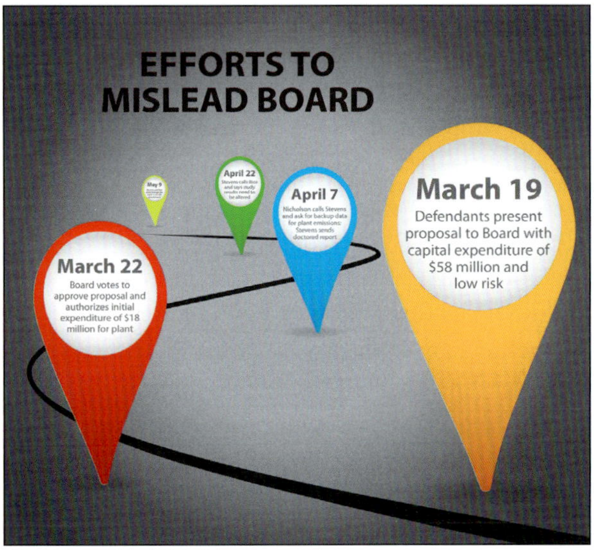

Timelines vs. Chronologies

Sometimes, it's a close call whether to convey a point through a timeline or through a simple, chronological list of events. The primary difference between the two is that, unlike a timeline, the simple chronology doesn't have a scale to visually depict the amount of time that has passed between events. Both timelines and chronologies order the data; they show you that A came before B. But it's a timeline that gives you a sense of *magnitude*—a visual image of *how long* A came before B. So, if you modify your chronology to depict this information . . . surprise! . . . you've created a timeline.

By eliminating the scale when what matters is only the order of events and not the amount of time that has passed between them, a chronology is usually quicker and easier to construct. That's obviously a huge benefit when you're pressed for time leading up to or during trial.

Familiar Symbols

As discussed in Chapter 5, using familiar symbols on timelines can add visual interest, aid recall, and quickly communicate new information when elements repeat.

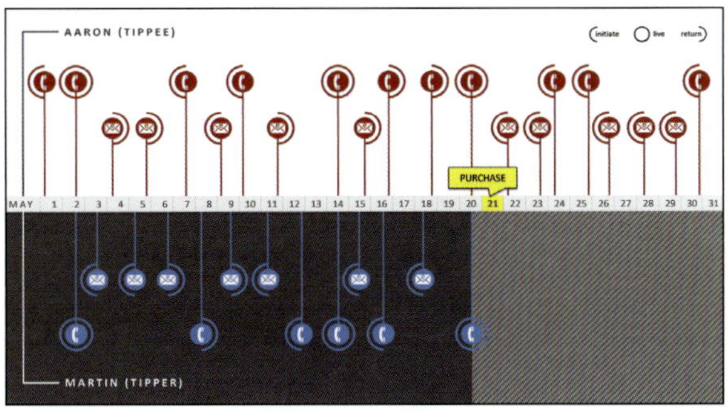

Even familiar text symbols—such as logos—can add visual interest to your timelines and make them more memorable.

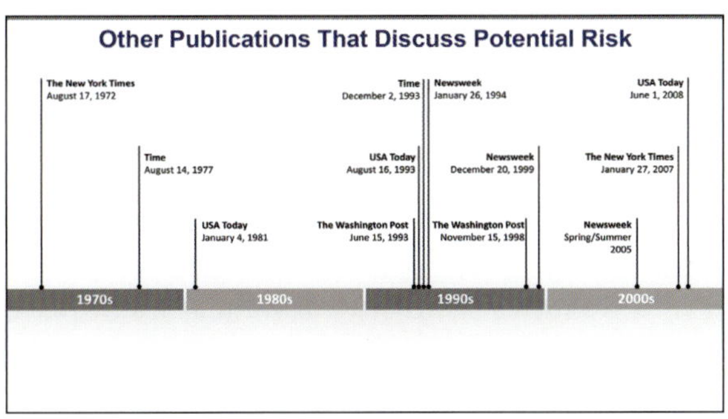

VS.

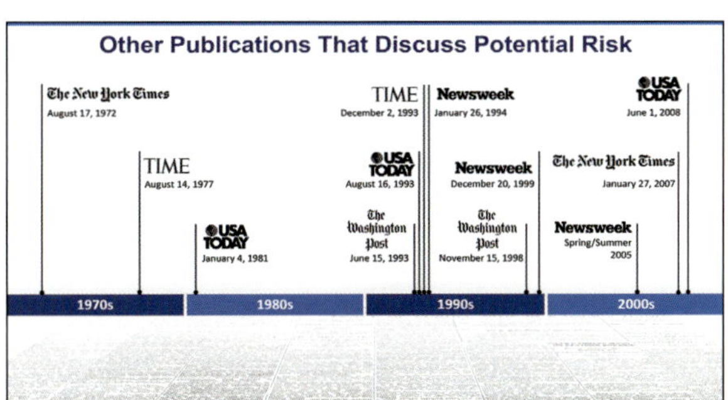

Adding a graphic component to the timeline can have a similar effect.

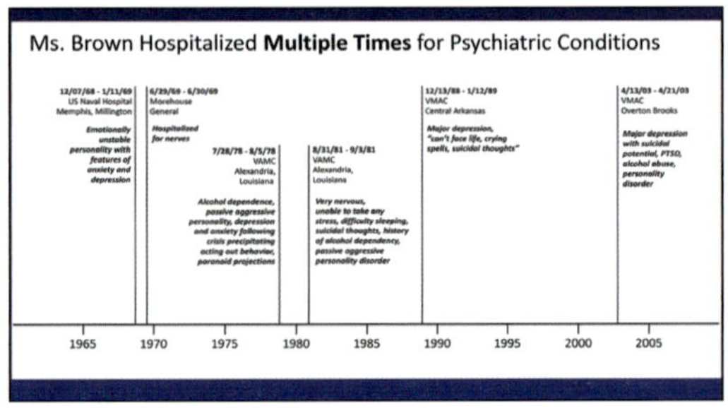

VS.

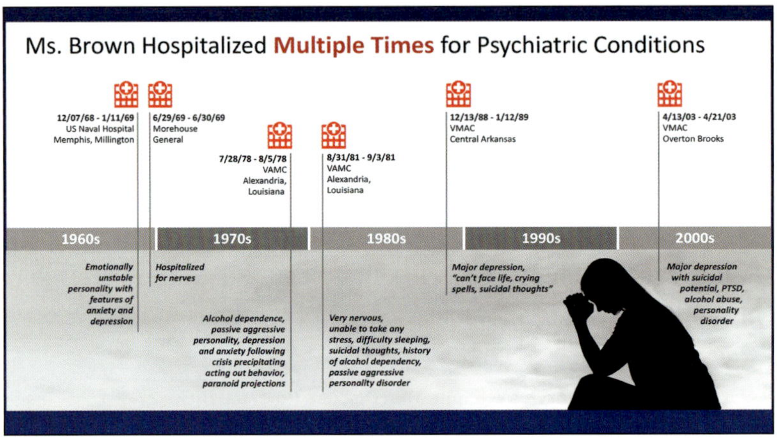

Timelines instantly convey a chronology, but they're of course not the only symbols that do so. A simple image of a calendar, for instance, is quickly recognizable and grounds the viewer in substantive familiarity as soon as it's displayed.

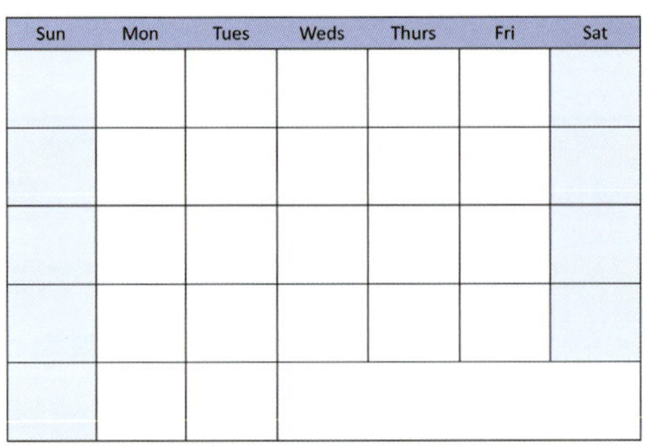

Sometimes a relatively short time interval is itself part of your theme—e.g., "these are all the things that had to happen within the span of a single week," or "these are all the opportunities the defendant had to correct the problem in the full month leading up to the injury," or "look at all that was accomplished in a single quarter." The calendar symbol might reinforce those substantive themes more than a generic timeline. By incorporating the image into your design, you create a visual memory that is inseparable from its meaning.

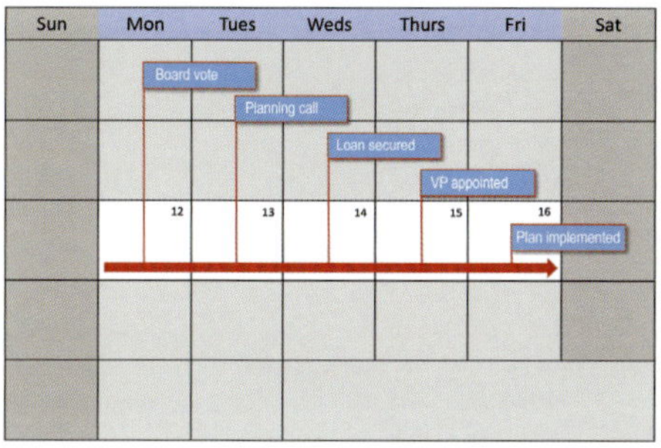

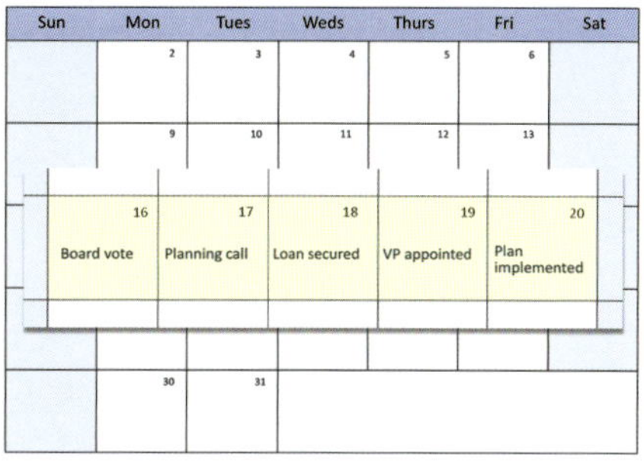

The point of using a familiar symbol is for instant recognition; it's one less thing the jurors have to comprehend, yet it conveys and supports your substance. Use that phenomenon to your advantage whenever you can.

8

MAPS

Maps answer the question "where" by visually depicting location and proximity. Typically, we're focusing on a geographical area and showing either what's located there or where something occurred within that space. We might depict what's there now, what used to be there, or where people, places, or things were located in relation to each other.

Diagrams are a close cousin of maps for depicting "where." For instance, a diagram of the human body, perhaps in a criminal or medical malpractice case, lets us "map" the location of injuries. A diagram of a building or an object can help us pinpoint where damage occurred. Since we can diagram literally anything, we can use diagrams to show "where" in virtually any context. I'll talk about diagrams separately in Chapter 10. In this chapter, I'll focus on maps as they're used to depict geographic locations.

Maps to Show Where Something Happened

If it occurred (even allegedly!), it can be depicted on a map. For crime or accident scenes, catastrophes, weather events, or encounters between people—when location matters, consider using a map with your jury to aid recognition, understanding, and recall.

Once you've decided to use a map to show where something happened, you'll need to determine how zoomed in or out your map needs to be, which is the starting point for your design. As with any other communication tool, start by determining what you're really trying to show.

In a case where environmental damage is at issue, you might need to show the impact range of an event. A map with a broad aerial view might work best, depicting an area large enough to capture the event, its impact, and enough surrounding area to put the location in context.

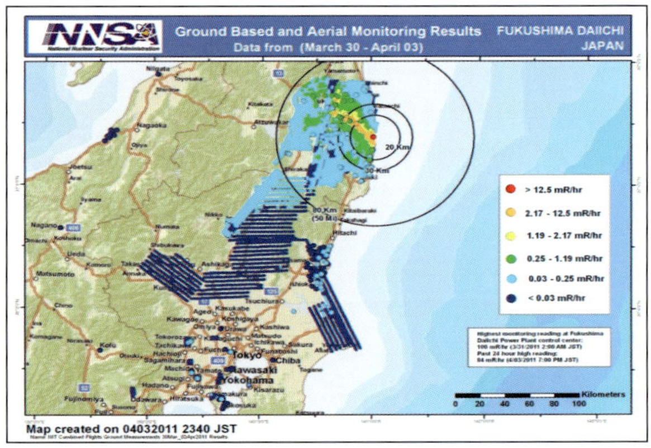

In another case, perhaps your goal is to show where people were standing in relation to an event. An aerial view depicting key streets and buildings might work just fine. You'll need to be "close" enough to depict the scene and the locations of the witnesses, but you might also want to provide a broader view for context. Enlarging a specific area from a broader map can work well to accomplish these dual goals.

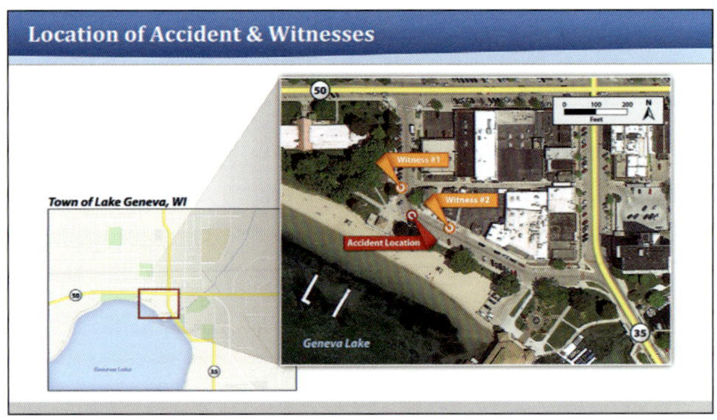

The enlarged, zoomed-in map shows the exact location of the accident and witnesses at issue. But the aerial map puts the event in a broader geographic context, showing its relation to known landmarks. The labels are few and purposeful. Two major highways and a lake—each of which might be already familiar to the jurors—are specifically identified, and the location of the accident is outlined in the red box. Nothing else needs identifying, so nothing else is labeled.

Notice that neither map requires a key. Instead, the labels are directly on the map image, in proximity to what they're labeling. You certainly could use a key instead. You could mark the location of each witness and the accident with a letter or symbol, and then translate the symbols in a nearby key. But by putting the labels directly on the map, you'll save the jury the effort of cross-referencing to decipher the message, and there's less clutter on the slide.

Calling out a specific area from a broader map is useful even when the called-out area, itself, is broad. Consider using it whenever context will aid understanding.

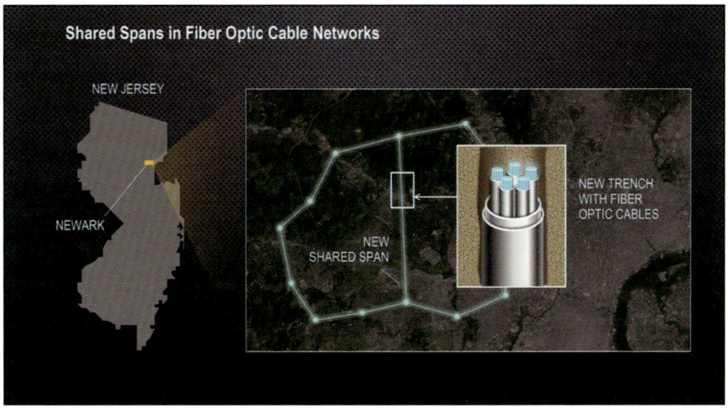

When depicting a relatively small area on a map, you can also consider departing from an aerial view and instead use real perspective from the ground. I've had a few cases in which the proximity of various employees in an office mattered. In one such case, several employees were involved in wrongdoing, even using a company photocopier to aid in forging the boss's signature on a contract. My client testified that he neither saw nor heard any improper activity, so I wanted to show where he sat in proximity to the bad actors and the copier. In another case, I needed to show the opposite—that employees sat exceptionally close to one another at open desks, which helped explain why there were so few emails between them.

Rather than use a basic blueprint of the office layouts, which admittedly would have worked just fine, scale drawings with key locations clearly marked allowed jurors to picture themselves in the space, adding to their visual memories of the theme. Below are some samples, in different design styles, to illustrate this approach.

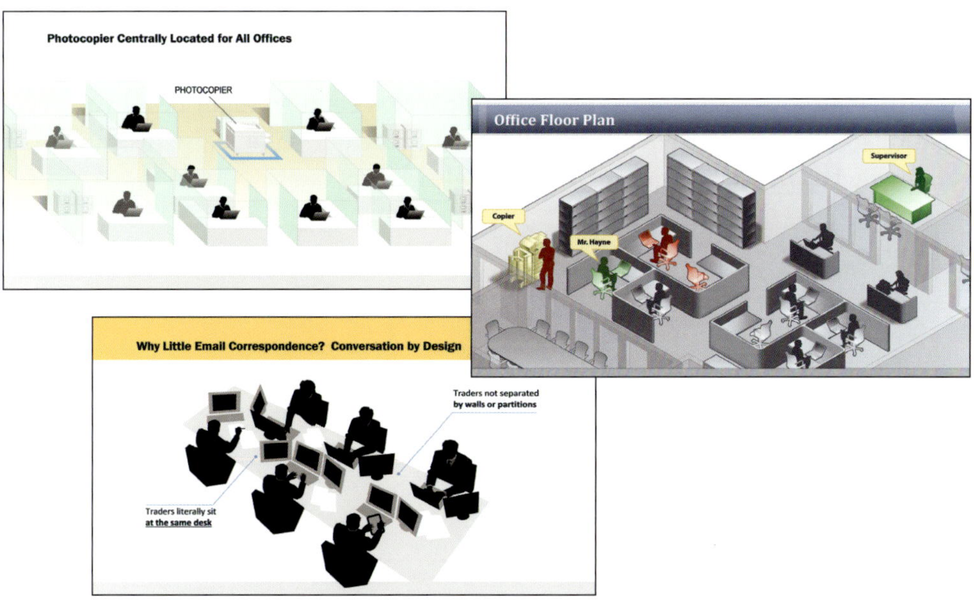

Alternatively, you could use photographs taken from the appropriate angle. But photos would likely contain a lot more detail than is necessary, which could distract from the main point of the visual. With a diagram, you can eliminate the extraneous by not including those details in the first place. Fewer distractions will keep the emphasis on the main point; jurors won't lose focus because they're busy examining the office wall art, carpet, lamps, desk toys, or whatever other irrelevant objects naturally appear in a photo of office space.

Photos as Maps

In other situations, a photo can work well as a map. In a murder case, I wanted to depict where a shooting occurred, where a key witness was standing, and where various people were entering and exiting the scene (according to that key witness). I took a photograph of the critical area from where the witness observed the shooting and turned it into a map, marking key buildings and streets.

In trial, I enlarged the map onto a foam-core board and used it with each eyewitness who testified. I had the witnesses mark where they were standing and what they saw happen. It was a great opportunity to interact with the witnesses, and to some extent even with the jury as I repeatedly turned the map toward them to make sure everyone could see it. When it was time for closing arguments, there was no need to explain the map. Jurors had seen it repeatedly, and it served as a perfect visual aid to support the argument. The jury acquitted on all fourteen charges, and in interviewing them after the verdict, it was clear this photo map exercise was worth the effort. Not only did it provide a visual image of the scene to aid understanding and recall, it also made sure everyone had the *same, accurate* visual image.

If you can't take the photo yourself, it's possible Google Maps can come to your rescue. With the satellite view and 3-D display on which you have significant control over the angle and direction of view, a simple screen capture might be all you need. Here are some views of New York City's Central Park from varying distances and from various angles, all screen captures from Google Maps.

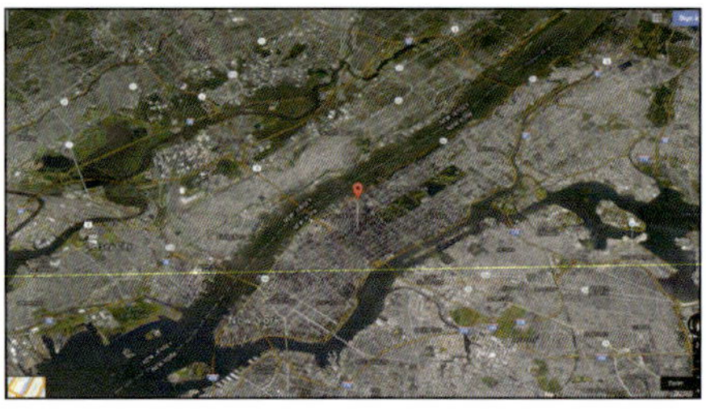

Maps to Depict a Route

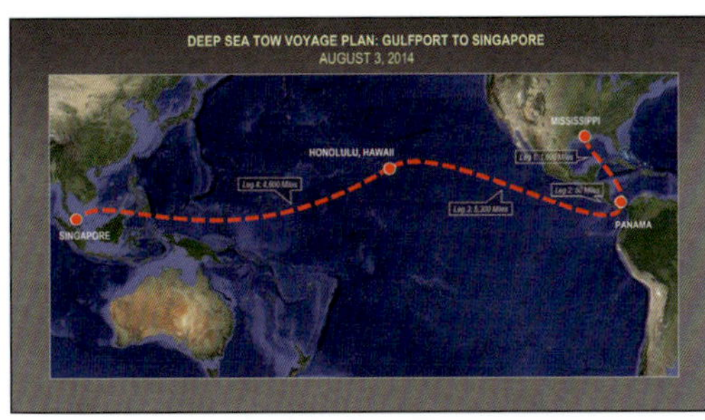

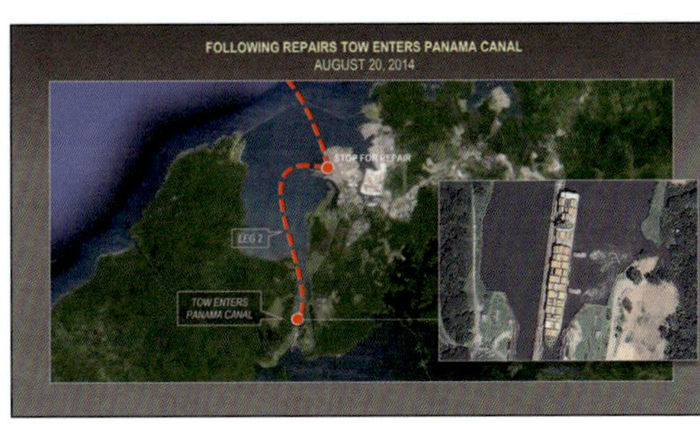

Maps are also effective for visually depicting a route—where someone traveled, where money was moved, where goods were shipped, or even where computer signals were sent.

When I use maps to show a route, I often build each step in front of the jury chronologically. If something else of importance was occurring at the same time, I can depict that on the map, too, with date labels as necessary. As with any other type of visual conveying multiple pieces of information, building the route along the map allows me to control the information flow and helps keep the jurors engaged.

Map Symbols to Convey Substance

Just like the size of a bar on a bar graph conveys quantitative information, so, too, can symbols on a map. Designed to fit a specific scale, the width of an arrow, the density of dots, or the size of marking pins can convey substantive meaning such as size, volume, density, or quantity.

"Heat maps" are a great example. They often use color to symbolize quantitative information, often depicting varying intensities. We see heat maps all the time, even if we don't know their name. Weather and radar maps, for example, use color to convey information such as temperature or the likelihood of rain or snow. Electoral maps use color to show which candidate or party has won in a particular geographic area (states, counties, etc.). The substantive information is numerical data, but showing it in a spreadsheet would have no visual impact. Instead, the colors provide an immediate and memorable visual representation of the information.

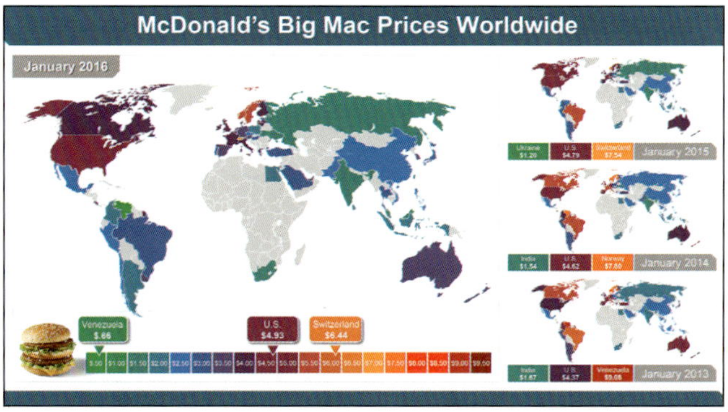

In the above example, a spectrum of colors from cold to warm conveys increasing prices for the same product around the globe. Once the viewer understands the simple key, it's easy to scan the map and instantly identify where prices are higher versus lower in different parts of the world.

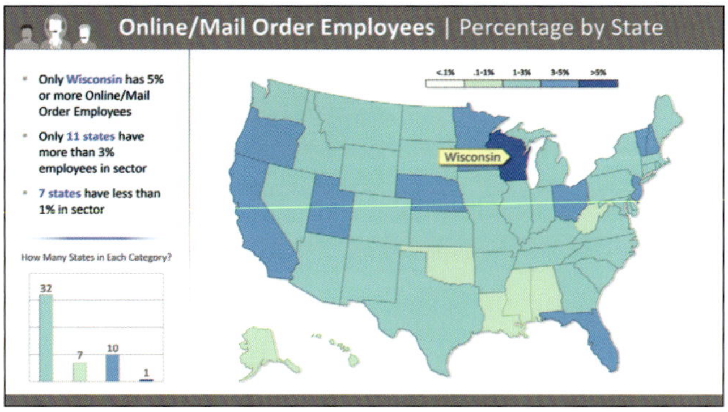

Similarly, the heat map at the bottom of the previous page uses colors of increasing intensity to represent the percentage of employees in each state who work in the online or mail order sector. The color key is simple and quick to comprehend, and the only text label on the map emphasizes the state of particular interest, discussed in the accompanying text.

Heat maps are also useful for depicting changes over time. Below, comparing the colors in the 1973 map with those in the 1999 map reflects an increase in states with legalized lotteries, casinos, or both. The map is more visual and memorable than a textual list.

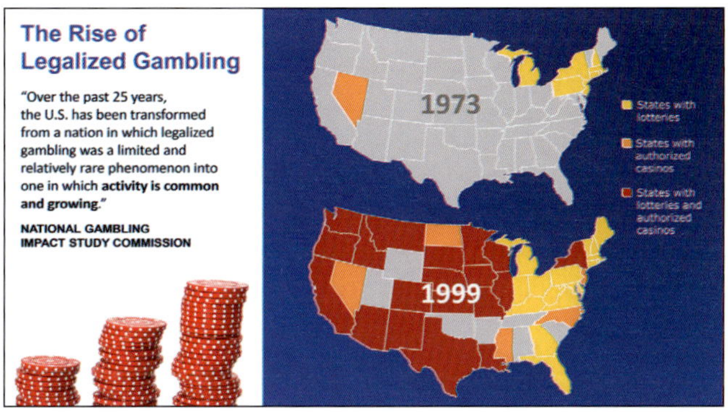

When using heat maps, be careful with the colors you choose. If you're using gradations of a color that don't contrast enough with one another, then you won't effectively communicate your message. Make sure the colors or symbol transformations are different enough to be perceived.

Minimize Text and Clutter

Maps can be stunningly beautiful. People collect them, study them, and display them. They can be clunky or elegant, cursory or detailed, simple or elaborate, and sometimes extraordinarily so. Cartography is both science and art and too often is taken for granted.

But this is not the time to display your cartographic prowess. As you design your map for trial, begin, as always, by focusing on the key question: "What's the point?" The answer to that question is what you map and what you emphasize.

Take a basic map of the United States. The design possibilities are daunting, and there's always more detail you could include.

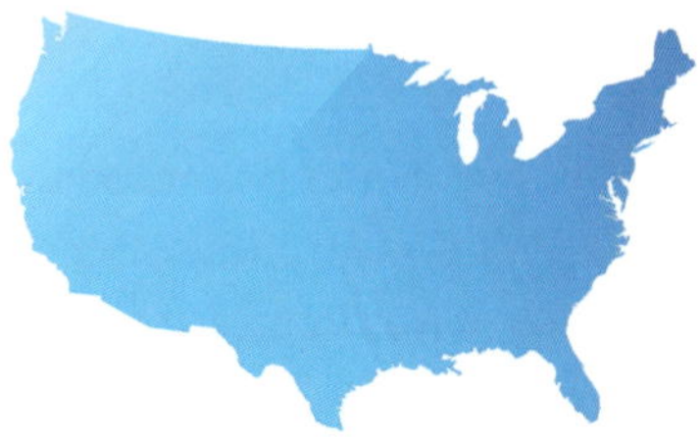

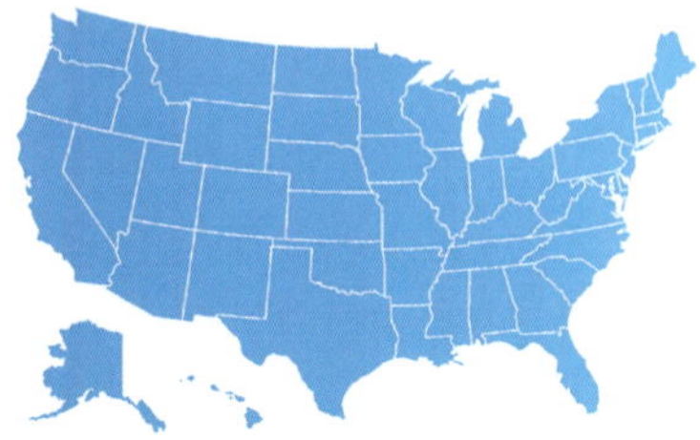

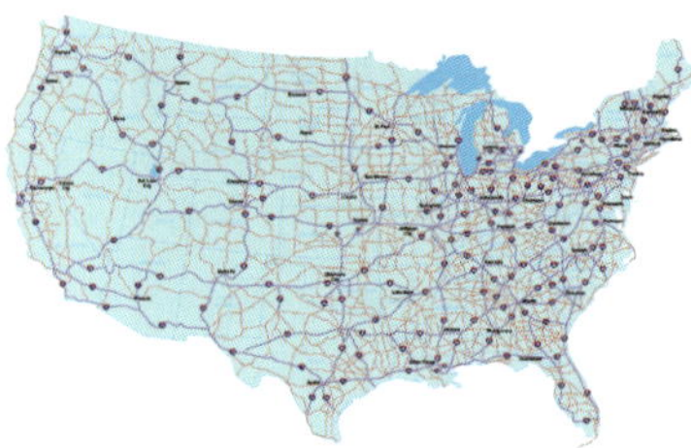

But what do you *need*? Are you showing an overseas trading route between the United States and Europe? Then you might only need basic outlines.

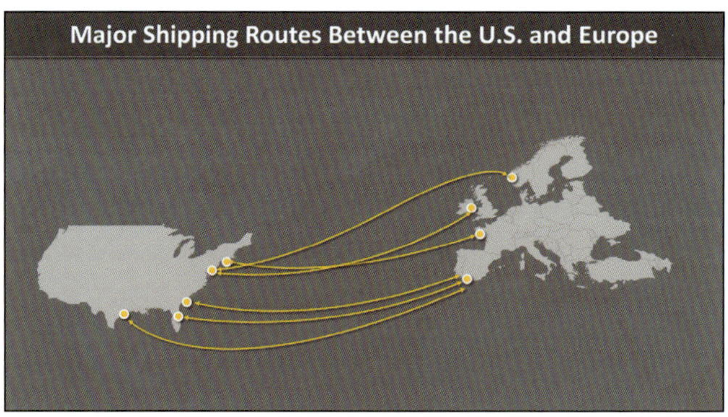

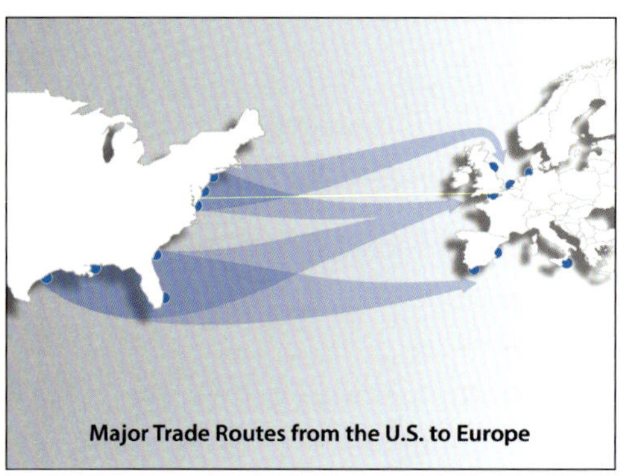

Perhaps you're depicting a national distribution chain. Lines dividing the states might be important enough to include, but they still don't need to be emphasized to the same extent as relevant city labels.

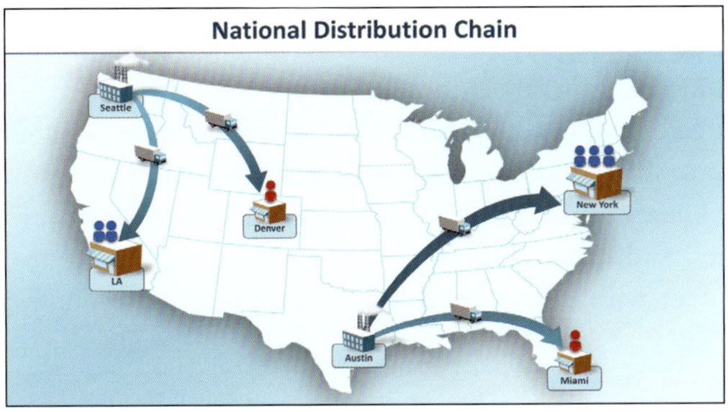

You could, of course, include state names or label the oceans and other bodies of water. But no one is making product in the Atlantic Ocean, so why label it? The map includes only necessary information to convey the message or provide important context.

Depending on what you're substantively depicting, you might not need to show the whole country. If you're showing the locations of key competitors from Maine to Florida, a map of just the east coast will suffice:

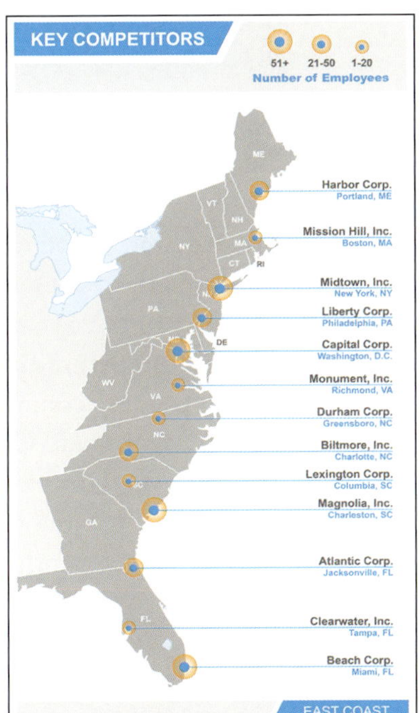

So far, none of these examples has necessitated depicting roads, lakes, mountains, or other similar detail. So start at the beginning. Design the map for what you need. That's exactly what the cellular phone companies do with their coverage maps. They have no labels at all. The outline of the United States is immediately recognizable; it doesn't need labels. There are no rivers, mountains, or other topography. Even the state borders are just dark enough to be perceived. That detail is not the point of the map, so it either isn't included or isn't emphasized.

In a recent case, a map was helpful for illustrating the geographic market for a service. I *needed* to show: (1) where my client and its various competitors were located throughout the United States and (2) which of three service types were offered at each of the companies' multiple locations.

Here is the map (with identifying details changed) that was initially provided to me:

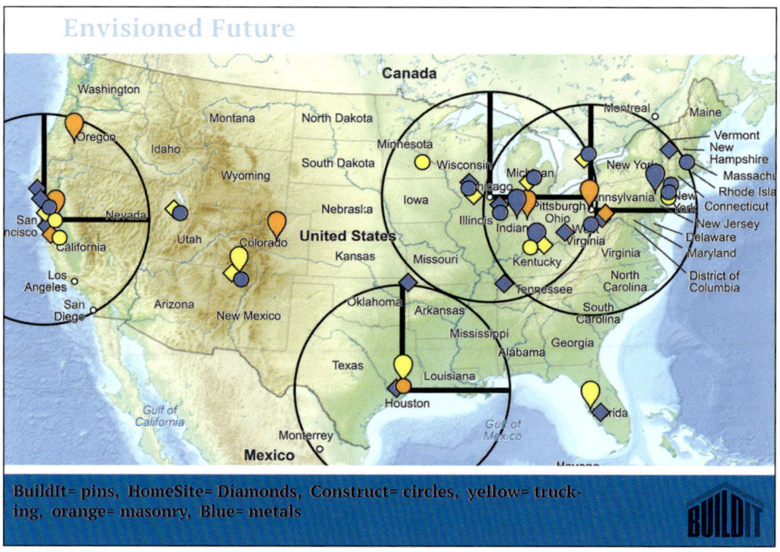

The map was overwhelming, confusing, and unfocused. The slide is filled with irrelevant information, and important information isn't presented clearly. The viewer has to work way too hard to figure it all out.

Lakes and mountains appear on the map, but they're entirely irrelevant to the case.

There are labels for every state, including those containing no company and no service area. The same is true of the Gulf of Mexico and Gulf of California.

The key at the bottom of the slide, black on dark blue, is extremely difficult to read, as there's not enough contrast between the text and background.

Why is the company logo (bottom right corner) on the slide at all?

The key relies on words to explain symbols. Why? Rather than spelling out "diamonds" and "circles," *why are we not using a diamond and a circle?* The same is true for colors. Why spell out "blue" and "yellow" when you can just use the colors? Think about how nonsensical this is. Can you imagine a key on an ordinary map stating "rivers = blue squiggly lines; mountains = brown triangles"? Don't do this.

Moreover, this long, run-on key is actually *two separate keys*—shapes and colors—which means there are two variables that require cross-referencing.

The large, black circles with the radius lines were an attempt to depict a third (ultimately unnecessary) piece of information—the 500-mile service area for four specific locations. The circles are dark and thick, and on the real map they even covered text and symbols. The radius lines are even worse. I have no idea why they're there, or why they're thicker than the circles and nearly everything else on the slide. As it turned out, we didn't need the circles on the map at all, but even if we did, the radius lines within the circles are completely unnecessary, and their angle within the circles is completely random. They could have been drawn in any direction and in the real image they were not even consistent across all four circles. Yet, they're the darkest, most emphasized elements on the slide, second only to the words "United States," "Canada," and "Mexico" (each of which also were unnecessary).

What's more, many symbols are covered by other symbols, defeating the purpose of having those symbols there at all. Those hidden symbols—which represent the companies we're trying to depict—are the whole point of the visual.

States in the Northeast are spelled out and cluttered, and a few are even cut off of the map. If words on your visual are so irrelevant that you don't care whether they're literally cut off in the middle, that should be a pretty good clue that they shouldn't be on the map in the first place.

There's also an odd and arbitrary band of white space between the map and the key, cutting off the label for Havana and introducing another distracting positive element to the visual.

So, the slide was redesigned.

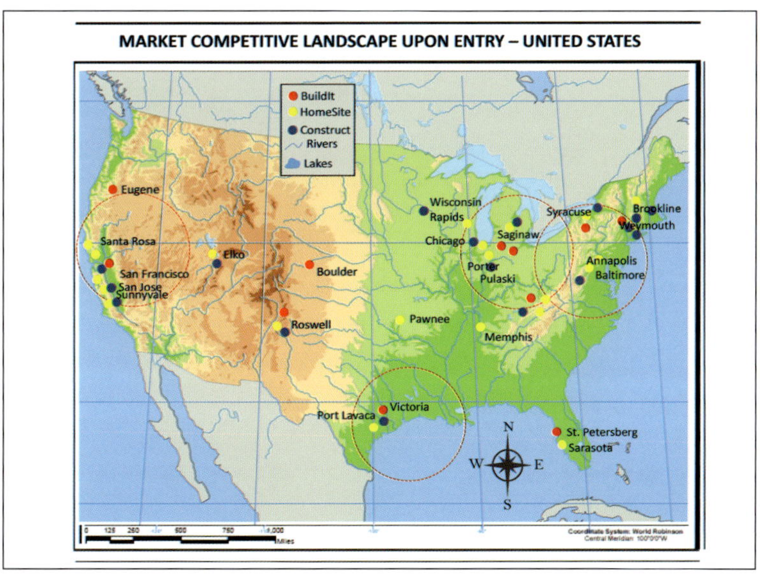

It's arguably better, but there's still a lot of unnecessary information. For example, there was no relevance whatsoever to the locations of lakes and rivers. Yet, they're included and even have their own labels in the key. There's no need for longitude or latitude lines, yet there they are. And why is there a compass? Is there any confusion about which way is north? Likewise, we simply don't need topographical information on this map.

Note that this redesigned map went too far when it eliminated state outlines. While it's good that not every state is named, without the outlines it's actually hard to tell where the companies are located. Those outlines provided important context. Now, there are random cities labeled on the map, which is arguably helpful but really just adds more confusion. It's not always clear whether the city label corresponds to a facility location (i.e., the company marker is in that city) or whether the city label is in that location and the company marker is off to the side. State outlines would have been a cleaner and clearer way of providing this important context.

We've lost other important data we wanted to communicate, as well. There is no longer any indication of which facility provides which services. We could create a separate map for that information, but then we lose the benefit of an immediate visual comparison.

So, I redesigned the map to eliminate the extraneous information. I also wanted to eliminate the need to cross-reference the data with multiple keys. The more information I could convey on the map itself, the less I'd need a separate key to explain my symbols. I hand-drew what I wanted, and a professional graphic designer brought it to life. Here's the result:

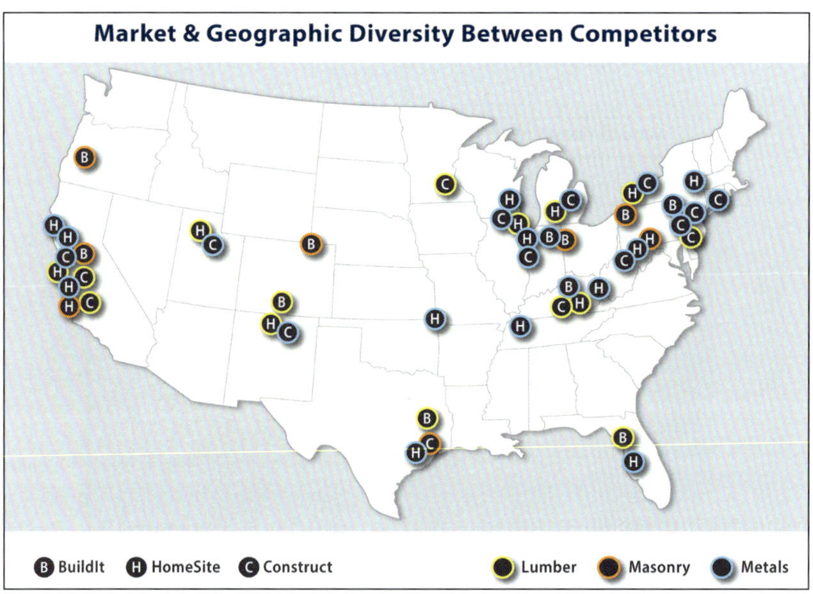

There's no extraneous information on the page. The title is limited to only necessary text. State outlines are back, but not over-emphasized. Mountains, rivers, roads, and other irrelevant geographic and topographic information is gone. A simple key lists the company names, but they also appear abbreviated directly on the map as plot points, reducing the need to cross-reference the key. I used color to denote the different service offerings, and I used those colors in the key rather than spelling out the color names (because that's just ridiculous). I also separated the keys—company names on one side and service lines on the other—so they're less overwhelming for the viewer. And, there's no compass, scale, longitude or latitude, logo, or giant, distracting circles.

Side by side, the difference is striking.

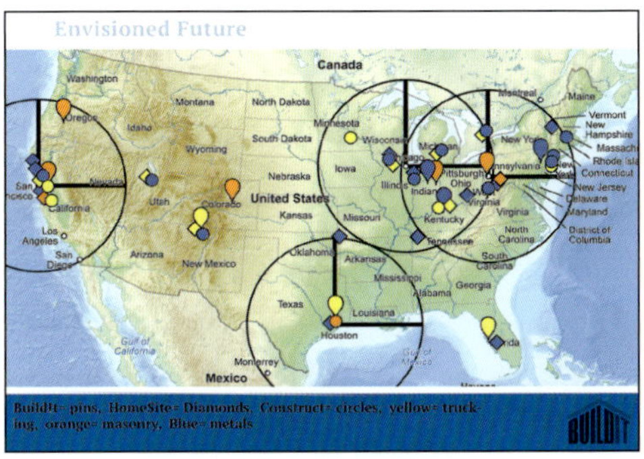

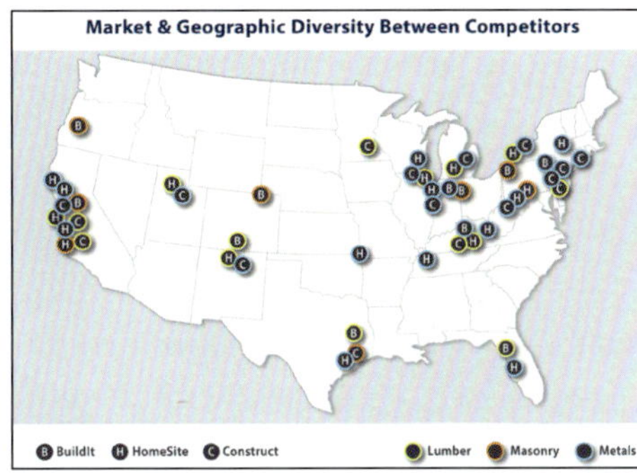

Design maps for what you need, and review them carefully for details you've included as a matter of habit but can eliminate for the message you're conveying. When designed well, maps can distill a lot of information into an immediately familiar, manageable, and memorable visual image.

9

Photographs

Photographs are visual by definition, and they stand out—particularly in trials that are otherwise document-heavy. In expanding upon his Brain Rule Number 9—"Vision trumps all other senses"—Medina explains that our brains are not as good at identifying letters and words as they are at identifying and remembering pictures.[1] It's not surprising, then, that photographs are an exceptionally useful trial tool.

When presented appropriately, photos can satisfy all of our jury communication goals—they aid understanding, boost credibility, and increase retention. In this chapter, I'll talk about some helpful uses for photographs in trial, design considerations, tips for dealing with Rule 403 challenges, and where to get photographs for your trial slides.

Uses for Photographs

Depicting Case Evidence

Photographs often are used and admitted as evidence at trial, as long as they're fair and accurate representations of what they purport to capture. In criminal cases, for example, photographs of crime scenes, injuries, autopsies, stills from surveillance videos, or even photos of undercover drug buys might be used with a jury. In intellectual property cases, you might use photographs to compare the plaintiff's and defendant's products to bolster an argument for or against an infringement finding. In a product liability case, a photograph might show the jury the manufacturing defect that led to the plaintiff's injury. Or, a series of photographs might effectively depict how something changed over time, such as improvements made by the defendant, ongoing property damage due to neglect, or decay due to disease.

Photographs aid understanding in these cases because something visual is directly at issue. Without the photos, jurors would be left to "picture" the evidence for themselves, based on a verbal description. And when the verbal description is open to interpretation, that doesn't always work out so well. For example, if a witness testifies that the defendant was "behind the fence," that testimony could sound credible or not, just based on the mental image the juror has of a fence.

By using a photograph of the actual fence at issue, you can get everyone on the same page, and there's no room for descriptive error.

Creating a Visual Memory of a Theme

Sometimes, a photo can provide a great background while you're speaking, or even while you're displaying documents. But the photo must be *relevant*. If it's not, it fights with your actual message.

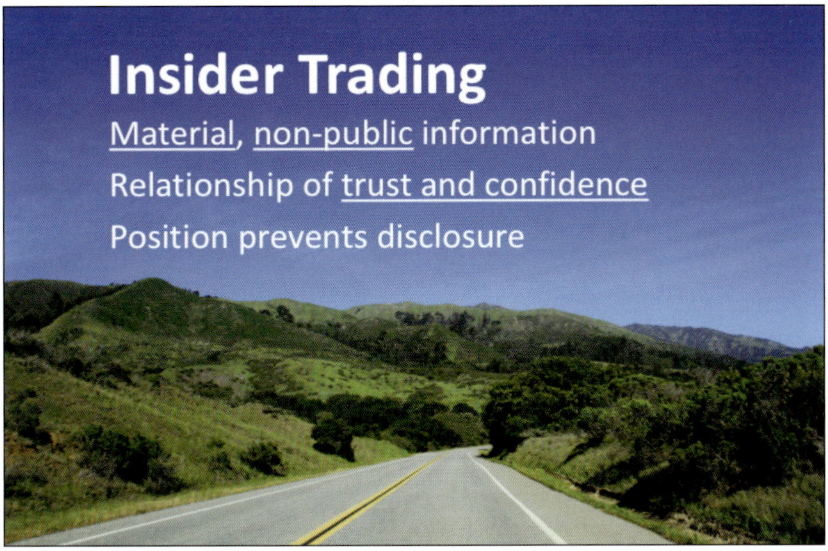

With some brainstorming, we might be able to articulate a reason why this winding road relates to insider trading. But we wouldn't want our jury trying to do that when they should be focusing on our message. Dissonance is a distraction.

On the other hand, when the photo is relevant, as it is with evidentiary photographs, it can be very effective. Think about print advertising or the motivational products industry. They'll feature photographs in magazines or on billboards, or they'll print them on mugs, posters, or mousepads, and the photo captures an entire concept.

A silhouetted man against a sunset embodies "contemplation."

A picture of an old radio is a symbol for "nostalgia."

A kayaker conquering rough water signifies "exhilaration."

Ever wonder why? Why does the silhouetted man suggest contemplation instead of loneliness? Why doesn't the old radio symbolize obsolescence? Why doesn't the kayaker evoke fear, or even recklessness?

Often, it's because the text—and context—tells you otherwise. Text defines the image for you. Using the photos above for their purported themes isn't a stretch (unlike the winding road and insider trading), but the text solidifies the photos' relevance where the image could have multiple thematic interpretations.

Keep this in mind for your trial visuals. Present thematic or conceptual photos together with text or spoken words that immediately characterize the photos the way you want the jury to view them. A picture might very well be worth a thousand words—*but which thousand?* Text helps ensure that the jury's interpretation matches yours.

A recent ad campaign for HSBC Bank illustrated this point beautifully. The ads were full-color photographs with a single word featured on each image. Sometimes the same photograph was repeated two or three times, but each image featured a different word reflecting a completely different interpretation of the photograph. The images were set side by side, juxtaposing the different interpretations. Another variation used alternating but identical meanings for two different images set side by side, again emphasizing that the same photograph can mean very different things to different people. Here are a few examples I created.

The extent to which you'll be able to use thematic images in the trial setting will vary. But even when your judge allows it and you've selected a relevant, tone-appropriate photograph, remember your setting and your audience. Overdone, the approach can alienate the jury and suggest that you aren't taking the case seriously. Used in moderation, a photograph emphasizing a theme can be an effective communication tool.

Aiding Evidence Presentation

When case evidence is too small or too large to effectively display it for the jury, a photograph can save the day. I've had both extremes in patent cases. In one case, the patent involved a semiconductor chip less than an inch wide. In another case, the patent was for a highway guardrail, a large and heavy item that would have been difficult to bring into court. By taking a photograph of the object at issue, you can display it as large or small as you need. A witness can explain the parts of the object and how it works. You can even add labels or other markings to turn the photo into a diagram and create a visual memory for the jury, which might be quite valuable, depending on your case facts.

Increasing Recall of Witnesses and Trial Evidence

When trials are long or when a lot of witnesses testify, consider using photos in your closing argument to help jurors remember key evidence and testimony. In one trial I had lasting almost four months, fifty witnesses testified in the government's case. Twelve testified in the defense. I put nine character witnesses on the stand in a single day. For the closing argument, I designed slides that would use testimony from daily transcripts and a photograph of the testifying witness. Text builds walked the jurors through the testimony at a controlled pace.

Getting photos of character witnesses is generally pretty easy. They're friendly witnesses, and they'll either give you an existing photo or let you take their picture. Use a neutral, trial-appropriate image. Alternatively, if the witness testified through a video deposition, you can use a still shot from the video as your photograph. Here, too, select a neutral image. Don't use one where the witness is in the middle of a word, or has his eyes closed, or looks particularly angelic or particularly evil. Jurors will see through that and will resent the attempt at manipulation, which harms your credibility.

Adding Credibility

We all know photos can be manipulated. We hear about it all the time. We can even do it ourselves in the comfort of our homes using basic photo editing software. But despite knowing that photos can be altered, the old adage remains true. Generally, seeing is believing. Using photographs can therefore add credibility to testimony and even attorney argument. Jurors know the trial context is adversarial—if one side uses a photo and the other side doesn't object or point out something misleading about the image, the credibility of the photo (and the lawyer sponsoring it) is that much stronger.

Design Considerations when Using Photographs

When using evidentiary photographs—e.g., a crime scene or the burned-out shell of a home—you take the photos as you get them. But in other contexts, you'll have to make some choices about whether and how to use photographs in your trial. Some of these considerations are discussed below.

Choose Between Photographs and Stylized Images

Emotions evoked through photographic images tend to be stronger than emotions evoked through clip art or drawn diagrams. Usually, I prefer a photograph to a stylized image. But not always. Sometimes, a photo will contain too many distractions. It's like the difference between showing a city block in satellite view versus in map view.

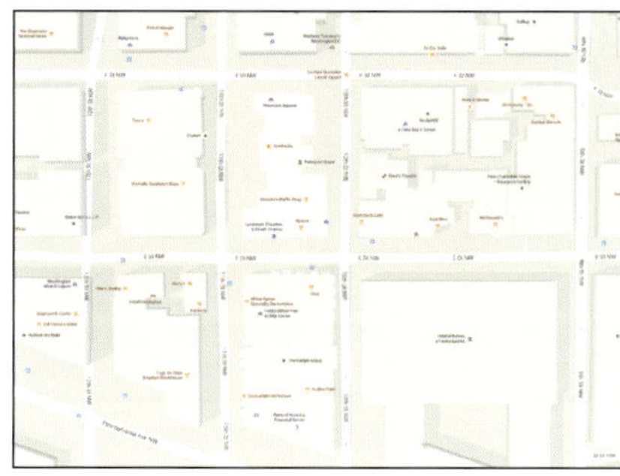

If a photo will be too busy, a diagram lets you control the level of detail you present to the jury.

Similarly, in some instances a photograph might be too emotional, risking Rule 403 exclusion. Using a diagram instead will allow you to control the tone of the image.

Whenever possible, pick one image style—either photos or drawings—and stick with it throughout your presentation.

If you need to switch styles, do so purposefully and try not to do it on the same slide. Contrasting styles so close to each other usually looks disjointed.

Place Photographs with Purpose

Like other elements on your slides, where you place a photograph should be a considered decision, not a random one. When the placement of a photo leaves oddly spaced borders, seems too small for the slide, or is itself enclosed in a heavily emphasized border, the result can look unprofessional or even like a mistake.

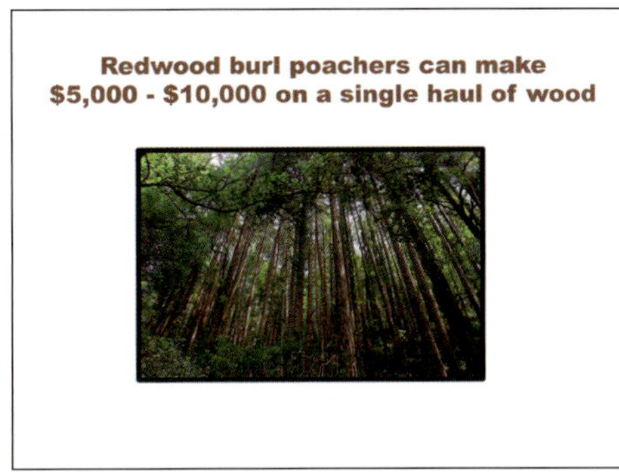

If you intend for the photo to take up the whole slide, then take up the whole slide.

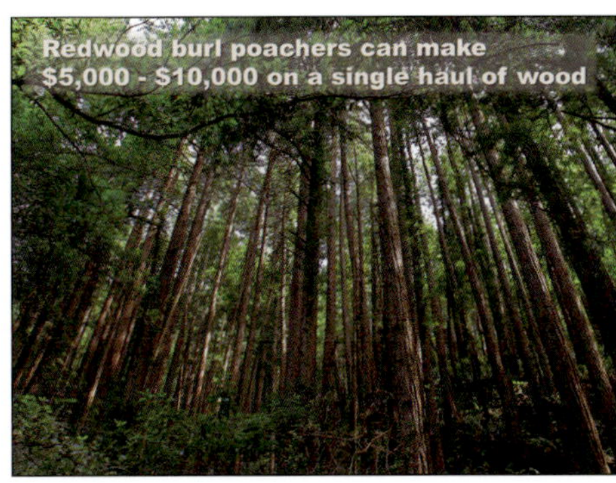

If you can shorten the heading, even better.

In addition, the photo should guide the jury through your message. If people are in the photo, have them looking at your text and not away from it or off the slide entirely. If there's no text on the slide, then think about where you'll be standing when you display the slide. When you can, position the photograph so the person is looking (or directing action) in the direction you'll be standing.

Likewise, if you're using a photo of an object or a scene, consider whether it is "pointing" or "facing" a certain direction and, if so, take this into account when you choose where on the slide to position the various elements.

Don't Use Poor Quality Photos

Using bad photos does nothing to help your communication. With evidentiary photographs, you're usually stuck with what you have. But with demonstratives, it's almost always better to not use a poor quality photo at all than to use an image that's grainy, blurry, overexposed, too dark, etc. If you can appropriately improve the photograph with editing software, go for it. But if you can't, let it go. Select a different photo, consider using stock imagery or a diagram, or go without.

Remove Extraneous Detail and Distraction

Photos with extraneous detail can undermine your communication goals by distracting jurors from your message. There's just too much other stuff in the picture to look at and think about, and before they know it, the jurors have been so focused on your busy picture that they've totally lost track of your argument.

So, before you use demonstrative photographs, consider whether there's anything you should de-emphasize or omit from the image. Again, you obviously cannot misleadingly manipulate an evidentiary photograph, such as a picture of a plaintiff's injuries. If you do, you're likely committing both a felony and a violation of professional ethics rules. But the landscape is different for demonstrative photographs. Removing clutter, improving lighting, and making similar edits are acceptable and even helpful as long as you aren't misleading the jury on a relevant point.

Basic photo editing software can do wonders to improve lighting in photographs by lightening shadows and darkening highlights. With a slightly more advanced understanding of these programs, you can select an area to darken or gray so areas deserving less emphasis recede into the background and areas on which you want to focus the jury's attention advance to the foreground. You can also sharpen photographs and adjust their contrast. If you're working with a graphic designer, keep in mind that they are usually quite facile with Photoshop and similar photo editing programs, and can improve less-than-perfect photographs effectively and efficiently.

But sometimes, reducing the emphasis on something in a photograph isn't enough. You need to eliminate it from the picture entirely. There are three primary ways to eliminate information from a photograph: crop it, cover it, or edit it.

Cropping

Perhaps the most common (and easiest) way to remove irrelevant detail from a photograph is to simply cut—or "crop"—what you don't need. For instance, if you're showing a photo of a building where a witness works, why show a photo of the whole block? If that's the only photo you have, you can simply crop the photo to eliminate the other buildings. Similarly, if you're focusing on an aerial layout of a particular block or set of buildings, you likely don't need to show an entire town. By cropping what you don't need, the relevant buildings are the focus of your photo, and the focus of your message.

The image above on the left is an aerial photo of the National Mall in Washington, D.C. By zooming in on the Washington Monument and cutting the remaining image, I created the image next to it. I used the same technique for the third image, this time focusing on the Jefferson Memorial and Tidal Basin.

Be careful with this technique, though. If the change is too dramatic and the photo resolution was low to begin with, the quality of your enlarged image will be too poor to use in the enlarged size you'll need for trial.

Cropping can also be helpful with evidentiary photographs, as long as you're cropping irrelevant information and not altering the meaning or context of the picture. For example, on many occasions, I've photographed physical evidence collected by law enforcement. I'm usually pretty cognizant of my composition, but every now and then I capture more in the picture than I intended—a random set of keys sitting on the table; a police officer walking in the background; or a portion of another item of evidence I failed to move completely out of the shot. In each example, cropping out the irrelevant detail has been a quick and easy fix.

Covering

If you can't crop out the extra detail, perhaps you can cover it up. Text, boxes, lines, and other graphic elements can do double duty, providing contrast with the image so text is legible while also hiding elements in the image that aren't relevant to your substantive message.

Editing

A third way to eliminate information from a photo is to use photo editing software to remove or minimize emphasis on the irrelevant. We do this in our personal photos when we eliminate redeye, which typically occurs when light from the camera's built-in flash bounces back into the lens. But we can eliminate more than redeye. Anything from a piece of trash on the road or a buoy in the water to an entire building or a person can be completely erased. We can even swap out one image for another. And, yes, it bears repeating that I am not talking about doing this with evidentiary photographs.

Suppose you took a photograph of a location but didn't realize a person was in the corner of your shot. Or imagine you want to show photographs of witnesses in your case during closing argument. You ask your witnesses to give you photos, and one gives you a picture of himself standing with a distracting painting behind him. Using editing software, you can eliminate these types of distractions from your photographs. Ultimately, if you can't eliminate the distraction from a photo, you can consider using a stock photo or an illustration instead.

Adjust Size Proportionally

When sizing a photograph or any other image, be careful not to distort it (unless distortion doesn't matter). When the height and width of the photo are scaled differently—called anamorphic scaling—the results might be amusing but they're not particularly usable.

To avoid this result, adjust the image from one of its corners and not from the top, bottom, or side. Your software's crop tool can be your friend during this process. You can keep the correct proportions of the image but eliminate excess from the edges if you've had to enlarge the photo beyond the dimensions you need to display it.

Rule 403 Considerations

Most of the graphic design books I've referenced (and love so much) discuss the tremendous benefits of using photographs in presentations. Primarily, their reasoning is that photographs have a heightened potential for emotional impact, particularly as compared to black-and-white text or even drawings.

And therein lies the problem in the trial setting. In the business context (and nearly all other contexts), a photo-heavy approach can make for an appropriately powerful, attention-grabbing, and memorable presentation. But in trial, a photograph's greatest asset can be its biggest vulnerability. The more the photograph appeals to emotion and the less direct relevance the photo has to the case, the bigger the risk it will be excluded under Rule 403 for its prejudicial effect outweighing its probative value. So, be careful with your photo selection and how you use the images to increase your chances of prevailing in a Rule 403 challenge. Here are some tips.

Trust Your Gut

If you think your illustrative image is extraordinarily powerful, emotional, etc., it probably is. And that could be a problem. Either select a different image, or have a backup in case that one gets excluded. A well-designed and professionally drawn diagram still might be better than no image at all.

Avoid Faces

Images of people, especially faces, appeal to emotion more than images of things. If you're concerned about Rule 403, consider using an image of a thing or a place instead of an image of a person. In fact, eliminating faces from photos can also minimize distractions in the visual. Our eyes are naturally drawn to pictures of people and to people's faces in particular.

Look at the photograph to the right. Did you feel yourself drawn to looking at the young man's face? Maybe even before you read the text? It's a very natural instinct. If you want (or need) your jurors to look at the person in the photo, fine. But if not, then using a picture without a discernible face eliminates a powerful and distracting area of focus. Instead, you can use a photo with no people; crop the image to start at the shoulders; show a person from the back; or use a photo where the faces are small or obscured.

De-emphasize the Photo

If a photograph risks Rule 403 exclusion (or even if it just risks being distracting), one option is to lessen its emphasis on your slides. The photograph's placement on the slide, the background you put behind it, the text you use with it, and even the amount of color and salience in the photo can impact how much it is emphasized.

Use a Smaller Size

Featuring the photo in a full bleed—taking up the entire slide with no borders around it—is more powerful and engaging than using a smaller version of the photo. So, you might successfully defend against (or avoid altogether) a Rule 403 challenge simply by displaying the photograph in a smaller size.

Use Neutral Text

The nature of the text you use with photos can also impact the power of the image. As discussed earlier in this chapter, words associated with an image can affect how that image is perceived. And, of course, the words on our visuals will be subject to their own Rule 403 scrutiny, perhaps slightly less so in closing argument than during witness examinations. Regardless of when in trial such images are used, carefully consider the text you pair with powerful photos. Using neutral text can help tip the balance in your favor on a close Rule 403 judgment call.

Background

Dark backgrounds tend to emphasize and even dramatize a photo more than light ones. Whether emphasis is helpful or harmful will be a determination for each visual, but knowing the impact of a dark versus a light background can help you adjust the emphasis when it's called for.

Color

Repeated studies in the advertising industry have shown that color ads hold more interest and elicit a stronger emotional response than black-and-white ads. Applying those principles here, converting a color image to grayscale (an easy task with photo editing software) turns the image into a black-and-white one while preserving its tone, and ultimately reduces its emphasis.

Don't Disregard the Law

If you wouldn't be permitted to show the jury something live, then don't show it in a photograph. For example, in 2016, a Missouri appeals court in *State v. Walter*, sitting *en banc*, reversed the defendant's conviction and remanded the case for a new trial due to the prosecution's use of the following visual in its closing argument:[2]

The problem was the inflammatory nature of showing the defendant in his prison jumpsuit—which he could not have been forced to appear in during trial—combined with the obvious mugshot and the word "GUILTY" emblazoned across his face. Initially, the appeals court had found error, but it held the error harmless in light of other evidence. Still, the court was offended by the use of the photograph, stating that "it defies logic why even an overzealous prosecutor would tempt the grant of a mistrial during closing argument on a case where the evidence of guilt is this overwhelming. The display of the photograph alone raises serious concerns and the addition of the large red letters across the photo reading 'GUILTY' increases the concerns exponentially. Such egregious conduct on the part of the prosecutor is unwarranted and cannot be condoned by any court."[3] The appeals court explained that, even "[g]iving the State the widest possible latitude," there was "no rational justification" for the use of such "irrelevant[,] prejudicial matters" that "otherwise tend to confuse the jury," the photo "added nothing" to the state's argument, and the only purpose for its use was to "inflame [the] jury."[4]

On review *en banc*, the court held that the use of the photograph warranted reversal. The court noted that "forcing a defendant to appear at trial in prison-issued attire undermines the presumption of innocence and the fairness of the fact-finding process," and that a defendant is not required to appear at trial wearing prison attire "because of the possible impairment of the presumption so basic to the adversary system."[5] The *en banc* court went on to acknowledge that Walter "was not forced to appear physically in prison attire during his trial," but found that "the altered photograph the state presented during its closing argument compelled the same *de facto* influence upon the jury."[6] Indeed, as is evident in the photo, Walter "is wearing a bright orange prison jumpsuit and the word 'GUILTY' is superimposed in large, block, red letters, running diagonally across Walter's face and filling the frame of the photograph."[7]

Thus, the *en banc* court found the "state's use of the altered photograph of Walter impinged upon the presumption of innocence and the fairness of the fact-finding process by juxtaposing the photograph of Walter wearing prison attire and 'GUILTY' stamped across his face with him sitting at the defendant's table in plain clothes."[8] Recognizing the power of visuals, the court stated "'visual arguments manipulate audiences by harnessing rapid unconscious or emotional reasoning processes and by exploiting the fact that we do not generally question the rapid conclusions we reach based on visually presented information.'"[9]

The prosecution in a Washington state case used a similar approach with a photograph, which the court likewise found improper. In *State v. Walker*, the prosecutor used a PowerPoint presentation with 250 slides, over 100 of which displayed the heading "DEFENDANT WALKER GUILTY OF PREMEDITATED MURDER."[10] Several other slides included photographs that were admitted into evidence, coupled with inflammatory captions, headings, and superimposed text.[11] The presentation concluded with the defendant's booking photo, superimposed with the words "GUILTY BEYOND A REASONABLE DOUBT."[12] The trial court found the defendant guilty, but the appeals court reversed and remanded for a new trial, citing the prejudicial effect of the slides.[13] The court stated that the prosecution "committed serious misconduct" by including multiple exhibits that were altered with inflammatory captions and superimposed text, and by repeatedly expressing a personal opinion as to the defendant's guilt.[14] *Walter* and *Walker* are not alone in their treatment of this approach with photographs.[15]

Selecting and Obtaining Photographs

Getting case-related photos is usually pretty straightforward. You might receive photos from someone else (e.g., pictures of a crime scene taken by law enforcement) or you might take them yourself (e.g., photos of property damage you allege was caused by the defendant).

Fortunately, getting thematic photographs nowadays can be just as easy. You might be able to take them yourself, controlling the composition. For instance, you can intentionally take the photo from an angle that blocks a logo, or a face, or anything else you want to avoid displaying on your trial slide. You can even control the orientation of the photo based on how you intend to use it on your slide (horizontal vs. vertical), what direction the photo is facing (as discussed above), and the placement of empty space to allow for headings, labels, graphics, or substantive text on the photo.

If you can't take the picture with your own camera (or if you don't have the time or just don't want to bother with it), there is a mind-boggling number of photographs available from stock photography companies and elsewhere on the Internet. Some images are available for free through WikiCommons and Google Images, both of which allow you to search for images that are licensed for reuse, even for commercial purposes. Well-known and trustworthy stock photography companies with broad and deep libraries of images include Shutterstock (www.shutterstock.com), iStockphoto (www.iStockphoto.com), flickr (www. flickr.com), Depositphotos (www.depositphotos.com), Fotosearch (www.fotosearch.com), and Stock XCHNG (www.sxc.hu). Although buying images from some of the larger photography agencies might be cost prohibitive, many of the smaller companies sell images royalty free—so with a one-time payment, you can use the image repeatedly and however you like. Some of these services also offer subscriptions, so if you do a lot with images, this might be a cost-effective approach. Regardless, if there's a fee, which is usually a modest one, pay it for the rights to use the photo.

Paying the fee has the added benefit of eliminating the watermark these companies appropriately put on their photos. Using a photo with a watermark looks (and is) unprofessional and cheap and adds yet another distracting element to the slide.

Finally, since you're likely going to take pictures with a digital camera (or purchase digital images), keep in mind the importance of resolution. The resolution of a digital image is determined by its pixels—the tiny squares that make up the image. The more pixels there are per inch (ppi), the better the image quality. Generally, you should aim for 300 ppi for images you'll use in a presentation. If you're taking the pictures yourself, make sure your camera is set to the best resolution possible. As you change the size of the image, the ppi also changes. So if you take a photo at 300 ppi and then crop and enlarge it, as we saw above, the resolution will diminish. Enlarge it enough and you'll actually see the individual pixels in the image. This effect, called "pixilation," contributes to the unprofessional look of the photo.

At bottom, the pictures you use in your trial presentation should look good. If you take a picture and it doesn't look good, don't use it. Overexposed, blurry, and grainy images are hard to see, which defeats the whole purpose of using them.

Photographs have an unparalleled ability to communicate powerfully, persuasively, and immediately. We certainly must bear in mind our limitations under the evidentiary rules when we use photographs in our trial visuals. But when used thoughtfully and in moderation, photographs can do wonders for translating our case themes into visual images.

10

Graphics, Drawings, and Diagrams

As a general matter, I use the term "graphics" to describe everything on the slide that isn't text—from a tiny bullet point to a large, intricate diagram. I view graphics as falling into two categories—design or substantive—and depending on how it's used, a single graphic can span both. Graphic elements such as lines, boxes, and arrows often serve a design function, helping to organize the slide or move the message along. At the other end of the spectrum are substantive graphics—those that convey meaning. Substantive graphics are the essence of what it means to turn messages into visual images. I tend to put diagrams, drawings (also called "illustrations"), and "information graphics" (or "infographics") into this "substantive graphics" category. In this chapter, I'll talk about substantive graphics and share suggestions for how to use them.

Diagrams and Drawings

I naturally convert information into pictures. It's how I tend to organize the information and how I process it into my long-term memory. I'm quite confident that at least some of my jurors do the same thing. I've even seen diagrams that real jurors have created (when I've interviewed them in the jury room after a trial) to help themselves process information. I've also watched mock jurors whip out pens and paper and start drawing during their deliberations.

For ease of reference, I think of a drawing as an illustration of something, and a diagram adds labels to the drawing. But a diagram is also a kind of drawing, and a drawing can also be a diagram (with or without labels!). The terms we use aren't critical. For purposes of jury visuals, just keep in mind that drawings and diagrams can help our communication tremendously. So, here are some considerations for using these tools with your jury.

Drawing the "Nonexistent"

Drawings are essential when a photograph or data display just isn't an option. We can't photograph something that doesn't exist in the real world or a view that would be impossible to capture. But we can draw it. Likewise, we can't always photograph a process or method, but we can draw that, too.

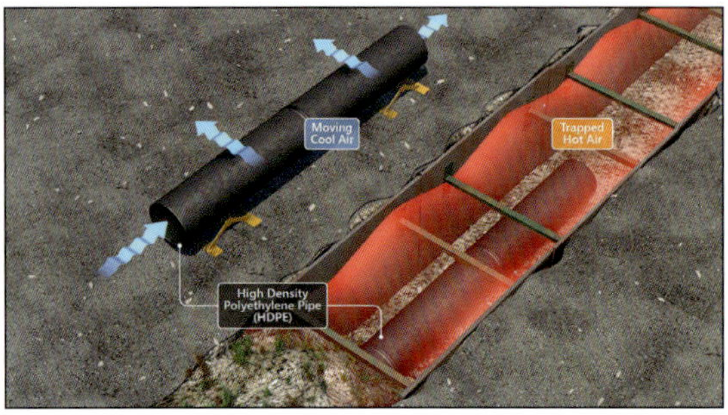

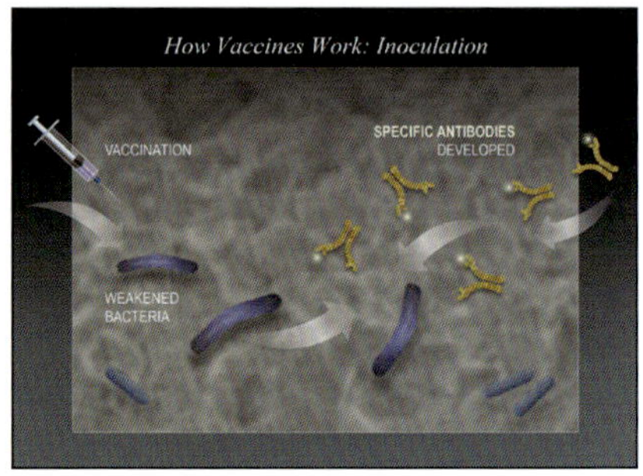

Drawings to Eliminate the Extraneous

When the subject does exist, drawings let us control content more than we can with photographs, which have limitations. Photos can include too much clutter, you might not be able to take the picture from the angle you need, or the subject might be too large or too small to effectively capture. Drawings can solve all of these problems. You can draw and diagram anything, from any angle, and with as much or as little detail as you need.

VS.

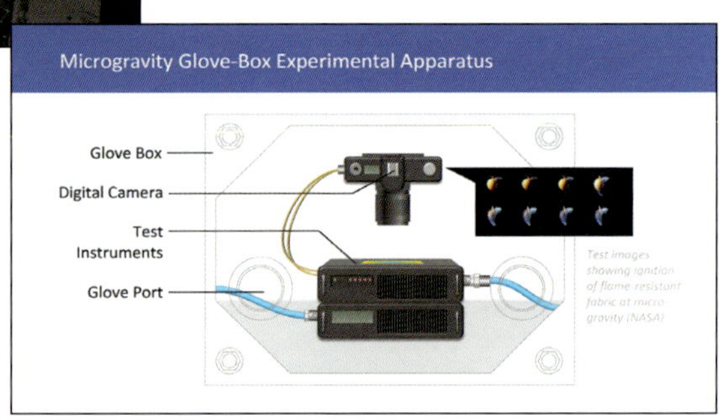

Drawings also let us focus on generic versions of our subject when we want to avoid showing a brand. It's hard to photograph a generic plane, box of cookies, or person's face. A drawing can solve that problem.

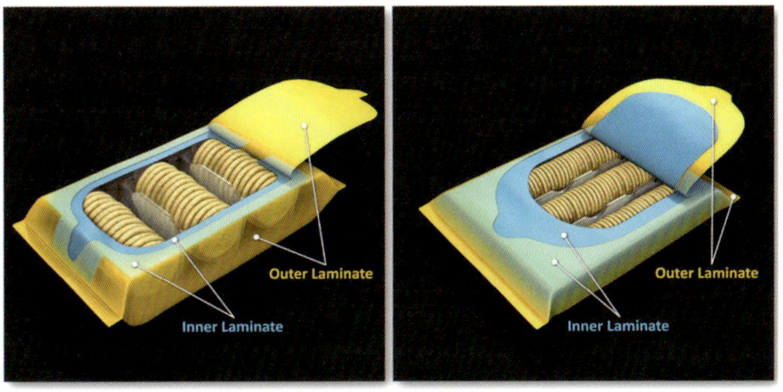

Leave Background Details in the Background

When designing diagrams, make sure the explanatory information doesn't distract too much from the message. Keep background information in the background, while making sure it's visible enough to be perceived by the jury. (Otherwise, why is it there?) If everything is equally emphasized on the slide, jurors won't know where to look first.

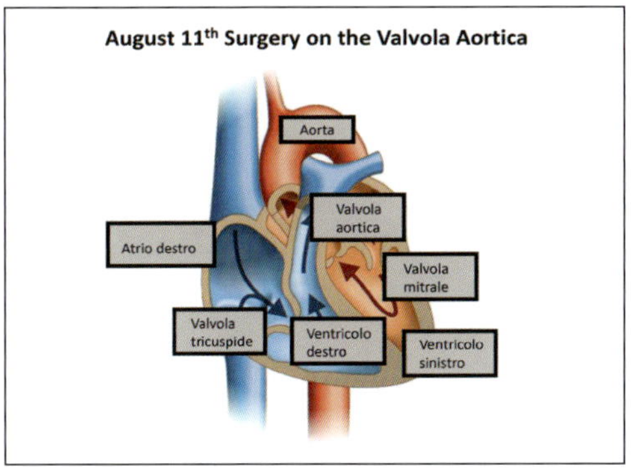

Here, with all the clutter from gray boxes with thick outlines, it's impossible to tell precisely which part of the heart every label is describing. The arrows in the diagram contribute to the confusion, as it's tough to tell in some instances whether the arrow is an anchor for the label or has substantive meaning. And, the extra graphic elements around the labels hide much of the diagram.

By eliminating the extraneous elements and using unobtrusive, organized anchor lines, the labels are clear and the diagram on the whole is less overwhelming.

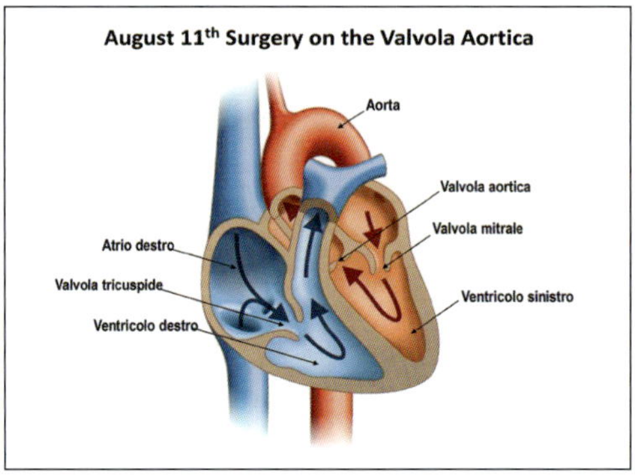

Without a hierarchy to the visual—in which some pieces of information are emphasized over others—jurors might miss the key message entirely. Take simple steps such as reducing the weight of secondary text and graphic elements. In Tufte's words, "[m]ake all visual distinctions as subtle as possible, but still clear and effective."[1] He calls this using the "smallest effective difference" between the primary message and the secondary organizational elements on the slide.[2] The design then helps lead the viewer's eye toward your core message, giving it emphasis over everything else.

Where Possible, Eliminate the Key

As a general matter, I try to place diagram labels close to what they're labeling, rather than in a key off to the side. I've certainly used keys on diagrams that I've submitted with significant briefs or motions or even when working with an expert on a diagram submitted with a report. But for jury visuals, I try hard to eliminate the need for jurors to cross-reference a key. By labeling the diagram directly, jurors have less work to do to comprehend the image and its components.

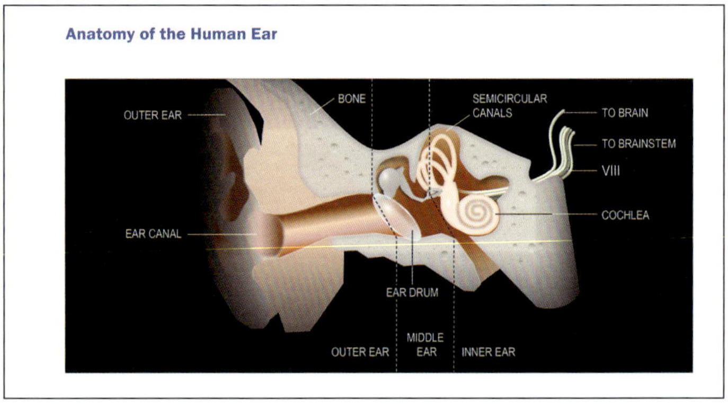

In the previous slide, jurors can see the label and its object at the same time, so it's easy to connect the two. The less effort the jurors must go through to understand a diagram, the better. In contrast, a key requires the jury to cross-reference and work harder to decipher the visual:

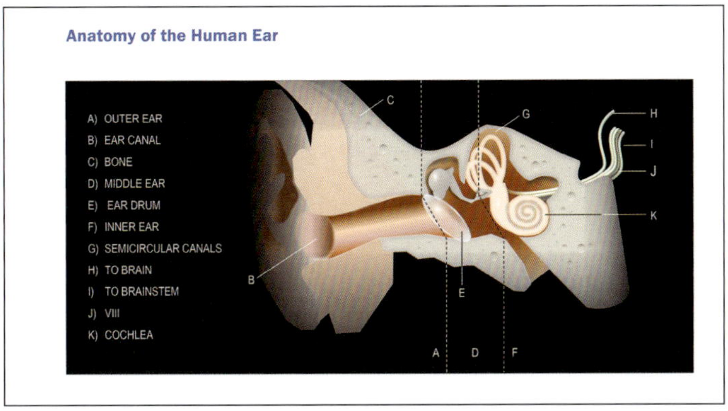

That said, sometimes you need a lot of labels. Including them all directly on the diagram could confuse or disrupt the flow of information or even obscure something else on the slide. When I have a lot of labels, I still try to avoid a key. I'll use fewer words or smaller symbols, and I'll introduce contrast between the labels and what they're describing. Using a lighter-weight font can work well, and different colors can help separate the labels (and their accompanying anchor lines) from the diagrammed object.

Here's a great example for effectively dealing with a lot of labels on a single diagram using a key.

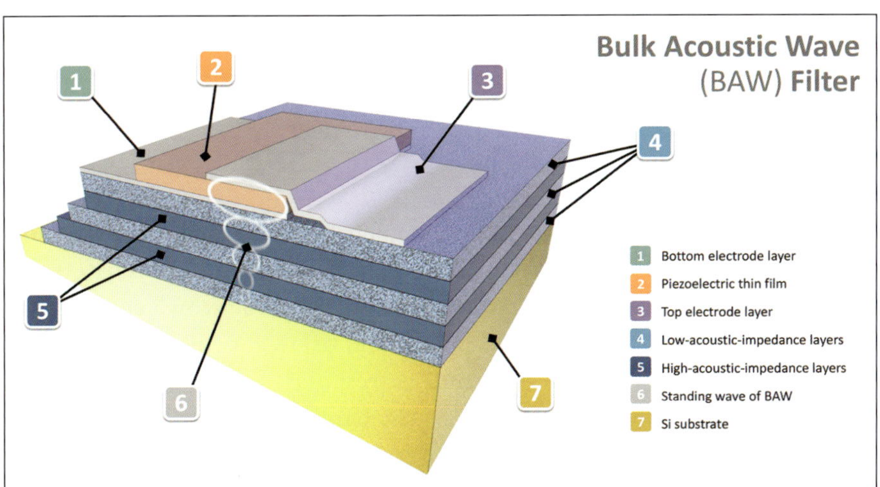

When there are a lot of labels, each requiring multiple words, the key helps keep the diagram from looking overwhelming. In the previous slide, the colors are coordinated—the color in the key matches the corresponding number on the diagram, which in turn matches the color of the item being labeled. There is a clear visual hierarchy to the diagram, and empty space around the labels calms the overall design and underscores the purposeful nature of each positive element. When a diagram has even more labels than this one does, this approach is even more effective.

Infographics

Information graphics aren't new. One of the most famous infographics in the design world was created in the 1860s by civil engineer Charles Joseph Minard (1781–1870). Minard pioneered the use of statistical and engineering graphics, creating many phenomenal data depictions. His most well-known and widely praised infographic depicts Napoleon's ill-fated invasion of Russia. It has been called "the map that made a nation cry," and Edward Tufte has said it "may well be the best statistical graph ever drawn."[3]

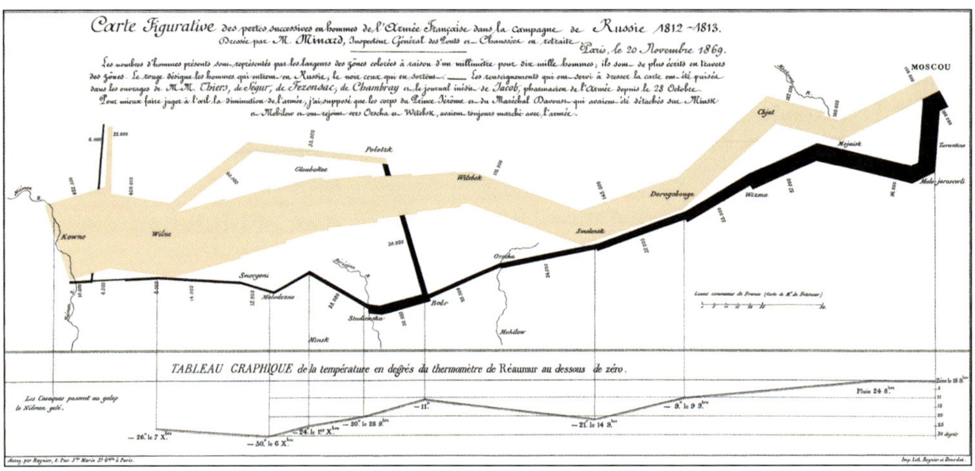

In a single image, this graphic instantly depicts Napoleon's disastrous losses, with troops plummeting from 422,000 at the start of the invasion to only 10,000 when they returned to Poland. Specifically, the tan band depicts the army's entry into Russia (progressing from left to right), and the black band below it depicts the army's retreat (from right to left). The width of the bands corresponds to the number of troops in the army at any given time and location. As the bands narrow, the number of troops diminishes, as well. At the invasion's start in June 1812, at the Polish-Russian border, the tan band is at its widest—the army was 422,000 troops strong. At the far right of the graphic, when the army began its retreat from Moscow in October, the number of troops had declined to 100,000. The line graph at the bottom of the graphic shows the corresponding temperatures during the troops' retreat, which were frequently far below zero (reaching –37.5° C on December 6). By the time the army returned to Poland (where the narrow black band returns to the far left of the image), only 10,000 troops had survived the hunger, injuries, and freezing temperatures.

With just one image, Minard effectively depicted a multitude of variables characterizing the doomed invasion: the soldiers' direction, their location, the temperatures they faced on their retreat, their shrinking size, and even the movement of auxiliary troops. Minard had an uncanny ability to translate complex data into easily digestible images. His work, which included over 50 informational graphics, is studied by cartographers and graphic designers alike. It's not hard to see why.

As innovative and successful as Minard's graphic was, it's rather obvious that it would not be an effective *trial* graphic without some modifications in both design and presentation. Using larger type, adding contrast to create a visual hierarchy, and building the graphic piece-by-piece would help make this graphic more digestible for a jury given the uniqueness of the trial setting. Regardless of these adjustments for trial, however, the overall importance of Minard's innovation to the advancement of visual data explanations is undeniable. Indeed, it's easy to see why Minard's work is still studied today and to spot Minard's influence in modern infographics. For example, in this Department of Transportation map, a red line of varying thicknesses depicts the estimated annual truck traffic for major U.S. highways.

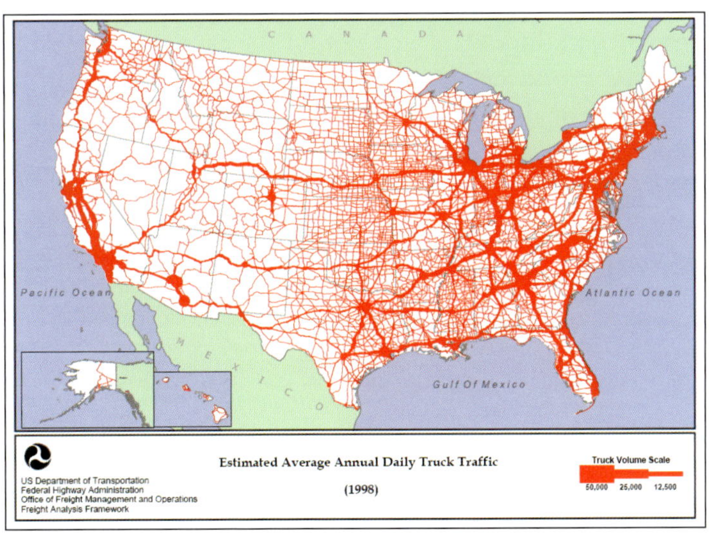

Today, infographics are gaining in popularity. They're in magazines, on billboards, on television, and all over the Internet. Even government agencies use them to communicate successes, initiatives, updates, and responses.

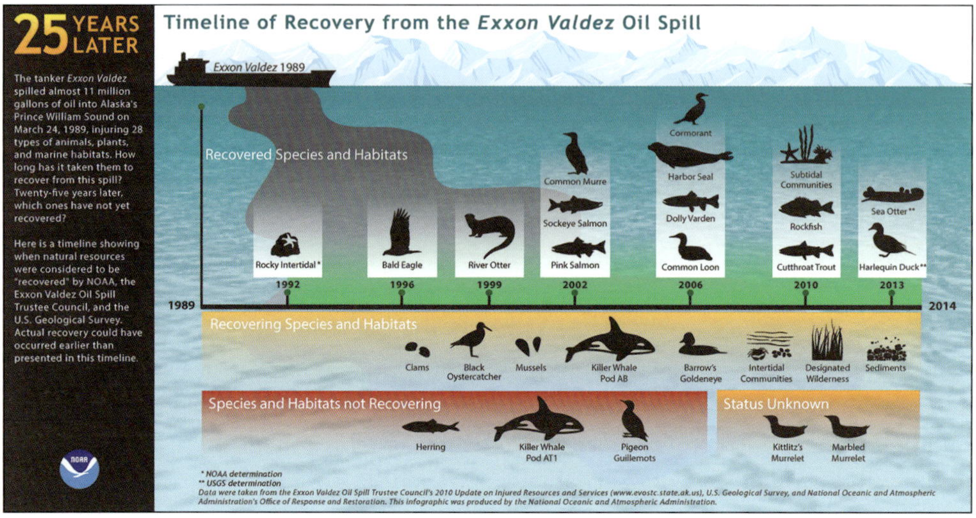

A common infographic used by millions of people every day is the public transit map. Its utility is undeniable. Understanding how to get around on the Metro in Washington, D.C., the BART in San Francisco, the T in Boston, the L in Chicago, or the subway in New York is exponentially easier thanks to these graphical images hanging in every station. Indeed, were it not for the expertly designed Tokyo Metro map, I might still be wandering Shinjuku, wondering if I'd ever see my family again. Instead, this informational graphic reduced a complex transit system to an understandable, usable format, and I navigated the subway lines with ease.

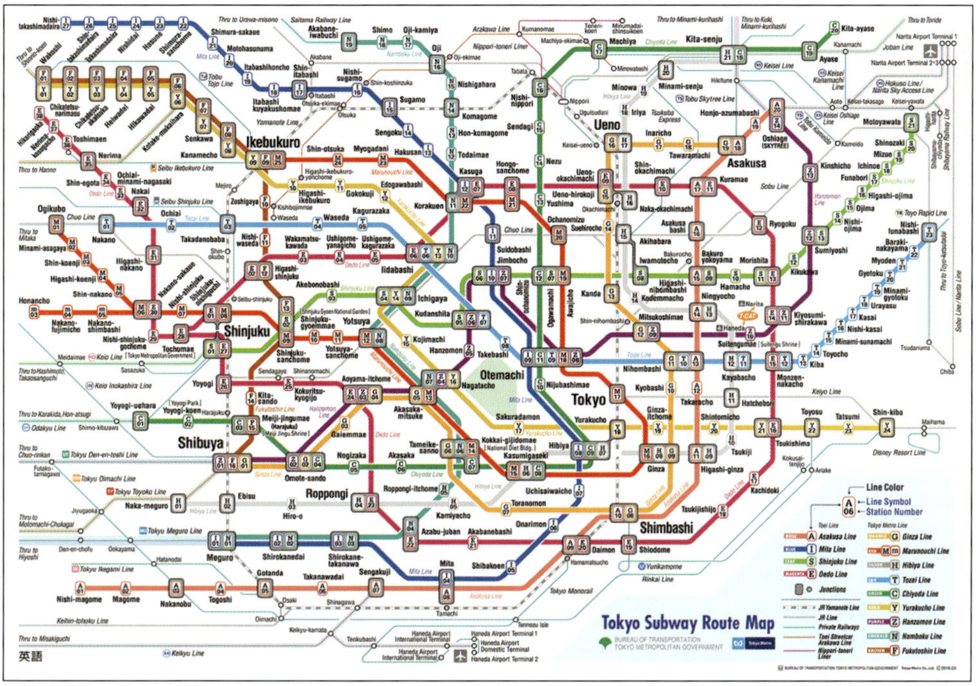

There seems to be some dispute as to what constitutes a "pure" infographic versus a traditional diagram or a picture graph. For our purposes, again, the labels aren't critical. Whether they're diagrams or infographics, they're hugely helpful. They can be used to display all sorts of data, from explaining diseases to tracing the steps of a destructive fire. Below, for example, is an infographic regarding types of scientific evidence.

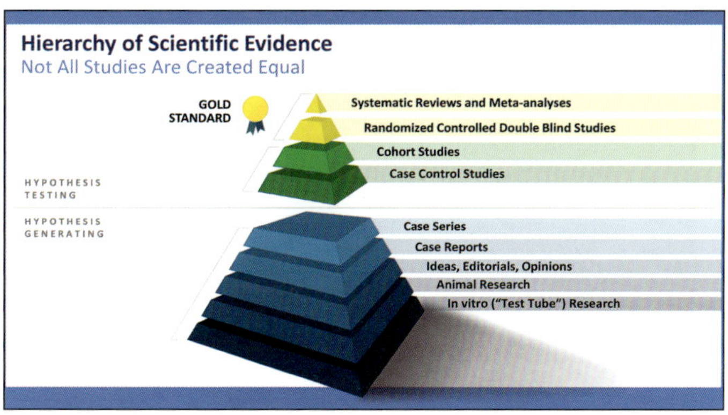

There are tons of infographics on the Internet and even on stock image sites, which can be useful for brainstorming. But be careful. Many are eye-catching and visually memorable, but what works well on an informational poster or handout won't work as well in court, particularly when the information is presented all at once.

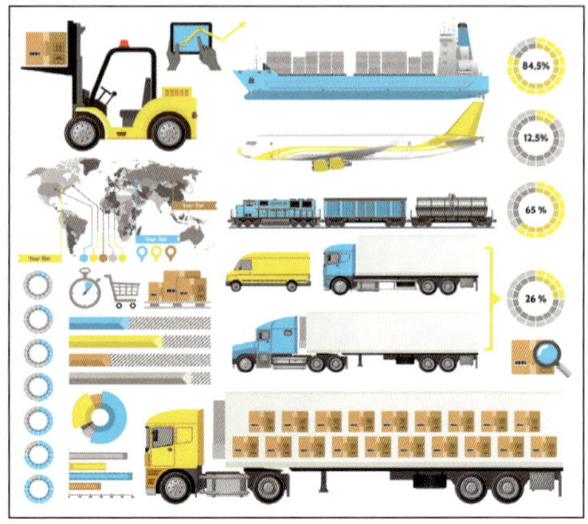

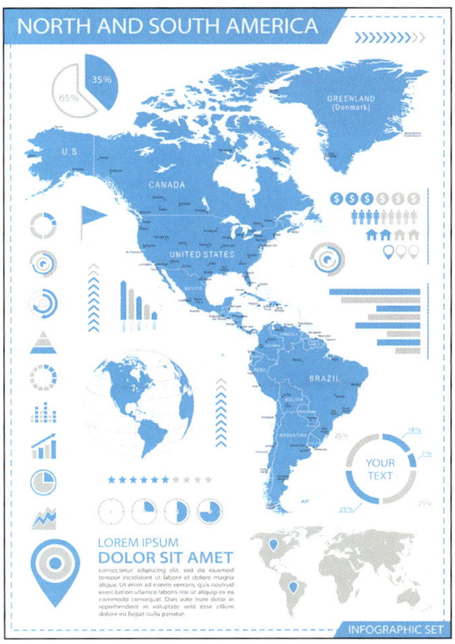

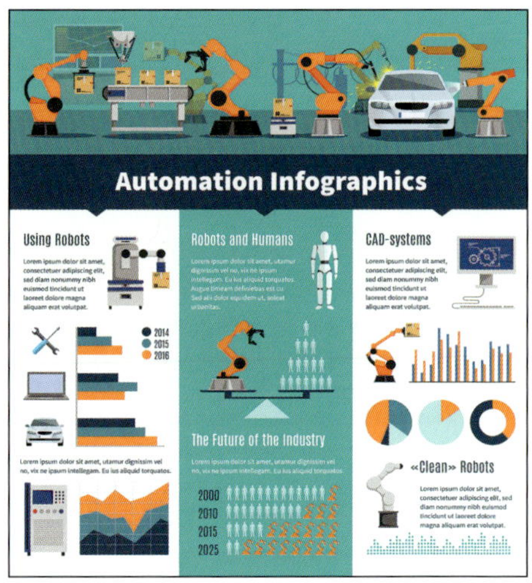

If the jury will be able to take demonstratives into deliberations (more on this in Chapter 24), we can get away with a busier visual. But break the visual into components if you're showing it during closing and jurors have one chance to comprehend it.

As with any other visual, be careful that form doesn't overtake function. This infographic about Medicare fraud prosecutions is eye-catching, but upon closer review, the graphics in the image area are not particularly informative.

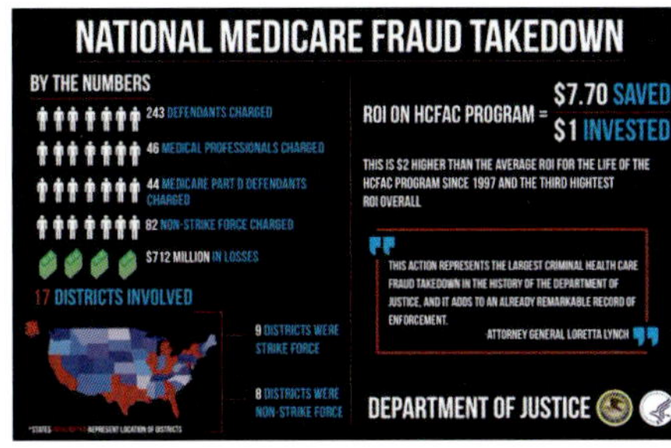

For example, the same graphic image of seven identical people is used to represent seven dramatically different numbers. The map of seventeen districts uses six discernible colors in fifty different states, but there's no key to decode the meaning in the colors. The visual makes a substantive distinction between nine districts and eight districts in two different text blurbs, but there's no way to tell which nine or which eight correspond to the text. Every word on the slide is in capital letters, and nearly every word is in the same font size and weight. The result is a visual lacking in hierarchy or organization. The largest lettering after the heading is reserved for the Department of Justice credit at the bottom of the slide, which cannot possibly be the most important information being communicated. Overall, the viewer has to work hard to decipher the details and is left unable to do so for several of the substantive messages on the slide.

There's no one "right" way to design an information graphic for any particular theme, but keep in mind the other design and presentation tips in this book for using information graphics with juries, given the uniqueness of the setting. Here are some additional tips to consider, and a few case examples, for converting trial themes into graphical representations.

Pay Attention to the Image That Comes to Your Own Mind

Take a moment during your trial preparation and try to *picture* your trial themes. What comes to mind visually when you talk about causation? What do you picture when you think about motive? What image do you see when you're explaining to a colleague your core claim or defense, or even key facts? In a case about different airline ticket prices for the same flight, the image at right might come to mind. Showing the image visually illustrates the content, and is more memorable than a textual slide listing the prices.

A few years ago, I participated as a faculty member in an American Bar Association "boot camp" on the False Claims Act. In addition to panel discussions, the program faculty (plaintiff, defense, and government FCA lawyers) put on a minitrial over several days before a mock jury and the conference attendees. My role was to deliver the defense closing argument.

The case involved an off-label marketing claim. Pharmaceutical representatives had been giving doctors unsolicited information about off-label uses for a drug, and prescriptions for that use of the drug were increasing. At the same time, however, doctors were learning of this off-label use from many other sources, including medical journals, conferences, and even other doctors and their own patients.

The case boiled down to correlation versus causation. Was the increase in off-label prescriptions *caused* by the pharmaceutical representatives' improper marketing, or was the increase simply *correlated* with that marketing? From the very beginning, I had a strong visual image of the defense theme. The picture that consistently came to my mind when I thought about the case, which I've shown you in earlier chapters of this book, was of a doctor surrounded by information coming at him from every direction.

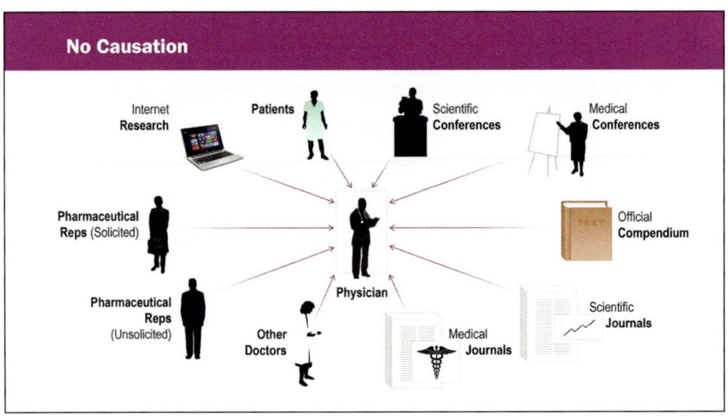

Each source on this slide was supported by evidence in the mock trial. There was no suggestion that any one source was more influential than the others, so I was careful to give each source equal weight on the slide. The source images are essentially the same size, the same distance apart from each other, and in the same artistic style. If I had emphasized a source when the evidence didn't support it, the slide could be misleading. It might be excluded, or worse, my opponent might focus on the slide's misleading nature and damage my credibility. I still visually depicted a lot of information sources, but I did so without manipulating the information display. There's no magic to this particular design; another designer might have a different stylistic approach to the same theme.

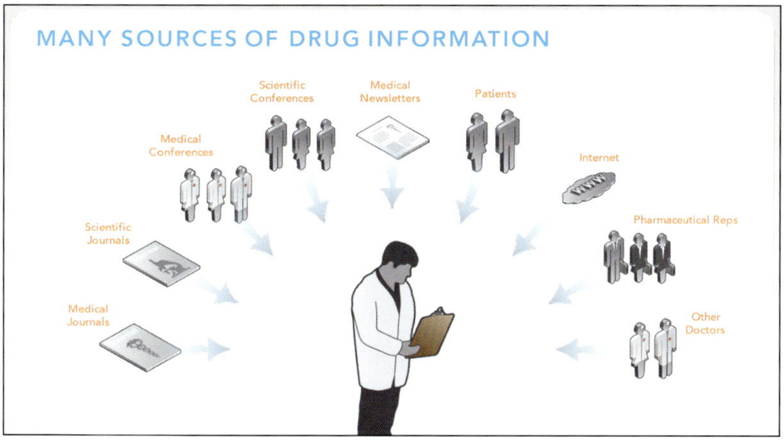

Whatever your design choice, a graphic approach is certainly more effective than a simple text build listing the inputs:

Physician Learned of Off-Label Use from Multiple, Recurring Sources

- Other physicians told him about the use
- Patients reported using the drug for an off-label use and feeling better
- Pharmaceutical representatives reported the information on their own and in response to the physician's questions
- The off-label use was discussed at medical and scientific conferences
- Medical and scientific journals reported on the off-label use
- Physician conducted his own internet research on the off-label use and determined it was successful

Unlike the list above, the picture is a memorable, visual translation of the message I was trying to convey. If the jury remembered the picture—even if they didn't remember every source—they would remember the theme. Our mock jurors (who voted "no liability") unanimously voted this informational graphic the most effective visual in the trial.[4]

There were, of course, other ways to convey this theme. For example, I could have used a timeline, assuming there was evidence of when the doctor learned each piece of information.

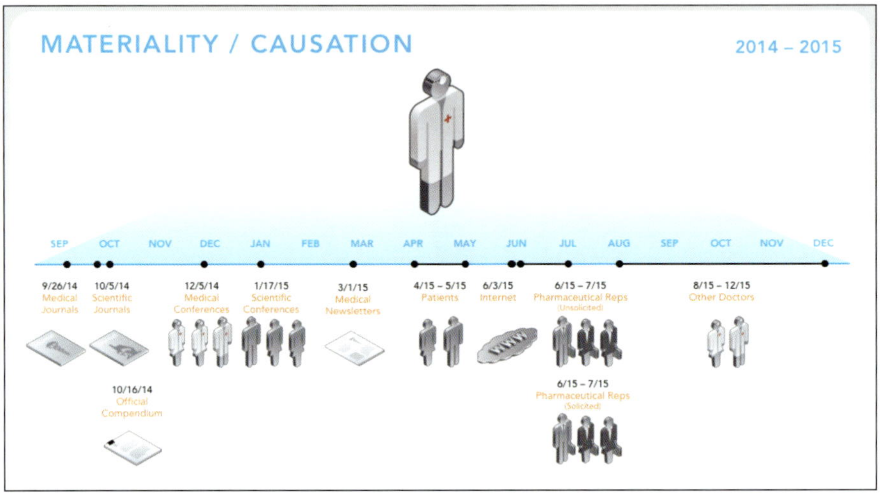

But the core theme I wanted to capture wasn't *when he learned* the information (which we didn't actually know, anyway); it was *the volume of sources* he'd learned it from. My goal was to visually emphasize the fact that all of this information was swirling around in the doctor's mind when he prescribed the drug. There was no way to know which source of information—the pharmaceutical representative or otherwise—made the difference in the doctor's decision to recommend the drug to his patients for an off-label use. The visual maintained focus on my theme, and the jurors quickly and easily digested the message.

The Literal Can Become the Visual

In Chapter 4, I described a case in which my client was accused of fraud in connection with a $3 million contract that spanned three years. We pointed out to the jury that the company was making $100 million per day at the time, undermining any allegation that the company depended on this contract. But the jury still could have thought my client's own professional advancement depended on the contract—if, perhaps, it was the only contract he was working on at the time.

But it wasn't. To the contrary, while he was working on the contract at issue, he was also working on or supervising *104* other contracts worth a total of *$584 million*. Again, I could have just listed these figures on a slide.

But I wanted to turn this concept into a memorable visual image.

We gathered the logos of every company in all 104 of those contracts and organized them in a table. Next to each logo, we listed the dollar value of the contract. We included the total number of contracts at the top—104—and the total dollar value at the bottom—nearly $584 million.

After walking the jurors through the slide and giving them time to digest the information, we enlarged the two key points: 104 contracts; nearly $584 million.

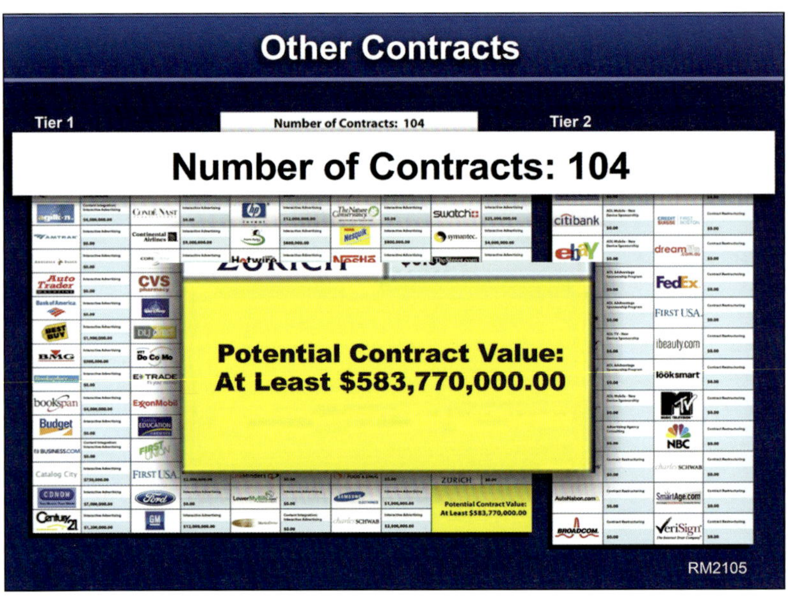

Jurors would remember the visual image, and if all that image triggered was a recollection that the client was working on a lot of other contracts worth a lot of money, we'd have made our point, and the jurors would remember our theme.

Illustrating Context and Comparison

Graphics also are exceptionally useful for putting unfamiliar concepts into familiar context. Numbers are a great example, as without a familiar context, their significance is often hard for jurors to appreciate: parts per billion; population growth; birth and mortality rates. We often default to explaining numbers through charts and graphs, but taking a pictorial approach can be even more effective. Jurors can relate your theme to a concept they already know.

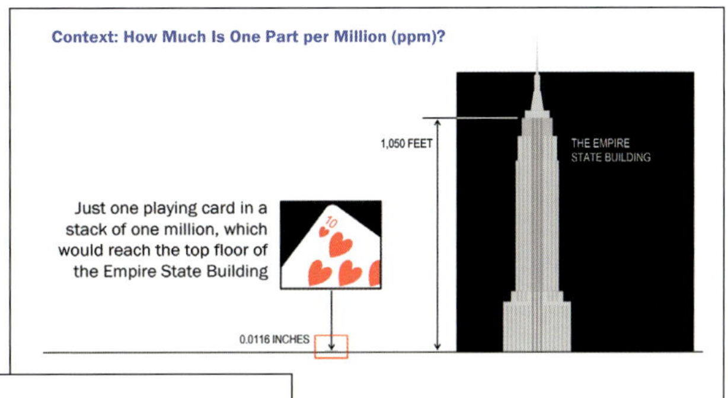

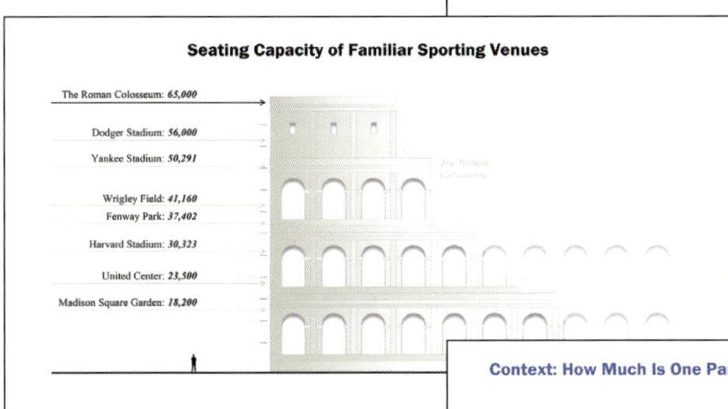

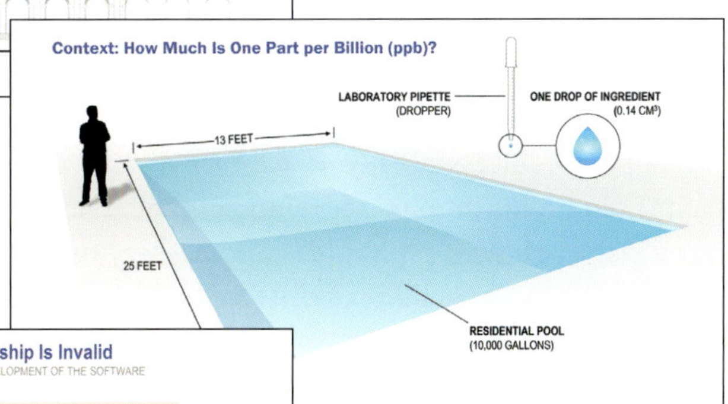

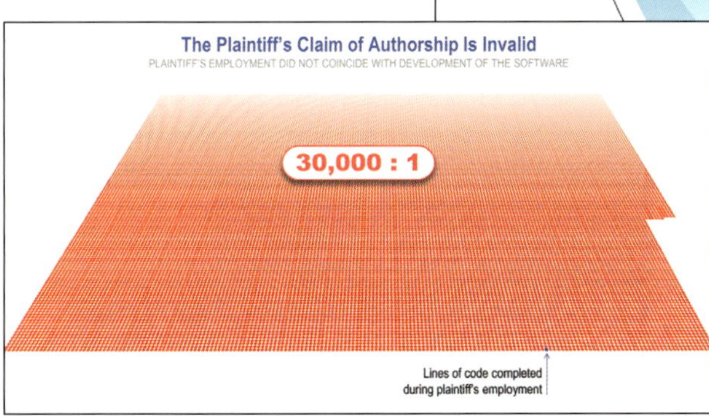

Consider using graphics to underscore key legal points, as well—those themes that it's essential the jury understand and remember during their deliberations.

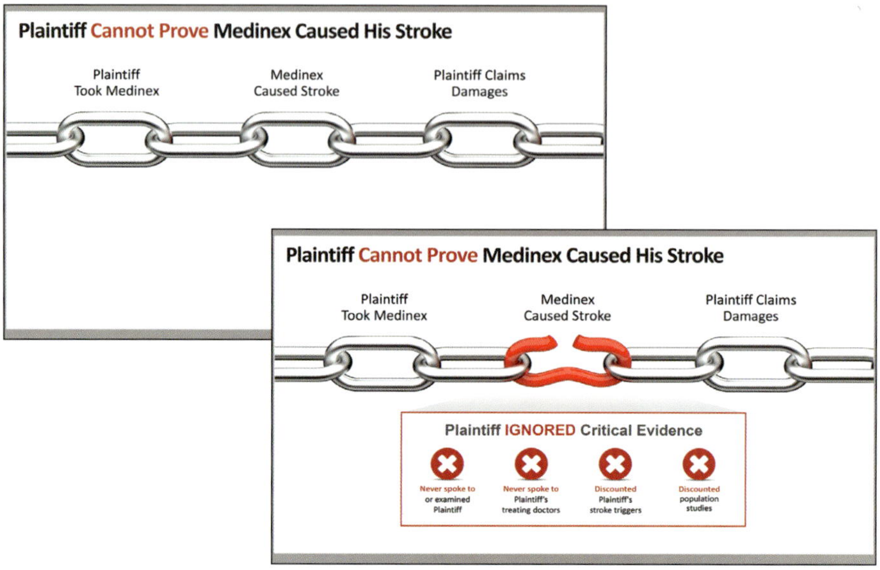

General Tips on Using Graphics

Basic Design Elements Can Convey Substance

Simple graphic elements can convey substantive meaning. For instance, as Minard did with the width of his tan and black bands, gradually adjusting the size of a graphic symbol such as an arrow can convey information about the size of the data you're displaying.

Suppose, for example, you want to visually depict something increasing—complaints, communications, accidents, crime, revenue, pollution, etc. If the increase is quantifiable, a line graph would be an easy way to display that upward trend. But if you already have multiple line graphs in your presentation, another one won't stand out. Instead, with a graphical approach, you can create a simple, memorable visual.

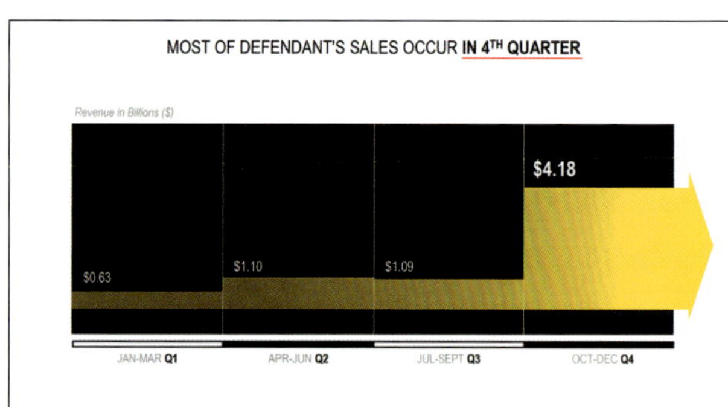

Here's another example. Say you want to break down how the price of an item is divided amongst the manufacturer, distributor, wholesaler, and retailer or even just between different inputs. A simple graph could do the trick:

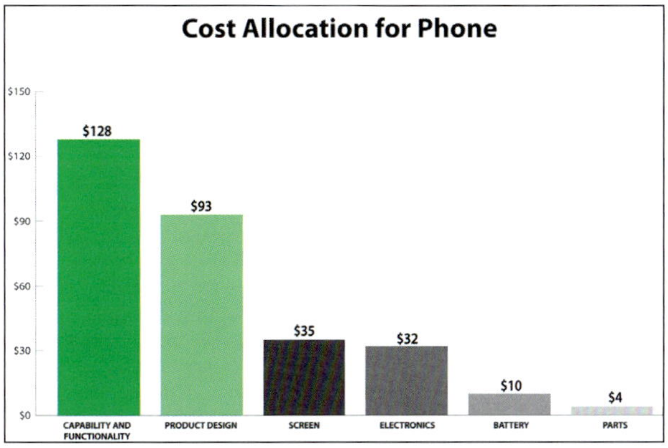

But if this theme is central to your case, think about using graphics to make the theme more memorable and more intuitive. Instead, you could do something like this:

You could even vary the size of the column widths, graphics, and text to correspond proportionally to the payment for that step, such that the design elements themselves convey substantive meaning on the slide. If you do, though, make sure everything is large enough to be readable.

As mentioned earlier, images of calendars convey instant substantive meaning. Incorporating them into your slide design when conducive to your message can visually reinforce that message with a familiar, meaningful symbol.

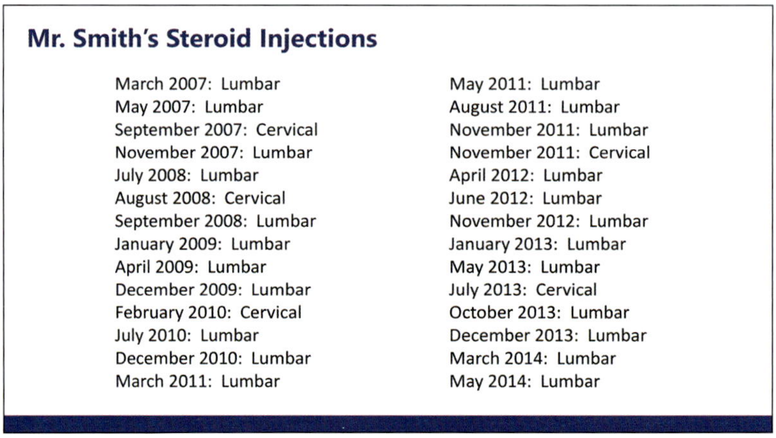

VS.

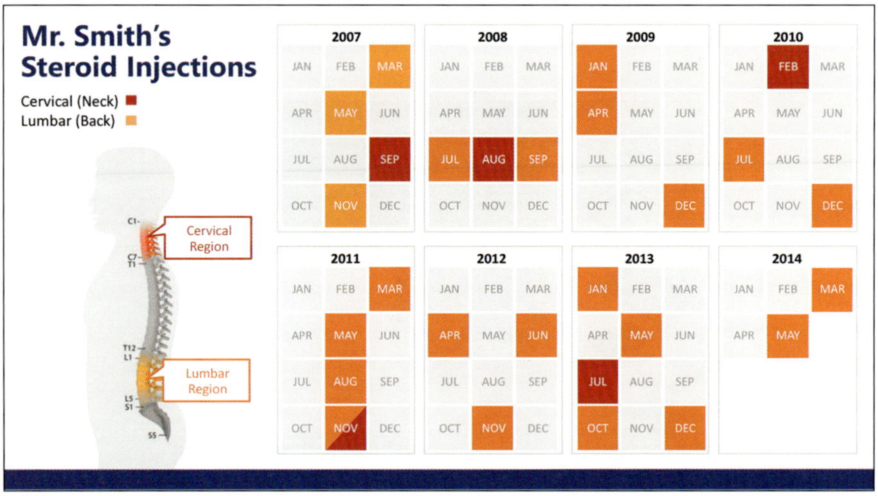

The difference between the text slide and the infographic for creating a memorable trial visual is undeniable. Both visuals convey the volume of injections, but the infographic, in addition to being visually interesting, conveys even more. The design is calm and organized, yet it instantly allows the viewer to compare the number and timing of cervical versus lumbar injections, and to put each injection into chronological context with all the others.

Relevance Is Critical

Substantive graphics should be relevant to your message.

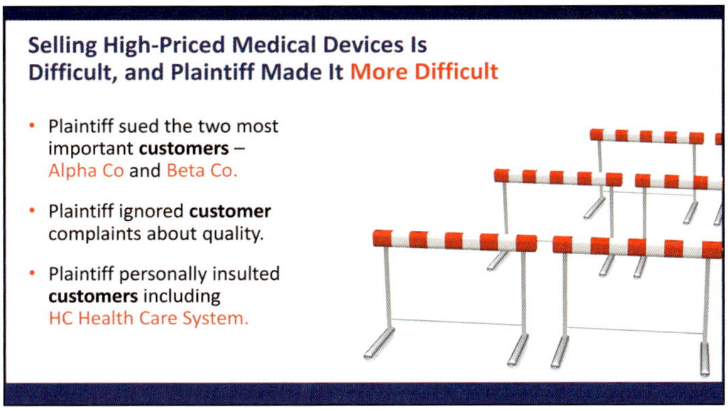

Here, the simple illustrations of hurdles conceptualize precisely what they're depicting. There's no track, no runner, no trees—no unnecessary distractions. The image is also tone-appropriate; it doesn't seek to exaggerate the issue with a photograph of a steep mountain and an exhausted climber.

I'm always amazed at the random images people put on their slides—from scales of justice and piles of cartoony-looking coins to swirls and sunsets. If they're not relevant, leave them off your slide. The same goes for design graphics. If you're using bullets, lines, or swirly things, make sure they're adding to the clarity or organization of the slide. You shouldn't be using graphic elements just to fill empty space. Every graphic element, substantive or not, must be processed by the viewer. It's better to have no graphics at all than corny or irrelevant graphics that distract from your presentation.

Be Careful Not to Offend

If your graphic might offend the jury, think very carefully about whether to use it. I see this issue arise most often with purportedly humorous graphics. Humor can be a terrific asset, but if it's used inappropriately or falls flat, it can undermine you and your message. Whether to use humor, or any other graphic, is a stylistic and strategic choice. When you make that choice, consider the consequences if the graphic isn't received by the jury the way you intend to present it. If the outcome would be dire—even if it would just *approach* dire—don't use the graphic.

Leave Off the Logo

Logos are graphics. There are many, many people who insist on having their logo on every slide. Think about how many conferences, CLE programs, business pitches, and even internal firm or company meetings you've been to where every slide in the deck has a logo. On some slides, the logo is fully or partially hidden by text or graphics. On others, the logo covers part of a word or a graph. Sometimes the logo affirmatively fights with the substance of the slide, commanding too much attention. And sometimes the logo is subtle—an ever-present but barely noticeable element in a far corner of the slide. It's either not perceived, so its presence has no point, or it's a nagging distraction.

Fortunately, this book is not about business presentations, so I don't have to take a strong position on whether I think your logo should be on every single slide in that setting. I don't have to comment on whether it would make more sense to feature your logo on the first slide (the one on the screen while everyone enters the room and stays there until you've begun your presentation) and the last slide (the one that stays on the screen while everyone's standing around talking after your presentation). I don't have to question the utility of a logo being on every slide when everyone already knows who you are because they hired you to be there, or they chose to attend your talk, or because you *work in the same company and it's an internal presentation.*

Instead, I can just compliment most lawyers who don't feature a firm's logo on their *trial* slides.

For the few folks who still insist on including a logo on trial slides, just a couple of thoughts for your consideration. By leaving off the logo, you'll avoid imposing color, space, and style constraints that you then have to design around. You'll free up valuable space to enlarge text or other graphics, or you'll simply have more empty space to calm and organize the slide. You'll also minimize the risk of having your own name, firm, or agency negatively associated with adverse information when those points are being made on the slide. (Just picture a six-slide closing-argument build with "FRAUD" at the top, displayed on a five-foot screen, and your law firm's logo in the corner of every slide.)

At bottom, eliminating the logo means you'll have one less element on the slide competing for the jurors' attention. (And if you're figuring that putting the logo on *every* slide alleviates that problem because eventually jurors will just ignore it, ask yourself why you're including an element that you expect—or even hope—jurors will eventually ignore.) Unless you can articulate a case-relevant reason the logo needs to be on every slide in your trial deck, don't include it.

The uses for graphics are endless. They're a terrific way to visually represent your theme, and they bring complex and unfamiliar concepts within your jurors' grasp. Think about graphics carefully and creatively, and don't be afraid to use them as long as you can articulate why they're relevant or how they help the design of the visual.

DEFENDANT'S EXHIBIT 72
EXHIBIT 154
EXHIBIT 112
EXHIBIT 14
DEFENDANT'S EXHIBIT 11
EXHIBIT 72
DEFENDANT'S EXHIBIT 98
DEFENDANT'S EXHIBIT 42
EXHIBIT 297
DEFENDANT'S EXHIBIT 27
THE ELECTRONIC COMMUNICATIONS AND PRIVACY ACT OF 1986 (ECPA)
DISQUALIFICATION OF JURORS BASED ON RACE
AUTOMATIC REVERSAL OF A CONVICTION FOR DENYING DEFENDANT A PAID LAWYER
SENTENCING JUVENILE OFFENDERS
PROBATION
INTERMEDIATE SANCTIONS
OTHER SITUATIONS ON THE MIRANDA WARNINGS
SITUATIONS THAT REQUIRE THE MIRANDA WARNINGS

11

Using Exhibits

Entire claims, arguments, and case themes can boil down to a single contract term, a discrete series of emails, or a small subset of photographs. You'll have used these key exhibits during trial, probably repeatedly. Most of your jurors will likely remember those key exhibits, but, realistically, some will have tuned out or fallen asleep during trial. Embrace this inevitability, and show them the key exhibits again. Using trial exhibits in your closing is an easy and effective way to enhance both the visual impact of your presentation and your credibility.

What's more, jurors who do remember the exhibits might have developed a visual memory of *where on each exhibit* the key information appears. Take advantage of this in your closing slides. If you marked up an exhibit in trial—circling or highlighting text, for example—try to use that version of the document in closing. You'll reinforce the jurors' already-developed visual memory.

If you didn't mark up the exhibit during trial, you can still create a visual memory for the jurors. Design the slide to emphasize key portions of the exhibit or use other graphic design techniques discussed in this book to add relevant visual interest to the rest of the slide.

Callouts and Highlights

Enlarging (calling out) or highlighting key language is an easy and effective way to focus jurors on particular language in a document. Used effectively, this technique can help create a visual memory of an important document we want jurors to review and even of where to find key information on the page.

I use this technique with all types of documents admitted into evidence. I'll also do it with jury instructions, particularly when I know the judge will give jurors a hard copy. I use callouts with transcripts, as well. I order daily trial transcripts, and my judges typically let me display portions of those transcripts during closing argument. Likewise, if a witness testified by deposition or if I played a portion of a video deposition during the trial, I can use that transcript, too. For critical testimony, showing jurors the official transcript page—typed by the court reporter the jurors have seen every day in the courtroom and who is associated with the court and not with the parties—enhances my credibility. I'm not asking jurors to rely on my (or their own) recollection of what a witness said. I'm showing them the official record.

When enlarging text from a document, try to set the enlargement sufficiently apart from its source so jurors can see both at the same time. Highlight, underline, or put a box around the original text even when you're separately enlarging it; this lets jurors know where to look for it on the page.

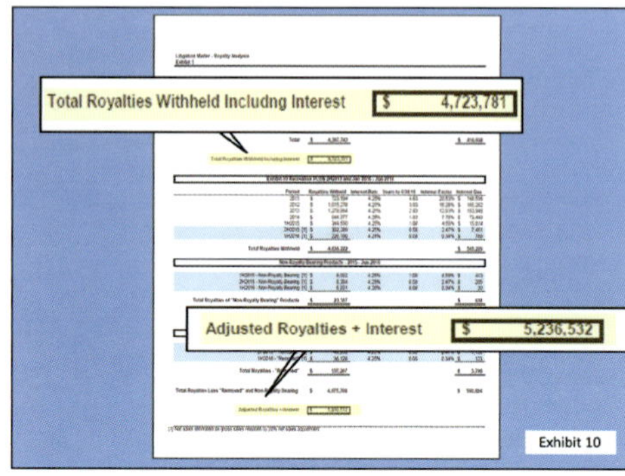

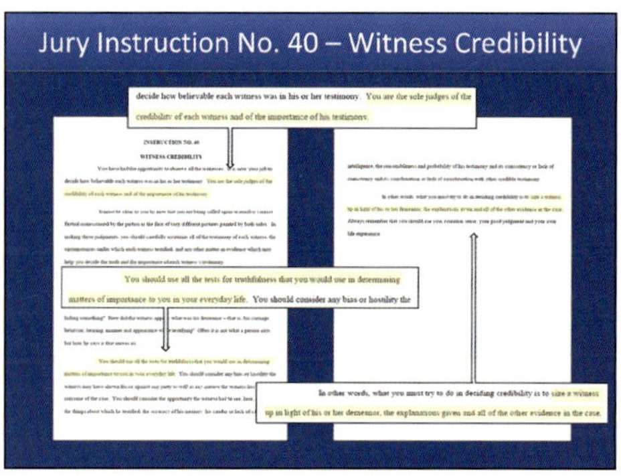

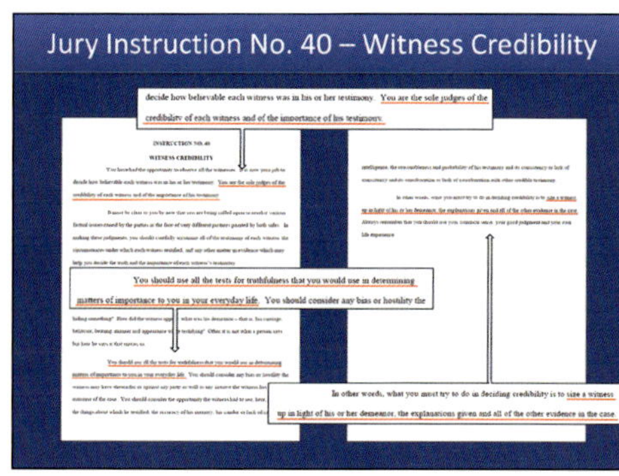

If I don't want jurors distracted by the rest of the document, I might display the page in a smaller size so they can't read the rest of the text. This way, I'm controlling their focus only on the callout. And even with the page much smaller on my slide, I can still identify where the key text appears by using graphic elements such as lines and boxes and by including a page citation on the slide.

Sometimes, the key language you'll want to emphasize is buried deep within a contract or a multipage email chain. When that happens, you'll need to decide whether to show the front page of the exhibit, the page from which you're calling out key information, or both. If the first page of the document is visually memorable—or at least distinct from other trial exhibits—displaying that page might itself create an effective visual memory.

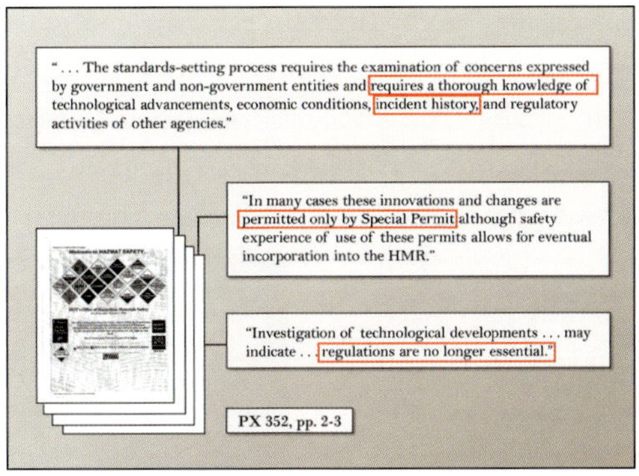

In the example above, the first page of this document might look much different from other trial exhibits, so displaying it as you enlarge key language is a constant reminder of the document. Including the exhibit number and the particular pages the callouts are drawn from both allows and encourages note-taking jurors to jot down the information. I still recommend displaying one callout at a time, controlling what information is displayed and when.

Combining Callouts with Creative Slide Design

When I use trial exhibits during closing, I try to give the slide some visual interest, particularly when the exhibit itself has none. Otherwise, I'm just projecting images of text documents.

In this example, the key data appears in a spreadsheet, and that's the exhibit that would have been introduced in trial. But graphing the data is what visually tells the story. Combining the two approaches—showing the trial exhibit and the visual graph—lets us organize the information presentation and simultaneously bolster our credibility, while providing a visual translation of the true message within the data.

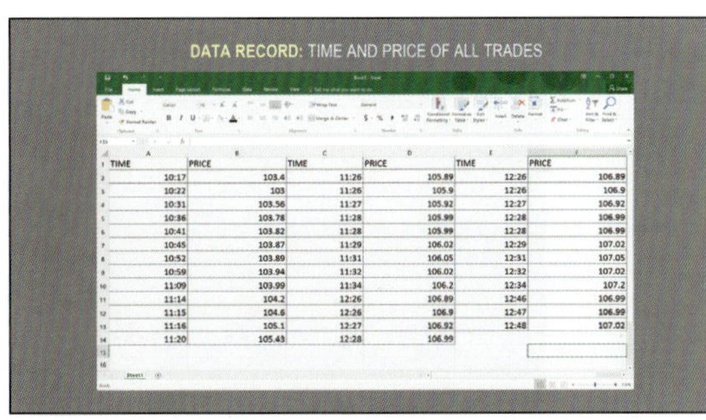

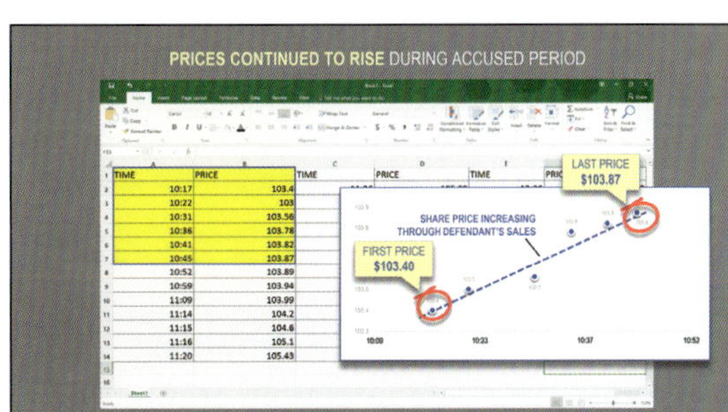

In one case, several emails were introduced into evidence that effectively contrasted my client's motivation with the motives of others. My client's emails were benign, while the emails of the true perpetrators (who themselves had pled guilty) revealed financial desperation and personal panic.

I certainly could have just argued that others had a motive, and my client did not. I could have generally reminded jurors of the emails they saw in trial. I could have even put the emails on the screen and highlighted key text. Instead, in light of the importance of the emails, I opted for a more visual presentation of the exhibits.

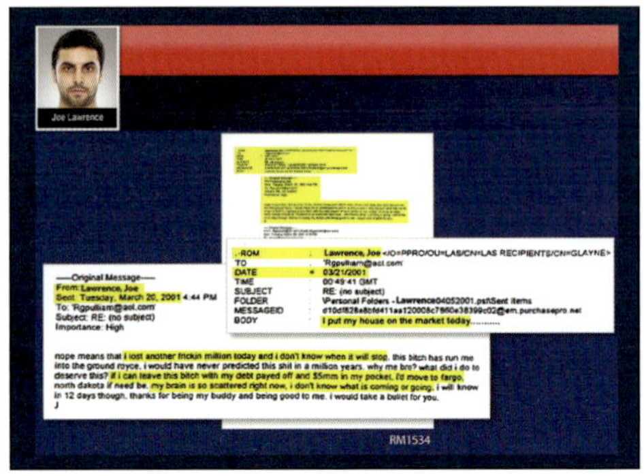

The exhibit (the email) is in the background, with the exhibit number underneath it. The relevant text is enlarged, with the key portions highlighted. I also happened to have photographs of the executives who sent these emails, so I used them, too—it reminded the jurors of which witness we were talking about and added visual interest to the slide. Finally, the color scheme in this slide was consistent throughout the presentation—blue for benign information and red when discussing the fraud.

Evidentiary photographs can even be paired with key testimony describing them to provide visual, memorable context to the photos.

Proof Timelines and Context

As discussed in Chapter 7, combining timelines with real trial exhibits allows you to re-prove your case in closing argument in an organized, memorable way. You're emphasizing key evidence while simultaneously putting it into context. When I use exhibits as part of a proof timeline, I'll still call out or otherwise emphasize the key text. And I'll make sure that the design for any hyperlinked proof slides complements the design of the timeline to visually reinforce their connection.

Comparisons and Context

Displaying trial exhibits also lets you credibly and directly compare evidence. This technique naturally lends itself to comparing before and after photos, comparing copyrighted, patented, or trademarked products against their alleged infringers, comparing an altered document with the original, or even comparing statements in emails or text messages. I've also used it to compare trial testimony with prior testimony or an inconsistent document, putting the two versions side by side and highlighting material differences.

Presentation of Exhibits to Enhance Credibility

How we display and use trial exhibits can add to or detract from our credibility. When we rush through exhibits, only show bits and pieces of documents, or otherwise don't seem transparent about the material we're presenting, our jurors think we're hiding something. Sure, some jurors might give us the benefit of the doubt and assume we were under time pressure, we forgot, or we were just saving them from reading boring, irrelevant material.

But many aren't so forgiving. Instead, they assume we're being underhanded, and they may draw their own "adverse inference" from material they haven't seen. Fortunately, there are some easy ways to counter this assumption.

When showing only part of a document, tell the jurors outright that you're focusing on part of the exhibit (due to time limitations or whatever), and encourage them to review the exhibit themselves for as long as they like when they deliberate. Include the exhibit number on the slide, and call the jurors' attention to it. If you're showing a portion of a lengthy document, give jurors the page number, as well. Make it easy for jurors to review the full document on their own. It doesn't matter whether they actually do; what matters is showing them that you're not afraid of the document or the jurors' careful scrutiny and that you're not trying to hide anything. What matters is your credibility.

The bottom line is that showing rather than telling boosts credibility, and it's easy to do this with case exhibits, jury instructions, and testimony transcripts.

STILL
PICTURE
PUSH

12

Animation and Simulations

Until now, this book has focused on two overlapping categories of courtroom visuals: "static images" such as charts, graphs, photos, diagrams, and "enhanced images"—those documents we manipulate in an obvious way by, for example, highlighting or enlarging part of the text.[1] But there's another world out there—a world of visuals that move.

At the more high-tech end of the spectrum are computer-generated simulations (or recreations) and computer models.

1

2

3

4

Simulations allow us to re-create an event—or at least our version of an event—such as a house fire, a car accident, or a crime scene.

In contrast to simulations, computer models are often created by expert witnesses to test hypotheses using the model. The expert then forms opinions based on the results, and the model may or may not be something that can be shown in court.

At the other end of the spectrum from simulations are visuals that are mostly static images, but some part of them moves on the screen. When used purposely (and sparingly), animation can enhance the effectiveness of otherwise fixed images.

Broadly, "animation" is a general term for anything on your slide that's moving, whether it's something blinking, flashing, or swirling; a person walking; or a plane flying across the screen. Animating information tells the viewer where to look. Our eyes are attracted to the movement.

Uses for Animation

On a busy map, animation can help call attention to a location. Or, it can trace a path taken by a person, a product in a distribution chain, or even money. In criminal cases, for instance, animation on a map can help depict the movement of money in a complex scheme or trace the movements of someone who was under surveillance.

Animation can also put a location into context effectively by zooming in or out, depicting both the broad and the narrow view of the place at issue.

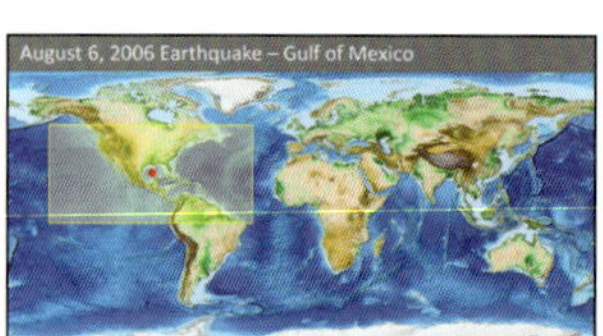

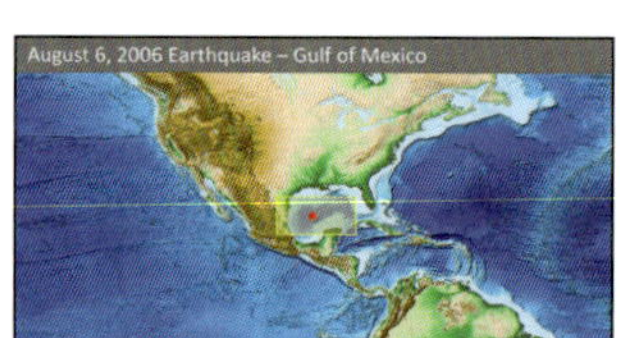

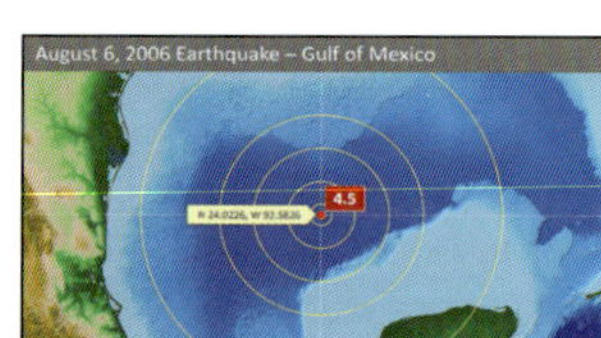

In patent or product liability cases, animation can help us demonstrate how a product works or is manufactured, how one part affects another, or how one product differs from another. Similarly, we can use animation to show changes in an object, whether internal (e.g., due to aging or disease) or external (e.g., due to fire or impact).

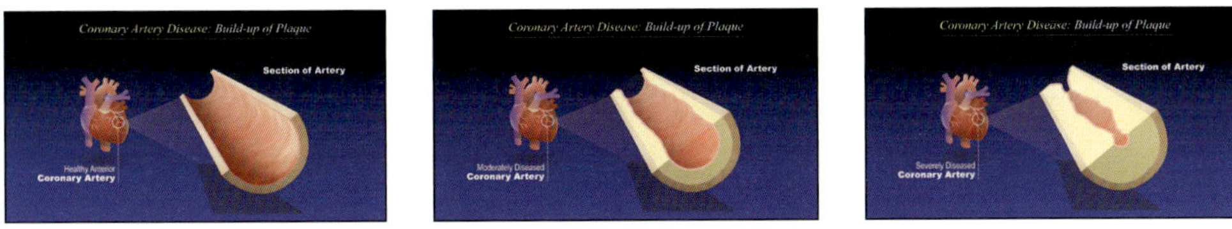

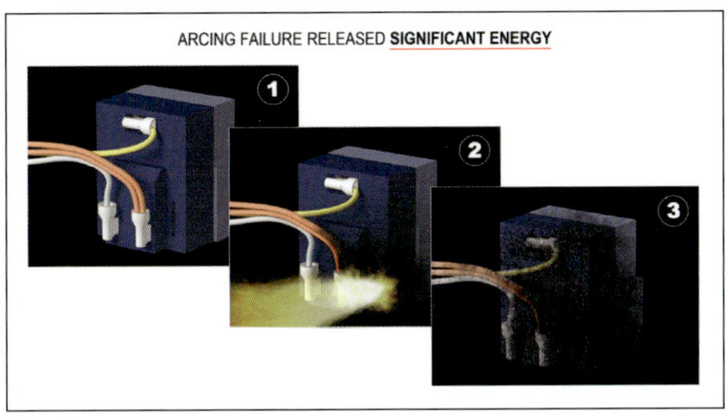

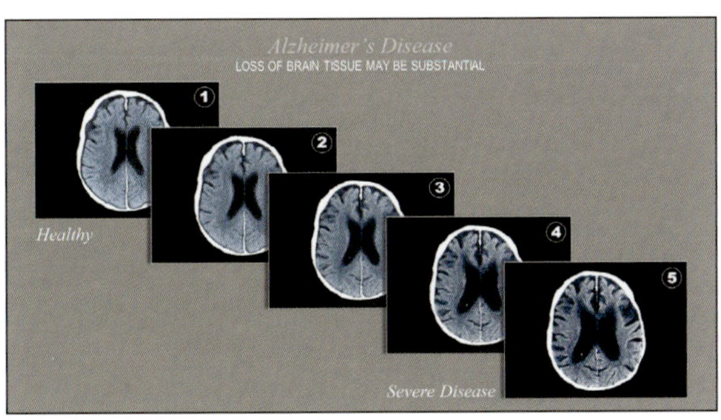

Animation can also help us explain industries or processes that might be foreign to most jurors, such as the trading process on the New York Stock Exchange, the approval process for pharmaceuticals, or the interdependent steps for constructing a large medical office building. Likewise, animation can be effective for depicting mathematical or scientific concepts, such as the effects of erosion, parts per billion, or a double-blind control experiment.

Shown here in a series of captures, in this animation the conveyor belt moves the package through the quality control process.

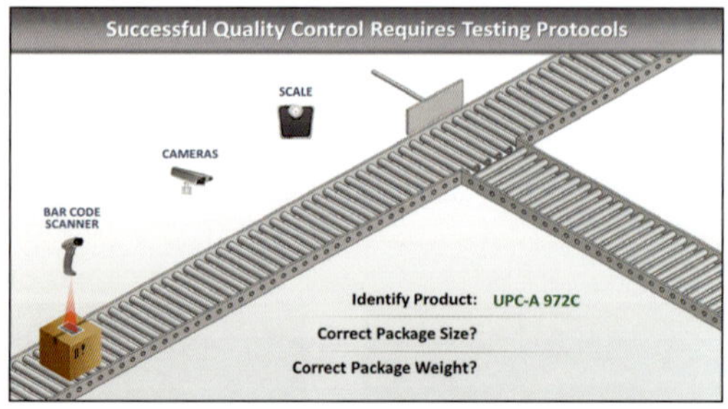

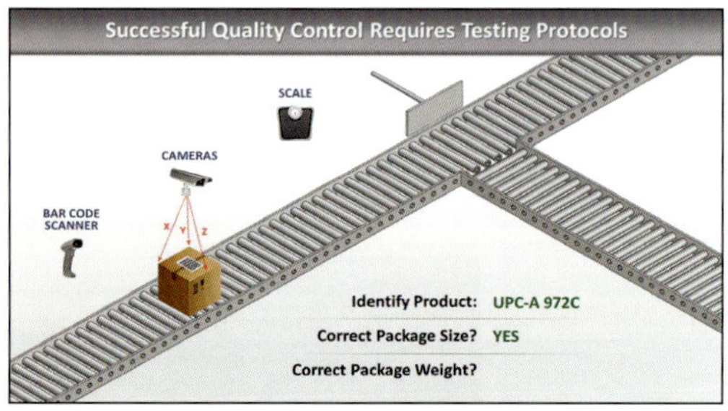

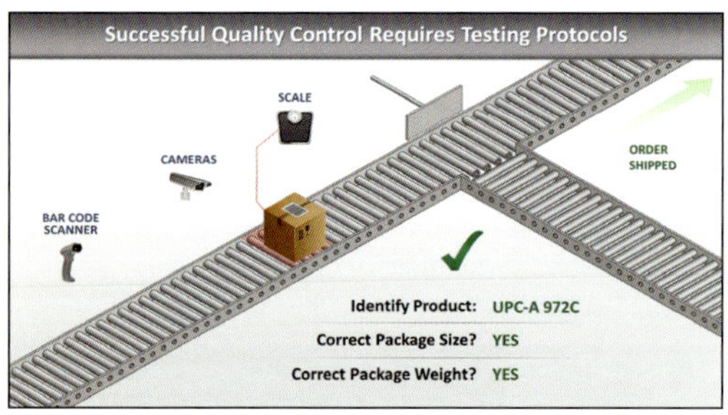

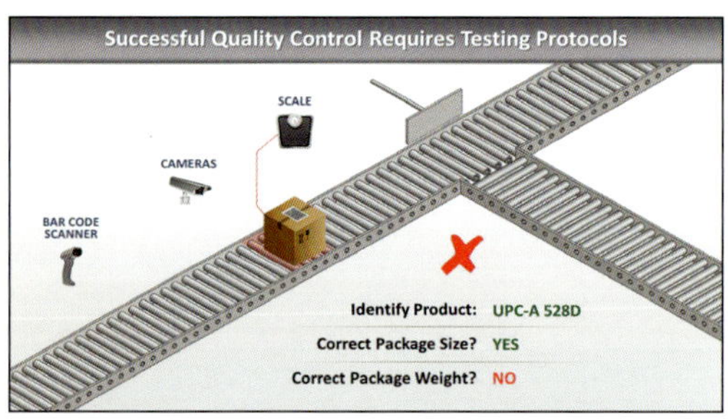

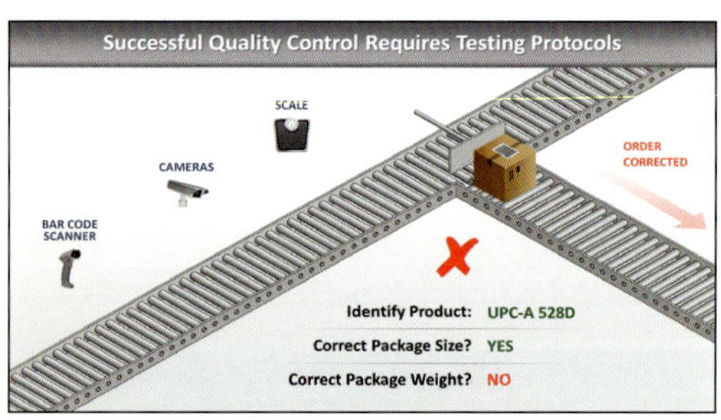

In this animation, the blue dot representing the lines of computer code the plaintiff completed during his employment gradually shrinks into place—and into context—amidst the rest of the code lines represented by the red dots.

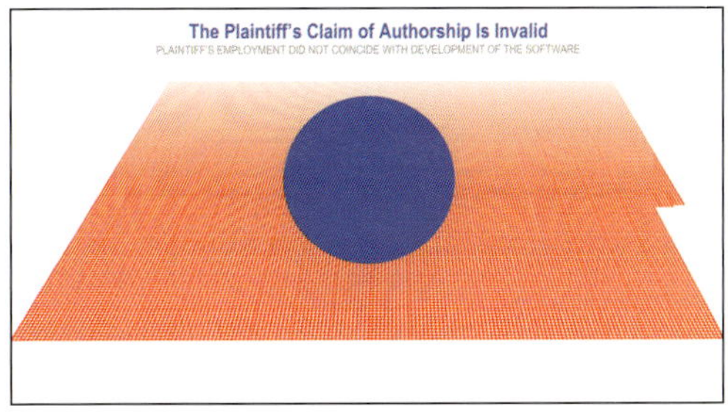

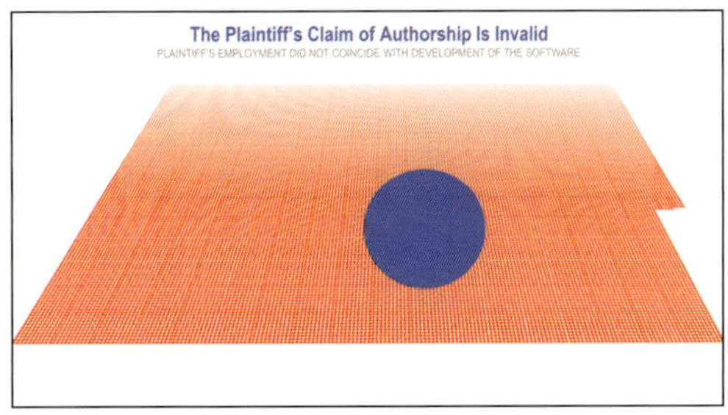

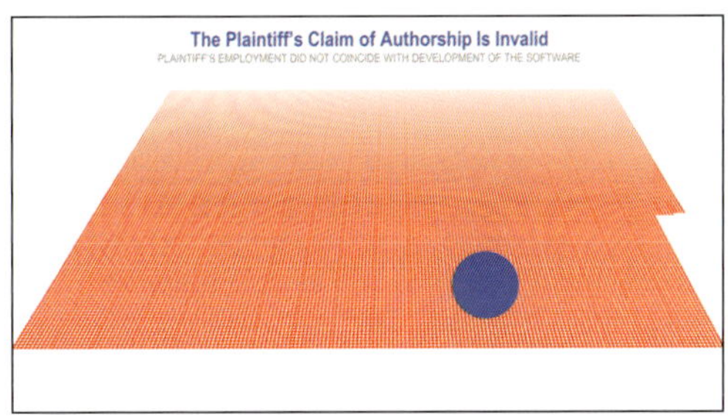

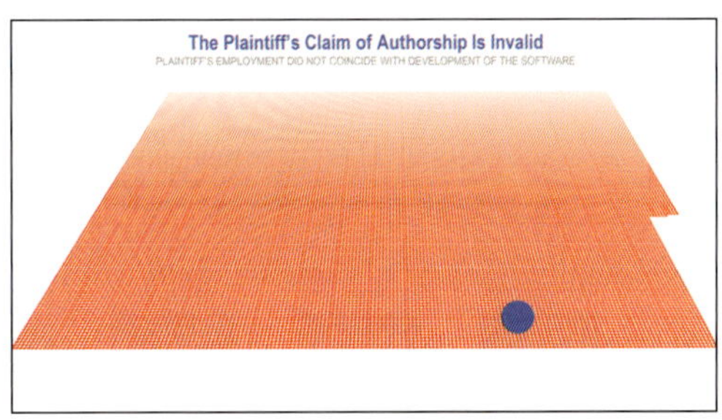

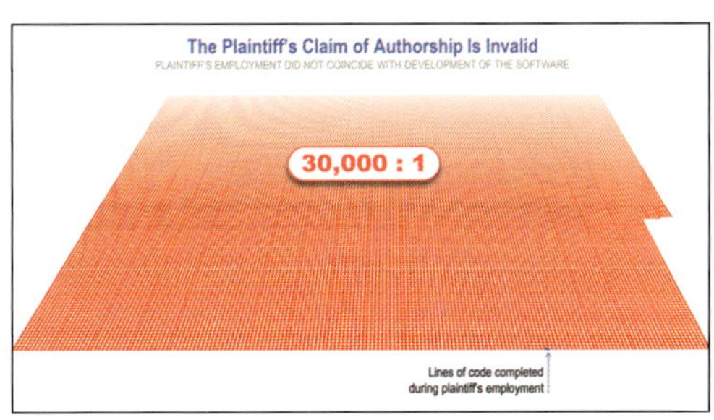

In the animation at right, the only movement is the green contaminant seeping into the water supply. Thus, the key message is immediately perceived and is visually memorable.

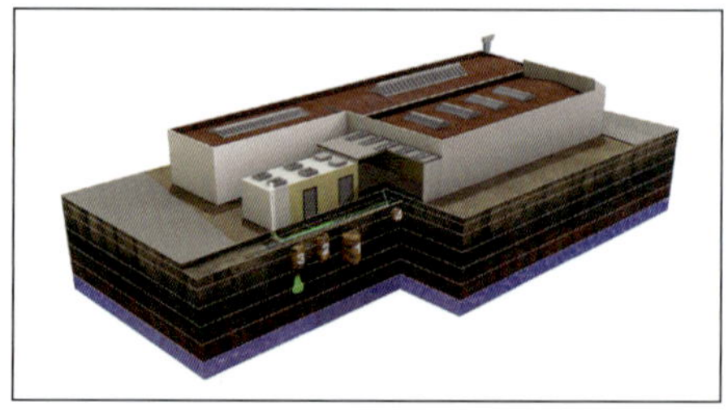

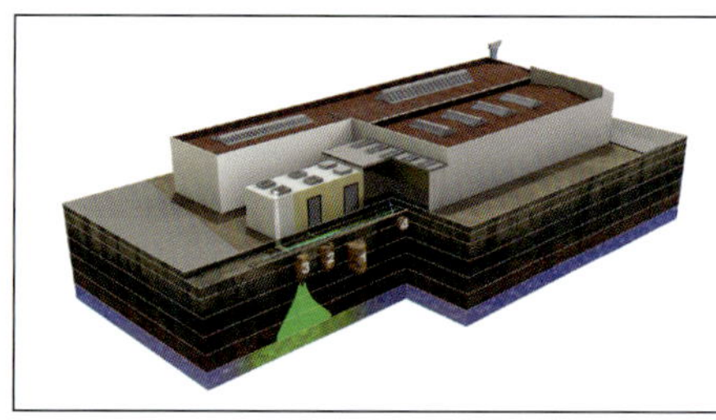

Below, each step of this flowchart appeared on its own, with some element moving within it. The cell undulated, the DNA strands slowly spun, and the damaged cell in the black box moved in the progression illustrated on the visual.

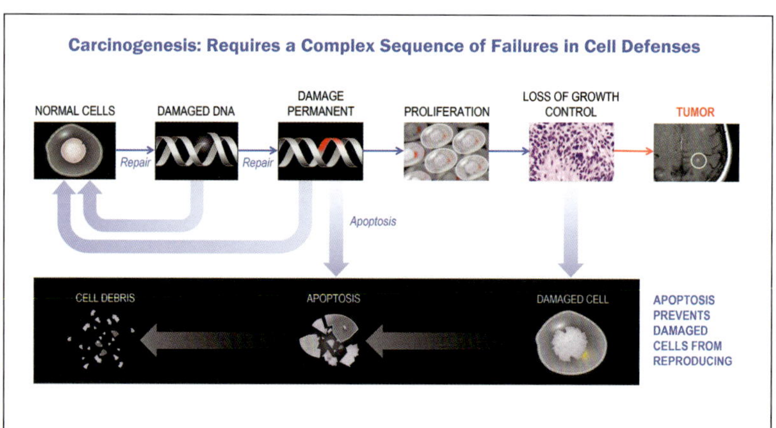

In the animation above, when the computer on the left was the focus, the dial-up connection wire glowed and the recognizable sound of the connection played. When the computer on the right was the focus, there was no sound, and the wi-fi lines and the lights on the router flickered.

Use animation in a relevant way, and in moderation. Animation that cheapens the look of the presentation does nothing to endear you to the jury. Just because our software allows us to make things blink, bounce, or zoom around the screen doesn't mean it's a good idea to do so.

Transitions Between Slides

When we move from one slide to the next, we have many options for what that change can look like. Software programs allow us to use an animation effect—called a transition—when we advance to a new slide. In trial, most often I see lawyers using no transitions between slides. Instead, with the click of a mouse or the press of a key, one slide is instantly replaced by another. My own view is that there's nothing wrong with this quick change between slides in the trial setting. But some designers and presenters find the instant switch too abrupt, and they advocate using a transition. If you're in that camp, just be careful. While some of the transitions our software offers are arguably cute for a presentation to elementary school students, nearly all of them are totally inappropriate for trial. For instance—

The "origami" transition will fold your current slide into a bird and you can watch it gleefully flap itself off the screen. I can't really capture the flapping wings with static images, but trust me. It doesn't exactly scream "professional."

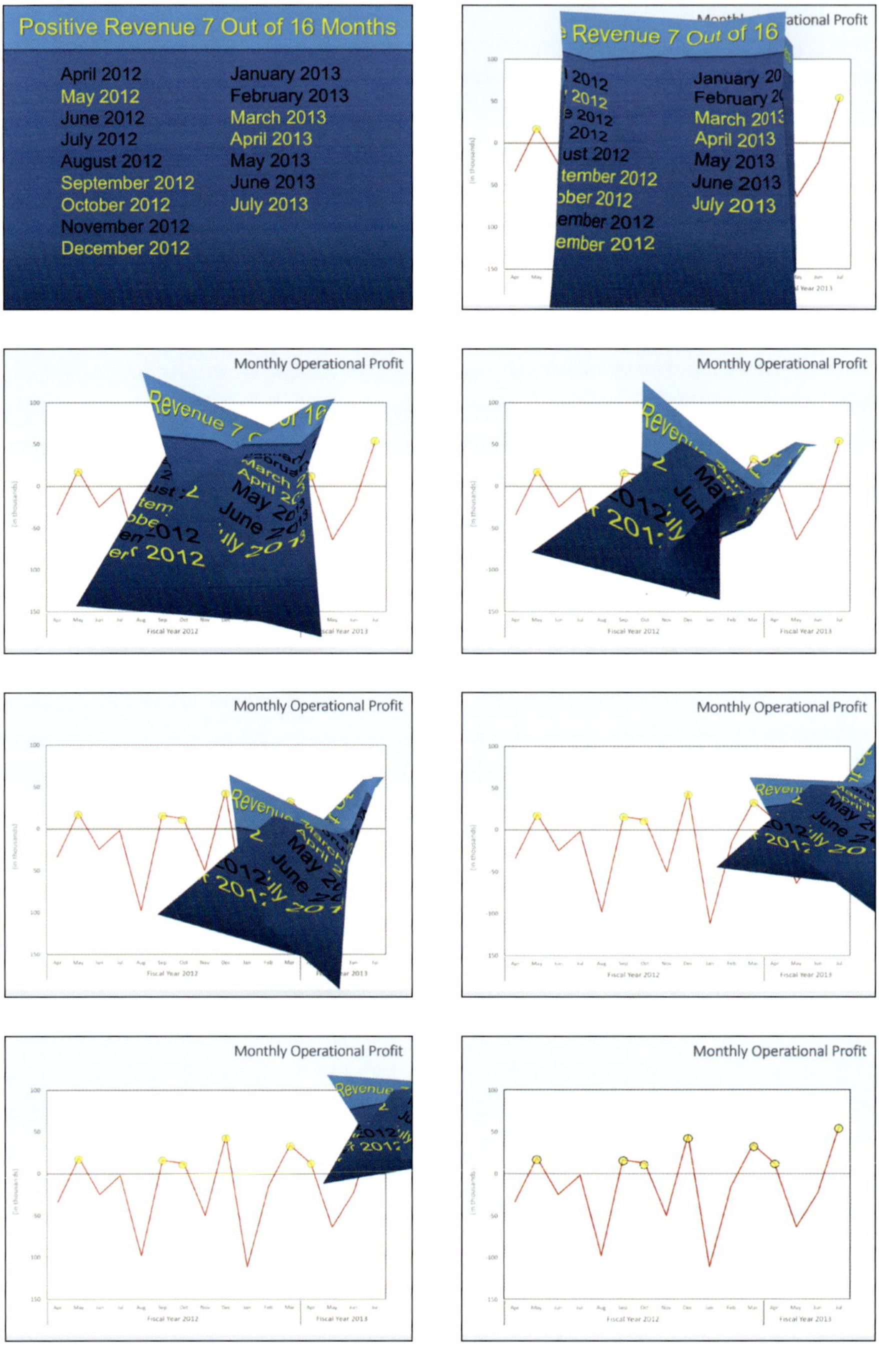

The "crush" transition crumples the current slide into a ball and drops it off the bottom of the slide, as if into an awaiting trash can. Great message to send to your jury about the information you just presented to them.

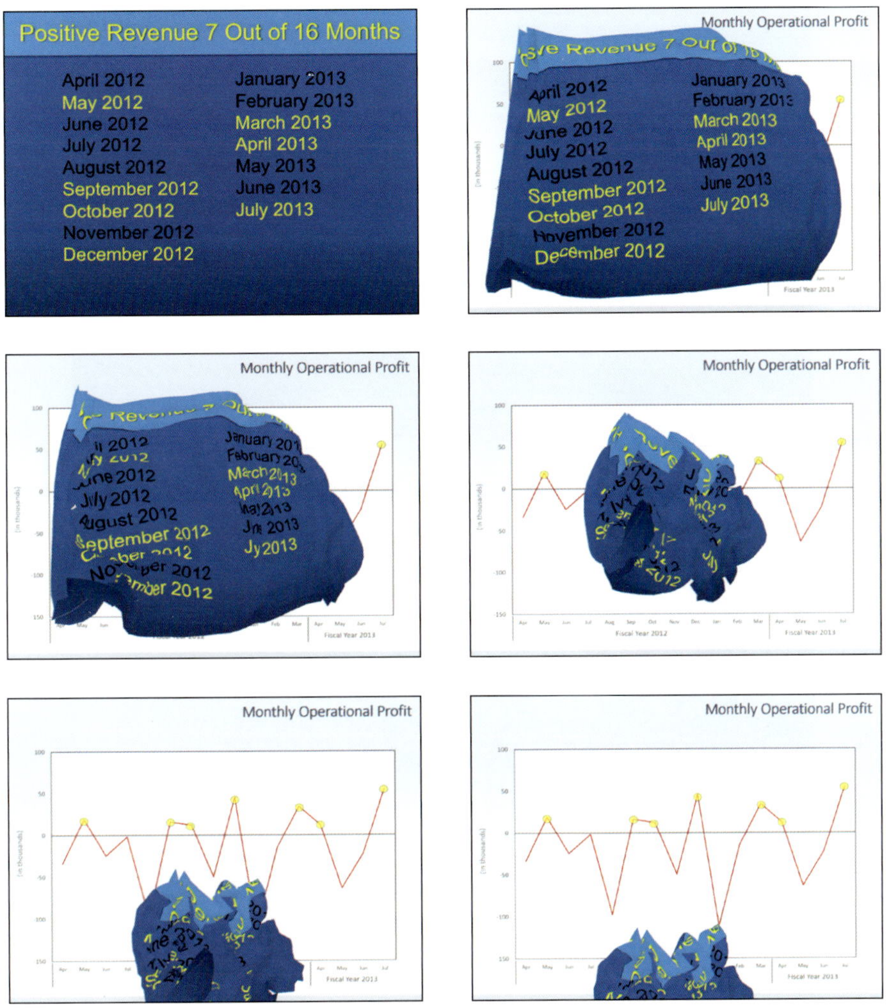

The "vortex" transition splits your slide into thousands of little squares that zoom all over the screen. I have no words.

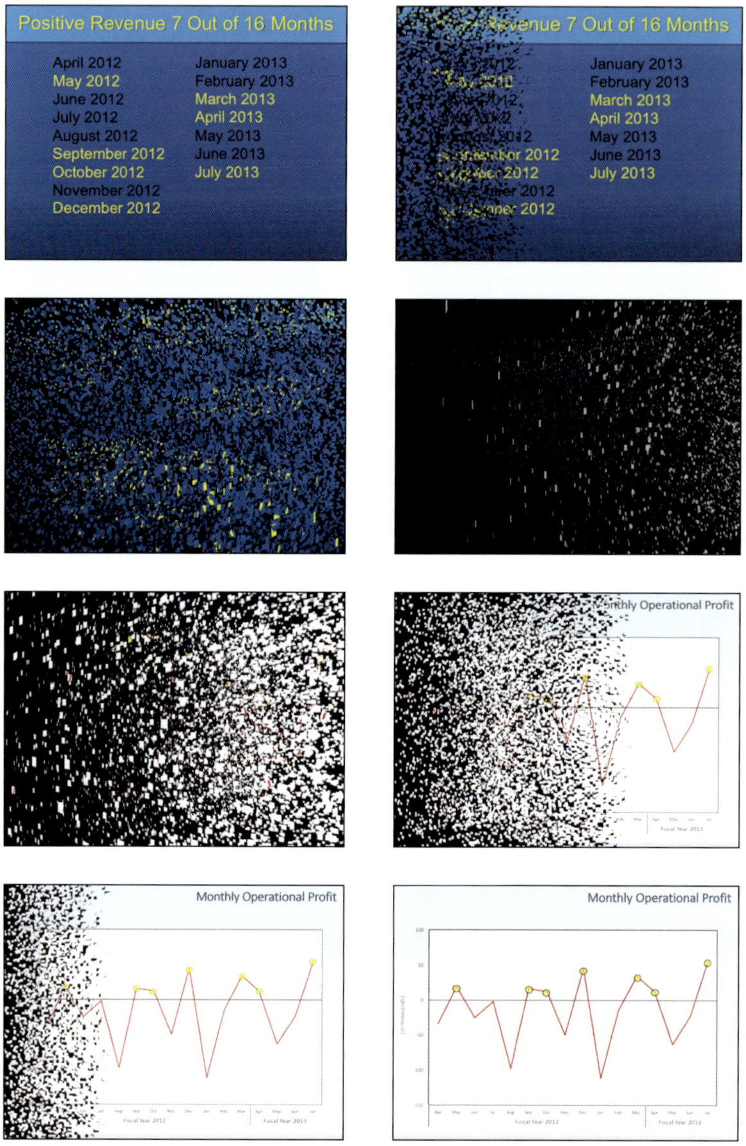

Do not use any of these.

Our software programs also offer a plethora of sounds that can accompany the transitions between your trial slides, such as a bomb, a hammer, a typewriter, a drum roll, and applause.

Do not use any of these, either.

There are a few basic transitions that would be fine in a trial setting. A simple fade, where one slide subtly fades into the next, is one example.

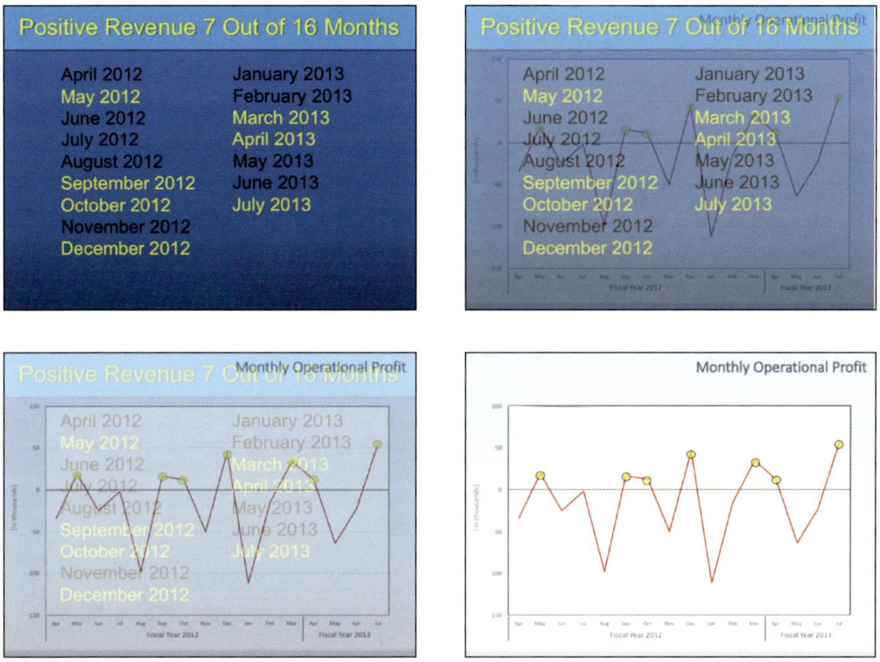

When used with restraint, transitions can help signal to the jury that you're moving to a new topic. For example, you might use a one-second fade between elements of a claim (e.g., when moving between duty, breach, causation, and damages), but a quarter-second fade (or none at all) between slides discussing the same element.

If you do choose to use transitions, follow a few simple rules. Make sure the transition is tone appropriate (no slides spinning into outer space). Don't take too much time to get to the next slide. Pick one style and stick with it—don't use a fade out *and* a fade in *and* a slide left *and* a slide right all in the same jury presentation. And if I wasn't clear before, don't add the little sounds.

Don't Compete with Motion

Keep in mind that just about any change in the slide will be perceived, even if the change was unintentional. If you create a text build with bullet points and one of the bullets is out of alignment on one slide, the jurors will notice that bullet jump out of, and then back into, alignment. As subtle as that movement is, when all else remains the same, it will be noticed and will distract from your presentation.

So, when you intentionally include movement on your slide, the jurors will notice it. That's a good thing, as it's the whole point of using animation. Knowing the jurors naturally will be drawn to the movement, don't compete with it. When there is action on the slide, you have two choices. Either stop talking, or talk about what's moving. When you compete with the animation on the slide, the animation will win.

Ultimately, animation should clarify your message and aid jurors in understanding it. When used effectively, animation creates a focus. It tells jurors where to look, so you can call attention to a particular part of the slide. It takes time to create animations and to use them during trial. Use animation sparingly, so it has an impact and so you aren't wasting valuable time before or during your trial.

Hopefully, this section of the book has given you some ideas for how to visually translate your trial themes and facts using common and creative tools. But if you find yourself stuck at the beginning—knowing the substance you need to display but having no ideas for how to display it—don't be above searching the Internet for a little inspiration.

Google Images and even stock photography websites such as Shutterstock.com and iStockphoto.com have many data display examples including charts, graphs, infographics, and timelines. With some targeted searching, you might get a sense of how others have organized similar information into a visual display. Be careful not to get seduced by overly fancy techniques and designs; most (if not all) of the visuals you'll find in your searches were not designed with the uniqueness of the jury trial setting in mind. But sometimes these ideas can do wonders to get you thinking about your own themes and even data in a new way, and you'll end up with a jury visual you would never have thought of otherwise.

PART III

The Basics of Graphic Design

Graphic designers have the training and experience to create powerful, professional, and memorable visuals. They know what tools are available and how to use them effectively. Designers who create jury trial visuals have seen many examples of how lawyers have visually conveyed case themes. Ideas often come from exposure, and they've had a lot of it.

But sometimes, you just have to do it yourself. This section is for those times. Not having a budget for a graphic designer is never an excuse for using poor visuals or none at all.

That's not to suggest it's easy. Most of us know what we like when we see it, but we can't quite articulate why a particular design works or doesn't work. We might say an image is "too busy" or "confusing." Or maybe it's "hard to read" or "the colors are awful." Learning some basic design vocabulary and principles lets us fix the design flaws that we already know, at some level, lessen the effectiveness of our slides.

In the following chapters, I'll share some of the principles I've learned from design professionals, my own study of graphic design, real and mock jurors I've interviewed, and nearly twenty years of observing what's worked and what hasn't, in my opponents' slides and my own. Before the jury ever gets to the substance of our message, where and how the pieces of the message are placed on the slide impacts how clearly the information is received. If jurors are overwhelmed, confused, or frustrated by the design, then even if they remember the image, they won't remember the message. It's like remembering a vivid TV commercial, but not what was for sale.

Ultimately, the effectiveness of your visuals doesn't stem from how many bullet points you can cram into a single slide, how colorful your graphs are, or whether anything moves. Their effectiveness depends on how clearly they communicate your message, and how the visual tone impacts the jury's perception of your credibility. Effective visuals require effective design.

13

Typography

The process of selecting a typeface for a presentation can seem overwhelming. Basic word-processing programs typically offer around two hundred built-in font options, ninety-five percent of which are completely inappropriate for a trial. And that's just the tip of the iceberg when it comes to what's available in the marketplace, where you can purchase (or get for free) thousands upon thousands of fonts.

So how do you choose an appropriate one for a presentation? It's a tough question, and it can be the subject of serious debate. I have heard colleagues in my office engage in boisterous discussions about fonts for appellate briefs versus trial briefs. I can only imagine the scathing arguments that must ensue among real graphic designers!

And I can't say I blame them. Typography is an art. It is the subject of its own books and design courses. The typeface and spacing you choose for your text impacts its legibility and, therefore, the viewer's comprehension and understanding of your message. Typography also impacts the overall tone of your visual. It's not surprising, then, that the effective design of jury visuals demands some consideration of typography. So, that's what I'll discuss in this chapter.

Font Styles

A font is a collection of type characters. Times New Roman, Arial, and Garamond all are well-known fonts. A font family is a collection of design variations on a font, such as italic, bold, narrow, or condensed.

Arial

Arial Black

Arial Narrow

Calibri

Calibri Light

Lucida Bright

Lucida Calligraphy

Lucida Handwriting

We tend to talk about fonts in groups or categories. One of the most common characteristics is whether the font has serifs, which are the small lines at the ends of the strokes on each letter.

Those with serifs are serif fonts, and those without serifs are sans-serif fonts. Serifs come in different shapes and sizes. Some are flat and angular (modern serifs), others are rounded (old-school serifs), and still others are thick (slab serifs).

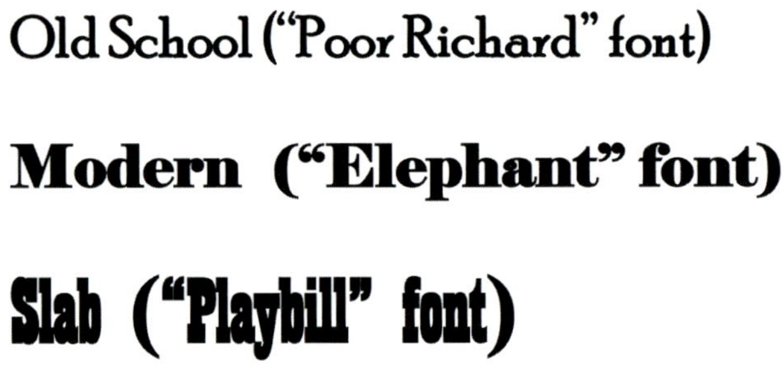

Stylistically, serif fonts tend to look more authoritative and formal than sans-serif fonts. Functionally, serifs help guide the eye horizontally across text, making it easier to read when there's a large amount of text to comprehend. Most text-heavy books and newspapers use serif fonts, and most of us are used to reading serif fonts in briefs and court opinions.

Sans-serif fonts, on the other hand, can be cleaner when there's less text to read. I usually use sans-serif fonts for headings and for labels in diagrams, tables, charts, and graphs.

Another common font category is script fonts, in which the characters look like cursive handwriting or calligraphy. Lucida Calligraphy and Lucida Handwriting, shown on the first page of this chapter, both are script fonts. These fonts are usually (but not always) formal and elegant. They look nice on wedding invitations, but they're rarely useful for jury presentations. They can be tough to read, and they generally won't match the tone of a trial.

The same can be said of another common font category—novelty fonts.

ALGERIAN
Bauhaus 93
Broadway
Chiller
Colonna MT
Curlz MT
GAUDY STOUT
Harlow Solid Italic
Jokerman
Mistral
Playbill

These fonts will rarely ever match the tone of a trial, and they will almost certainly reduce the professional look of your presentation.

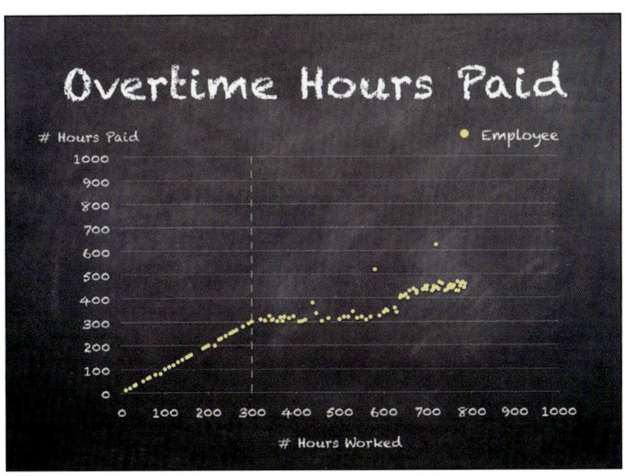

Trials generally are not fun and light, at least not for our clients. So don't use a fun and light font for trial visuals unless you have a really, really good reason. Make the font (and the overall design) match the message and mood.

Font Weight

The weight of a font refers to how thick the letters are. Using a bold version of a font increases its weight. A heavier-weight font can be useful for legibility and emphasis.

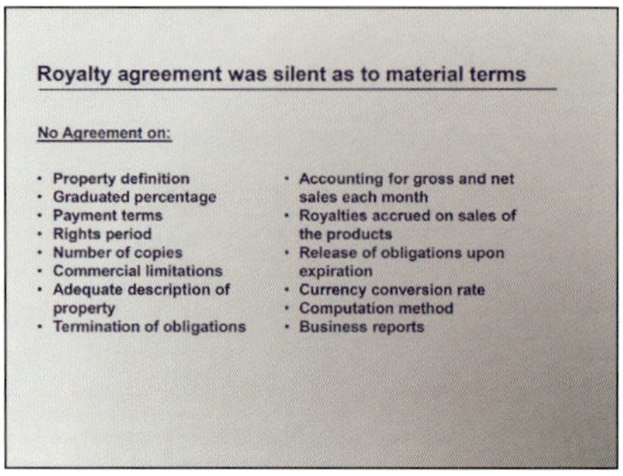

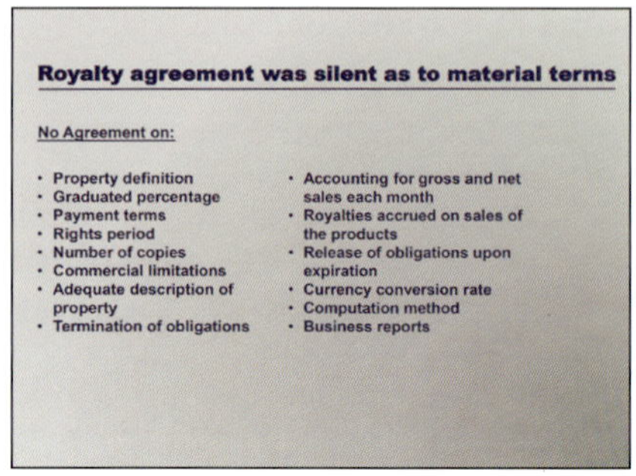

But be careful. If you heavily weigh everything on the slide, then nothing is emphasized. With enough lengthy text, this can be tough to read.

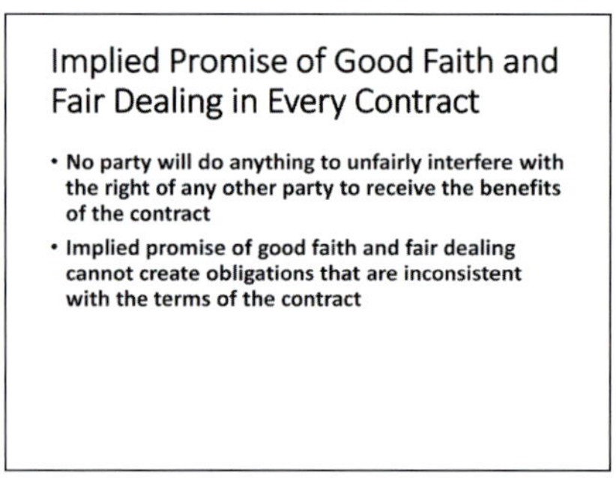

VS.

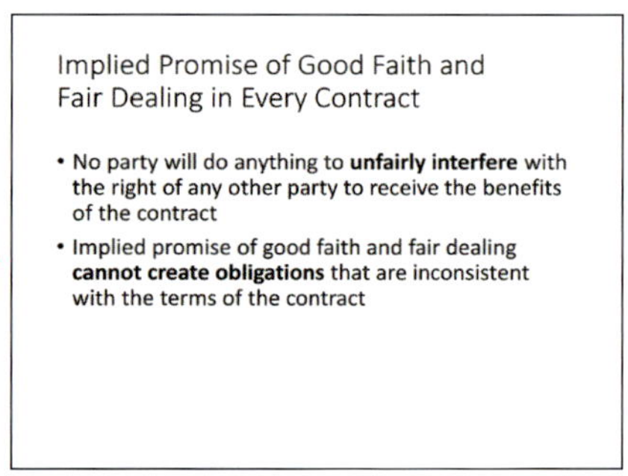

If you're using a lot of text within a chart—even if the lines themselves aren't particularly long—consider a light- or medium-weight, condensed, sans-serif font. All of these characteristics work together to help maintain the text's readability.

Finally, and not surprisingly, remember that the thicker the letter, the more space that letter consumes. Using a lighter-weight but still readable font will give you more space on the slide for your overall design, including leaving calm, empty space around your text.

Font Spacing

After you've selected a font, pay attention to how the words and letters are spaced on the page and adjust them as necessary. The space between two letters is called "kerning," the space between all the letters is called "letterspacing," the space between words is "tracking," and the space between lines of text is "leading" (or, more vernacularly, simply "line spacing"). Each will impact the legibility of your text. If letters, words, or lines are too close together, jurors have to work too hard to discern them. If the spacing is too far apart, the visual impact can be clunky, confusing, and unprofessional.

Each of these adjustments is relatively easy in most word processing or presentation software programs. Use the advanced font menu to adjust kerning and tracking, and the paragraph menu to adjust leading.

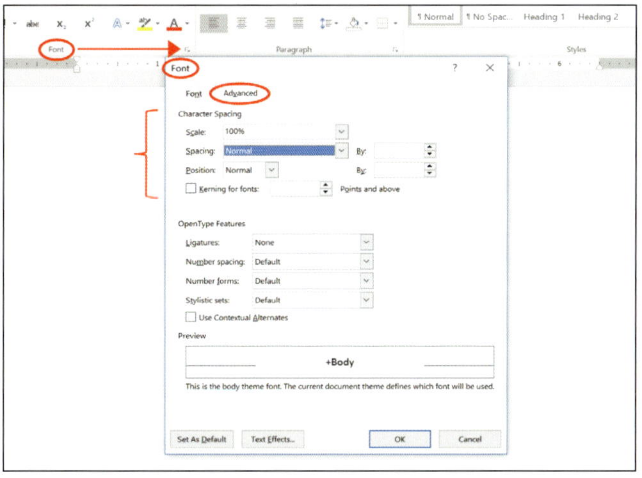

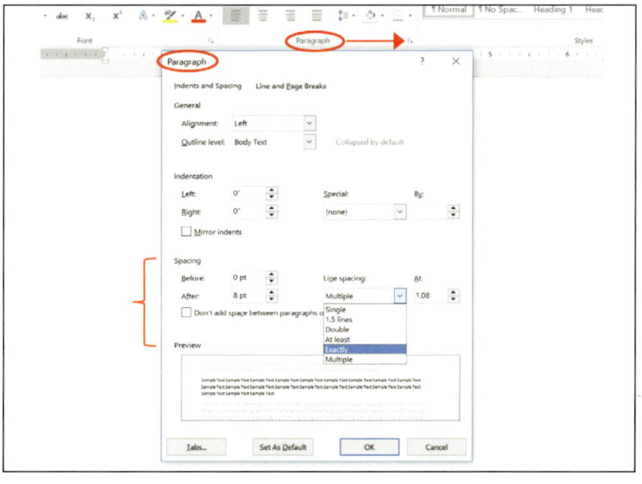

Text Size

The size of your text also impacts its readability. If your text is too small, the jurors can't see it. If you have older jurors or jurors with poor eyesight, that risk is heightened. And, jurors sitting farther from your display will have a tougher time reading the words than those sitting close by.

Design your slide with those farthest away in mind. Indeed, one benefit of eliminating extraneous information is the ability to make the rest of your slide elements bigger and thereby more readable and memorable.

Text Alignment

There are four basic ways to align text, and we're familiar with all of them: left justified, right justified, centered, and fully justified.

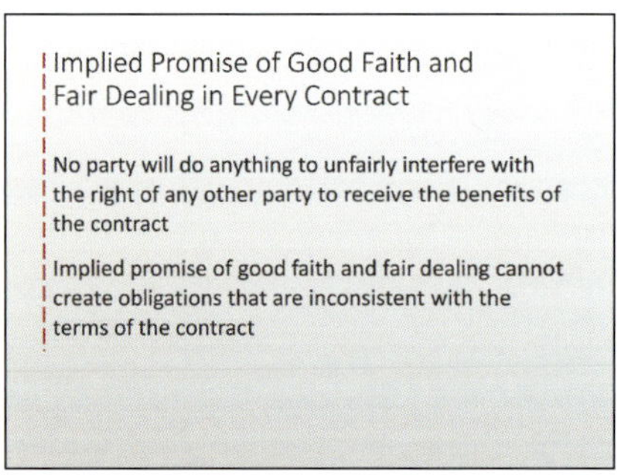

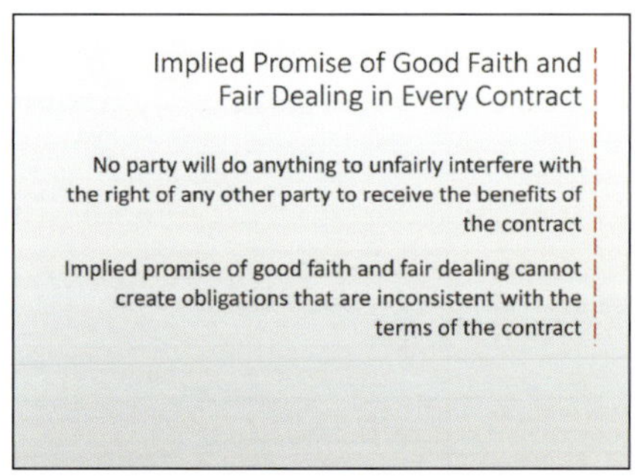

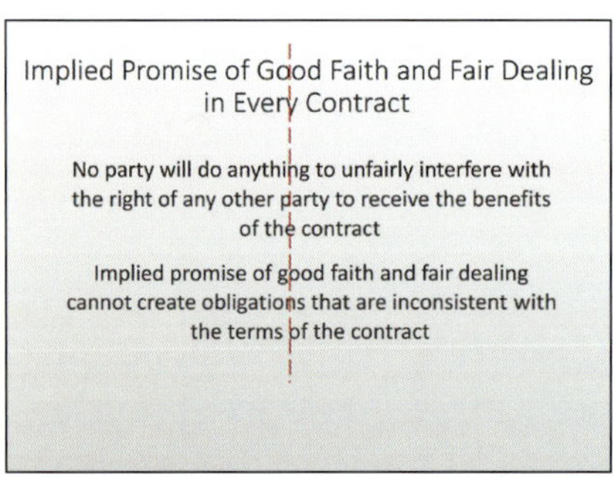

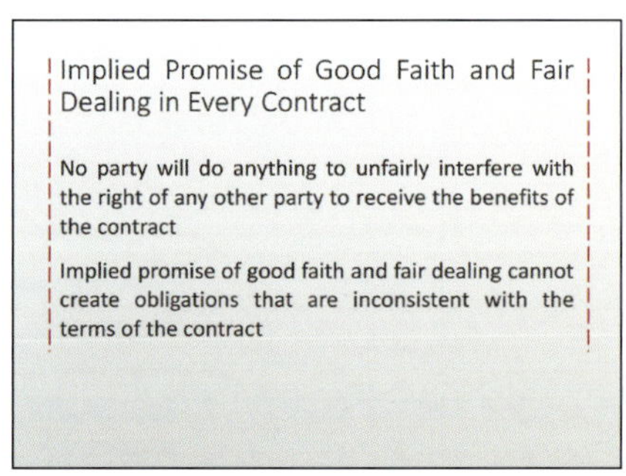

We're used to reading text that's left or fully justified, so I usually prefer those alignments for trial visuals, at least for text in the body of my slide. I'm not a fan of center justification. I rarely use it for body text. When I do, it's usually when there are only one or two lines of text on the slide. The eye prefers a fixed return point for ease of comprehension when reading. When each line starts in a different spot, it takes extra effort to find the new starting point each time you finish a line. It's annoying, and it makes jurors have to work harder to comprehend text.

Another tip for professional-looking alignment is to pay attention to the edge of your text when it's not fully justified, and try to balance the line lengths as best you can.

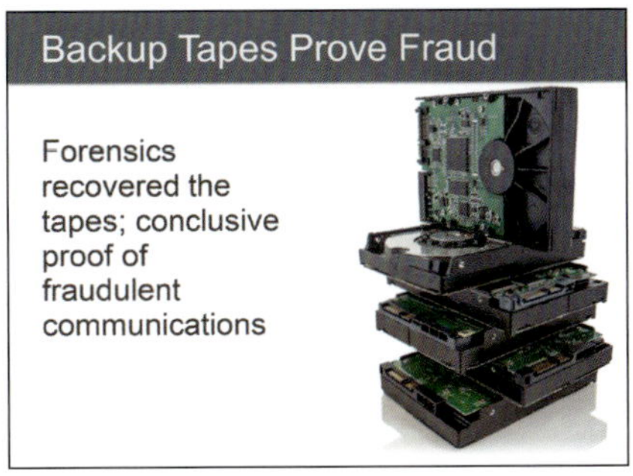

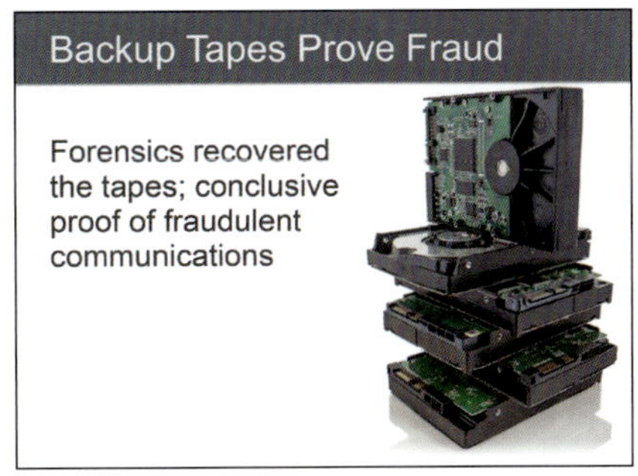

The text above on the left breaks in an awkward way, creating a distracting shape in the empty space between the text and the photo. Typographers call the shape at the nonjustified edge of text the "rag." Watch for an unnecessary but pronounced contrast between the positive lines of text on that rough edge and the negative shape they leave in the background. If you even out your lines as in the slide on the right, you'll have a less-pronounced rag, and the result will be a smoother overall look.

Of course, it's not just about the aesthetics. As we do for headings in briefs and motions, consider breaking the line endings in your visuals where they are meaningful, not just wherever the text conveniently fits. You might need to play with the font size and spacing to accomplish both a calm alignment and a meaningful line break, but it's a worthwhile exercise. The goal is to focus the viewer on the substance of your words and not their awkward spacing.

Capitalization

Rarely will you need to write anything in all caps. Yes, acronyms and some brand names are written in capital letters. If you're using an acronym, by all means, write it correctly and capitalize it. But we can write pretty much anything else in initial caps or lowercase. And most often, we should.

Unless we're talking about just a few letters, text in all caps is generally harder to read than text in lowercase or initial caps. Here's the slide I just showed you—with the improved line justification (the rag)—in all capital letters. You'll see it's harder to read than the version above. That difficulty is magnified the more text you have on your slide.

The eye reads words by identifying their shapes, skimming the ups and downs of the letterforms. With capital letters, all the words are rectangles, generally the same height and width, taking up the same amount of space. When reading words in all capital letters, our reading comprehension is slowed.

WITH MOST FONTS THAT WE'RE LIKELY TO USE, CAPITAL LETTERS ARE GENERALLY ALL THE SAME HEIGHT, WIDTH, AND VOLUME, SO THEY DON'T CONTRAST ENOUGH WITH EACH OTHER TO STAND OUT. THIS REDUCES THE OVERALL READABILITY OF THE TEXT—JURORS HAVE TO WORK HARDER TO READ AND COMPREHEND IT.

Oh, and writing that way FEELS LIKE WE'RE SHOUTING, which is annoying and unnecessary.

Finally, capital letters take up more space than lowercase letters. When I changed the slide on the previous page to capital letters, I also reduced the font size from 36-point to 28-point to capture the identical line breaks and to take up approximately the same amount of space on the slide. In other words, simply by using lowercase letters, I put the same words in the same places and increased the point size substantially.

Italicized Text

Italicizing text can add emphasis by providing contrast with non-italicized text on the same visual. But if you italicize all the text on the slide—which I see presenters do much more often than you'd think—that benefit is lost. And just like it's difficult to read a lot of text in all caps, it can be tough to read a slide full of words all italicized. So use italics sparingly and with purpose.

Text Color

I'll talk about color in more depth in Chapter 19, and all of the principles discussed there apply equally to colored text. For now, just keep in mind that the color of your text and how well it contrasts with the background will undoubtedly affect how easily the jury can read it. I am continually amazed at the color combinations people put together on their slides for no articulable reason, leaving text that is virtually illegible. Use color strategically in your text. If you struggle to read it, so will your jury.

Yellow (or any light color) on white is hard to read. That should be obvious. Don't do this.

Dark colors on black are also hard to read. That, too, should be obvious. Don't do this, either.

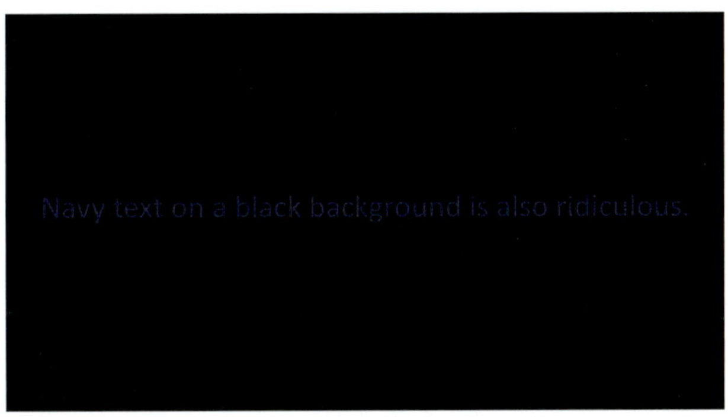

A light color on a dark background is generally legible, but if there's a lot of text it can get overwhelming, and jurors have to strain to read it. When I use this "reverse type" approach, I typically have few words on my slide. Reverse type—typically white text on a black background—can be easier to read when the viewer's eyes are far from the image and when the amount of text is minimal. It's also unusual and dramatic and so commands attention. At the other extreme, dark colors pop out on light backgrounds. If I have a decent amount of text, I'll opt for this approach—just like we see regularly in books and newspapers.

The strongest color contrast is black and white, which is why that combination is used most often with text. But be careful with too much black and white on screen. The contrast is clear, but it can induce eyestrain and fatigue when shown on a monitor in a lit room. One way to reconcile these competing issues—fatigue-inducing black and white versus the need for stark contrast—is to use a soft, solid color such as a pale yellow or blue as your slide background instead of stark white.

Finally, don't forget about color blindness. Typically, those who have it cannot distinguish between red and green (8%–10% of men, and less than 1% of women), though sometimes color blindness affects the ability to distinguish between blue and yellow. With red-green color blindness, both colors may appear brown, so that slides in that color scheme are exceptionally difficult, if not impossible, to read. Indeed, if someone cannot distinguish between the text and the background, it's as though the text isn't there at all.

For example, someone with red-green color blindness cannot distinguish the figure 74 in the middle of this circle:

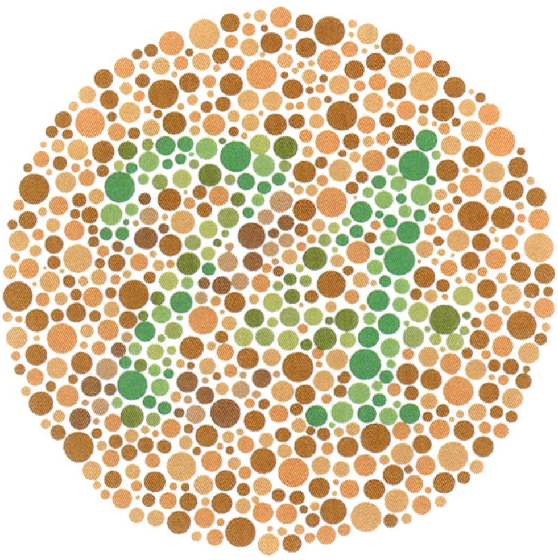

It's not worth taking such an unnecessary risk that some of your jurors won't be able to read your text (and will become frustrated with you in the process). Simply avoid using this color combination for text and background.

Consistency of Typography

Select one or two fonts to use throughout your presentation. Frequently changing fonts on your slides is unnecessary and distracting.

Likewise, mixing a serifed font with a sans-serif font can look out of place. I've seen it done successfully when it's the heading and body text that differ or when body text is in a serif font and the text content of a chart is sans serif. Usually, though, I prefer to select one font and stick with it. I can still make the headings stand out by increasing their weight. I can also distinguish subpoints by decreasing point size or italicizing text. But by using the same font, or at least the same font family, the presentation looks unified and the fonts aren't a distraction.

Vertical Text

Unless you're typing in a language that actually reads vertically—such as Chinese, Japanese, or Korean—don't align your text vertically. I don't see this often in court (thank goodness). But I have seen it. Lawyers stack letters and even numbers vertically to display exhibit numbers, axis labels on charts and graphs, and even the names of witnesses next to an image of transcript testimony. Avoid doing this.

All these typographical considerations boil down to one key point: make sure your jurors can read your text. Make it big enough, legible enough, and visible enough that they can do so without struggling. And if you limit your text to just what you really need, you'll create a thematic road map that note-taking jurors will copy down and take with them into the jury room.

清酒
登録商標
末廣
富貴萬代寿
会津清酒
清酒
金水晶
醇良清酒
花の露
ハナノツユ
一抹千歳
東一
三井の寿
七賢
芳醇清酒
谷櫻
高級清酒
盛升
HANANOMAI
花の舞
静岡極みの酒
開運
縁起清酒
長寿
蓬莱

14

Alignment

Alignment is a fundamental graphic design principle. It applies to all the elements on your slide—text, graphics, bullet points, charts, photos, etc. Alignment defines how these various elements are lined up with each other.

The importance of alignment is best appreciated when it's missing. Consider, for example, a slide like this—something I see with frequency in the courtroom.

Notice how much your eye jumps around on the slide, trying to make sure you've seen everything. Even when you're done, do you feel your eyes still wandering around, just to make sure you didn't miss something important? Can you imagine a juror doing this while trying to listen to you at the same time, and maybe even take notes? By adjusting the alignment (and eliminating the irrelevant photo) . . .

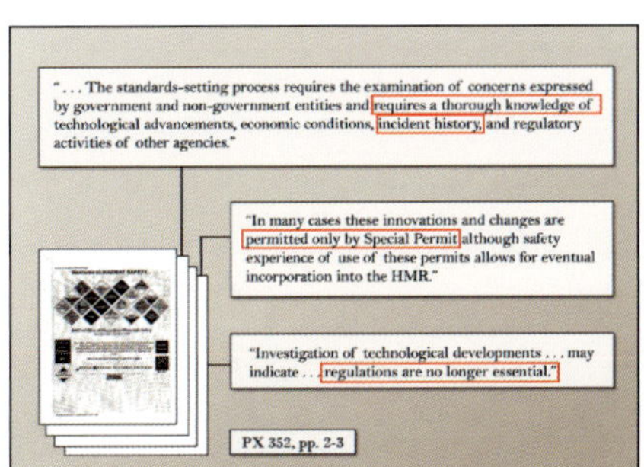

. . . we make the slide remarkably calmer. Now your brain doesn't worry about missing something because it knows it has seen everything. The information is organized, and therefore processed, much more cleanly and easily. That's what we're trying to accomplish with alignment.

Here's another example:

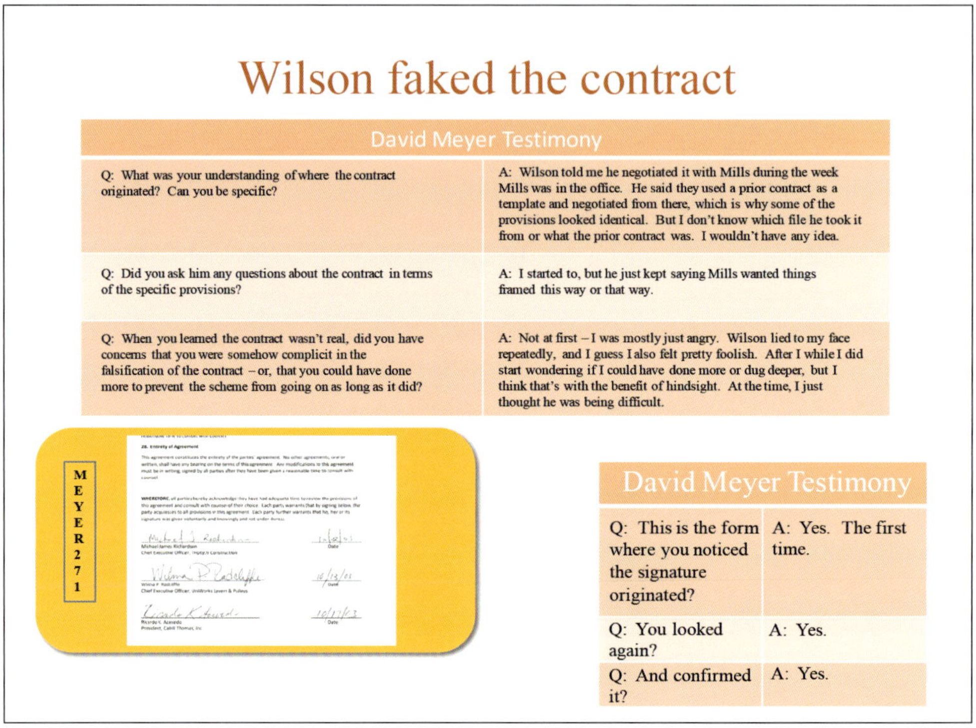

This slide design was inspired by one I saw a lawyer use in trial. The substance of the real slide—the story it was telling—was exceptionally compelling. But the design was so difficult to read, for a host of reasons, that the visual was counterproductive. There's a lot to fix on this slide, but we can start with the alignment.

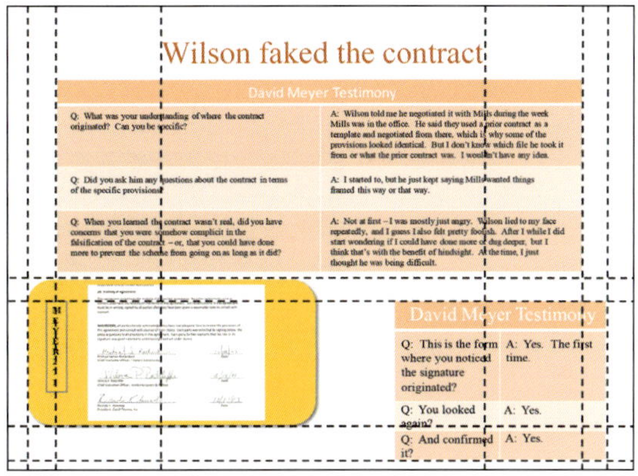

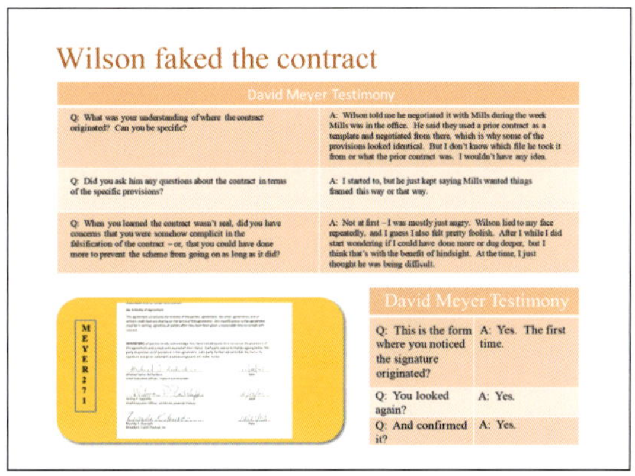

The goal when bringing elements into alignment is to visually connect everything on the slide with something else on the slide, whether it's a heading, a picture, a graph, or even a line of text. You don't need everything aligned along the same line, but everything should be lined up on at least one side with *something* (assuming there's more than one element on your slide). Robin Williams, author of *The Non-Designer's Design Book*, suggests picturing a straight edge, such as a ruler, running across and up and down the page. Every time the ruler hits an element on the slide, look to see whether it lines up with anything else. In essence, you're following along an imaginary grid.

If every element hits a different grid line—as is the case here—the visual has no hierarchy and no organizational structure. Adjusting your layout to align the elements improves the flow of your message. It also improves the overall aesthetic, creating a more professional-looking and calmer presentation.

Center Alignment

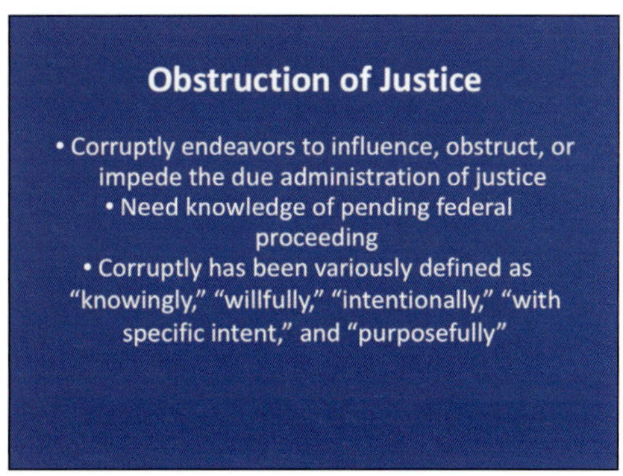

Steer clear of center alignment, particularly with more than a line or two of text. Aligning text or other elements along the center of the slide often produces the least organized alignment of all. There are no straight lines on either side of the text to guide the viewer's eye.

Simply left-aligning the text and lining up the heading instantly organizes the elements.

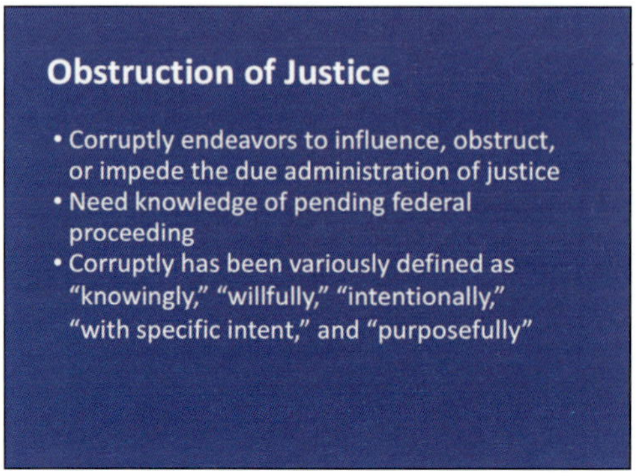

Breaking Alignment

Although our default should be to align the elements on our slide, occasionally breaking alignment can have a powerful effect. It adds interest and emotion to the visual, and can emphasize a substantive point.

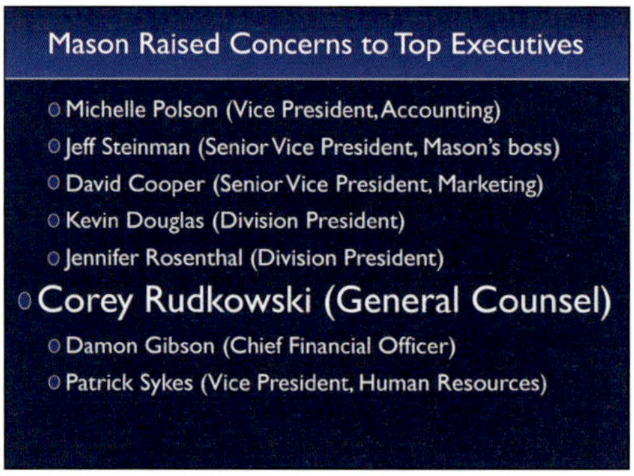

Like anything else, of course, if you use the technique too much it loses its impact and, frankly, can get a little annoying. But don't discount the possibility of using broken alignment in moderation, particularly with overview or introductory slides that feature a graphic element. For the right slide, in the right case, it can be very effective.

Finally, if you're going to break alignment, make it obvious. If it's too subtle, it looks like a mistake, which looks unprofessional and, more important, is distracting.

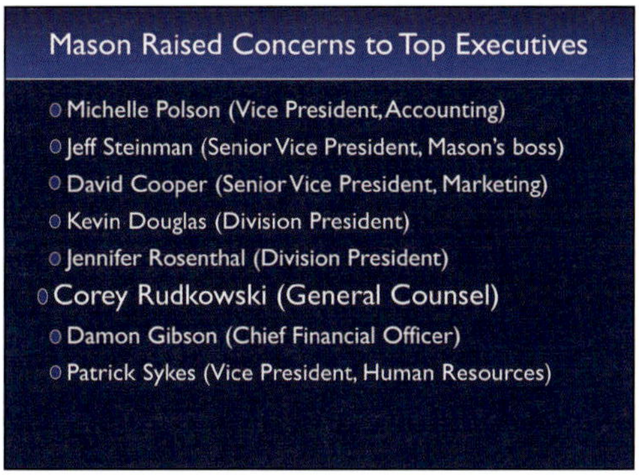

At its core, alignment is about organization and clarity. When elements are placed on a slide at random, jurors are overwhelmed by the disorganization and might miss the point altogether. By organizing the elements, we direct the viewer's eye and control the message. It's much easier for jurors to understand and remember a visual's message when that message isn't fighting with poor design.

15

Proximity

While alignment addresses how items are lined up with one another on the page, proximity is about how close the elements on your visual are to each other. Alignment and proximity both organize and clarify the design, but proximity has a substantive meaning—one that is perceived naturally and immediately by the viewer.

Intellectually, we assume that items grouped together have some similarity or relationship to each other. Conversely, we assume that items spaced apart are dissimilar or unrelated. The jury draws conclusions about items on our slides based solely on their location, which means the space between elements impacts jurors' immediate understanding of their relationships.

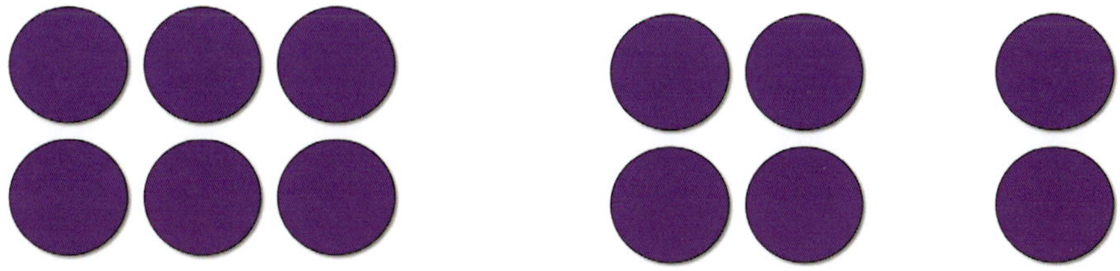

The closer elements are physically, the closer they seem intellectually. As they move farther apart, they separate intellectually as well. Look carefully at the silhouettes in the photograph to the left. The proximity between one silhouette and another suggests the relationship between those individuals. When the proximity between two or more individuals is unclear, so is their relationship.

Knowing jurors will make these relationship assumptions naturally, you can use proximity affirmatively as a communication tool. When you're trying to show similarity or a relationship between items, consciously design the slide to place them closer together.

This slide features two transcript quotes and a signature page from a contract, but it's hard to tell if they're related. The boxes all seem to be set off on their own. The box at the bottom right is in the largest text size. Perhaps it's the most important? Overall, it looks as if these are three separate thoughts, all related to the heading.

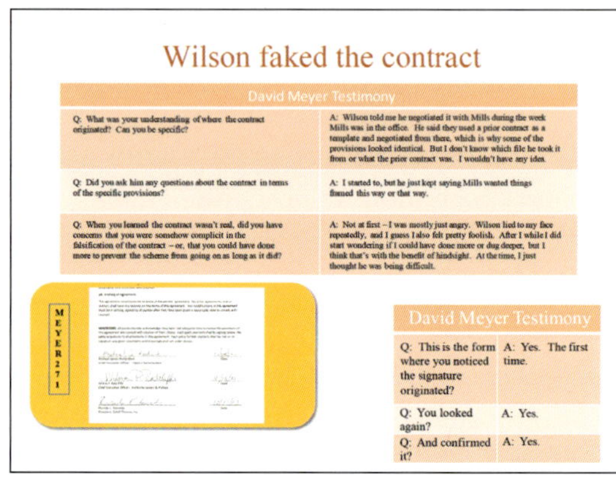

We already fixed the alignment on this slide in the last chapter, which calmed and organized the slide, but the true substantive meaning isn't captured.

In reality, the testimony on the bottom right is *about* the contract signature on the left. Those two items are directly related, but their proximity suggests nothing about their relationship. What's more, the testimony on the bottom right—in the largest font with the largest heading—is actually the *least* important element on the slide.

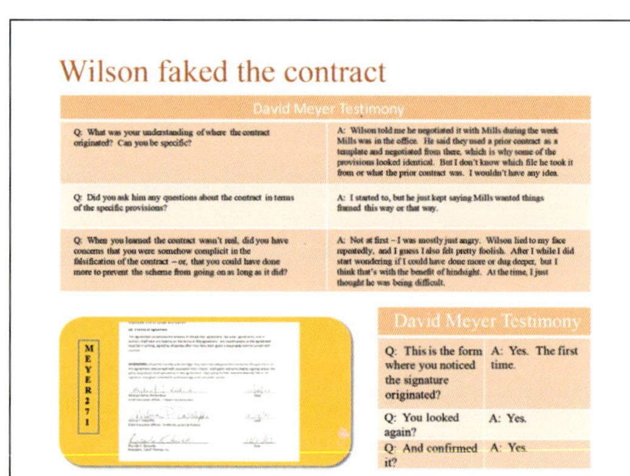

If we adjust the proximity, the relationships instantly become clearer.

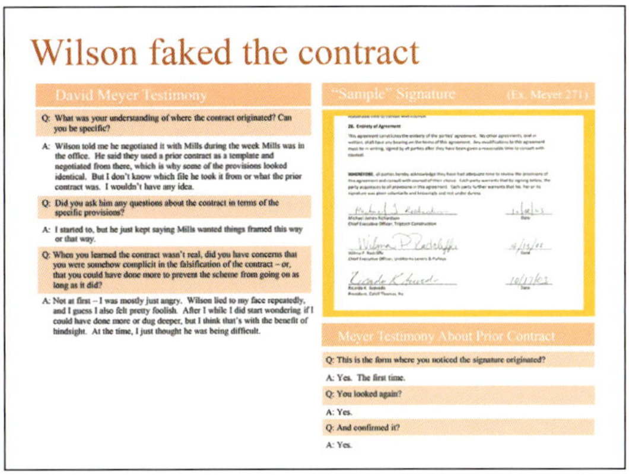

Now the key testimony is on the left (where, in Western culture, we tend to start reading). That testimony is separated from the contract and the testimony about the contract, which are now meaningfully connected on the right. Reorganizing the slide also let me fix the oddly formatted testimony Q&A, which ran from left to right. Now each question appears directly above its answer, which is how we're used to reading transcripts and even interviews in magazines and online. Any other layout just makes the jurors work harder. (I also changed the exhibit label to read horizontally instead of vertically, and I reduced the prominence of the distracting light orange box with the rounded edges. Yes, the visual is still terrible. Baby steps.)

You should even be thinking about substantive proximity in the context of how you space text on a slide, especially your line and paragraph spacing. The proximity of words, sentences, paragraphs, lists, and labels all convey meaning. Make sure labels on diagrams, for example, are placed in close (or at least logical) proximity to what they're labeling. The placement is critical to the viewer's understanding.

Consider this list of logistical steps for an overseas move:

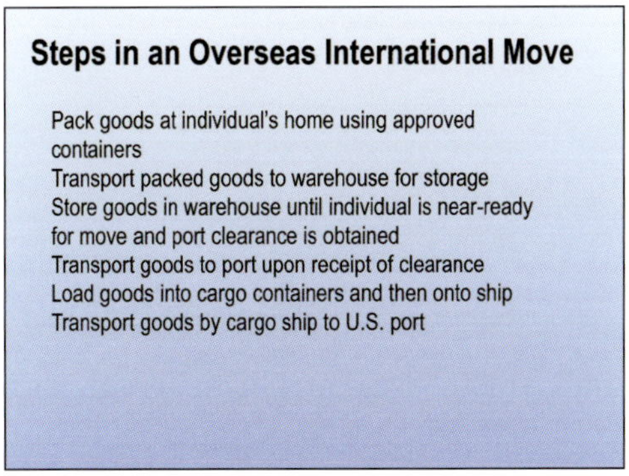

Just listing all this information on a slide doesn't tell us much. There's no hierarchy (other than top to bottom) and no organization to the information. In reality, there is an inherent organization in these steps. The first three steps are part of an initial packing and storage process; the next two steps take place near the time of the move, when the goods are taken to a port; and the last step is the final transport across the ocean.

Changing the basic line spacing on the slide—both between groupings and between individual steps—keeps related steps together, emphasizing the relationship. Eliminating extraneous words opens up layout options and makes it easier to convey substance with design.

Adding simple headings makes this even clearer:

Turning the slide into a more visual graphic diagram, with steps placed in proximity to where they occur, will aid juror understanding by turning a simple text list into a memorable visual image. The following image diagrams the steps in an overseas move using photographs along with basic text to describe each step. It was printed on foam-core board, which is easily displayed on an easel for the jury.

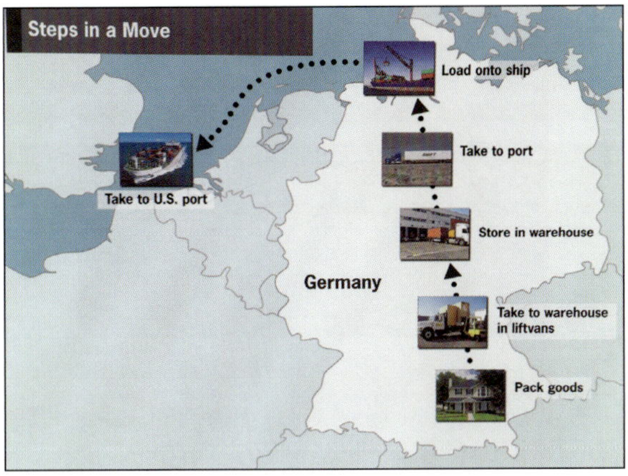

Below is the fully centered text slide that I mentioned is typical of what I see in court, as well as in other presentations.

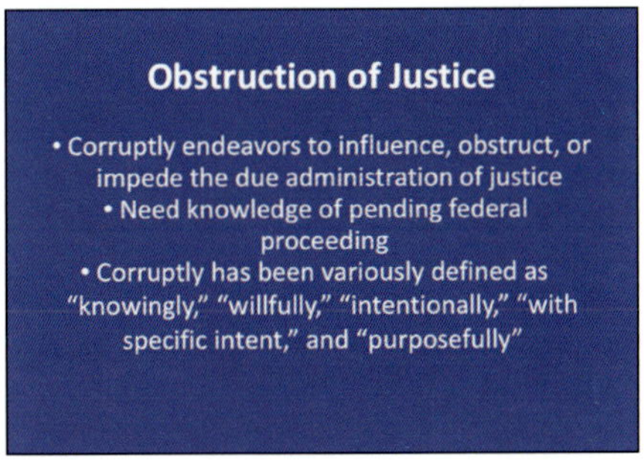

We fixed the alignment in the last chapter . . .

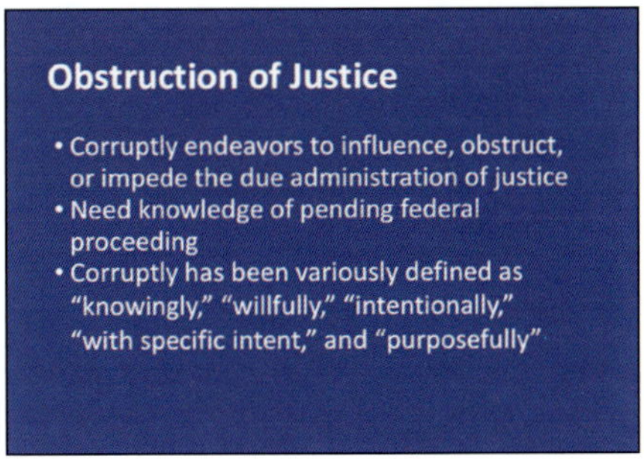

. . . but the spacing is still unclear. The three bullet points suggest three separate thoughts, but you'd never know that based on the proximity of each line to the line above it. If we make that one adjustment . . .

. . . the slide is instantly clearer.

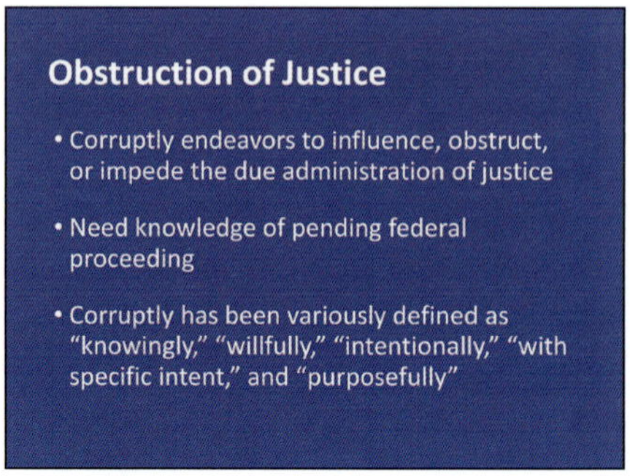

Without even reading the text, the viewer knows there are three distinct points at issue, each described with relatively few words. By making it clear we're conveying the information in digestible pieces, the slide is organized and less overwhelming. Note-taking jurors are much more likely to jot down key language simply because it's presented in a manageable format.

The same principle holds true when the slide features multiple elements in addition to text. Consider an organizational chart, for instance. It's a classic example of a visual entirely designed to convey relationships. But we miss an opportunity when we count on lines or arrows to do all the work. Unless we think carefully about the proximity of the names (or whatever else) we're displaying, the jurors will have to work harder than they should to understand the organization.

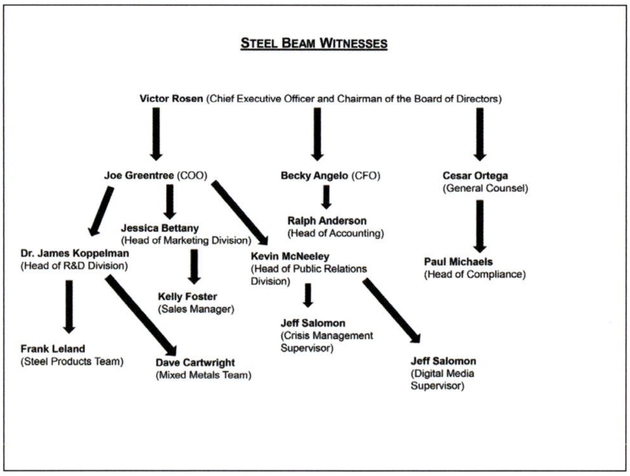

Instead, arrange the elements in proximity to one another based on their substantive relationships.

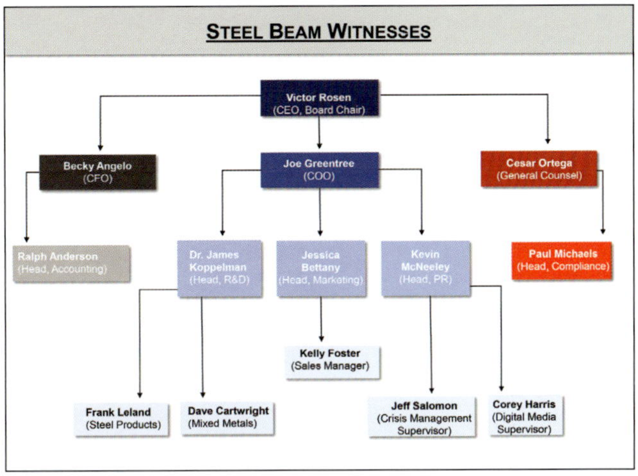

It might mean the slide isn't perfectly symmetrical, but symmetry (design) is not our goal. Rather, the goal is the content. We must design the slide to accurately—and clearly—depict the relationships we're displaying. Here, the groupings communicate three or four distinct areas of focus. Proximity is the graphic design principle that informs these groupings. The close placement of related information suggests the relationship between those elements and reduces the number of independent thoughts being conveyed in a single slide.

Consider proximity when you design the layout of all of your visuals. Even with timelines, keep in mind that if there's text above and below your line, your layout could suggest a relationship between the entries on top and a separate relationship between the entries on the bottom. If that's not accurate, consider another design. For example, if you simply don't have room to put all of your text entries above the line, consider moving the line to the bottom of the slide.

An appreciation for proximity in your designs is useful on several fronts. It organizes visuals to make them easier for the viewer to comprehend. It also ensures that we accurately convey the relationships between design elements. And, when we recognize the design is conveying an inaccurate relationship, we know how to fix it.

16

Contrast

Contrast is what it sounds like—making things look different from each other. Sometimes the differences are slight, and sometimes they're substantial. We can create contrast in many ways, including using color, size, shape, and even location—where elements are positioned on a slide.

Contrast is perceived almost immediately, and as soon as it's perceived, it focuses the jurors' attention by guiding them through the visual.

Consider a typical text slide:

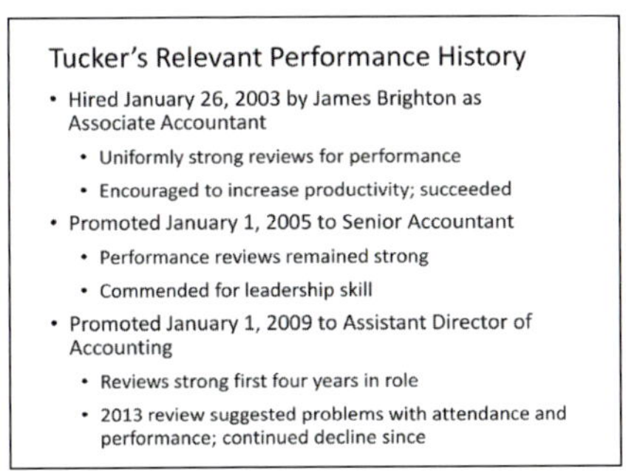

By introducing contrast with color, spacing, and font weight and size, we instantly guide the viewer through the slide and call attention to where we want jurors to focus.

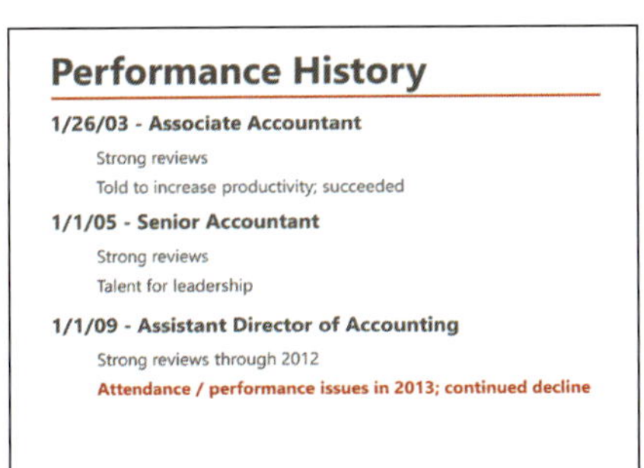

Contrast can also provide substantive clarity. We saw this in the "real fraud" timeline slide in Chapter 7.

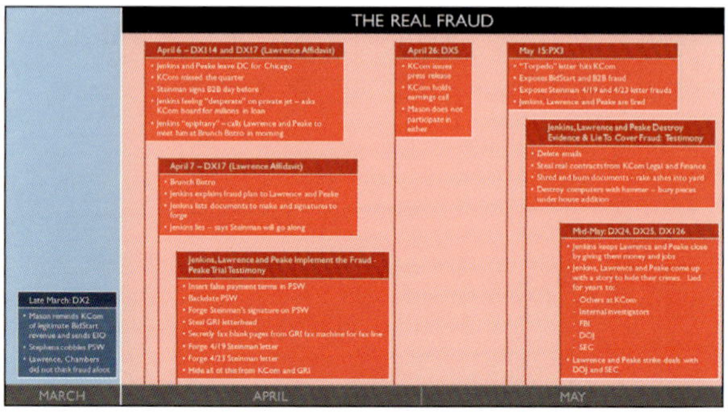

The contrasting colors instantly communicated a difference between the timing of my client's actions and the actions of the other executives. That contrast alone was a substantive visual tool that helped turn the theme into a memorable image.

Let's take a look at this slide again:

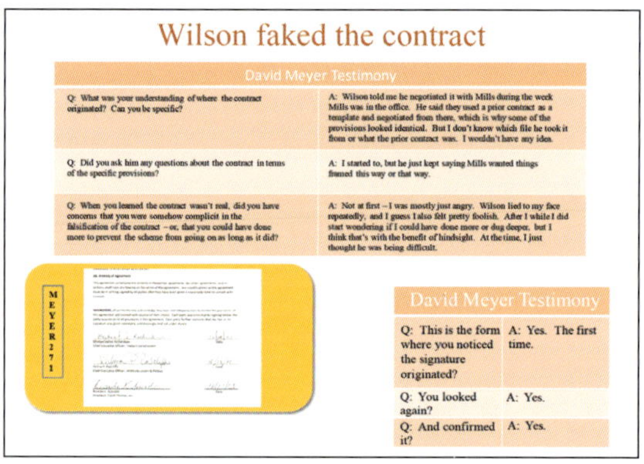

So far, we've addressed alignment and proximity.

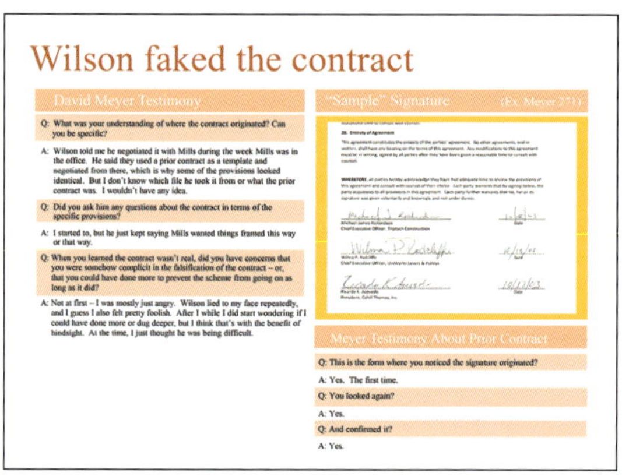

But we obviously still have a contrast problem. The light orange color doesn't contrast enough with the white background, and the bright orange and muted orange don't contrast enough with each other. In fact, I'm not sure what the bright orange is even doing on the slide. It adds no value and instead is just another element on the page that will take some of the jurors' attention.

By adjusting the colors to contrast more strongly with the text, the slide is less overwhelming, and the text is more legible:

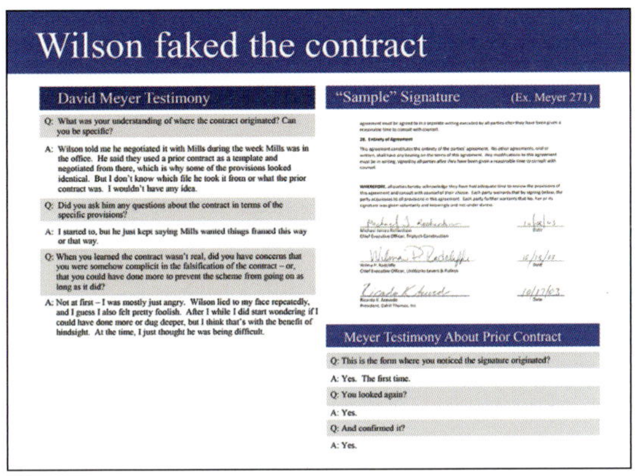

Because the slide is still very text-heavy, I could also use a contrasting color to draw attention to the key language I would read to the jury. If I use the same color to emphasize key language throughout my visuals, I'll essentially color-code the information I want the jury to write down and to remember.

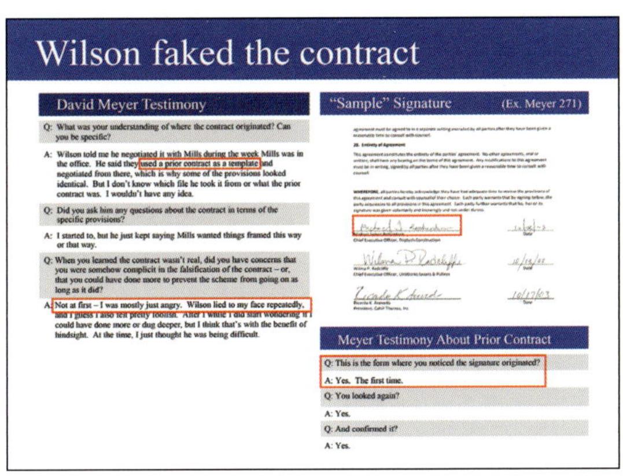

Ultimately, although the resulting slide with fixed proximity, alignment, and contrast is easier to read and understand than the original slide, it is still not a particularly effective trial visual. Instead, I would strongly recommend breaking this visual into its component parts, building each piece of evidence on a separate slide. Your design options open up for displaying each exhibit, and you can bring the pieces back together in the end to emphasize the volume of evidence that supports your story.

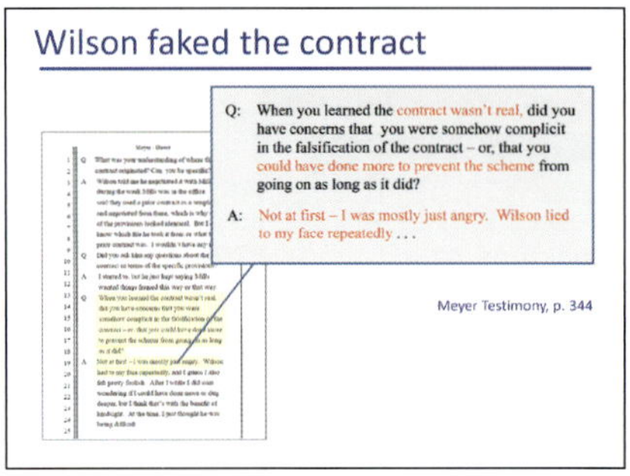

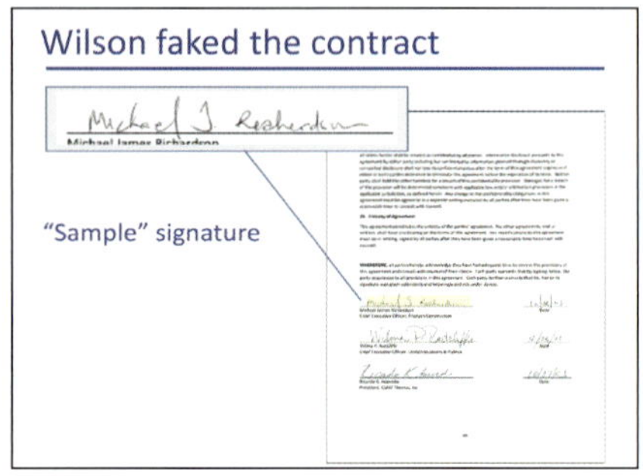

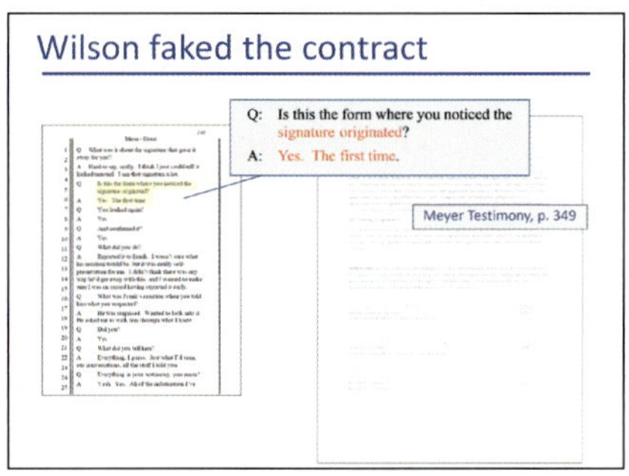

Now, you certainly need to be careful not to overuse contrast in your design.

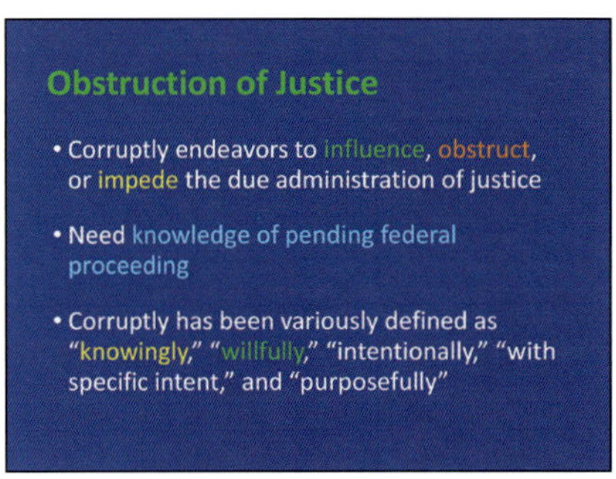

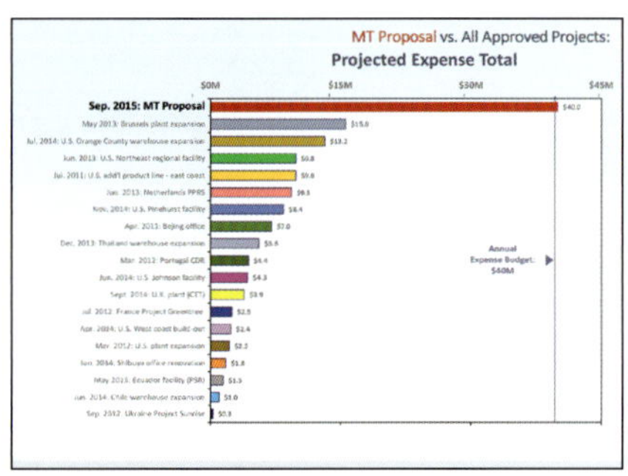

When elements contrast too much, the effect can be counterproductive. The point of contrast is to help organize the slide. If there's contrast everywhere, we're back to square one—overwhelmed and not knowing where to look first.

But it's a delicate balance. You also need to make sure the contrast is different enough to matter.

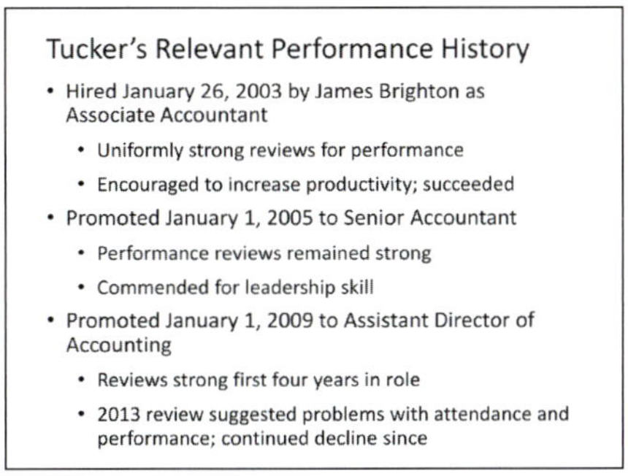

Part of the problem with the above slide is that the bulleted text is in a 27-point font, and the sub-text below it is in 25 point. The contrast between those two font sizes is not substantial enough to make a difference. The contrast is either not perceived, in which case it serves no purpose, or it is subtly perceived and looks like a mistake. Stronger contrast and the elimination of unnecessary text helps calm and organize the visual.

In Chapter 5 on volume builds, I showed you this slide depicting communication between two witnesses before a stock purchase and then one-way communication after the purchase.

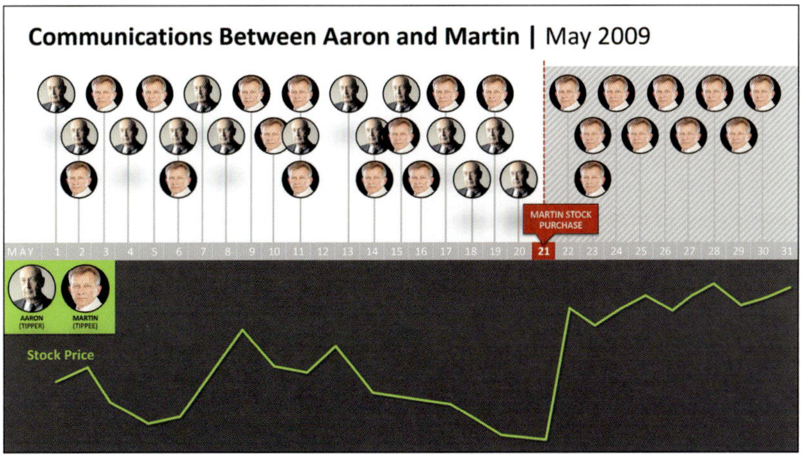

The contrasting photographs were purposeful. One has a dark background while the other is light, and only one of the witnesses is bald. These pictures are easy to distinguish even when they're small and viewed in the aggregate.

But what if the photos you have don't actually contrast with each other very much?

If you can't immediately distinguish between the two people in your design, the visual impact of the slide is diminished, if not eliminated.

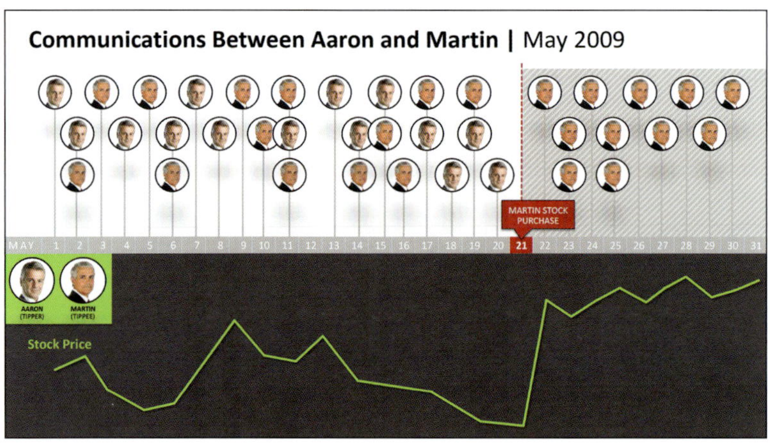

In this visual, *it matters* that the jury can easily distinguish the pictures. Without contrast, it just looks like the communication diminishes after the stock purchase. But that's not the point of the slide. The point is that communication from one of the witnesses *ceases entirely* after the purchase. To communicate that, the photos must contrast with each other enough to easily be perceived.

So, if you're stuck with the less-contrasting photos (but still want to use them, such as in a long trial with a lot of fact witnesses who start to blend together), just add some simple contrast.

Here, we can use contrasting color to enclose the pictures. Carrying the relevant color (red) into the post-purchase period of the timeline visually emphasizes which witness was continuing the communication. We preserve the substance of the message while keeping the visual memorable, compelling, and instantly perceivable.

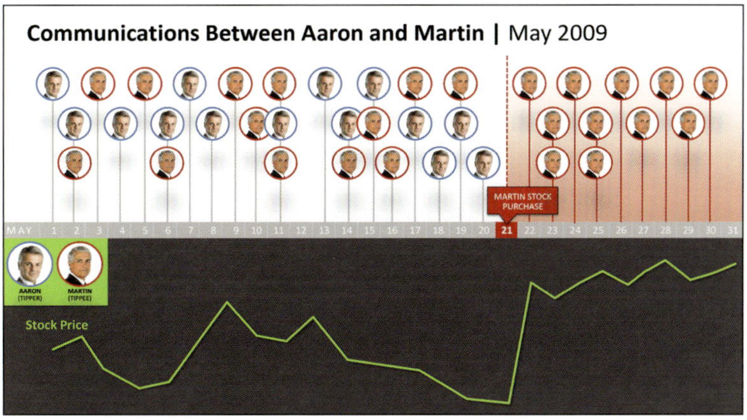

Of course, there are other ways to design this slide while still using photographs of the witnesses. If you weren't as interested in showing the stock graph on the same slide, you could use the design I showed you in Chapter 5, with one witness's communications above the timeline and the other below it, but this time include prominent photographs next to the time entries.

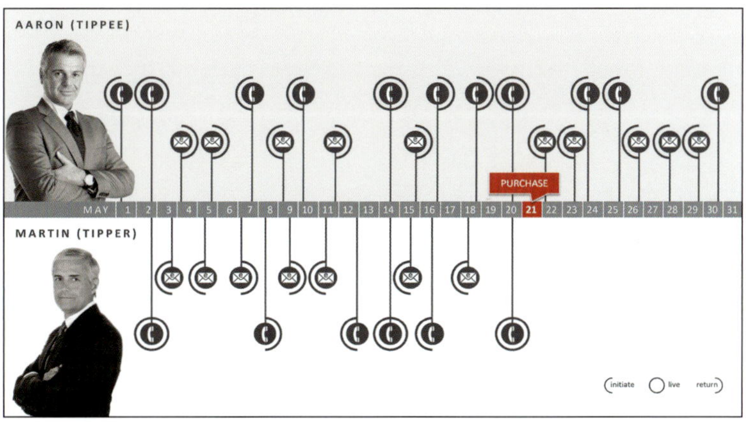

It's now immediately apparent that one person's communication ended after the stock purchase, but the contrasting pictures are still helpful for creating a visual memory of *which witness* stopped calling.

At bottom, contrast is one of our most powerful tools for creating visual memories for the jury. When you're rooting through the papers on your desk to find that one handwritten note on the yellow paper with the doodle in the upper-right corner, you're picturing the image of that page as it contrasts with other papers, both those in your mind and on your desk. Use contrast deliberately, strategically, and in reasonable moderation. But use it.

17

White Space

Everything on your slide commands some of the jurors' attention. Whether it's a paragraph of text or a single word, a full-screen photograph or a small image in a corner of the slide, everything you choose to include on the slide must be perceived, interpreted, understood, and remembered by the viewer. Presumably, that's why you put it there.

But in order for those positive elements to stand out, they need to contrast with the rest of the slide. And that's where white space comes in. White space doesn't have to be white; it's just the area on your visual that's not taken up with text or graphics. The contrast between the white space and the positive elements helps organize the slide and emphasize what actually matters—your message.

Despite this reality, most nondesigners view white space—also called clear, empty, blank, or negative space—as a failure. I certainly used to fall into that camp. When we see empty space, we instinctively want to fill it. So, we take a perfectly fine slide and add more text, squiggly lines, or clip art for no reason other than to fill the void.

This:

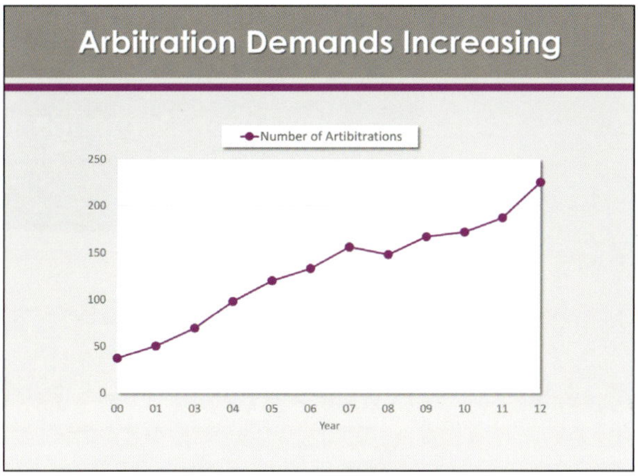

Becomes this:

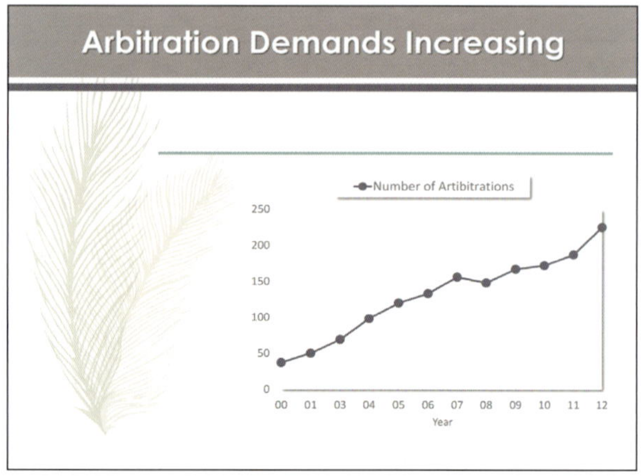

Or this:

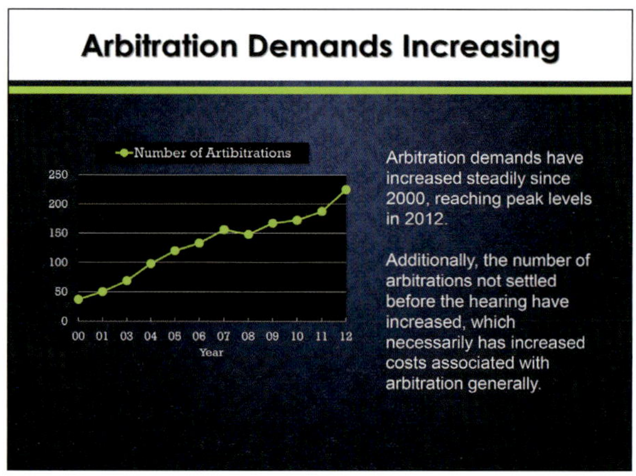

Or this:

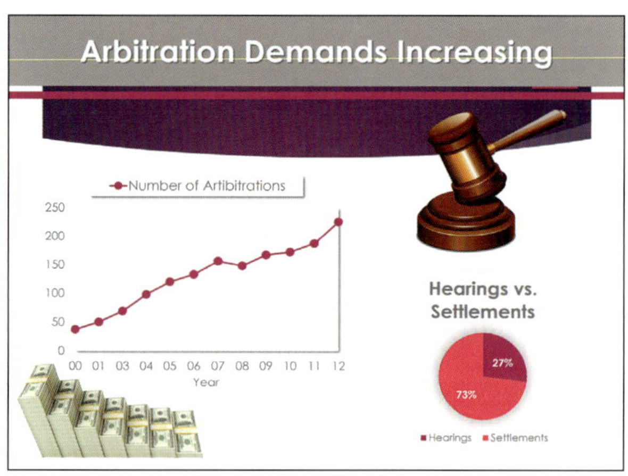

Don't do this. Footers, logos, and decorative items create noise. If an element on your slide isn't purposeful and adding value, it's not neutral. It's distracting and counterproductive. It clutters the visual, making it difficult for the viewer to discern the positive elements. Don't put something on a slide for no other reason than to fill white space. You need calm, empty space to direct the viewer's eyes to your message.

Organize the White Space

When you lay out your visual, pay attention to white space the same way you pay attention to the positive elements on the slide. It's easier than you think to inadvertently create distracting shapes. When you enclose something in a border, for instance, you increase the risk of "trapping" white space within the frame. This can create distractions that would not otherwise appear.

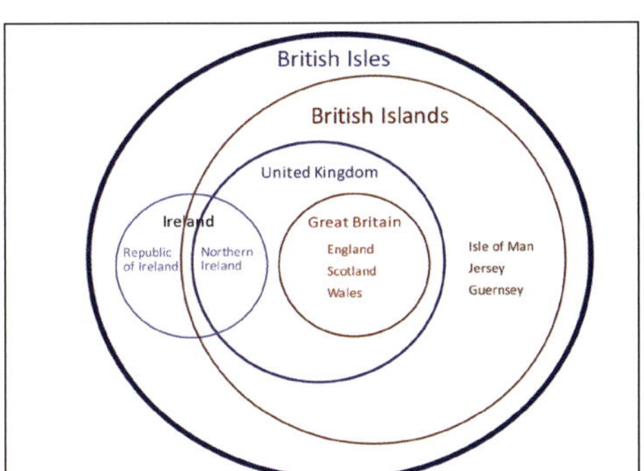

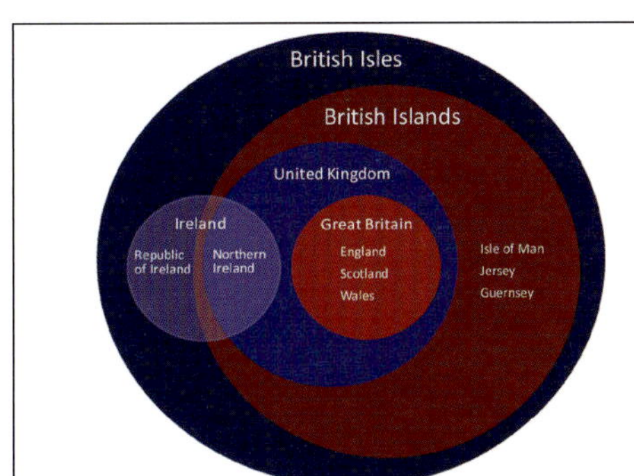

The visuals on the left aren't as calm as those on the right because the trapped white space creates more shapes we have to perceive, sort through, and discard. With the Venn diagram, in particular, the message is communicated through the substantive information contained within the circles. If we fill in the circles, we eliminate the (many) extra shapes created by the overlapping outlines, and we calm the slide.

Tufte, citing Josef Albers' 1969 writings, calls the phenomenon of creating new shapes with white space "1 + 1 = 3."[1] Two positive shapes create a strong negative shape, and now those two positives produce three shapes with similar levels of emphasis. This phenomenon isn't limited to trapped white space. It also occurs when our elements aren't aligned well.

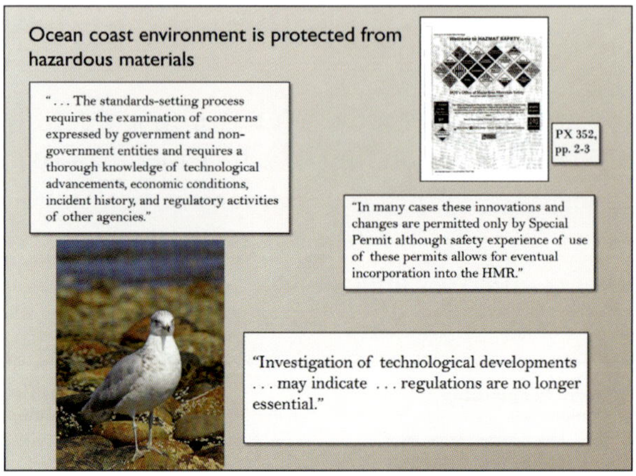

In the slide above, the problem isn't really that white space is unnecessarily trapped within a border. It's that the lack of alignment on the slide leaves the white space just as prominent as the positive elements it surrounds. The white space is, effectively, turned into another positive element.

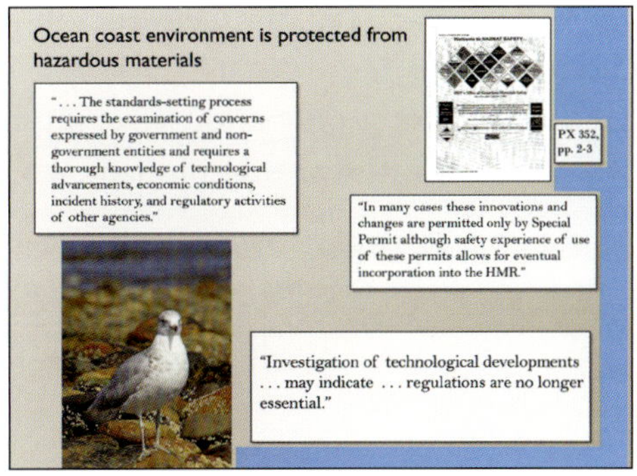

The same problem can occur with any graphic element. Even misaligned text can create oddly shaped, distracting white space. We discussed this in the context of text that is not fully justified, leaving a jagged edge (the rag).

Fortunately, organized white space flows from effectively implementing other design concepts such as alignment and proximity. The empty space surrounding the organized positive elements is then itself organized.

White Space as the Message

Empty space can even convey substantive meaning. For instance, if you're comparing the size of two objects that differ substantially, the white space around the smaller object emphasizes the distinction.

White space can also help convey an absence of something. Say, for example, a defense theme in my case is "guilt by association." I want to emphasize in my closing argument that the only evidence of my client's involvement in the alleged wrongdoing was that he worked at the company with the admitted wrongdoers.

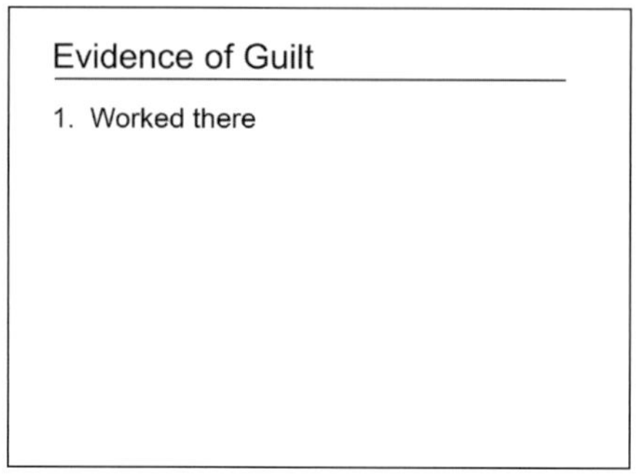

Here, the white space, which shows the absence of evidence, is a material part of the message. In fact, it's what dictated the size of the text. I wanted to leave as much white space on the slide as possible. If the text were too large or if I used too many words to describe this one piece of evidence, I would defeat the purpose of the design.

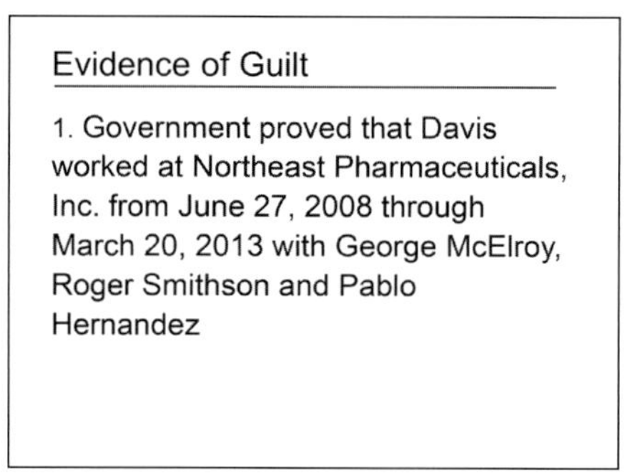

By adding more (unnecessary) words, the evidence against my client visually takes up much more of the slide. Where white space had been a visual manifestation of my theme in the prior slide, that's obviously not what's happening here. A text-heavy description of evidence against my client certainly isn't the visual memory I want to create. Fortunately, it's easy to avoid. The jurors already know who the wrongdoers are, what the company is, and that the government is trying to prove my client's guilt. The jurors just sat through the trial, and even the sleeping jurors will have picked up on all of that. (If they didn't, a long sentence in a text slide isn't going to help them.) In delivering my closing, I'd likely say something such as "all they've proven is that he worked there." So that's all I need on the slide: "Worked there."

That said, I don't want to make the size of the text too small, or I'll risk looking like I'm trying too hard.

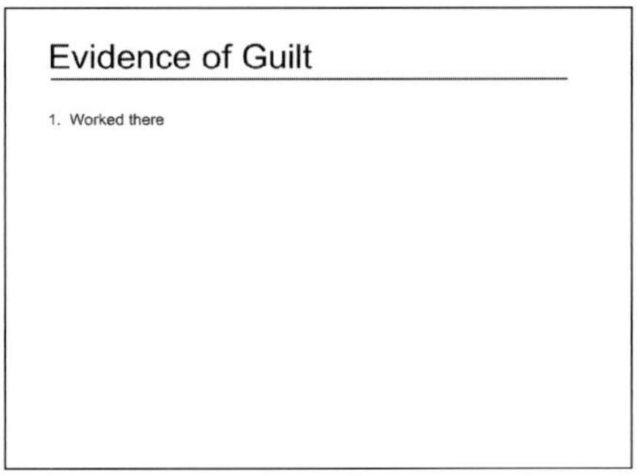

With the text so obviously small, I may damage my credibility. Using a reasonable font size shows I'm not afraid of the evidence that did come in, but there's nothing more.

Finally, I'd argue this is one of those times when the use of a bullet point would be perfectly justified, as it would have a substantive purpose and add value to the design. Bullets denote lists. For that reason, a bullet would convey substantive meaning (just as my use of the numeral does). The bullet or numeral suggests the beginning of a list, but it stops with only one item. And that's exactly the point.

When you eliminate the excess, empty space naturally appears on the slide. By streamlining text, deleting squiggly lines and flowers, and resisting the impulse to include irrelevant clip art, you leave calm, empty space in its stead. The result is worth the effort. Your jurors can focus their attention on the message you're working so hard to help them understand, believe, and remember. The empty space is just as substantively valuable as the positive elements it surrounds.

18

Repetition

In its simplest form, repetition is consistency. We repeat elements all the time in our visuals without even thinking about it. We naturally use the same font, text size, color, and heading style, particularly when we rely on templates in software programs such as PowerPoint and Keynote.

For example, a template might default to displaying text in 12-point Times New Roman next to an 8-point solid round bullet point in the upper-left portion of the slide. We type a bunch of words, and when we run out of room we go to the next slide, where we type more words in 12-point Times New Roman next to an 8-point solid round bullet point in the upper-left portion of the slide. With virtually no purposeful decisions by us other than what to type, the presentation looks consistent (if boring), thanks to this repeated design style.

As with all of these graphic design principles, though, we can maximize the effectiveness of repetition by using it purposely, rather than stumbling into it by happenstance. As a design element, repetition unifies the look of our visuals, making them feel like they belong to the same presentation. Our slides look more professional, and the design is less distracting. If we're constantly changing colors, fonts, backgrounds, and headings or placing exhibits or testimony excerpts in random places on our slides, we risk overwhelming jurors and detracting from our message. Here are some tips to keep in mind when you're thinking about repetition in your visuals.

Layout

Repeating the style of layouts can be critical to the viewer's understanding in the context of a jury trial, where jurors don't control the amount of time they have to absorb any one slide. Repeating where information appears from slide to slide helps the jury process that information on the new slide quickly and easily. Edward Tufte discusses this concept in the context of presenting data. He calls it using "small multiples."[1] When we use the same design format and structure from one slide to the next, we allow the viewers to learn the design once and then focus their attention on what changes in the next slide—the substantive message. They don't have to relearn a new design with every slide just because we chose to use a different layout.

Imagine trying to compare data in two charts, side by side, but with the columns in a different order.

1998

Offense	Fines	Avg. Fine	Jail range	Max Jail	Mand. Jail	Avg. Jail Term	Public Service
1st DWI	$200-$500	$200	2-180 days	180 days	None	2 days	24-48 hrs
1st DUI	$600-$1000	$650	5 days-1 year	1 year	None	10 days	48-96 hrs
2nd DWI	$600-$1000	$725	45 days – 1 yr	1 year	10 days	27 days	48-96 hrs
DWI w/ prior DUI	$800-$1200	$950	60 days – 1 yr	1 year	6 days	18 days	52-104 hrs
DUI w/ prior DWI	$900-$1500	$1125	70 days – 1 yr	1 year	7 days	12 days	56-112 hrs
2nd DUI	$1000-$1500	$1300	90 days – 1 yr	1 year	10 days	15 days	60-120 hrs
1st UDD	$100	$50	None	None	None	None	Up to 24 hrs
DWS Alcohol	$500-$1000	$550	30 days – 1 yr	1 year	30 days	54 days	TBD
DUI w/ BAC >.200	$1000-$1500	$1425	10 days – 1 yr	1 year	10 days	72 days	60-120 hrs

2013

Offense	Jail range	Mand. Jail	Max Jail	Fines	Public Service	Avg. Fine	Avg. Jail Term
1st DWI	5-180 days	None	180 days	$300-$700	24-48 hrs	$300	2 days
1st DUI	8 days-1 year	None	1 year	$700-$1500	48-96 hrs	$800	15 days
2nd DWI	45 days – 1 yr	20 days	1 year	$700-$1500	48-96 hrs	$875	31 days
DWI w/ prior DUI	75 days – 1 yr	10 days	1 year	$900-$1400	52-104 hrs	$1200	20 days
DUI w/ prior DWI	80 days – 1 yr	12 days	1 year	$1000-$1800	56-112 hrs	$1250	29 days
2nd DUI	90 days – 1 yr	10 days	1 year	$1200-$1800	60-120 hrs	$1500	23 days
1st UDD	None	None	None	$150	Up to 24 hrs	$70	None
DWS Alcohol	45 days – 1 yr	45 days	1 year	$600-$1400	TBD	$775	62 days
DUI w/ BAC >.200	20 days – 1 yr	20 days	1 year	$1500-$2000	60-120 hrs	$1800	48 days

The comparison would be a lot easier and more efficient, not to mention less frustrating, if the basic structure and rules remained the same from one chart to the next.

The same is true for all of our communication tools. If you're using keys for charts, graphs, or maps, try to put them in the same location throughout the presentation. Similarly, put exhibit numbers in a consistent place in proximity to the corresponding document. You'll save the jurors from having to hunt around on the slide for the number because sometimes it's in the bottom-right corner below the exhibit, sometimes it's above the exhibit, sometimes it's on the exhibit itself, and sometimes it's not provided at all. If they're busy figuring out your new structure, they aren't focused on whatever you or the witness happens to be saying at the same time.

In sum, when there's no reason to change a layout, don't. It just means more work for the viewer. Unless there's an articulable reason to put an element in a different spot, repeating the way in which the same type of information is presented to the jurors will do wonders to aid them in quickly finding the information they need and not distracting them from the rest of the message.

Backgrounds

Repeating backgrounds helps tie together the presentation. We do this all the time with basic backgrounds, as when we use a solid color. But you can use a busy (relevant) background as a repetitive element, too. We've already discussed techniques for ensuring that text and other graphic elements are legible on a busy background. Repeating the background on subsequent slides and using the same legibility technique and layout can effectively signal that you're discussing information relating to a similar topic. Then, when you change the background, it's purposeful and signals a meaningful change.

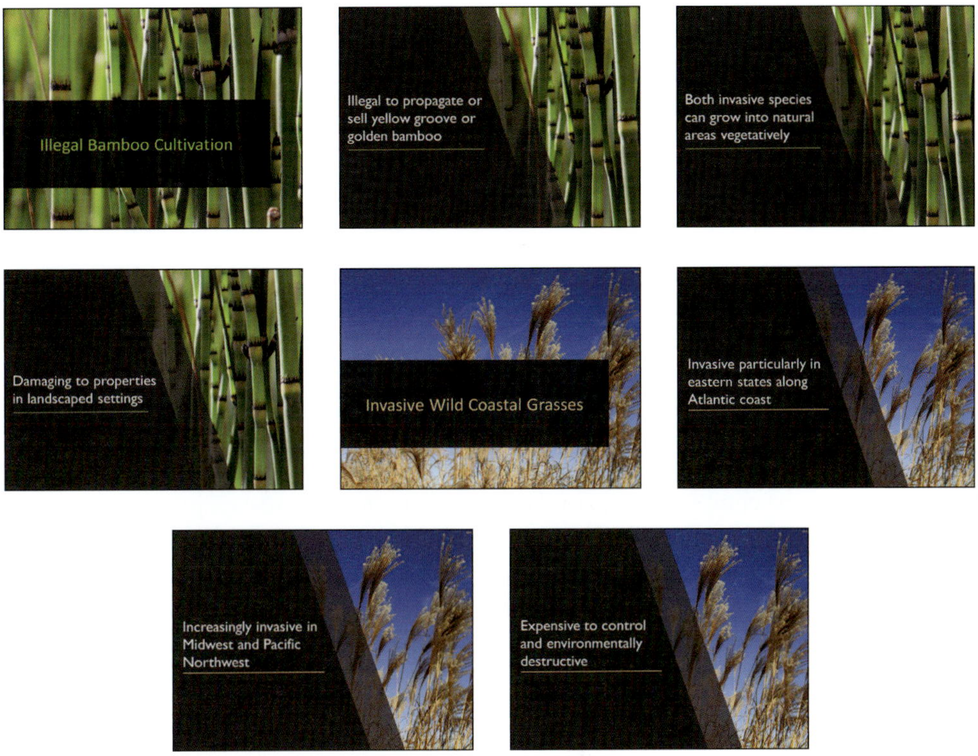

Headings

Repeating the style of headings—the same font, point size, and color—is often second nature. But by making them graphically interesting, they become repetitive, unifying elements in the presentation. A box of color behind the text or a line of color beneath the text that emphasizes your slide alignment can add some purposeful graphic interest where there otherwise is none.

Bullet Point Style and Layout

If you do use bullet points, pick a style and stick with it. Don't start out with little circles and then move to arrows and then switch to stars. Likewise, if you put periods at the end of your bulleted (or just listed) statements, do so consistently. If you're using incomplete sentences, do so throughout your visuals for that presentation. Using a mix of complete and incomplete sentences is noticeable and looks sloppy. (In fact, start by asking yourself why you're putting complete sentences on your slides. Nine out of ten times, you're better off with less text.)

Repeat your layout choices with bullet points, too. Use the same amount of space between the text and the bullet and between the bulleted text and the heading. And, be consistent in where the bullets are aligned along the margin.

Image Style

If you include images in your visuals, use a consistent style. As we discussed in Chapter 9, using illustrations and photographs on the same slide, or even randomly switching between the two in the same presentation, can look unharmonious.

Contrast

Repeating contrast choices helps to unify the presentation and to ease jurors' substantive understanding of your slides. For example, if you use several bar graphs with a consistent data element or theme, consider using the same contrasting color each time. Then, if you switch to using bar graphs to depict something else, you can repeat the style of the graph but introduce a new color scheme to emphasize that the new graphs are communicating a different point.

Here, red and blue horizontal bar graphs depict comparisons among different projects, with red emphasizing the key data point on each graph.

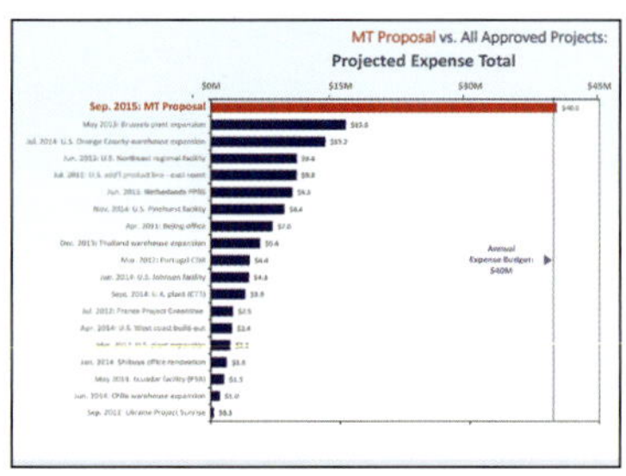

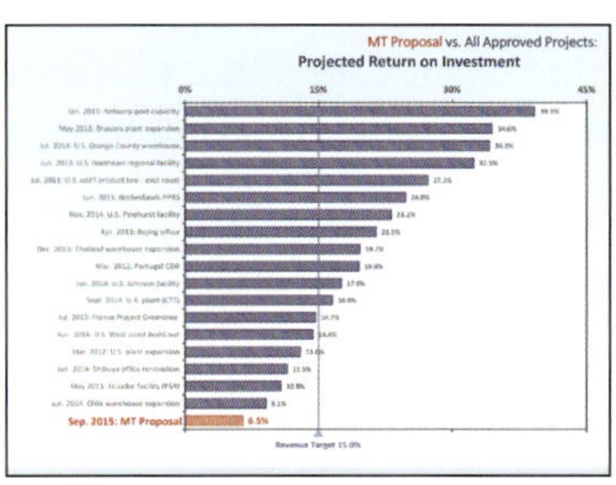

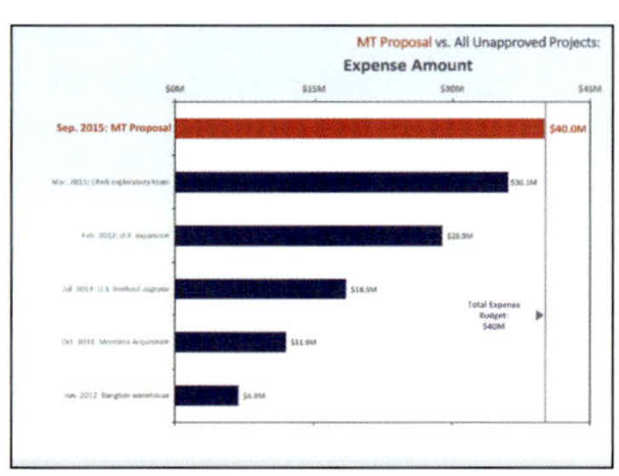

I can then use the same style and layout to depict comparisons between expenses for a single project. I've switched the color scheme to signal the change in comparison, but I've repeated the use of an accent color (white) for the key data point, while using a single color (gray) to depict all remaining data.

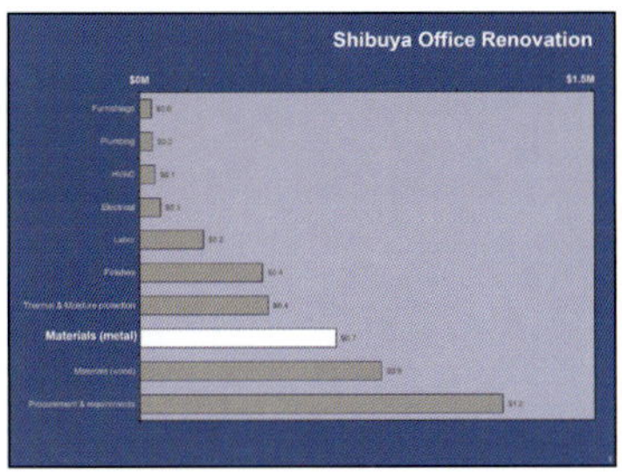

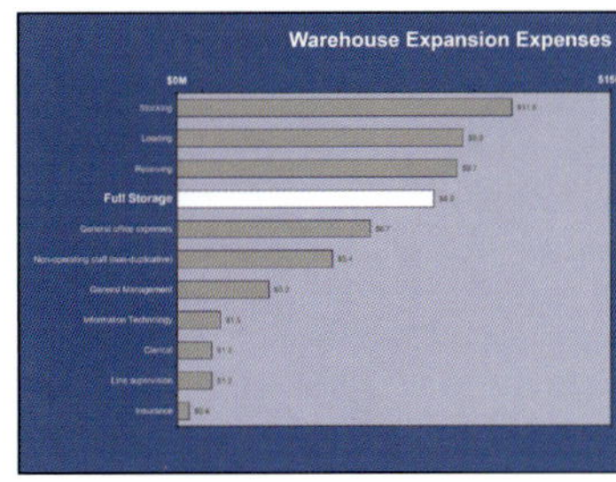

Substantive Repetition

In addition to helping with the design of the visuals, repetition of substantive themes reinforces them and helps the listener remember them. Medina puts it succinctly in his Brain Rule Number 7: Repeat to remember.[2]

Information naturally repeats in trial. At minimum, most key evidence is raised in opening statements, then again with a witness, and again in closing. Often, more than one witness will testify about the same evidence. Certainly, you don't want to waste everyone's time with needless repetition; indeed, at some point you'll come head-to-head with Rule 403's prohibition on cumulative evidence. But some repetition in trial is inevitable, so make it work for you in how you design and use your slides.

As you identify key case themes before and during trial, think about when and how you can appropriately repeat information in your visuals. As I'll discuss in Chapter 23, one way to do this is to build visuals with multiple witnesses, creating the visuals right in front of the jury during the examinations. The repetition is purposeful and appropriate, as each witness adds his or her knowledge or perspective. In addition to reinforcing the theme's substance, you're building a lasting visual memory of the theme.

Ultimately, despite the many virtues of repetition, breaking away from a pattern can also be impactful. Too much repetition can lead jurors to tire of the presentation and stop paying attention. There's a fine line between repeating design and substance, which aids memory and organizes the presentation, and habituation, where information is repeated so often that it becomes monotonous and jurors tune it out.

So, aim to strike a balance. Keep in mind the substantive and stylistic value to repeating elements and maintaining consistency throughout the presentation. And when you do change things up, do so purposefully and with an eye toward keeping jurors engaged and interested.

19

Color

Color matters.

Psychologists, advertisers, and graphic artists consider color one of the most important design elements there is. It is unique in its ability to attract and hold attention, code information, heighten emotional involvement, and help us remember what we have seen. Study after study has found that humans have a tremendous capacity to store pictures and that color pictures have a clear advantage over black-and-white pictures for retention.[1] Likewise, advertising researchers have found that color ads hold viewers' attention as much as 82 percent longer than black-and-white ads and have a higher retention value.[2] And a color image stimulates substantially more interest than a black-and-white one; indeed, one study found that color ads are read up to forty-two percent more often than the same ads printed in black and white.[3]

We sense color broadly and immediately. We also process color faster and at a greater distance than shapes, patterns, or words. Indeed, thanks to our peripheral vision, our eyes can scan a wide area and thereby take in a broad array of information. But our eyes actually focus on a very small area at the center of our field of vision. That is where our vision is at its sharpest.[4] In fact, we cannot read what we are not looking at *directly*.

Think about when you're talking with someone at a conference and you desperately want to sneak a glance at the name badge hanging around their neck. You have to be subtle, because as soon as they see your gaze shift to their badge, they'll know you've forgotten their name. But you *have to* adjust your gaze to read the name. Despite it being a mere twelve inches below eye level, you cannot read the text. What you *can* process, without having to adjust where you're looking, is the *color* of the badge. (Seriously—try it. Focus your eyes even just a few inches away from this text, and see if you can read it. I'm betting you can't; but I'll also bet you can discern the color of the paper beneath the text you can't read!)

Likewise, our jurors will be processing the colors on our slides throughout their field of vision. Your color choice is always perceived and always has an impact on the tone of your visuals. The converse is true, too—jurors will only process words and symbols if they're focusing their gaze directly upon those elements.

Keep these simple truths in mind in your slide design. Use color to focus attention, organize your message, and substantively emphasize themes. At the same time, you'll be creating visual memories for your jurors and maintaining a consistent and professional look and feel to your presentation.

But where to start? One of the biggest challenges when you sit down to create a presentation is choosing a color scheme. Sometimes the task is easier if you know you'll be using exhibits that feature certain colors. But we're often dealing with black-and-white documents and perhaps just a vague sense that we want at least two contrasting colors repeated throughout our slides.

What follows are tips that have helped me over the years as I've improved my own slide design. They include the basics of color vocabulary, associations and relationships, and a website that can help you quickly select fantastic color schemes for your presentations.

Color Vocabulary

Our lack of color vocabulary holds us back from attaining our best design—whether we're creating our own slides or communicating with a graphic designer. We might know we "don't like" a certain color, we might think something looked "drab," or we might realize a slide is "hard to read." But these imprecise descriptions aren't particularly helpful. Have you ever taken your car in for repairs and found yourself making grunting or clicking noises to try to explain what's wrong? If we don't have the words to communicate it clearly, then grunts and clicks are about the best we can do.

Knowing the relevant vocabulary to explain a problem is the first step toward solving it. We're empowered to improve our own slides more effectively, and we can describe our goals more clearly. When we can articulate what's wrong, we can fix it. When we can explain what we want, we can get it. And when we can communicate our design goals, we can achieve them. So, here are some basic color terms that will put you on the road toward your best design.

Color

What we think of as "color" is actually light in varying wavelengths that our eyes interpret as color. The human eye can distinguish about ten million colors, all of which are combinations of red, yellow, and blue. Scientifically, white contains all color, while black is the absence of color, or light on a surface that cannot reflect visible light.

Hue

The "hue" is the true, pure color. No black, white, or other colors have been added or subtracted.

Shade

When we add black to a hue, we make it darker. The term for a darker version is a "shade" of the original hue.

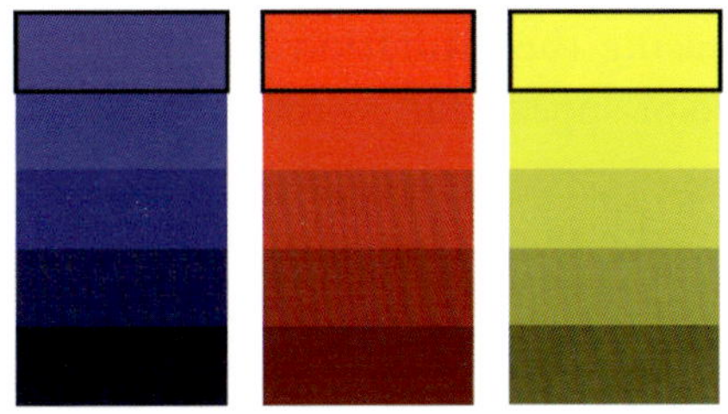

Tint

Conversely, when we add white to a hue, we make it lighter. The term for a lighter version is a "tint" of the original hue.

Sometimes shades and tints of a color have specific names, such as pink (a tint of red) or navy (a shade of blue). Paint companies typically name every shade and tint they offer, as keeping a consistent nomenclature allows consistency of purchase. Every store selling Sherwin-Williams, Benjamin Moore, and Behr paints uses the same color formula to mix Sparkling Morning Yellow (or whatever), and every time a customer asks for this color it will look (and actually be) the same. For our purposes, the key is just to remember that it's easy to lighten or darken a color by adding black or white, which can be an extraordinarily effective design tool for contrast, clarity, and tone.

Value

Value refers to the lightness or darkness of the color. Tints have a lighter value than shades. A color's value is not dependent upon its hue. Indeed, contrasting values are what add depth and emotion to black-and-white images.

Saturation

While adding white or black to a color adjusts its value, saturation refers to how intense the color appears in the image. Increasing the saturation makes the color look brighter and more vivid, and decreasing the saturation makes the color appear dull to the point of gray.

In the photographs at right, the original is in the middle, the saturation is increased in the top photo, and decreased in the bottom photo. (The difference in saturation is more clearly visible in the orange tones of the leaves and ground at the left of the image.)

When an image is fully desaturated, it is entirely made up of grays. It's essentially a black-and-white image.

Whether a color appears saturated or desaturated often depends on how it looks next to another color, so consider your individual color choices together with the other colors in your palette for a particular presentation.

Gradient

Gradients, in the design context, are gradual transitions between colors. Subtle gradients can work well for backgrounds.

Just be careful not to overdo it. If the transition is too stark, it can be distracting and can even interfere with the readability of the foreground text.

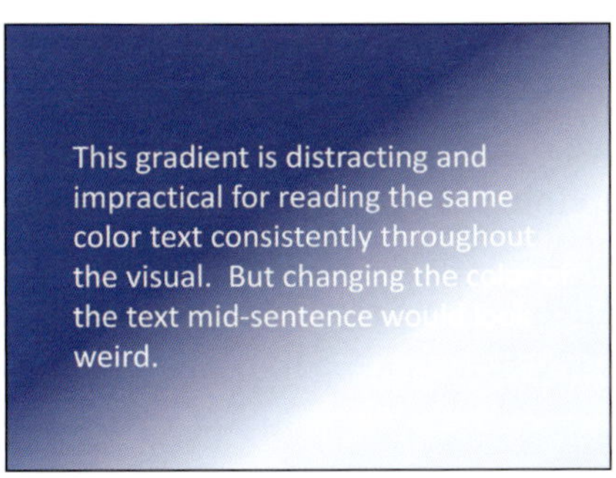

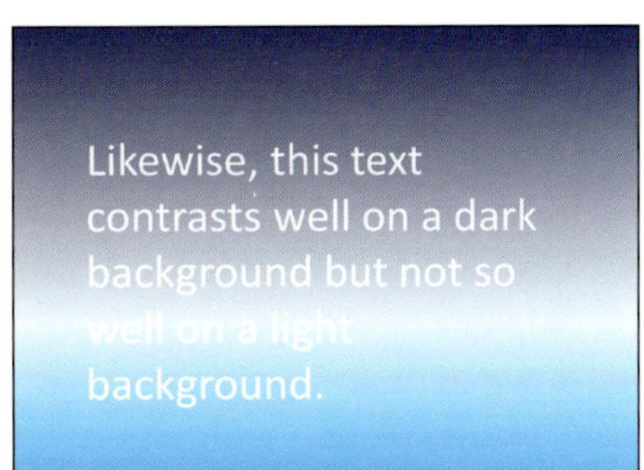

Gradients can also add a substantively meaningful dimension to a monochromatic color scheme (described below). Here, tints and shades of a single hue were used to convey information about state legalization of cannabis. Solid shades symbolized cannabis that was either fully legal or legal for medical purposes. Then, three gradients using the same hue depicted hybrids of full and pending legalization. In the fashion of a heat map, the graduated tones depict a combination of data.

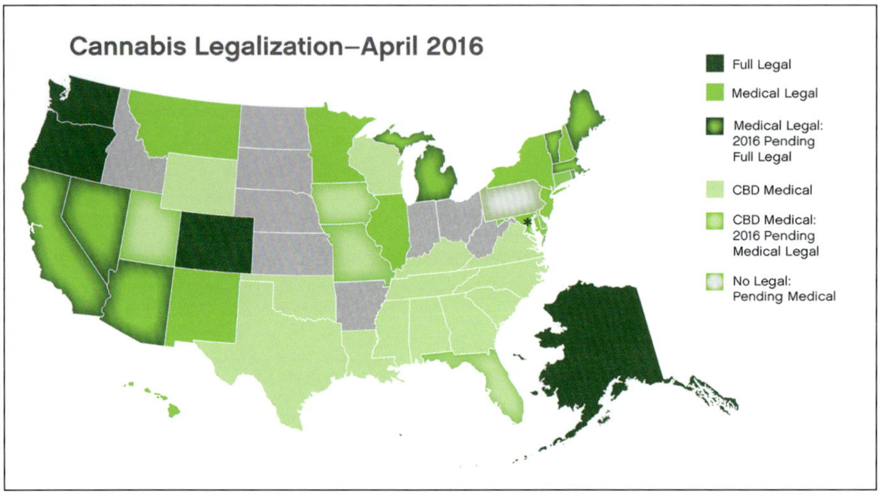

Color Associations

The meanings we associate with particular colors can differ by culture, age, gender, and a host of other factors. And the same color can have multiple meanings—some negative, some positive—depending on the context. For example, green is often associated with nature and the environment, but it is also associated with envy and greed. For professional presentations, blue can convey dignity and success, but blue can also be associated with depression. Yellow is often a cheerful color, but it also can be a color of danger or warning. Purple can convey royalty or death. The words and images you use on your slide will bring context to your colors and vice versa. When selecting a color scheme for your visuals, it's good to keep in mind the common, and sometimes inconsistent, substantive meanings commonly associated with certain colors. Doing so may help ensure that your color scheme furthers your message. But don't get too bogged down in this. How you use color in your visuals is more important than which color you choose to do it with.

Case-Specific Color Associations

Sometimes, color associations form during trial and are specific to the case. If you're using exhibits that feature a corporate logo, internal company documents with a particular color palette, or photographs with featured colors, those colors can be reinforced as appropriate in your slides. In fact, many software programs include a tool (usually an eyedropper) to select a color directly from an image. In Adobe Color (https://color.adobe.com), for example, you can upload a photo or other colored image, and the program will instantly devise a color palette to match it exactly. If you prefer a different color from your image, simply drag the little circles where you want them, and voila. As you can see from the screen captures below, I changed the light blue to a steel gray by dragging that circle over a different part of the image. The program helpfully enlarges the circle when it's selected so I could choose my color with precision.

Using this technique to capture a color in your background image is a great way to match text, boxes, lines, arrows, and other design elements directly to your exhibits or case photos. These days, most of the programs we might use to create our presentations (e.g., PowerPoint, Photoshop, Word, Keynote, etc.) have this eyedropper option. You can still adjust the color to a tint or shade that works with your design, but it's a useful option for at least starting out with the identical hue.

In this image, I used the eyedropper to capture the gray from the thin lines in the train, which I used for the boxes behind my text. I then ghosted the boxes (making them a bit transparent) so the photograph was still visible underneath. For the text color, I used the eyedropper to capture the exact yellow in the train.

But use common sense. If the case colors (in your client's product, for instance) are particularly ugly or are too aggressive or bright or dull for use throughout your entire presentation, don't use them in that way. Ultimately, what counts is the effectiveness of your color scheme.

Selecting a Color Scheme from Scratch

Adobe Color

If you don't have (or don't want to use) a photo or an exhibit to set your color scheme, you could consider a color scheme based on the industry at issue in the case, like the green colors in the cannabis map. If the case involves industrial machines, then metallic grays, silvers, or blacks with a contrasting accent color might work well and match the color associations that will naturally arise in the jurors' minds. If the case involves agricultural or property issues, appropriate thematic colors might mirror nature—greens, tans, reds, yellows, and blues in hues reminiscent of grass, sky, wheat fields, and flowers. Don't get too cute. It is a trial, after all, not a marketing campaign. But for significant presentations such as jury openings or closings, colors and their natural associations can help reinforce your themes.

The Adobe Color website I mentioned (formerly known as Kuler) offers thousands of color theme ideas, primarily generated by other users. The website integrates directly with other programs such as Photoshop, Illustrator, and InDesign, but it's also a great brainstorming tool even if you don't have these other programs. If you have one color you know you want to use, you can search for it (e.g., "cobalt blue" or "fire engine red") and a multitude of color combinations appear featuring that color.

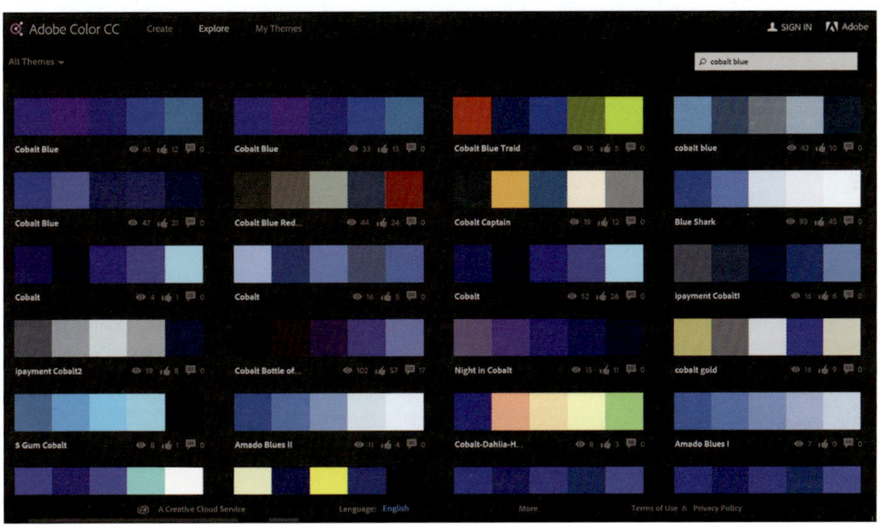

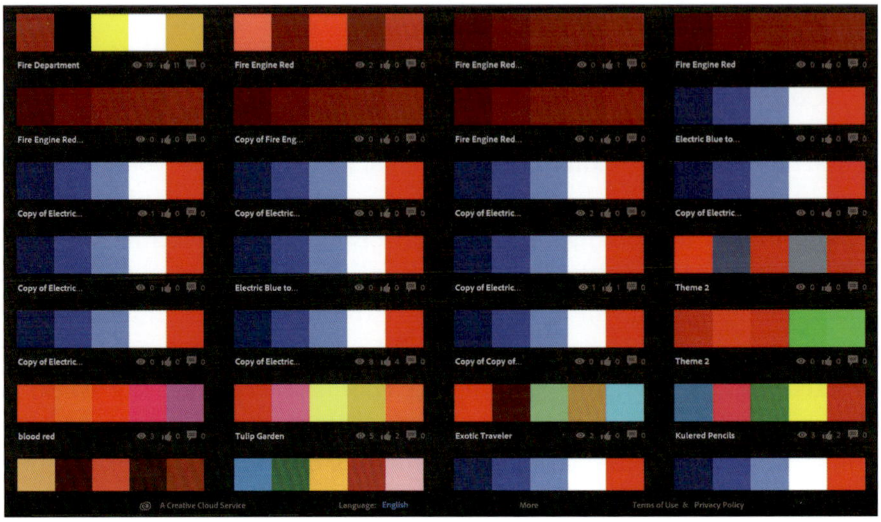

Or, instead of searching for a particular color, you can search for themes such as "industrial" or "autumn."

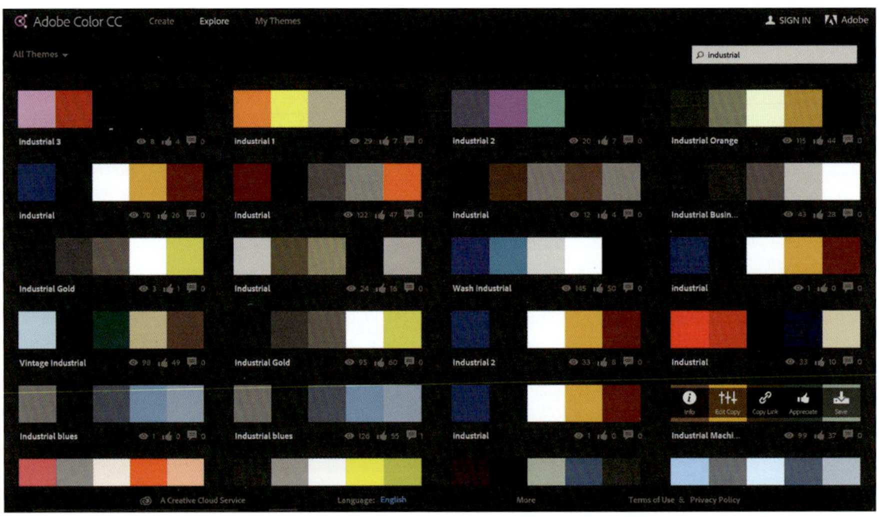

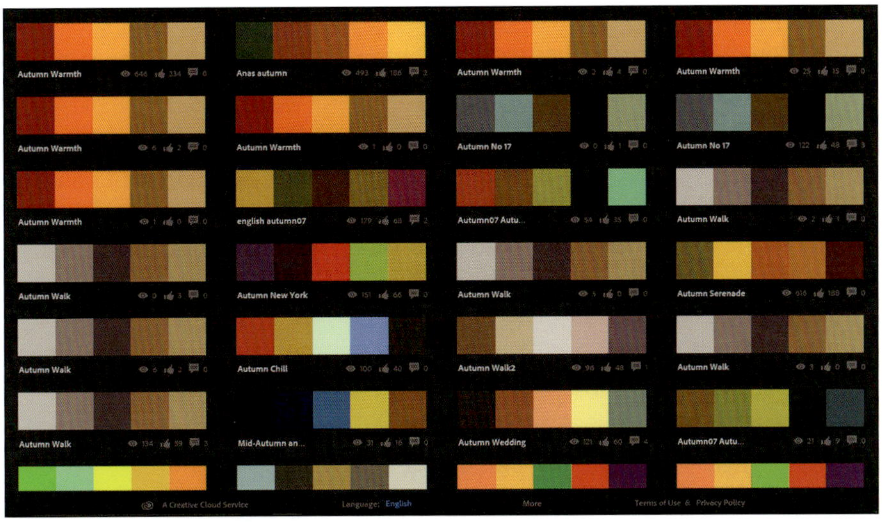

These combinations will spark ideas for headings, backgrounds, graphs, and even graphic elements in your slides. (And if you do have a program that integrates with Adobe Color directly, you'll be able to import the precise colors into your presentations.) There are other similar online resources for color ideas, such as Color Schemer (www.colorschemer.com), Paletton (paletton.com), and COLOURlovers (colourlovers.com). Whichever site you use, these tools are a great way to streamline the color selection process.

The Color Wheel

The color theory underlying the combinations in these online resources and much of color theory itself is reflected in the color wheel. Yes, the one we learned about in kindergarten. It starts with the primary colors—red, yellow, and blue—which cannot be made by mixing other colors together.

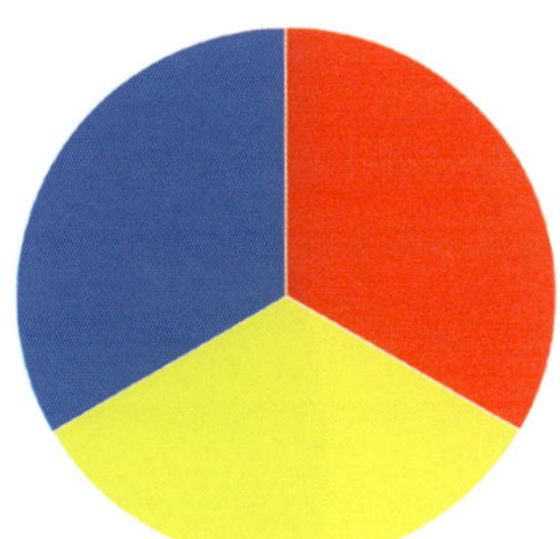

When primary colors are mixed together in equal amounts, we get secondary colors: green, purple, and orange.

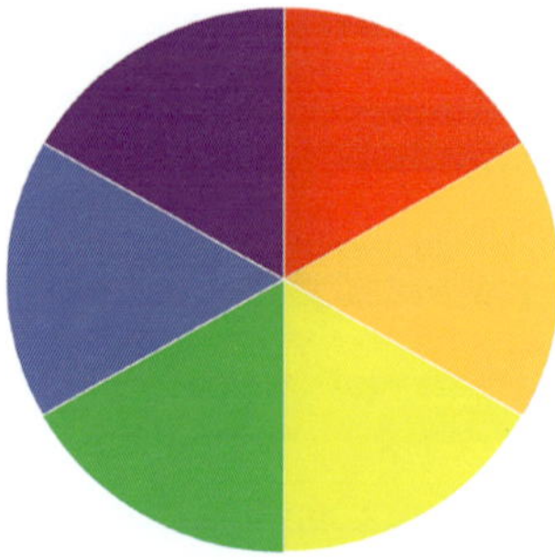

And when we mix those in equal amounts, we get tertiary colors: variously named red-orange, violet, bluish-purple, aqua, lime green, and yellow-orange.[5]

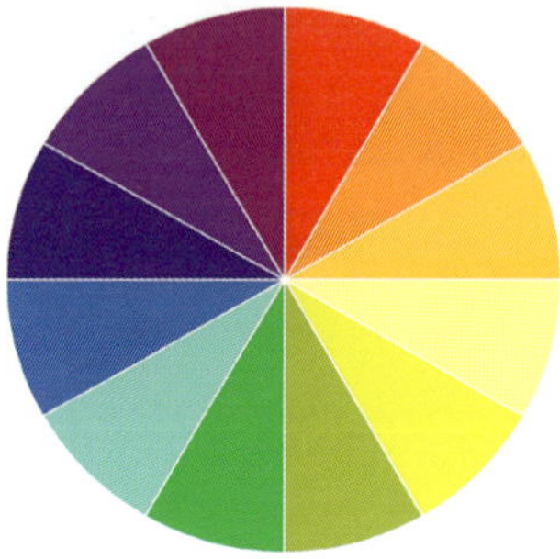

The wheel also divides colors by temperature, with warm colors the reds, oranges, and yellows and cool colors the greens, blues, and purples. When the color wheel is fully filled in, it includes shades and tints of each hue.

Basic Color Relationships[6]

Adobe Color and color theory in general have at their core some basic color relationships. Certain color combinations tend to work together well and are relatively easy to spot and select once you know they exist.

The color wheel images below are captured directly from Adobe Color, so you'll see how the program utilizes and depicts them. The circles within the wheel are default settings, which you can adjust however you like as you're creating color schemes for your visuals. The color blocks just below the wheel give you an immediate view of how the colors you've selected will work together.

Complements

Complements are colors directly across from each other on the color wheel.

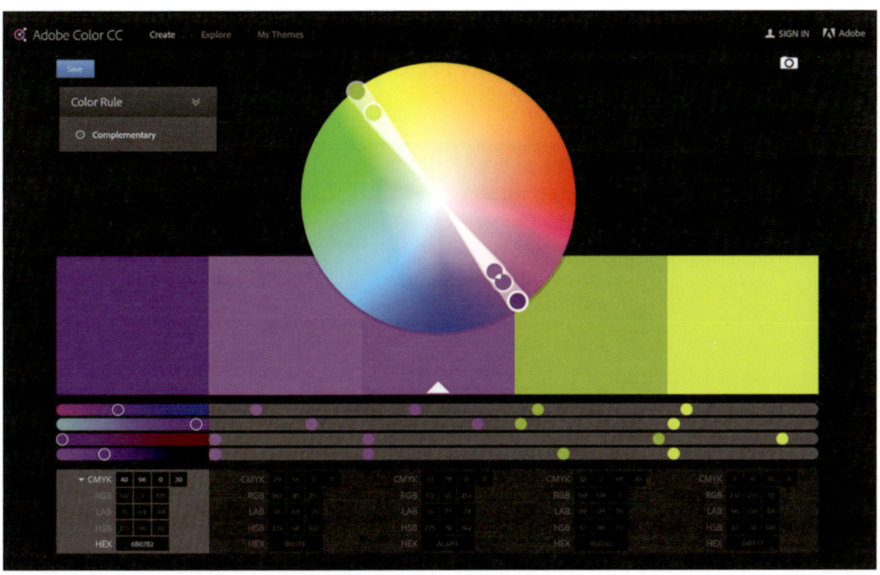

Be careful with complements—sometimes the contrast between complementary colors can be too strong and even illegible. You can mitigate this by adjusting tints, shades, and saturation, so the impact of the color contrast isn't so jarring.

Triads

Another successful color relationship is a triad of colors on the wheel—three colors equidistant from each other.

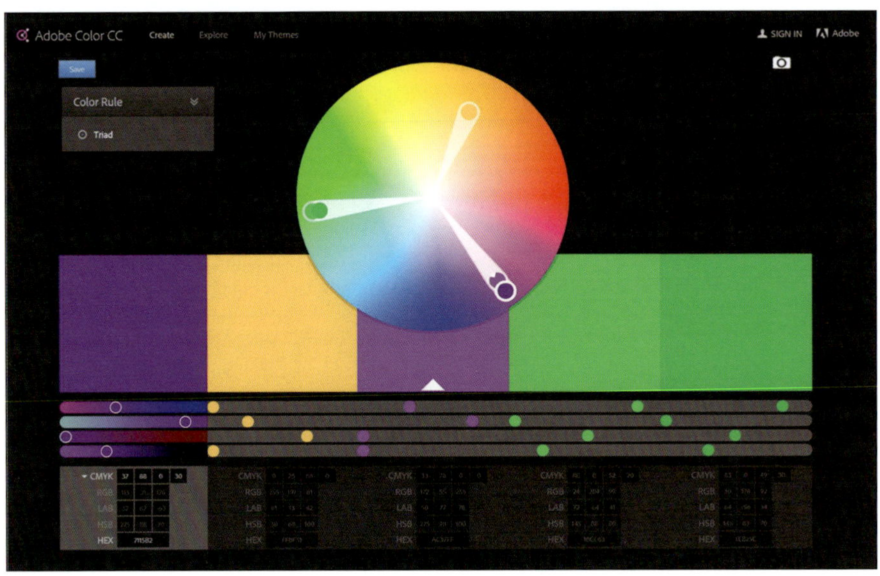

Analogous

A series of colors next to each other on the color wheel are called analogous colors. They work well together because each color is a blend of its immediate neighbors.

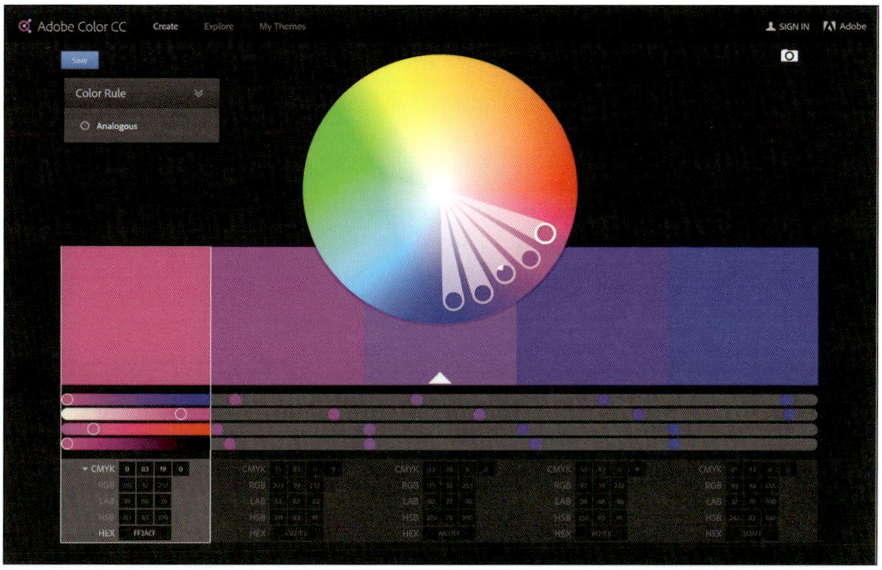

Monochromatic

Using one color in various shades and tints can create an obvious harmony in your slides, as the colors all originate from the same hue.

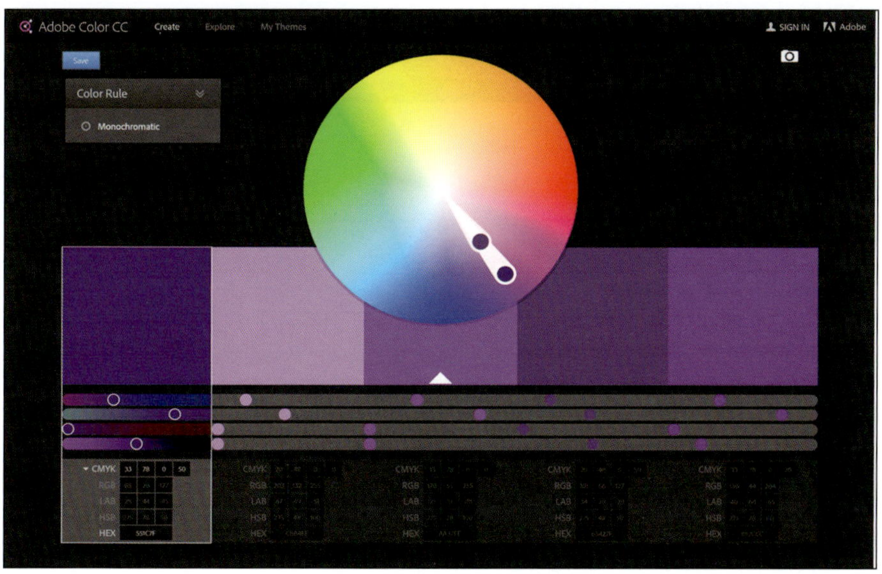

A monochromatic approach can be particularly effective for charts and graphs. In a bar graph, for example, if there's one data point (i.e., one bar) you want to call attention to, why make every bar a different color? With that approach, nothing stands out from the rest. Instead, using a monochromatic approach for less-important bars and a contrasting color for the point you want to emphasize will immediately direct your jury's attention to that key point. Just make sure the contrast between the shades and tints of a single hue is strong enough to be perceived when it matters.

Achromatic

Images are achromatic when the elements appear in black, white, and various shades of gray. Here, I set all colors to zero and simply selected five different shades along the continuum between (and including) black and white.

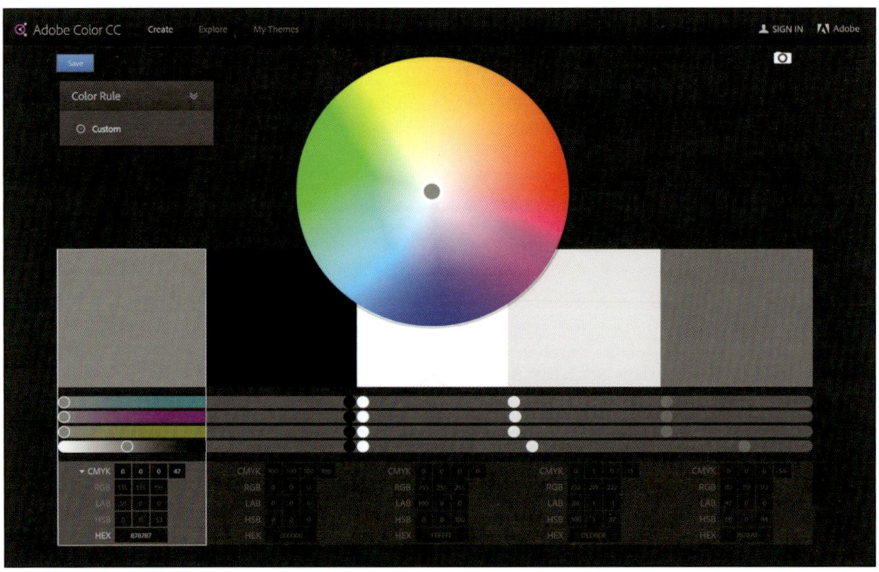

We can use an achromatic approach with just about anything, including photographs. With basic photo-editing software, it's actually quite easy to turn color photos into black-and-white pictures while still preserving the various tones. Simply convert the color to grayscale, and you're done. You could fully desaturate the image instead, but this approach tends to leave the image less vivid and mutes distinctions in tone.

For comparison, the original image is on the top, the middle image is converted to grayscale, and the image at the bottom is fully desaturated. The richness of the sky is maintained in the grayscale image but is nearly lost in the desaturated image.

Strategically introducing a single color or a specific area of color into an otherwise achromatic design will immediately focus the viewer's attention where you want it.

What would be Miller's motive?

Design and Presentation Tips for Color

Adjusting Color to Account for Trial Tone

Sometimes, you'll identify a color scheme you think would work well for your presentation, but the tone isn't quite right for trial. When that happens, try using shades or tints of your chosen colors. Adjusting the value of the colors can change the entire feel of the slide.

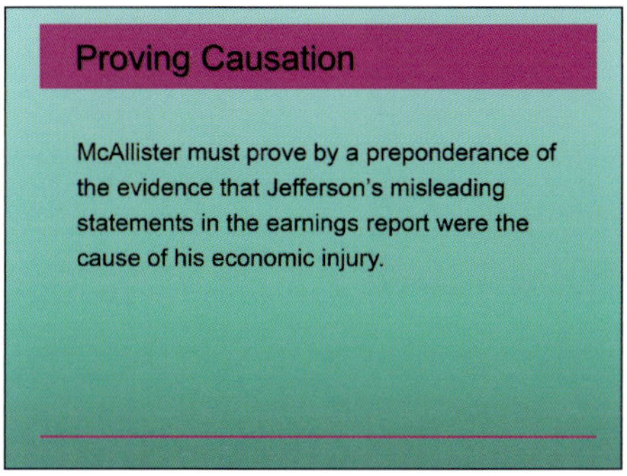

VS.

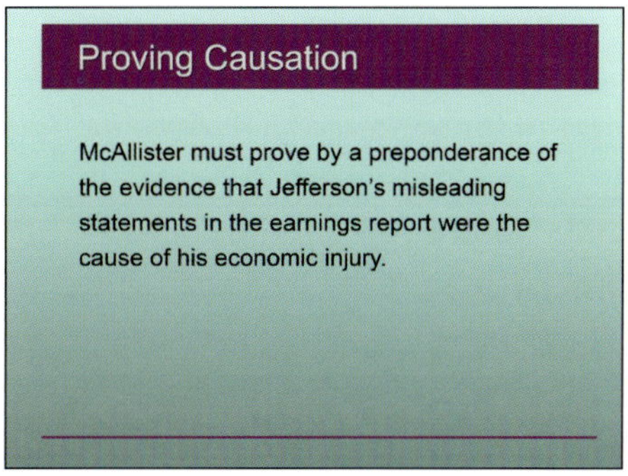

Color and Projected Light

Colors that work well together and provide sufficient contrast on your computer screen might look different when shown in the courtroom (or any presentation room). If you're showing the jury your slides on a computer or television monitor, there's less concern than if you're using a projector and screen. Light comes from behind a computer (or television) monitor and hits a viewer's eyes directly. So, there's a good chance that if you'll be showing your slides on a monitor, they'll look quite similar to what you created on the computer in your office.

The same is not true if you'll be using a projector and screen in court. With that approach, light leaves the projector, hits a screen, and then bounces off the screen to reach your eyes. As a result, colors aren't as bright and the contrast between them isn't as significant. What's more, the hue on the screen might not even look the same as it did on your computer when you created the presentation. These problems are exacerbated when the lights are on in the courtroom or when there's a good deal of daylight coming into the room through windows.

If at all possible, test how the colors will look in the courtroom, using the device you'll use in trial. You might need to adjust the projector or even adjust the colors in your presentation if they don't provide sufficient contrast. But even if you can't run a test, find out how you will be showing your images to the jury, and plan your colors and contrast accordingly. And if you just can't know too far in advance what your technology setup will be (e.g., if your courtroom or judge won't be assigned until close to trial), use a color palette with values and contrasts that will hold up regardless of the presentation method.

Color Interactions

Our perception of a color depends upon the colors around it, so colors look different in relation to one another. For example, light colors can look even lighter when they're next to (or on top of) a dark color.

Here, the same gray square looks lighter on the black background than it does on the white background.

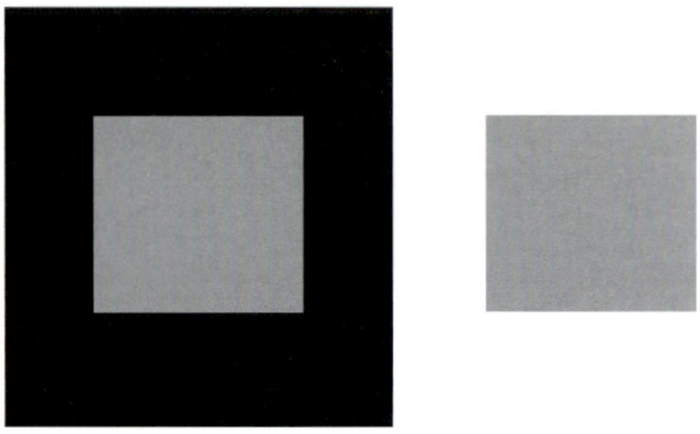

Even an object's size can appear different, depending on the color contrast between the object and the background. A white square on a black background will appear to be larger than the same size black square on a white background. These illusions can be even more pronounced depending on the image layout.

Color temperature—warm versus cool colors—can also impact how colors are perceived in relation to one another. Again, "warm" colors are the reds, oranges, and yellows, and "cool" colors are the blues, greens, and violets. Warm colors tend to pop into the foreground, while cool colors tend to fade into the background. (Neutral or crossover colors such as grays and beiges neither advance nor recede.)

So, when text is written in a cool color on a warm background, the slide tends to look flat. If you reverse the design, the warm-colored text floats on the page.

When you do use warm colors for backgrounds, consider adjusting the saturation or value to keep the slide from looking flat. But if you're looking for your text or graphics to pop, or even if you're just adding color contrast for emphasis (or to compensate for a tough courtroom setup), text in a warm color often works better. What matters most, of course, is maintaining a clear contrast between the background and the foreground elements of the slide.

Readability

Color contrast is powerful, but not if you can't read the text.

I mentioned this issue in Chapter 13. Yellow is typically the ideal highlighting color. Yellow is the lightest, brightest color in the spectrum. It is almost immediately perceived, even in low light. But if you're using a light background, then it should be obvious that putting the text in yellow doesn't provide enough contrast, and as a result it's difficult to read.

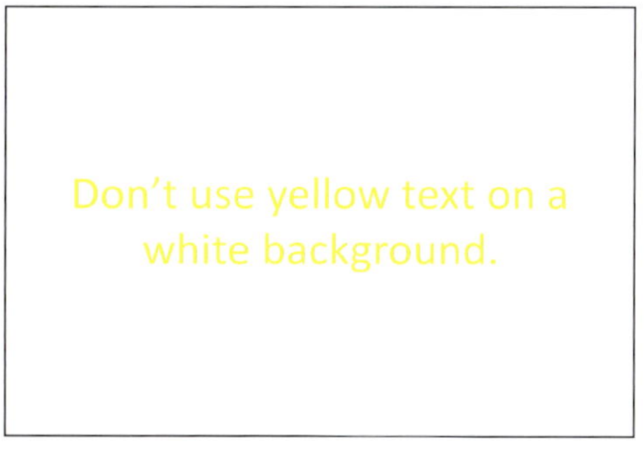

Another color effect to be mindful of involves "visual vibration." When we use bright text on a bright background—or really just two colors that are equal in their brightness value and which are essentially complimentary on the color wheel—the text is tough to read and can actually appear to be vibrating. The afterimages from the colors fight with each other.

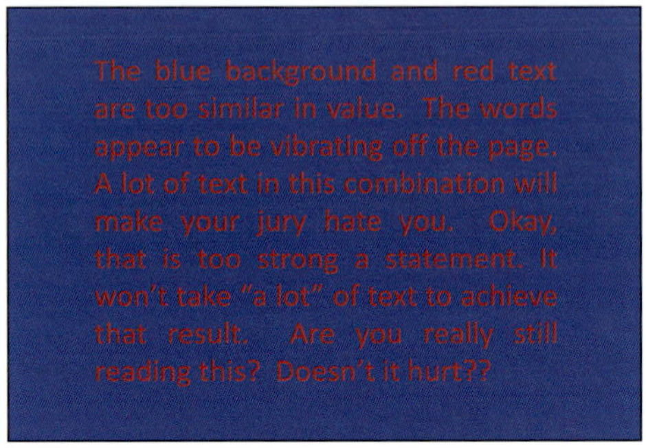

Once again, you can reduce this effect by adjusting the value of one or both colors. Use a lighter tint or darker shade, or consider inserting a neutral color between them so they aren't interacting with each other directly.

With text colors, just use common sense. If it looks hard to read, it is. Fortunately, it's not hard to fix this problem. One option is to adjust the value of the color to give it more contrast. Or, just pick a different color, one that contrasts more significantly with whatever's behind it.

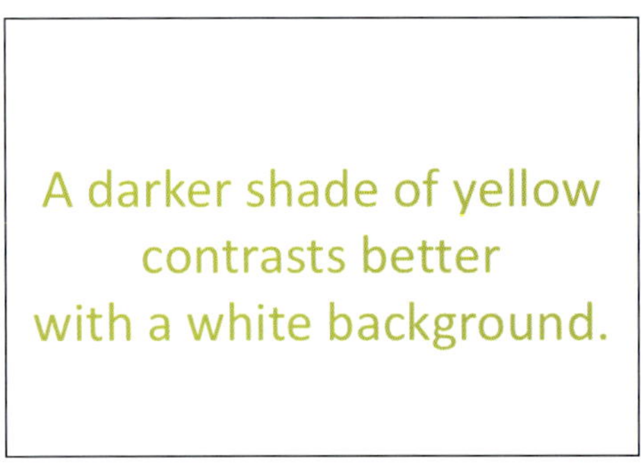

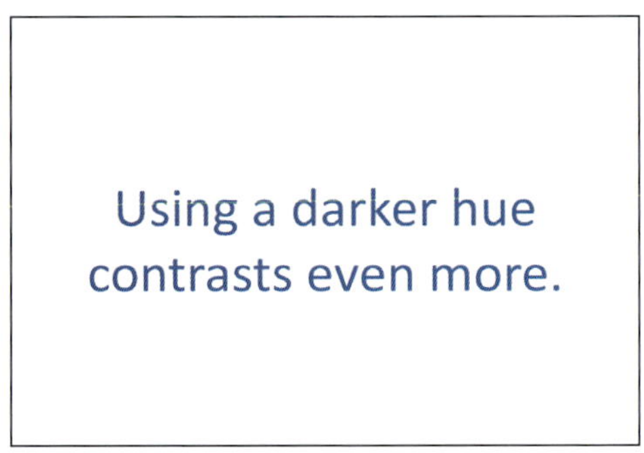

There are many other options, as well. You can use an outline or slight shadow behind each text letter or a larger shaded area behind the text in its entirety. With shadows, take care that they are not too pronounced. When done well, the shadow is barely noticeable. The goal is just to provide contrast, not to make our slides look three-dimensional.

Shadows work well when they're subtle.

Use too much, and you get an
annoying, nearly-illegible 3-D effect.

Color Vision Deficiency

As mentioned in Chapter 13 on typography, sometimes the legibility of your contrasting colors will differ by juror. If any of your jurors have a color vision deficiency (color blindness), your color choices might mean all the difference to them. Since the most typical color impairment is the inability to distinguish between red and green and distinguishing those colors from orange-yellow, avoid using a color combination of red or orange with green. Any color-blind jurors will miss the distinction. In her book *Slide:ology*, Nancy Duarte has a great tip to check for adequate color contrast before finalizing your color palette. She suggests printing the presentation on a black-and-white printer. If there are elements you can't distinguish from the background or from each other, then those elements could be indistinguishable for someone with a color vision deficiency.[7]

There's a lot to think about when working with color, but it doesn't have to be so overwhelming as to be paralyzing. Hopefully, with some color vocabulary and an appreciation for color relationships, the next time you create a presentation, you'll have a running start on selecting a color scheme that will best support your message.

20

Backgrounds

In earlier chapters, I talked about keeping certain design information in the "background" of your slide because it is less important than the substantive information you're communicating. Elements such as anchor lines connecting labels to what they're labeling or the row and column dividers in tables shouldn't command as much attention as your substantive elements. De-emphasizing that background information helps keep focus and order to the slide.

In this chapter, I'll address the literal background—the area of the slide against which we set all of our positive elements. Unless you're going to blindly rely on a default template in your software program, at some point you'll need to make a decision (and probably more than one) about the background you want to use for your visuals. When you do, consider three things: (1) is the background relevant; (2) is the information you're displaying over a particular background legible; and (3) when should you change backgrounds in the midst of a single presentation?

Relevance

Everything on the slide should be relevant to the topic of the slide. This includes the background. PowerPoint and other software programs provide templates that are busy and generally not relevant to most talks. Use common sense. I cannot begin to tell you how many slide presentations I've seen that incorporate odd shapes, swirls, and swooshes for no other reason, apparently, than to fill empty space.

If a background's relevance is not immediately apparent, the image fights with the text and will distract from your oral presentation. If you can't articulate what a background image has to do with your talk, don't use it.

Not only are these backgrounds irrelevant and distracting, they also present their own design challenges. Suddenly, you've introduced positive elements where there were none, which impacts the placement of your exhibits, text, graphs, or whatever else you were substantively hoping to communicate. Why in the world would you want to conform your entire presentation to irrelevant shapes on a random PowerPoint background template? You have also introduced a color scheme that may or may not make sense for your trial and that may or may not work with exhibits you'll need to display on the slide. These templates might be fine for party invitations, certificates of achievement, or the menu for your summer barbeque, but they're usually inappropriate, not to mention exceptionally limiting, for trial slides. Instead, carefully select your background to enhance your presentation.

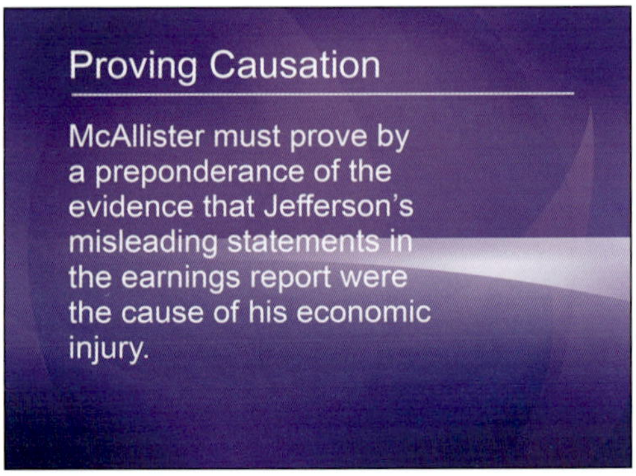

Legibility

Presumably, if you choose to place text on a slide, you want the audience to be able to read it. As I mentioned in Chapter 4, it should come as no surprise that text is tough to read on a busy background.

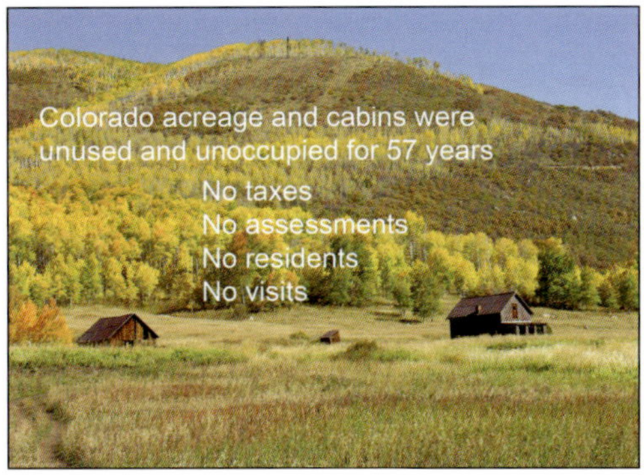

Generally, the busier your slide is, the simpler your background should be. But sometimes there's a good reason for using a busy background. A relevant photo might aid recall, or you might want to use a busy trial exhibit as the background on your slide when you're discussing its significance.

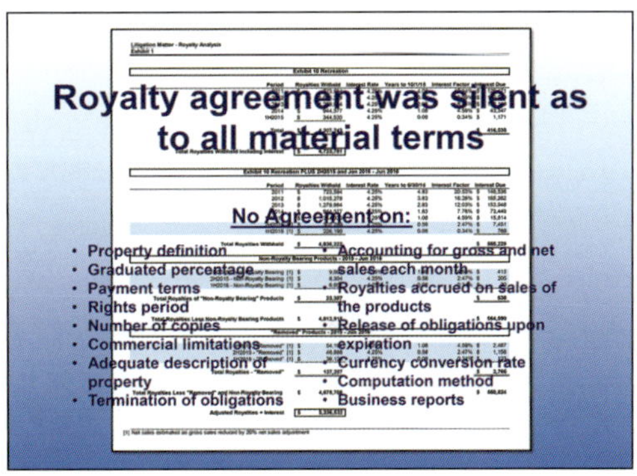

In one of my trials, for instance, an Excel spreadsheet was important substantively and memorable visually, as nearly every other exhibit in the case was a text-based email, letter, contract, or memorandum. I wanted the jurors to remember and potentially review the spreadsheet themselves during their deliberations. So, I displayed the exhibit during closing argument and kept it on the screen when I discussed its significance, using basic text to prompt note-taking jurors to jot down key points. The problem, of course, is that placing text over a spreadsheet can result in a readability problem.

One way to deal with this is to adjust the brightness, sharpness, and/or saturation of the image so it fades into the background, keeping emphasis on the foreground elements. In the bottom image on the right, I reduced all three characteristics of the background photograph, leaving the text much more readable than in the image above it.

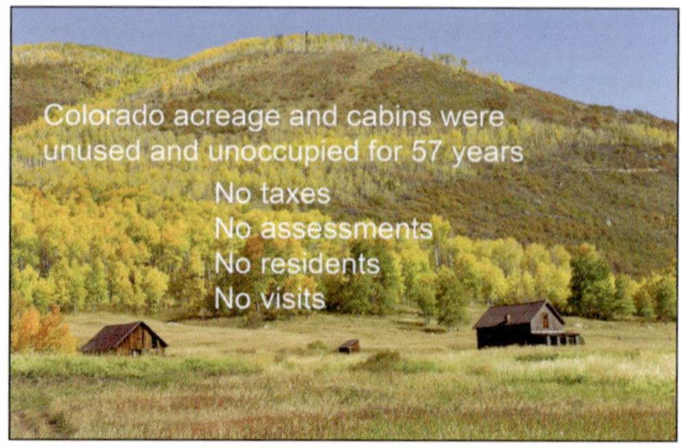

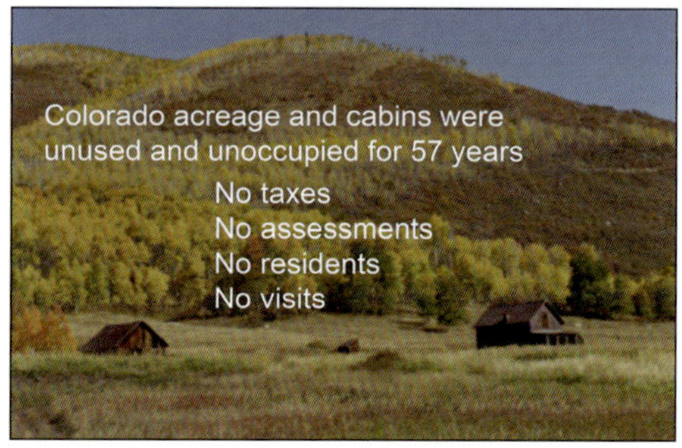

Don't forget why you're displaying the image in this context, though. If you want the jurors to remember it, make sure they can still see it.

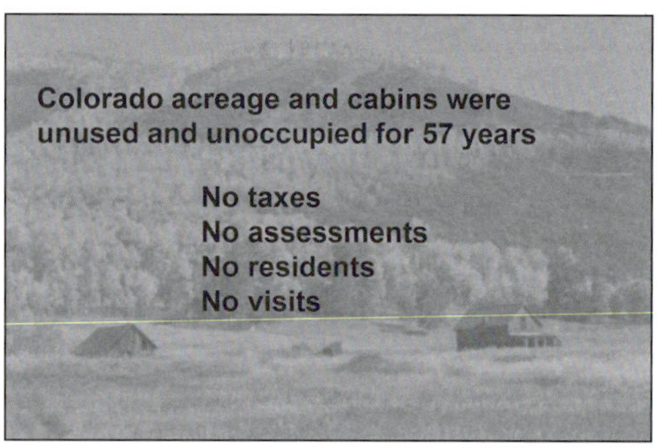

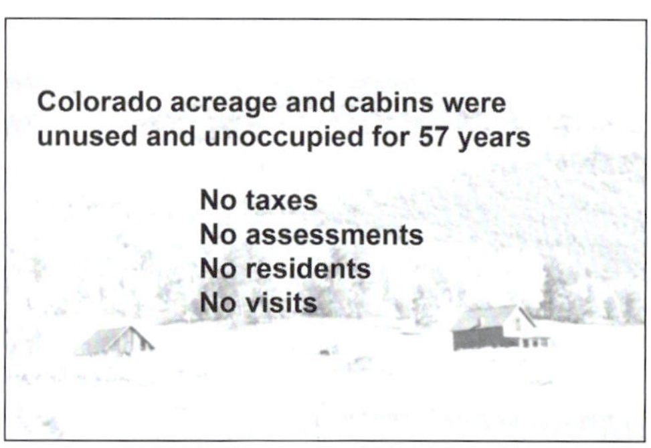

Converting the image to grayscale might match the mood of the slide more (it arguably does here, where the topic is abandoned property), but be careful it doesn't defeat the purpose of including the image at all. Moreover, when you modify an image so much that it's barely discernible, you create an unnecessary distraction as jurors struggle to figure out what the image is in the first place.

I showed you another option for keeping text legible over a busy background in Chapter 4. You can use boxes of color between the text and background. The color provides the contrast necessary to read the text. Alternatively, you can ghost those color boxes so the background image shows through subtly.

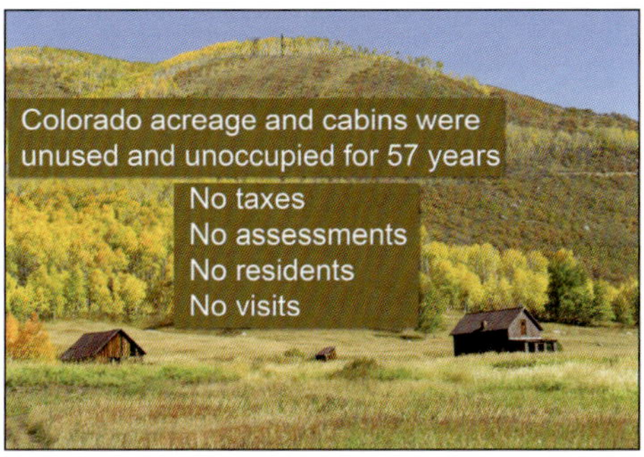

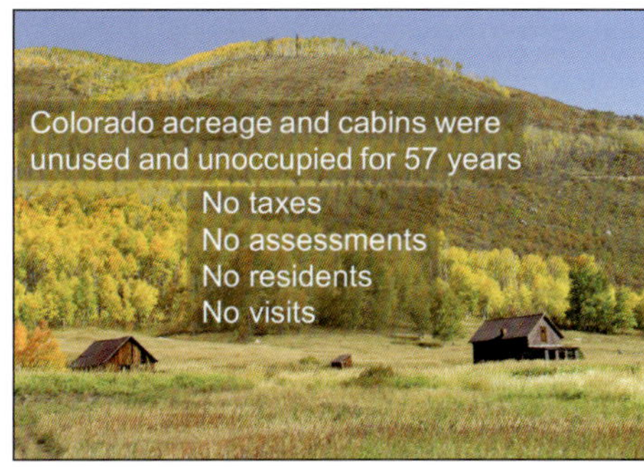

You can also consider leaving the exhibit or image on the screen, but shrinking it. There are many ways to design such a slide. Here are some ideas:

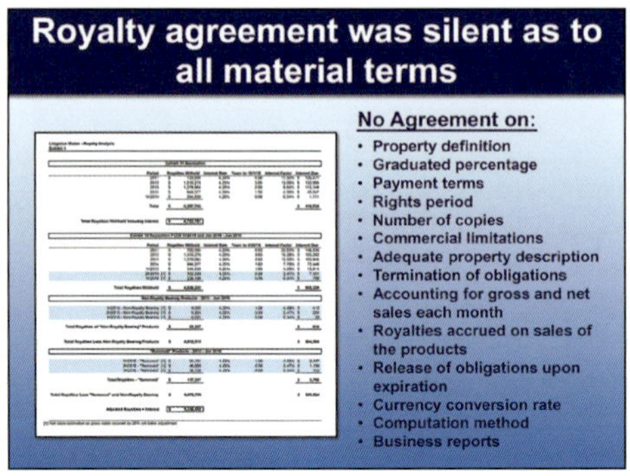

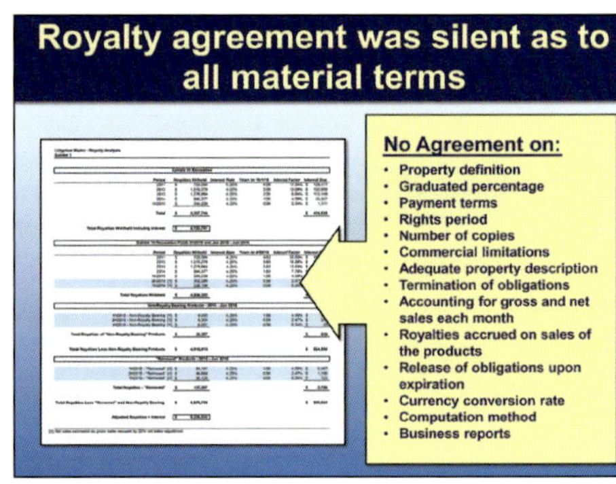

Whichever option you choose, just be consistent and use a similar technique throughout the presentation so everything looks purposeful and unified.

Changing Backgrounds

It's perfectly fine to use different backgrounds in the same presentation, as long as you can articulate *why* you're changing the background. As designer Robin Williams says, "[a] reason such as 'I'm tired of the blue spaceship background and now I want a green forest' is not a good reason."[1]

When you change the background on your slides, you're necessarily communicating a larger change to the jury. Typically, it's that you're about to cover a new topic, one that's not directly connected to the prior topic. This subtle message can be affirmatively useful *when you're actually changing topics.* I might use a different background when I shift from addressing factual claims in the case to addressing jury instructions. Or perhaps I might use a new background when I switch to a new case theme or when I'm discussing a different category of claims. There's certainly no rule that you have to change backgrounds, but if the change is purposeful and it's not a distraction from the presentation, changing a background can be a helpful tool for maintaining juror interest and creating visual memories.

PART IV

STRATEGIC CONSIDERATIONS

As with every other aspect of a trial, there are many strategic considerations in play with the use of jury visuals. In prior chapters of this book, I've focused on substance and design strategy. Now, I'll talk about trial strategy.

Obviously, strategic decisions are subjective. A lawyer's judgments will be informed by all sorts of factors—including the preferences and proclivities of each trial judge—that I couldn't possibly cover in this book. What I will provide, though, are considerations relating to jury visuals that will inform the strategic judgments you make in your own case.

For example, whether to object to an opponent's visual is a judgment call, but knowing your strategic options helps inform that judgment. Whether to use a computer-generated slide or draw on a flip chart is a judgment call, but knowing the benefits and drawbacks of both can inform that decision. And deciding when to start preparing jury visuals and how to staff your trial team to account for them are also judgment calls, but understanding the impact of that timing will, again, inform the decision.

In this section, I flag many of the ways in which visuals can be misleading, so you can spot them in your opponent's visuals and avoid them in your own. I also give you some ideas for using your opponent's misleading visuals to your advantage if you strategically choose not to object (or if your objection is overruled). I pass along practical tips for creating and proofreading your visuals and for working with graphic designers. And I share tips for using high- and low-tech visuals during trial and suggest backup plans, regardless of how you're presenting your visuals. Finally, in the last chapter I provide an overview of how federal and state courts around the country are treating demonstrative evidence and the issues that often arise from its use.

It's critical to appreciate and account for these issues before you embark upon a time-consuming (and in some cases, expensive) effort creating your visuals. Doing so helps ensure that you can actually use what you create. It also best positions you to create the most effective visuals possible for your jurors.

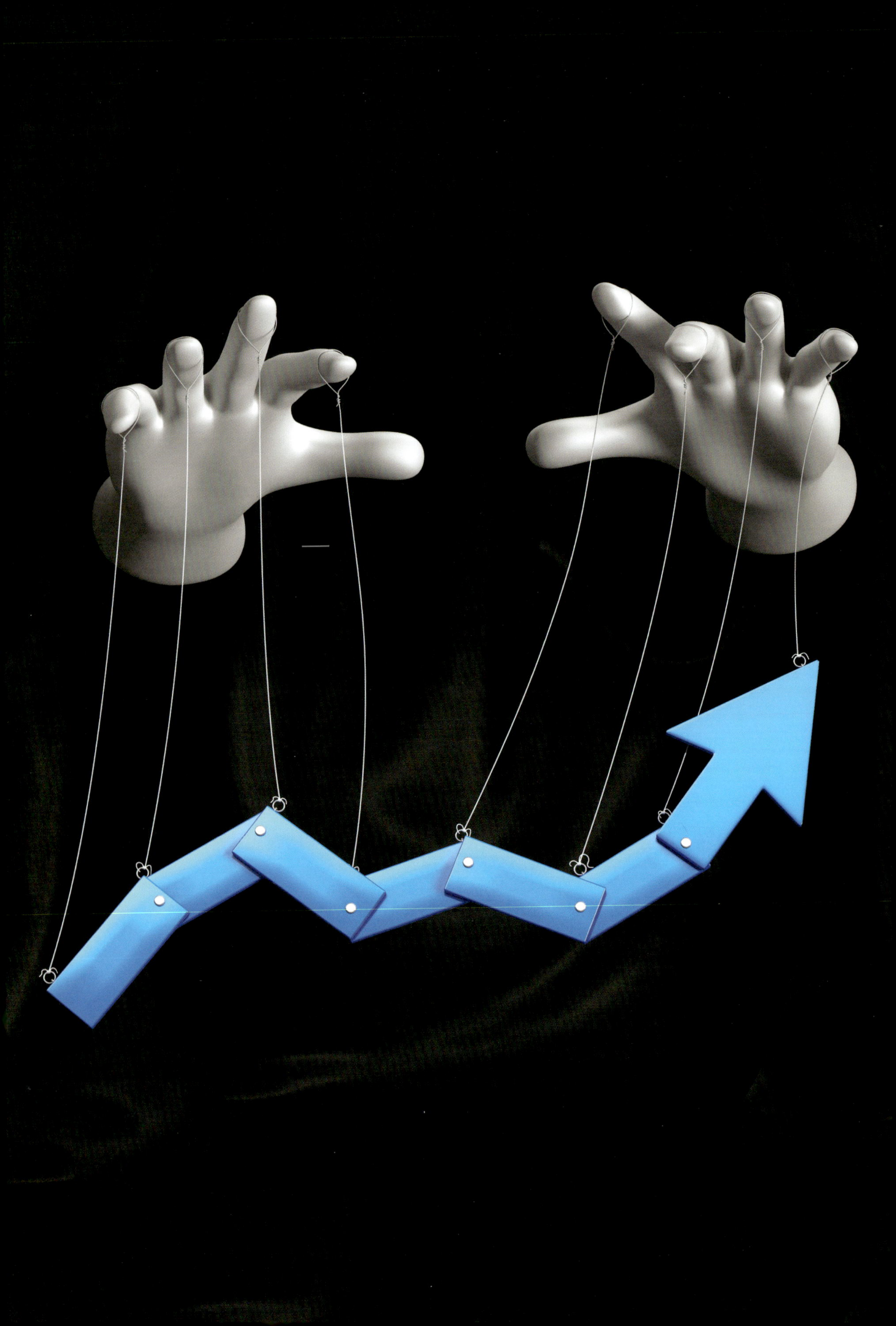

21

Spotting Misleading Visuals: Objecting vs. Using Them to Your Advantage

Many judges require us to exchange visuals with our opponent before we show them to the jury. The exchange might be weeks, days, or mere hours before the visuals are used. Other judges don't require an exchange at all. Lawyers just display their visuals, and opponents see them at the same time as the jurors do.

Whenever you see your opponent's visuals, if you have a visceral reaction to an image, carefully consider the most effective response. Your instinct might be to object immediately and seek exclusion (or a limiting instruction), which might be the most appropriate strategy. But consider whether, instead, you can use your opponent's misleading visual to your advantage.

If a visual is truly prejudicial, certainly one option is to argue for its exclusion. You can't unring the bell, and if the visual is egregious, you might need to keep it away from the jury rather than try to explain it away after they've seen it. If the problem is nuanced or tough to explain, the jury might infer that you're worried, desperate, or petty if you try to address it. And, of course, moving to exclude the visual might be the only practical option if your opponent might use it in rebuttal, such that you'll have no opportunity to address it afterward.

But often you can get a lot more mileage out of *using* your opponent's slide than you can from excluding it. If the slide is obviously and materially misleading, then simply pointing that out to your jury may be sufficient to damage your opponent's credibility. (And lest you think no lawyer would be foolish enough to chance this outcome by using such an egregious slide, I promise you, I've seen it done.)

Depending on the timing of the slide exchange, you might be able to do more than just point out the problem. You might have time to mark up your opponent's slide to highlight its deceptions or even to redesign the slide and show what it would look like if it weren't misleading. This, too, has the effect of harming your opponent's credibility in a more effective way. You're essentially creating a visual memory of your opponent's deception.

Strategically, if your judge doesn't require an exchange of visuals before they're shown to the jury, then your first opportunity to object will be in front of the jury. This, of course, raises its own strategic considerations. You'll call attention to the problem and might signal that you're worried. The objection is all the more dramatic if it occurs during opening or closing. And if your objection is overruled, the judge will have seemingly given the visual a stamp of approval.

Ultimately, whether to object is a strategic decision that will depend on a host of factors. You'll need to consider the law in your jurisdiction, your judge's temperament, the materiality of the slide at issue, appellate preservation, and even your subjective assessment of how trial has been going.

My focus in this chapter will be on identifying some of the common ways visuals can be misleading to help you spot them in your opponent's slides and avoid them when you design your own. I'll also give you an example of an opponent's slide I redesigned for use in trial, and I'll suggest some quick fixes if one of your slides is successfully challenged by your opponent.

What to Watch Out For

As you might imagine, there are a lot of ways to manipulate the visual display of data and information. Be on alert for these tactics, whether they're presented through a high- or low-tech medium.

Three-Dimensional Graphs

When your opponent introduces a graph using three-dimensional elements, review it very carefully. Three-dimensional bar graphs, pie graphs, and even line graphs can optically distort data. In a pie graph, for example, whichever slice is closest to the viewer takes up more space on the slide simply because it's depicted in three dimensions. That slice is emphasized over the others, and the data it represents may appear larger than it should.

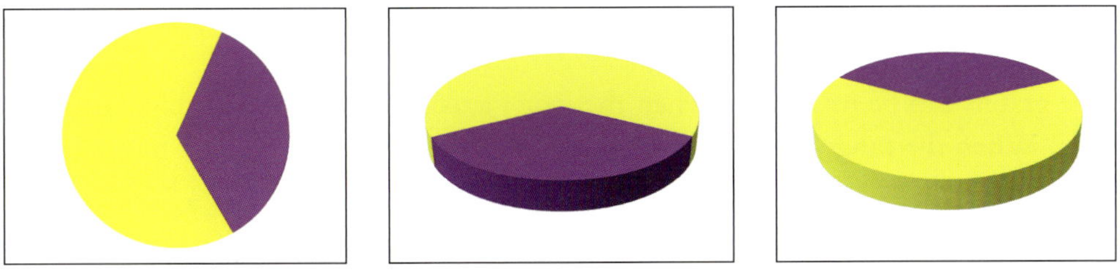

Above, the purple pie slice is the same size in all three graphs. But it looks larger in the central graph, thanks to the three-dimensional display. The same holds true for line and bar graphs, particularly when they're shown from odd angles and when combined with odd shapes.

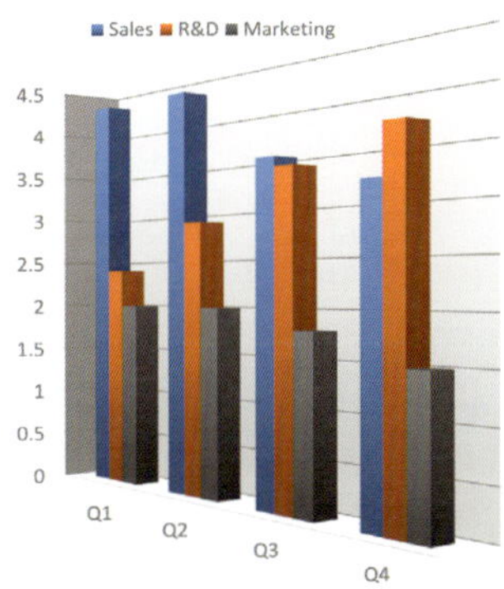

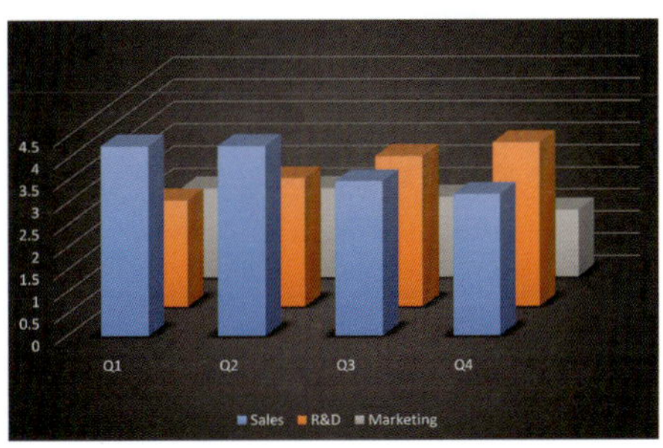

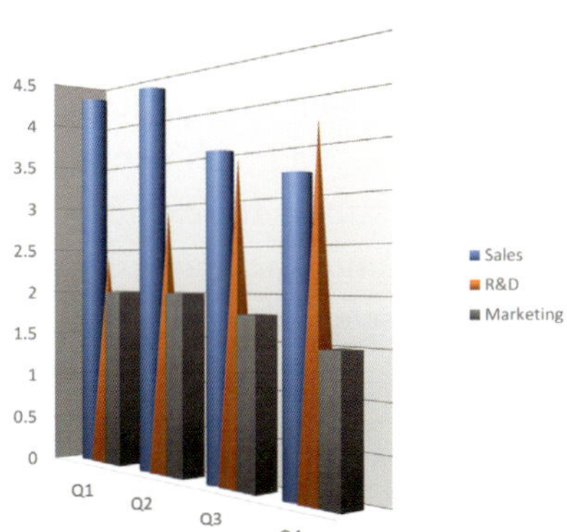

Unreasonable Axis Range

Line graphs can be misleading when the *x* or *y* axis range is unreasonably narrow or wide. When the range is too narrow, relatively small changes can look huge. When it's too wide, large changes look deceptively small. If data is changing by tens, then using *x* axis intervals of one hundred will make the change look very different than intervals of five.

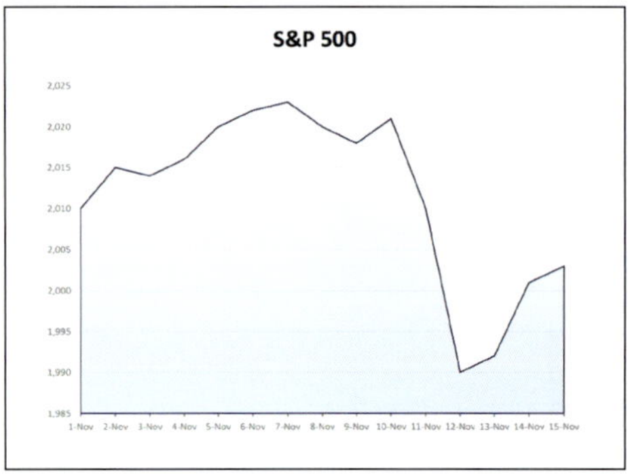

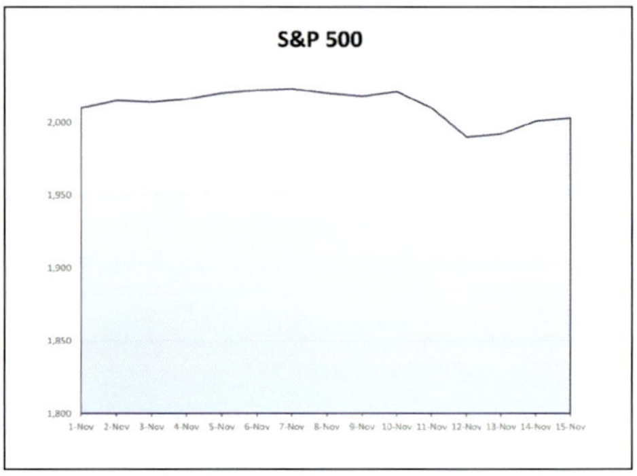

So, to avoid being misleading, ask yourself what range is reasonable to represent on a line graph. If daily data is critical, then depicting changes on a quarterly basis won't accurately depict the change that occurred during the five-day span at issue in the trial. (Showing the quarterly data might still be relevant, of course, if you're trying to demonstrate the lack of a long-term effect of that seemingly significant five-day data event.)

Moreover, we're used to the *x* axis beginning at zero. If you design a graph and the *x* axis does not begin at zero or at least at an otherwise logical starting point for the case (such as the first day of the quarter), make sure you've made that design choice obvious if it otherwise could be misleading.

Elimination of Context

Graphs are also misleading when they eliminate material context, such as when someone selectively uses the available data. If a graph depicts a single month out of a year, profits for one department in a company to the exclusion of others, or a data trend cut too short to show a change in the trend, the graph is misleading if the fuller data set matters to the interpretation of the selected portion.

In a recent trial, an important theme for my client's case was that a key division of the company was failing financially. My opponent, understandably not very keen on that theme, repeatedly emphasized that the division showed positive revenue in seven out of the last sixteen months.

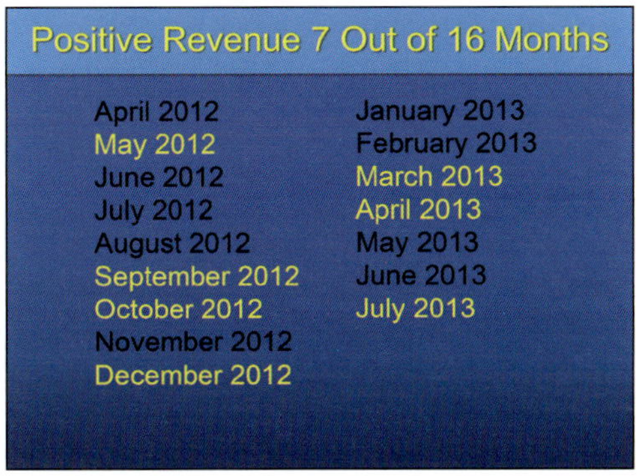

The slide above was not used by my opponent; rather, it's my own representation of their theme. I strategically chose a dark background and used black text for the unprofitable months, forcing that text to blend into the background. I used a warm color (yellow) in a midtone value for the seven profitable months so they would pop off the page. A clearer data depiction (such as a graph) would have revealed the misleading nature of the message, so I went with a basic text list and manipulated the design to underscore the theme, which my opponent verbally emphasized repeatedly.

Although the list is technically accurate, it is out of context and misleading. The division posted positive revenue in seven of the sixteen preceding months, but not by much. And those seven months were far outweighed by the other nine months of the relevant period, during which revenue dropped dramatically. *Context* revealed the truth:

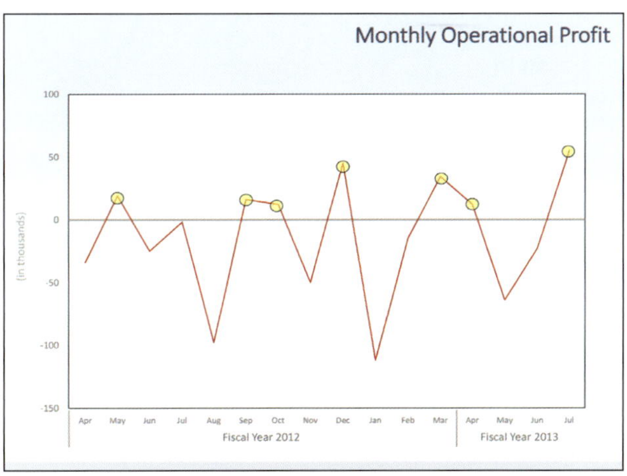

Viewing the data on a quarterly basis underscored the point even more. Indeed, the division was in the red in every single quarter, by a substantial margin.

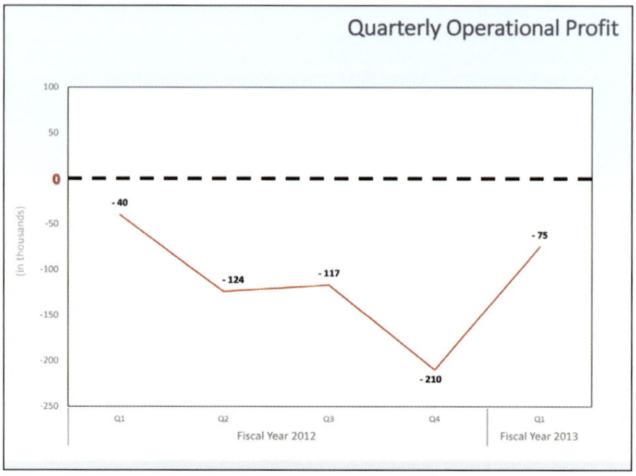

Order vs. Magnitude

Tufte reminds us that numbers have a magnitude in addition to an order.[1] Watch for this on your opponents' slides (as well as your own). While a diagram might arrange objects correctly in an order, that doesn't mean the diagram is accurately depicting the size of the objects' differences.

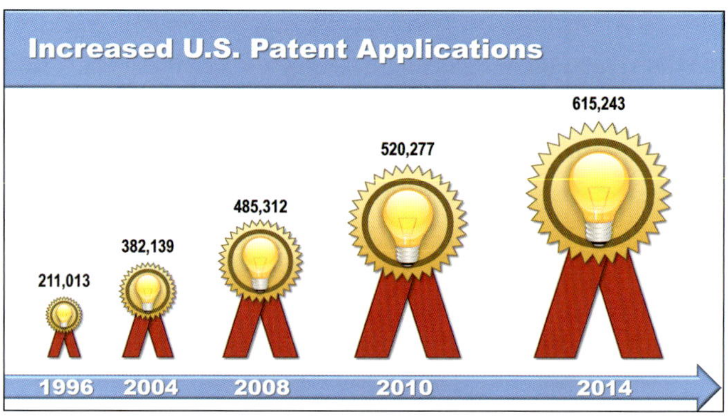

On this slide, for example, the ribbons are depicted in the correct order; each ribbon gets larger as it represents increasing numbers of applications. But the ribbons are not to scale, so they aren't accurately representing the *magnitude* of the increase from one listed year to the next.

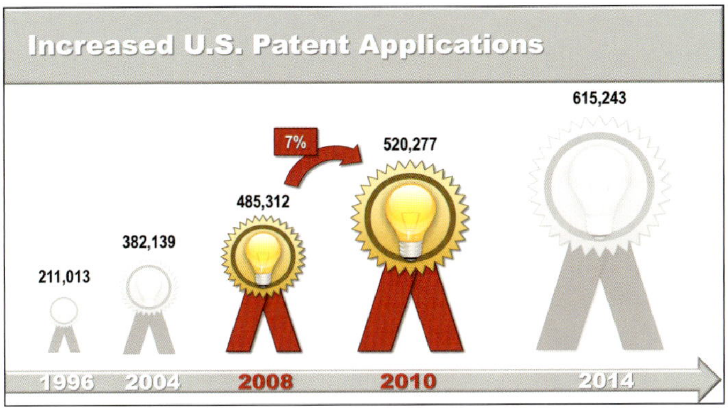

For instance, as illustrated above, between 2008 and 2010 the number of patent applications increased by seven percent (from 485,312 patents to 520,277 patents). So the 2010 ribbon should only be seven percent bigger than the 2008 ribbon, which would barely be perceptible on the slide. Instead, the 2010 ribbon is much larger than the 2008 ribbon, visually suggesting a larger increase than actually occurred.

The problem is even more stark when we compare 1996 to 2014, below.

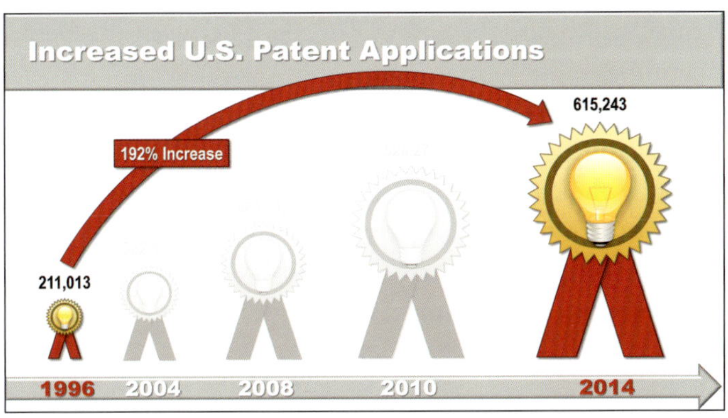

The increase is 192%. That's still just three times as large; so the 2014 ribbon should be about three times the size of the 1996 ribbon. But the 2014 ribbon is much larger—well over twelve times bigger.

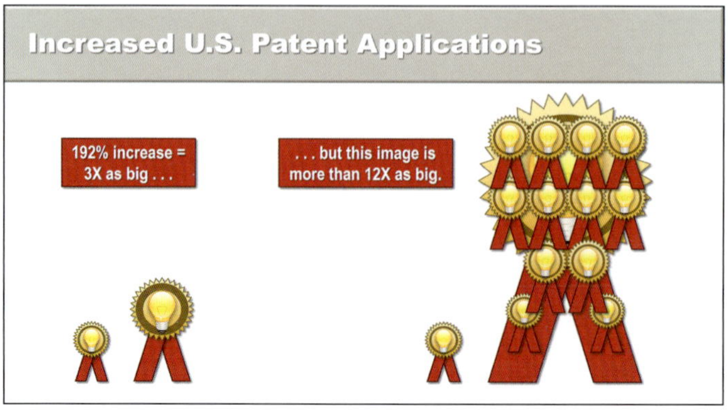

Once again, the size of the ribbons visually suggests a significantly larger increase in patent applications than the data actually shows.

Misleading depictions of magnitude often result from enlarging or shrinking an image proportionally—i.e., changing both the length and width—without accounting for the reality that we've now changed the size of the object by twice as much. We end up with a misleading image that suggests a greater or lesser difference than actually exists.

Similarly, when white space is used to imply a measurement of magnitude, such as the passage of time, make sure the amount of space between the elements accurately conveys that magnitude.

Notice the timeline at the bottom of the patent application visual. The years with the most amount of time between them—1996 to 2004 (eight years)—are placed the closest together along the continuum. The inaccuracy here is relatively glaring, since measurements of time (years) are directly reflected in the labels themselves. But be careful when the measurement is merely implied—when time, size, or anything else of substantive meaning is conveyed purely through the space between images.

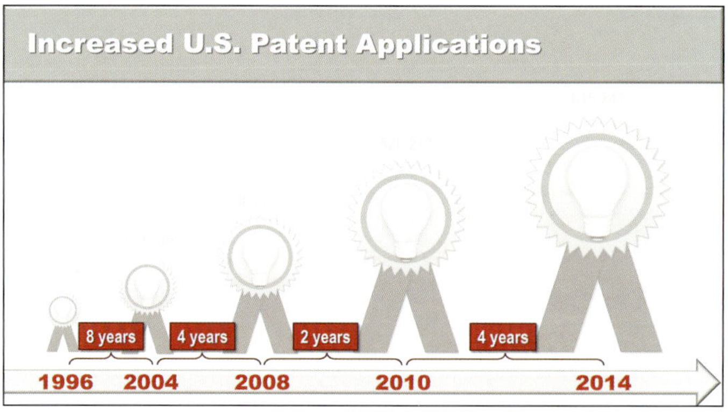

In the patent application slide, the spacing between the year markers (on what would be the *x* axis of the slide) is inconsistent. From a pure design standpoint, the years are centered under their corresponding ribbons. But the space between the years gives an inconsistent, and therefore misleading, sense of the passage of time.

Compare Apples to Apples

Most of us are used to scrutinizing textual statements to make sure comparisons are reasonable. But train yourself to look for this in visual depictions of data, as well. For instance, in the Medicare fraud infographic I showed you in Chapter 10 (page 145), an identical grouping of just seven "people," in the same size, is used to depict four different numerical data points: 243, 46, 44, and 82, respectively.

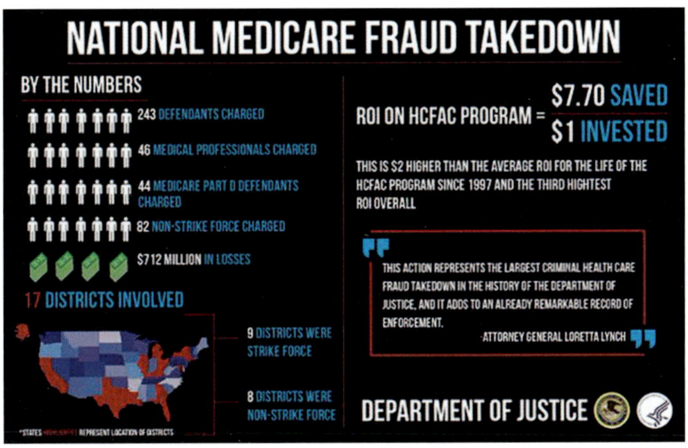

If those numbers matter in the case (and presumably they do or they wouldn't be depicted on the slide), then you'll need to make a strategic decision whether to object or whether instead to point out to the jury the misleading nature of the visual.

False Legal or Factual Implications

Blatantly incorrect statements of fact or law are relatively rare and usually result from a mistake. When your opponent does make an incorrect statement of law or fact on a visual, it's pretty easy to spot. What's tougher is spotting the subtle false implications that can creep into a visual's design.

For example, one of my opponents in a civil securities fraud trial sought to use slides such as this during closing argument:

The year before, after a nearly four-month trial, a jury fully acquitted my client of criminal charges stemming from the same conduct. In the subsequent civil trial, the plaintiff wanted to emphasize that the civil burden of proof, a preponderance of the evidence, was substantially smaller than the criminal burden to prove guilt beyond a reasonable doubt. Putting a percentage on the burden of proof wasn't allowed, so the lawyer chose to visually depict the burdens. But the difference between the liability sides of the "preponderance" scale was barely perceptible. And the guilt side of the "beyond a reasonable doubt" scale was nearly grazing the table. Both scales visually exaggerated the burdens, and both were misleading.

My team and I chose to object to these slides. If we'd allowed the plaintiff to use them and tried arguing to the jury why one side of the scale should be "a bit lower" or some unspecified amount higher, we could have looked petty and desperate. But the burden of proof is certainly not a collateral issue. So, we raised the objection with the judge, and she quickly excluded these slides.

Any element can imply legal or factual substance in a design, which means it can imply inaccurate substance. When illustrating a process, for instance, the way we choose to depict the flow suggests other things about the process than just the order of steps. The length of an arrow leading from one step to the next could suggest the amount of time that step takes when compared to other arrows in the chart. If most arrows are shorter, a longer arrow might suggest a longer time period. If that's not accurate, the visual is misleading.

Similarly, the size and placement of boxes or images in a flowchart could suggest whether those steps or inputs should be given equivalent weight or even whether they operate independently.

In this flowchart, the three stacked inputs are the same size, and they don't overlap. The visual might otherwise be accurate in that all three inputs do make their way into the final product, but the

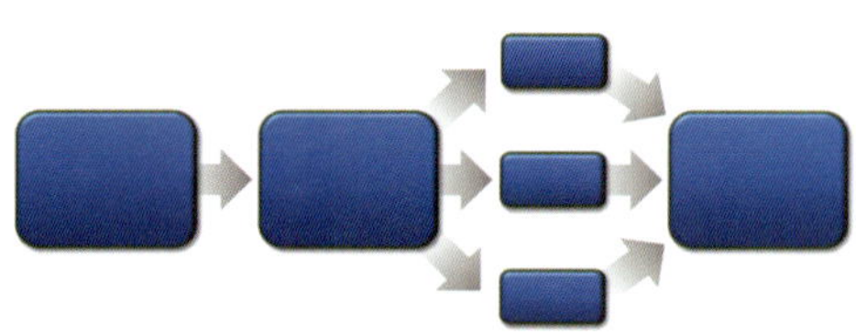

inputs might not be of equal weight, they might not occur at precisely the same time, and they might not be mutually exclusive. If the theme being depicted is causation, for example, then such a slide could imply more or fewer steps necessary to establish causation than are really required.

There are many other ways to misrepresent facts on a visual. Your opponents might quote a deposition transcript, play a video clip, or display a portion of a document out of context. They might even string documents or testimony together to imply a causal effect or another relationship when the implication is unsupported by the evidence.

My approach to these slides is the same as my approach to any misleading slide. If it makes sense to object, I will. But if I think I can use the slide to my advantage, highlighting or redesigning it, I often do that instead. This approach can be particularly effective when the misleading slides involve case exhibits. The jury will be able to examine exhibits themselves, so unlike thematic visuals or those depicting data analysis, I can simply point out the problem and direct jurors to another part of the exhibit.

Logical Fallacies

Errors in logic that sometimes plague written and oral arguments can also impact demonstratives. Non sequiturs, circular reasoning, exaggeration, and other logical fallacies we object to in a brief are just as objectionable in a visual. Watch out for these.

Sometimes the fallacy will be obvious, and it might even be an issue in your case. Causation versus correlation (a subcategory of *post hoc, ergo propter hoc*—i.e., after this, therefore because of it) is a common one. The plaintiff says the defendant's actions caused a particular event or injury; the defendant says his actions merely coincided with the event but didn't cause it. If it's a key issue in your case, you'll spot it in a demonstrative. To be sure, in that context the demonstrative might be perfectly appropriate, overtly setting forth the plaintiff's or defendant's view on that issue. But it still creates a visual memory for the jury that is contrary to your case point of view, so make sure to call jurors' attention to it if the fallacy isn't obvious.

Other logical fallacies are more subtle, but their use in a demonstrative can have a material impact on the jury. For example, a visual might imply a false dilemma, suggesting that only two or three options exist when in fact there are additional reasonable alternatives. A visual that relies on an analogy can introduce a false dilemma, or the analogy can promote other logical fallacies by virtue of its own shortcomings. (Analogies can be dangerous that way!) There are hundreds of logical fallacies. Knowing their names isn't nearly as important as recognizing when they've crept into your opponent's slides. So, when you're examining the other side's visuals, pay attention to conclusions that don't quite flow from the premise.

Misleading Text

Watch out for misleading text on visuals. Carefully read column and row headings in tables, axis labels on graphs, and even descriptions on diagrams. They all have the potential to mislead. Likewise, titles and explanatory text can unfairly characterize a document, a witness's testimony, a party's position, the results of data analyses, and just about anything else. And, of course, text that's purely inflammatory is objectionable for that reason alone.

One way to avoid objectionable text in your own slides, particularly when you want to include text that is not entirely neutral, is to use direct quotes. You can pull quotes from documents, expert reports, and witness testimony. In one of my own cases, multiple witnesses called by both sides testified about a series of industry bankruptcies that threatened to collapse a government program. I certainly would have been safe titling a summary slide "Bankruptcies" or "Industry Bankruptcies." But one opposing witness described the bankruptcies as "devastating," and that theme was consistent across every witness who testified about them. So, my heading was "Devastating Bankruptcies," and it drew no objection. Framing the heading as a question rather than a declarative statement, when appropriate, is another way to potentially avoid an objection.

Just don't ignore the obvious. If you'd object to a statement made verbally to the jury, the statement doesn't suddenly become acceptable because it's in a pretty font on a colorful slide next to a clip art image of a gavel.

Overcomplicated Visuals

Messy visuals can obscure data. Pay close attention to charts, graphs, and diagrams with so much extra stuff on them that it's hard to discern the conclusion or comparisons being depicted. Although disorganization, excess decoration, and other "chartjunk" might just be poor design, when the mess on the slide hides or even skews information, the visual might be legally objectionable.

When designing your own visuals to depict data, keep in mind that simple, organized visuals are usually more understandable and more credible. Messy data displays overwhelm the jury; they won't understand or won't trust the message. If jurors think you're purposely trying to conceal or distort information, your credibility is shot. What a shame it would be for jurors to assume you're intentionally hiding something when really you just have a messy slide.

Using Your Opponent's Visuals

As I mentioned at the beginning of this section, if you get your opponent's slides in time, you can use them in your own case to undermine your opponent's credibility. One approach is to copy your opponent's slide wholesale into your own presentation and add your own descriptions or emphasis to whatever is misleading. This approach is relatively quick, as all you're really doing is adding text or highlights to a preexisting slide.

Another option is to actually redesign your opponent's slide so it's not misleading, and show the jury how the slides differ. For example, I had a trial in which the government used a slide materially identical to this one in its opening statement:

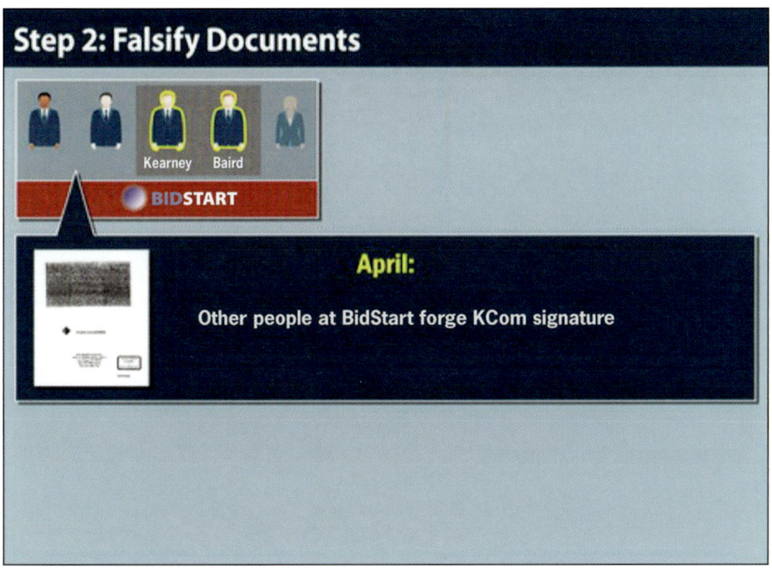

The descriptive text, that "other people" forged a signature, is connected to the box containing five generic characters. Two of those characters, highlighted and named, were defendants in the trial. The other nameless people who forged signatures are represented by a generic African-American man, a white man, and a blonde woman.

At trial, however, there was no question whatsoever that the two defendants named and highlighted on this slide had *nothing to do with forging signatures*. In fact, the three people who committed the forgery (presumably the other three generic characters on the slide) had already pled guilty and had begun serving prison terms. They even testified at trial pursuant to cooperation agreements with the government.

Of course, during opening statements (when this slide was used), before any witnesses testified or any documents were introduced, the jury had no way to evaluate the exceptionally misleading nature of the slide.

Rather than object, however, we let the government use the slide. We knew what the evidence would show, and we had plenty of time to redesign the slide for our own closing argument.

Trial went on for nearly two months, and as expected, the evidence unequivocally showed that the two highlighted defendants had nothing to do with the forged signatures. Not surprisingly, the government didn't use this slide again during its closing argument.

But in our closing, we reminded the jurors of this slide.

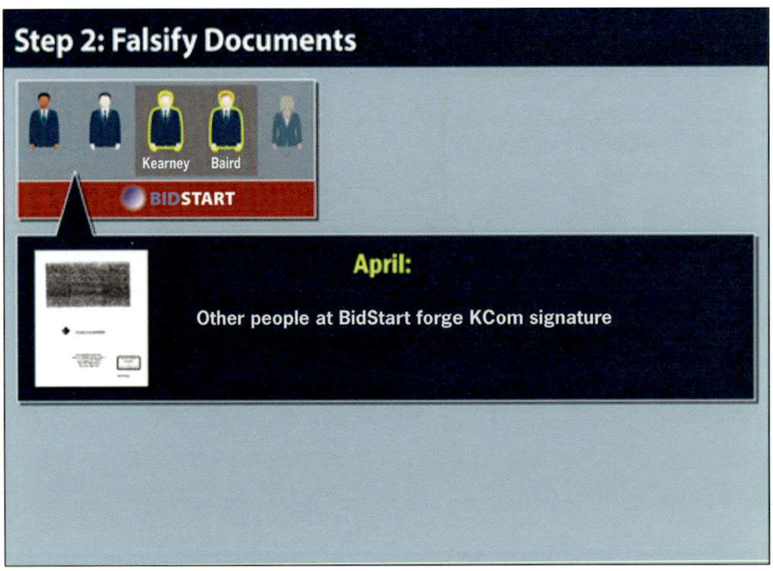

We pointed out that the two named and highlighted defendants had nothing to do with forging signatures.

And then we removed them.

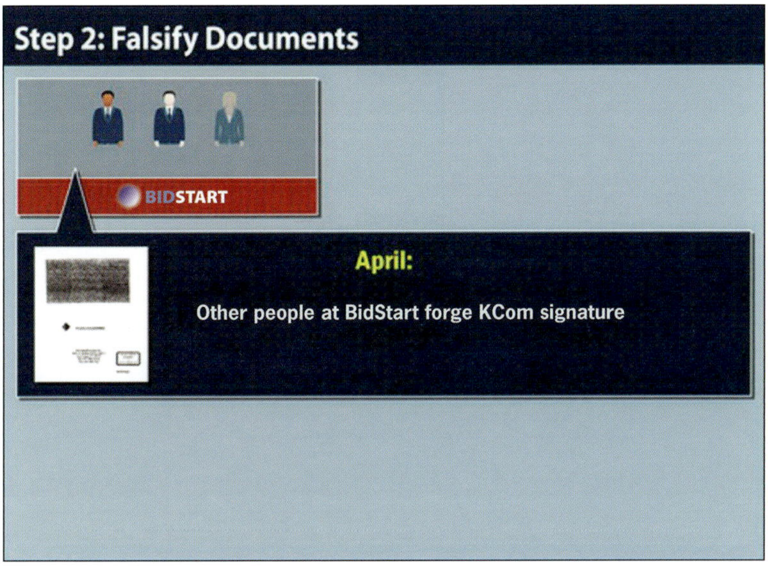

We next set our sights on the generic characters, the remaining nameless "other people" involved in forging signatures. Only now that we'd gone through the trial, the jury knew *exactly* who those three individuals really were. And, thanks to their mug shots, we had pictures.

So, we inserted them.

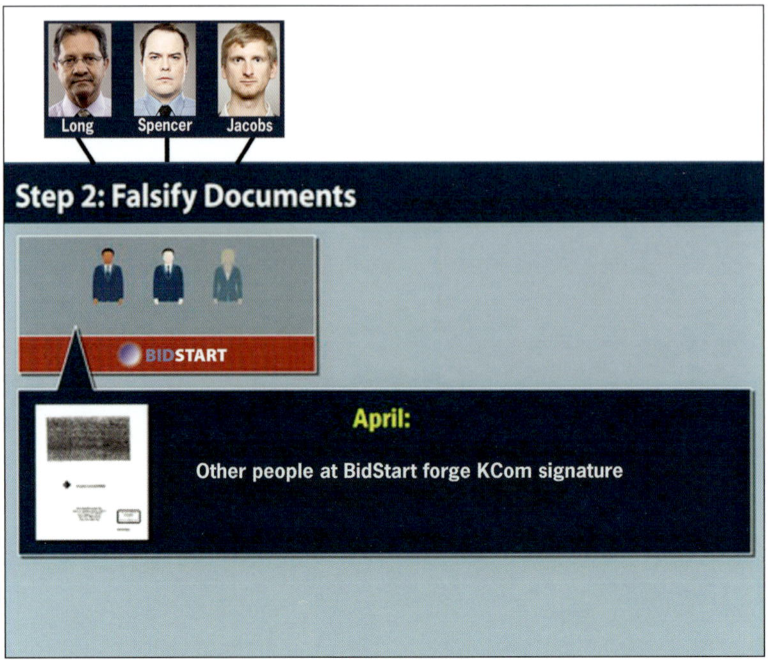

The generic African-American caricature was really Randolph Long (who was not African American). The generic white male caricature was really Kevin Spencer. And the generic blonde woman was really Roger Jacobs (who, while blonde, was not a woman).

There was no reason whatsoever why the government couldn't have named or even used photos of the real forgers. And there certainly was no reason to change their race or gender. We didn't have to make a snide remark, or really say another word. It left a poor taste in the jurors' mouths, and the government's credibility was damaged. (And our client was found not liable on all claims.)

Fixing Your Slides If an Objection Is Sustained

Hopefully, you'll never have one of your own visuals excluded for being misleading or prejudicial. But if your opponent successfully excludes all or part of a slide you designed, the slide may very well still be salvageable. Certainly, if it's an easy fix, such as modifying text, correcting a mathematical error, or adding a source citation, you can make the fix and use the slide. You might even be able to edit the slide quickly in the courtroom before a witness takes the stand or before closing argument begins.

Another quick fix (though by no means optimal) is to use a box of color to hide the offending portion of the slide, just as you would when redacting a document. If the problem is on a physical visual, such as a foam-core board, taping a piece of paper over the offending elements might fix the problem.

If the fix is more involved—for instance, if a photograph you're using is deemed unfairly prejudicial—then adjusting the slide to satisfy the ruling is just a question of time. If you have time to fix it, then look for a photo with less emotional appeal. (See the discussion of this issue in Chapter 9 on photographs.)

The best way to spot misleading substantive and design elements, particularly subtle ones, is to affirmatively look for them. It's not enough to skim your opponent's visuals passively and wait for obvious errors to jump out at you. Examine them as critically as you would examine a written brief, and then decide strategically what to do about a problem when you see one.

22

Practical Tips for Creating Visuals

Creating jury visuals isn't just a luxury to squeeze into your trial preparation if there's extra time (which there rarely ever is). Planning how to visually depict case themes, complex concepts, and key facts for the jury *is itself trial preparation*. In this chapter, I'll provide some practical tips for when to start thinking about your visuals, how to begin creating them, and what to look for when finalizing your visuals before showing them to the jury.

When to Prepare

Thinking through trial visuals helps you think through your case. As you figure out how to visually break down complex concepts, key trial themes, and important facts and evidence, you're also determining how to best present your case to the jury. That's not to say you're done thinking about it or that it won't be nuanced or tweaked during trial preparation and even throughout the trial. You might even choose to drastically alter or even abandon a particular theme. But when you have a visual sketch of something, even a relatively bad one, you'll have at least started down the path of nuancing that fact, theme, or concept. That preparation can never start too soon.

While the possibilities for communicating visually with the jury are seemingly infinite, the time we have to prepare for trial is not. I start thinking about jury visuals when I first learn about a new case. No, I don't draw my closing argument slides after my first meeting with a new client. But I do pay attention to how I process case information, including my client's industry, the players in the story, and the themes and theories I might want to present. More often than not, I'm already thinking about this information visually.

And I'm not alone. Most of us process and organize information visually by default, so you're likely doing so without even realizing it. You might find yourself picturing in your mind how various business lines or people are interrelated, diagramming something to explain it to a colleague, or creating a chart to meaningfully sort information. Each of these visual images might make for a useful jury demonstrative.

As I work my way through a case, I continually think about how a visual would help explain a concept or solidify a theme. I start a file for demonstratives very early. For me, a hard-copy file works best. I write "jury visuals" on a manila folder and use it to store my ideas. I keep a running list of complex facts and concepts that need to be broken down for the jury in a visual way. If I find myself drawing something as the case progresses, I put a copy in the file. If I think of a chart or graph that might be useful, I add that, too. When I visualize a concept in a new way as I review evidence, take a deposition, or even just talk with colleagues, I note it in the file. When a client, colleague, or even a mock juror or focus group participant uses a helpful analogy or explains something visually, I capture that in the file, too. I even keep visuals in mind when I'm taking notes during the trial itself. If an exchange occurs with a witness that I think would be useful enlarged on a slide, I'll mark my notes so I can quickly spot the soundbite, locate it in the official transcript, and incorporate it into my visuals for closing.

I also try to think outside the box when planning witness examinations, determining whether a demonstrative will further my communication goals. This is a common strategy with expert witnesses, who often must teach the jury before they can effectively testify about their opinions. Visuals can enhance experts' credibility while aiding the jurors' understanding and recall of what is often complicated and unfamiliar information.

But there's no reason we have to limit our use of visuals to expert witnesses. If a fact witness is explaining what he or she saw, how something works, where people were located, or anything else conducive to a visual depiction, consider using a demonstrative during the examination. You're only limited by your imagination (and, of course, your case facts!). You can even create visuals that build from witness to witness. If, for example, you're eliciting chronological evidence, such as when each witness arrived at a crime scene, started working for a company, or first learned of key information, each witness could mark a predesigned timeline. Because it's used repeatedly, jurors will already have a visual memory of the theme by the time you get to closing argument. So, I think about options for visuals when I'm preparing my fact witness examinations, as well.

This consistent attention to jury visuals is helpful on a number of fronts. It organizes and distills case themes to their essence. It exposes faulty logic or themes that need to be abandoned, such as when a volume build of evidence looks fuller or emptier than expected, a timeline turns out to tell an unhelpful story for your side, or a graph reveals something no one expected to see. Thinking through jury visuals early also helps identify evidence to go after in discovery—documents to request from the other side or to look for in our client's files, testimony to elicit during depositions, and potential areas of focus for our experts.

At bottom, early attention to visuals helps keep the process from being completely overwhelming, as we're not starting from scratch right before trial. When that happens, particularly when we're already insanely busy finalizing our trial preparation, it's just too easy to let visuals fall by the wayside. We either settle for unhelpful (or even counterproductive) visuals or we eliminate them entirely. If, instead, you have a cache of ideas, some of which are probably quite far along or even fully designed, it's much more manageable to finalize those visuals for trial.

Getting Started

Some of your ideas for visuals will arise very naturally. Enlarging key documents and testimony is now second nature for many trial lawyers. Likewise, you might instinctively look to an organizational chart when the relationship between witnesses matters, or a map when the route your client took is critical to the case. And, any diagrams you sketch out during the case, perhaps to assist with your own understanding of a thorny issue, can then be adapted for use with the jury.

But often you'll find yourself trying to figure out how to best express something visually, and the possibilities (or lack thereof) can seem overwhelming. How do you help a jury visualize causation or good faith? How do you create a picture of a lack of motive or your client as a scapegoat? How do you graphically illustrate constructive discharge, merger specificity, or one of a million other legal doctrines that might make or break your case?

For me, it starts with old-fashioned brainstorming. I'm a fan of the mind-mapping technique, which has been described in many books and articles. In a nutshell, it's a way of visually organizing your thoughts on paper. The main idea you're brainstorming usually appears in the center, and other ideas—which can be text, drawings, symbols, or anything else—branch off in all directions. Those ideas then branch into related ideas, and by the end, hopefully, you've got a number of good ideas to work with that can take your trial demonstrative in a few directions.

When I've decided on a concept for a visual and it's time to start designing it, I never start with a computer. Instead, I grab a blank pad of paper and a pencil, and I sketch out my ideas. I can think more effectively and creatively when I'm not constrained by my own limited knowledge of a computer program. When I'm creating visuals on the computer, my substantive train of thought is constantly interrupted as I look for the right menu button, adjust sizing, and try to figure out how to get a particular effect. I find the process works much better for me if I ignore the computer and just work on paper until I have a solid sense of what I want my visual to look like. I draw the diagram or sketch out the graph that works best for my message, and I avoid restricting my creativity because I haven't yet figured out how to translate an idea onto the computer screen.

Working with Graphic Designers

If I have money in my case budget, I almost always end up retaining a graphic designer to assist with my trial visuals. There are some terrific firms out there, large and small, with experienced professionals who not only have a mastery of graphic design, but who also have a wealth of experience with jury trials. Here are some tips on working with graphic designers. Not all of these tips will apply in every circumstance, of course. But when they do, they can save time, money, and headaches for both you and your designer.

Explain the Case

Unless you only want the most basic of visuals—enlargements and callouts from documents, for instance—tell the designer about your case. Explain your big-picture goals, case themes, theories, and weaknesses. They don't need to know the case as well as you do, but the more they understand strategically, the more they can brainstorm effective visuals or suggest helpful edits to visuals you're already considering. After all, the visuals are there to bolster your story, not the other way around. You have to know your case themes before you can start creating visuals to explain them. Including your designers as part of your case team, with everyone working toward a common goal, allows the designers to take ownership over their projects and add even more value to the case.

Provide Drawings

It can be really, really hard to describe visuals with words. When we're in the same room with someone, we usually will at least add gestures, drawing the visual we're describing in the air. But if you can just put your idea on paper, you'll improve your communication with the graphic designer exponentially. The drawing doesn't have to be "good," it just needs to convey the basics of what you're looking for. You'll save time (i.e., money), and you'll substantially reduce your own and the designer's frustration. The designer's first draft is likely to be on-point rather than something to redo because it wasn't what you had in mind.

Communicate Edits Clearly

Just as it's important to clearly communicate your initial ideas, it's important to get on the same page with your designer quickly about edits. You can, of course, print the slide and make edits directly on the page. But if that won't work (e.g., because the slide is too dark or busy to make notes on) or if you prefer to make notes electronically on the PDF, then you can use the sticky note or comment tool and insert your comments right where they go on the slide. The clearer you communicate your edits, the easier it is for the designer to capture precisely what you're looking for.

Keep an Open Mind to Design Ideas

Brainstorm ideas with your designers and be open to their suggestions. You might have an idea for a visual, but the designers, particularly those who specialize in trial visuals, will often have a much broader range of experiences to pull from. They might have prior experience designing visuals to convey the very legal concept you're struggling with. And they certainly will have important thoughts on your graphic design choices. You might love mint green. But if your designer tells you it won't contrast enough with your white slide, listen to that advice. It doesn't mean you can't use mint green if you really want to—it's your trial—but the designer can help make sure your mint green message is legible, so you don't tank your case.

Be Clear about Budget and Deadlines

This one's kind of a no-brainer. Clear communication about budget, deadlines, and other restrictions is always important. It's no less important when working with graphic designers. And to the extent you can, help prioritize the graphics you need and when you need them. If everything is presented as a rush, when really you don't expect to call a certain witness for another week, you might end up with unnecessarily rushed visuals that don't reach their full potential.

Be Responsive

Some visuals take little time to create; others are quite complicated. The sooner you review draft slides or let your designer know about a new idea or a change, the better. And remember, if you change something on a series of slides that build, that same change will have to be made on all subsequent slides in the series.

Be Careful if People Are Working on Visuals in Parallel

Sometimes it's efficient for more than one person to be working on a slide presentation. If you're taking that approach, just make sure the team is coordinated, and each person knows the instructions and strategy you gave to the other(s) to the extent necessary. You'll avoid having two (or more) people inadvertently creating different versions of the same visual or applying inconsistent edits.

Connect Designers with Your Case Experts

If you'll be using a graphic designer to create visuals for an expert, have the designer and the expert speak with each other directly. You can still participate in the discussion, but putting them together helps avoid miscommunications. It also allows the designer to brainstorm the best way to display information with the person who knows that information best.

Proofreading Tips: Substance and Design

Despite our best intentions, chances are pretty good that we'll be creating some of our visuals very, very late in the game. Trials aren't static. Evidence often comes in differently than you expected. A witness whom you thought would be called, isn't. The jury instructions or the verdict form are modified after the charge conference, and slides you'd prepared using the old text or format must be adjusted. It's just the nature of the beast. And because you'll be busy all day—you know, trying the case and all—you'll likely be modifying your slides in the evening, after a long day in court.

When you have a million other things to do to get ready for the next day, whether it's preparing witnesses, working through witness examinations and exhibits, drafting a motion, or working on your closing argument, you're already spread thin. Certainly, having someone on your trial team tasked with focusing on your visuals is a huge help. But rarely have I had a team member who wasn't also multitasking during a trial. When I'm working with a graphic designer retained for this purpose, these last-minute adjustments to visuals are much easier. But I still need to be the one directing the work and ultimately approving it.

The point is, this environment breeds mistakes—both substantive and design. Proofread your visuals carefully. Errors are distracting, look unprofessional, and can damage your credibility. Here are some tips on what to look for when proofing your visuals.

Substance

- **Text.** Check spelling, punctuation, and grammar for all text on your visuals, and check for consistency from slide to slide, particularly in builds.
- **Quotations.** If you've retyped a quote from an email or other document because enlarging it degraded the quality, make sure you've reproduced exactly what was in the original. Likewise, if you've typed the text of jury instructions, transcripts, or anything else, make sure you've captured it accurately.
- **Verdict Form.** If you choose to show your jurors the verdict form during your closing argument to walk through how to fill it out in favor of your client, proofread it carefully. This is always a good idea, but it's especially important when the form is complicated or if it changes after you've made your slide and you need to adjust the design.
- **Attribution.** Make sure any testimony or documents you use are attributed to the correct person, company, government agency, etc. Misattributing someone's statements looks sloppy at best and misleading at worst.
- **Exhibits and Exhibit Numbers.** Make sure you're displaying the correct exhibit number for any exhibits on your slides.
- **Redactions.** Confirm that you've appropriately redacted (or otherwise hidden) any portions of documents that cannot be shown to the jury.
- **Excluded Exhibits and Stricken Testimony.** When exhibits have been excluded or testimony has been stricken, pay careful attention to make sure you haven't mistakenly included such material in your slides.
- **Maps, Graphs, Charts.** Take a last, close look at your slides to make sure locations on maps are labeled correctly, the right people are in the right places on organizational charts, and the data looks right on your graphs. Avoid handing your opponent a way to take a shot at your credibility.

Design

- **Consistency.** Check for design consistency on every slide. Unless you've purposely chosen to do otherwise, confirm the consistency of font, size and placement of text, line spacing, the widths of lines and other graphic elements, and the placement of borders, callouts, exhibit numbers, documents, and other elements on your slides.
- **Layout.** Make sure you haven't placed an element (e.g., a graph) on a slide in a way that it unintentionally obscures another element.
- **Builds.** Click through slide builds to make sure information appears gradually and in the right order. As you're planning your examination or argument and moving slide sets around, it's easy to inadvertently misorder slides. This can really throw off an otherwise smooth witness examination or argument. Also check to see that anything you've shrunk, deleted, or grayed out on one slide stays that way on remaining slides in the build.
- **Interactive Slides.** For any interactive slides—slides on which you can click a link and bring up additional information—check each link to make sure it works, and that the document (or transcript, photo, video, etc.) it links to is correct.
- **Documents.** Make sure documents you're using, and any callouts from those documents, are legible. If they're not, and assuming you can't get a better-quality version of the document, consider retyping the enlarged text and indicate where you're pulling the text from on the page.
- **Photos.** Check the cropping and color on all photos and remove distracting objects when appropriate.
- **Document Callouts.** In the rush of trial, it's easy to put one document in the background of a slide and place enlarged text on the same slide that's actually pulled from a different document. So, if you're enlarging or calling out a portion of a document or transcript page, make sure the enlargement and the document match.

Start thinking about potential trial visuals from the earliest stages of your case. This ongoing exercise necessarily entails creative and strategic reflection that will naturally enhance the development of your core case themes. And, of course, the early preparation and close attention to detail will also greatly improve your ultimate jury visuals and your overall trial presentation.

23

Practical Tips for Using Visuals in Trial

Jurors see technology everywhere, including in their own workplaces, homes, and schools. And more and more, they also see it set up and ready for use in the courtroom. They know that virtually anyone can create semiprofessional-looking graphics and animations with home computers, tablet devices, and smartphones. As a result, jurors have gone from being suspicious of technology to expecting it, and the use of engaging visuals has gone from a risky move to a commonplace strategy. Indeed, at least one mock jury study showed that when lawyers used visuals effectively, jurors viewed the lawyers as prepared, and they were appreciative of the effort to teach.[1] In my own interviews with both real and mock jurors, they even voice frustration with lawyers who don't use simple visuals when doing so would have helped them understand unfamiliar or complicated material.

Most courtroom visuals, particularly in complex cases, will likely be in the form of slides created and displayed using computer software. Our in-court setup will involve monitors, projectors, cords, switches, and other high-tech equipment. Many of our visuals will be static images projected on a screen or shown on a monitor; others might be animations, simulations, or videos. But not everything we show jurors needs to be high-tech or needs to be shown to them in a high-tech way. There are many other ways to create and display trial visuals, using all of the same substantive and design concepts I've discussed throughout this book. I've used a variety of mediums in my own trials, including enlarged foam boards, blank paper on document projectors, and even easels with large pads of paper.

Each type of presentation medium has its own benefits and limitations. Some are great for interacting with witnesses. Some break up the monotony of trial by allowing you to move around the room or by letting you create a visual right before the jury's eyes. Some mediums allow you to get physically closer to a witness, developing a rapport and changing the tone of the interaction. And some mediums even allow you to get closer to the jury box, creating a connection with jurors that's not as easily established from behind the podium.

While most of this book has focused on *designing* visuals for trial, in this chapter I'll talk about actually *using* them. I'll pass along some general pointers I've learned along the way for dealing with technology in the courtroom. I'll also provide some tips for using computer slides as well as lower-tech presentation mediums. None of it is rocket science. But I've seen enough lawyers stumble in court when it comes to presenting their visuals—and I've had to learn some of these things the hard way myself—that I want to share these tips to help you avoid those "uh-oh" moments as much as possible.

General Tips on Using Technology

The concept of Murphy's Law—anything that can go wrong, will go wrong—has been around for a very long time. It certainly applies to courtroom technology.

Ask yourself, "What will I do if this doesn't work?" Answer the question. Then ask it again. The answers are your backup plan, and the best defense is a good offense. If you've really thought through how you'll need to recover if a projector bulb bursts, a computer won't wake up from sleep mode, or a monitor display is too dark for the jury to see key details in a photograph, you can plan for those eventualities. You might even prevent the problem from occurring altogether, but if something does go wrong, you'll have a solution.

Murphy's Law is cruel and unforgiving. Don't poke it in the eye.

Learn the Equipment in Your Courtroom

Make sure you're familiar with the technological capabilities in your courtroom. Determine what's already there and what you'll need to bring (which might be limited by what the judge will allow). See if there's someone at the courthouse you can meet with to discuss the available technology and learn how it works. Some courthouses routinely offer these meetings, and some even make it mandatory to attend.

If more than one person from your team can attend this meeting, all the better. Certainly, whoever will be running your equipment should attend, whether that's you, a colleague, or a vendor you've hired for trial. I try to always have at least two people on my team who know how to use the technology. Even if I'll be running the presentation, if I need help fixing something that isn't working or I need someone to get a replacement cable or bulb, it's helpful to have someone who already knows my technology setup, what courtroom I'm in, and other logistical details.

Learn the Layout in Your Courtroom

In addition to learning what's in the courtroom, you need an appreciation for where the equipment is and how its location impacts the jury. In fact, it's a good idea to sit in a sampling of the jurors' seats before the trial even begins. Ask the court's permission if you need to, but do it. Make sure you understand the jurors' limitations. Put a document on the document camera (often referred to as an "ELMO" after the brand), project it, and see how well you can read it from the jury box. Can you see the yellow highlighting on a black-and-white document? Do you find yourself straining to decipher the print on the page? If you're struggling, the jurors will, too. And some won't bother to try.

The courtroom layout might also inform your decision on the best way to present certain visuals. In a high-tech courtroom, there might be a monitor at each juror's seat. In other courtrooms, any visuals presented as slides might have to be projected onto a screen far away from the jurors, or at least far from some of them. Depending on what you'll need to display, using a lower-tech option such as an enlarged foam-core board might be more effective.

Test Your Equipment

Test whatever you're bringing into court to display your visuals. And don't just test each piece separately. Connect the projector to the monitor, load the actual presentation you'll use in court, turn on the sound if you're using any (e.g., for playing deposition video clips), and project the images onto a screen. Testing your equipment is the only way you'll find out, before it's too late, if one of your cables has the wrong connector, if the bulb in the projector has burst, if the testimony isn't clear through the speakers, or if the program you're using to run the presentation has been corrupted.

The same goes for other presentation equipment. If you're bringing a portable screen for your projector, make sure it expands correctly, and that the screen stays taut. Test your easel if you're providing one. Make sure the legs and support brackets lock in place and can adjust the way you want them. If you're using a dry-erase board, make sure you have an eraser, and that your markers are dry-erase and not permanent markers. And make sure they're new.

With electronics, try to test them in the courtroom you'll be in for trial. That way, you'll be using the actual equipment, in the actual lighting conditions, in the actual room layout that will be in place for trial. Plug everything in, and make sure it's compatible with the court's systems. See how your visuals look—especially from the jury box—on every monitor or projection screen in the room. If you need to make adjustments to brightness or contrast, it's better to know that (and do it) before you're in the middle of questioning your expert or delivering your closing argument. And if you can't adjust the technology, you can adjust your own design to use more contrast if needed.

Finally, test the positioning of your projector before you start your presentation. You'll need to position it just right so the image is clear and the full image is displayed on the screen. Set it up while the jury is out of the room, and check every position. Move the projector up and down, left to right, side to side, and even toward and away from the screen. If you can't leave the projector in place until you're ready to use it, ask the court to take a brief recess before you have to start your opening or your closing, and make the final adjustments. If the court won't agree to a recess, leave as much as you can set up and put a tape marking on the floor so you'll know where to put the projector when it's time for you to start.

Bring Extras

Many "extras" are pretty easy to bring to court: an extra bulb for the projector; extra batteries for your laser pointer, remote, and wireless mouse; extra dry-erase markers, cables, and extension cords. Think about what could go wrong, and what you could fix by having a spare. Then bring one.

Test the Extras

If your extras don't work, you have a material flaw in your backup plan.

Keep Your Technology Current

Electronics don't last forever. If you're using old equipment, you increase the risk it will fail when you need it most. The same can be said of really cheap equipment. Projectors, for instance, vary in brightness and resolution, which will impact your display. If the projector is dim, whether that's because it's old or it's cheap, the jury will struggle to see your slides, especially if there's not much contrast in the design.

Save Your Presentation in Multiple Locations

If you're using computer slides, don't just save your presentation on the hard drive, on a thumb drive, or on a CD. Do all three. If you know you need a thumb drive, save it on two (or three) thumb drives in case one is damaged. Redundancy is your friend when it comes to technology.

Embed Fonts

If you design a presentation on your own computer and then use a different computer to open the presentation and display it, you could be in for a surprise. If the program on the second computer doesn't have the same font options, the program will replace the font you selected in your design with a different font. This could be disastrous. A change in font can easily mean a change in size, which will translate into a change in spacing on any slide with text. So, either use the same computer to create and display your visuals, or make sure you select the option to "embed fonts" in PowerPoint (or the equivalent in whatever program you're using).

Tips on Using Computer-Generated Visuals

Visuals created with a computer program—what I've referred to as "slides" throughout this book—will be displayed in court in one of two ways: they'll either be shown directly on a monitor, or they'll be projected onto a screen. Here are a few things to think about if you'll be using computer slides during your trial, in addition to the general technology tips above.

Presentation Versus Litigation Software

PowerPoint is a type of presentation software, but it wasn't designed for trials. Instead, consider using software meant for trials, such as Trial Director 6, Trial Director for iPad (a downloadable app), Sanction, or TrialPad. These programs let you enlarge, highlight, or annotate documents on the spot, compare documents side by side, and generally present your visuals seamlessly. New technology options are being developed all the time, so stay current and select what works best for you.

Make Use of a Blank Screen

Unless I'm talking about the image I'm displaying or I have another affirmative reason for leaving a slide up, I prefer the screen to be blank. It shifts focus back to my argument or back to the question-and-answer colloquy between the witness and me. If I'm running my own slides, I usually just insert a blank slide where I know I'll want it. When I finish a section, I advance to the blank slide and leave it up. When I'm ready to move to the next topic with visuals, I simply advance the slides again and my next visual is displayed.

Some presenters advise using the B or W key in PowerPoint (or similar functionality in other programs), which blacks or whites out the screen. If you choose this method, keep two things in mind. First, you have to hit a key again (it can be the B or any other key) to bring the screen back up; you can't just advance the presentation. And second, when you do hit that key, the prior slide is still displayed. That can be distracting and interrupt the flow of an otherwise powerful presentation. That said, knowing about the B key is useful for emergencies—if you realize you have the wrong material displayed and you need to take it down as quickly as possible, the B key might be the cleanest and fastest way to accomplish that goal.

With a more sophisticated courtroom setup, which may involve someone else running your slides, blanking the screen can be more seamless. By controlling the display on the monitors, you can turn off select monitors while keeping the screen at your counsel table on. This allows you to work with the presentation in whatever way you need—changing the order of slides, bringing one up out of order, or even changing or redacting something—without the jury watching (and getting distracted by) what you're doing.

Notes Pages

Called "speaker notes" or "notes pages" in PowerPoint (depending on the version) and "presenter notes" in Keynote, this option allows you to add text below or next to your slides as a presentation cheat-sheet. The notes are not displayed on the slides themselves; they're hidden during the presentation and only the presenter can see them. You can even print out the notes, along with a thumbnail copy of the corresponding slide, to reference during your presentation. Notes pages can be a helpful alternative for people who put too much text on their slides as a presentation crutch.

But be careful. First, a dull presentation read to the jury off of slides doesn't suddenly come alive because you read the whole presentation off of notes pages. Use the notes pages for *notes*—quick reminders of points you want to cover with that slide. Try not to type a full presentation script into the notes pages and read it to the jury.

And second, mind Murphy's Law. Assume something will go wrong and your speaker notes, which are supposed to be hidden, will somehow be shown to the jurors. Don't put anything in those notes that you wouldn't want jurors (or the court, or your opponent, or press covering your trial) to see, such as "weak argument—consider cutting" or "make eye contact with old female juror." (Lest you think this would never happen, quite recently I was in a hearing where my opponent finished his presentation and went to close out his PowerPoint. But something went wrong. The notes pages were displayed, and he couldn't get the image off the screen for at least thirty seconds. So everyone saw the notes reminding him to "sit," "stand up," and say "Thank you, Your Honor." He certainly didn't give away the store with those notes, but it had to have been embarrassing.)

Move the Cursor Out of the Way

If you show slides or video using a program with a cursor, move the cursor off of the slide while you're showing it. I cannot tell you how many presentations I've sat through where the presenter brings a video up on his or her laptop and then steps aside while it plays, leaving a little hand or arrow in the middle of the screen. The little hand then covers someone's eyeball, or picks their nose, or hangs out in the sky, and is totally distracting.

It's too easy for an audience to lose concentration because they're waiting to see what the little hand (or arrow or whatever) will do next as the picture changes. The pointer automatically disappears on some programs after ten seconds or so, but if the program you're using doesn't have that feature (and even if it does!), just take a nano-second and make sure you move the cursor to a far corner of the screen to minimize the distraction.

Bring Hard Copies of Slides

I always bring a full-color hard-copy set of my slides to court. If any part of my display setup fails, the hard copy can save the day. This one I know from first-hand experience, having had a laptop quit on me only minutes before a closing argument. Fortunately, I had a hard copy of the slides with me, so I used the document camera (discussed further below) to display them for the jury. It wasn't ideal, but in my estimation it was much better than forgoing my visuals altogether. And, whether or not you're experiencing technical difficulties, the judge, courtroom clerk, or a witness might find it easier to look at (or for the court, take notes on) slides in a hard-copy format. Bringing a few sets with you lets you immediately respond to a request for one from the court.

Rehearse What You Can

Although trials are not amenable to rehearsal in the same way actors memorize a play, there are some things we can do in advance to make our trial presentation run smoothly, and some form of rehearsal is one of them.

Rehearse with your slide deck by playing the slides through, in slide mode, just as you will in court. Make sure everything's in the right order, all slides in a build are present and accounted for, and all animation and sounds are working properly. If someone else will be advancing your slides in court, run through the slides together. Get that person familiar with your style, give him or her a sense of when you want a blank slide (or a blank monitor), and point out key portions of documents you might want enlarged. Trial will run much more smoothly if you don't have to keep stopping during your argument or examination to consult with your operator.

Minimize Opportunities for Technology Failures

In other chapters of this book, I've cautioned against making something bounce, shake, or whizz around the screen just because we know how to do it. Without a substantive reason to add sound or movement to a slide, doing so can be distracting, can undermine our message, and can even hurt our credibility by making light of the seriousness of the trial. Here's another reason. You're inviting more technology to the party, which means more opportunities for something to go wrong. If you don't need the sound or movement, that's just another reason to think twice before adding it.

Tips on Specific Low-Tech Presentation Mediums

Lower-tech presentation options tend to allow more interaction with witnesses and even with the jury. You can approach witnesses with enlarged images on boards so they can write or mark key information. Experts can come down from the stand to draw a diagram on a flip chart or mark up a document on a board, creating a visual before the jury's eyes. And during closing argument, you can walk along the jury box with an enlarged image to make sure the jurors can see it. (All of this is subject to the court's permission, of course.)

Consider these low-tech options when using visuals such as maps, simple diagrams, and charts, particularly when you want to use the same visual with multiple witnesses. When it matters where someone was standing, where an event took place, or where someone traveled, having the witness mark the map rather than you doing so based on your interpretation of the testimony adds a level of credibility to the visual. The witness can place an X, his initials, or whatever other symbol you ask for directly on the board. Or, if you prefer (particularly for a hostile witness), you can have the witness point to the relevant spot and you can mark the board yourself.

Creating "spontaneous" visuals yourself or with a friendly witness is often easy to plan in advance, and I strongly suggest you do so when you can. Make sure you know how much detail you need in text descriptions or on diagrams, how much space you need to effectively capture what you want to display, and how large or small your writing or drawing needs to be in order to fit and still be legible. As with anything else, it's much better to work out the kinks in advance and be prepared rather than risk—in front of the jury—running out of space, writing or marking something you didn't mean to, or creating a freeform map or diagram that confuses the issues more than it clarifies them.

The preparation is well worth it. Low-tech options can be tremendously effective, particularly when they contrast with an otherwise high-tech trial presentation. Below are tips for using particular lower-tech presentation mediums in court.

Document Cameras

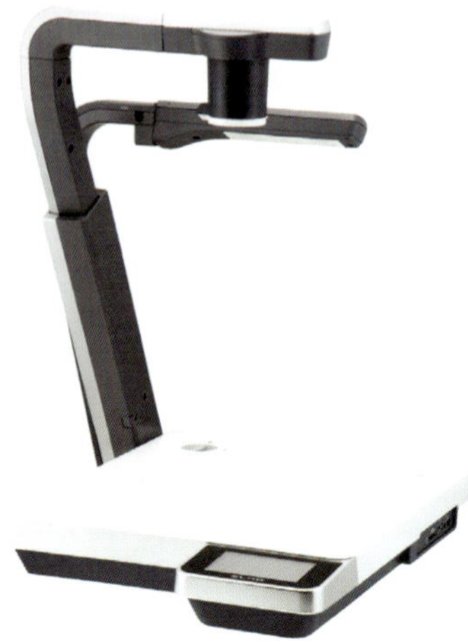

Document cameras are basically projectors. Similar to the old overhead projectors schoolteachers often used with transparency sheets, you simply place a document below the lens, and the document is projected onto a screen. If you write on or otherwise annotate the document, even if it's just a blank piece of paper, your markings are projected as well. Most document cameras will also allow you to zoom in on the document to enlarge a specific part of the page on the screen.

Document cameras have a variety of uses. They let us easily focus a witness on a particular part of a document. You can even use your pen or your finger to point directly to where you're directing the witness's attention and the jury can follow along. Document cameras are also great for creating real-time visuals during witness examinations. You can create a visual from scratch, such as a diagram or a list, or you can annotate an existing document. I'm a fan of both approaches. In one of my cases, a significant word appeared over and over again in a key document; circling each instance of the word as I read through it with a witness was impactful and created a visual memory for the jury. Later, I could take that same annotated document and put it on a closing argument demonstrative, making a broader point.

I've also used document cameras to display and enlarge tangible evidence. Yes, the jury will have it in the deliberation room. But if I want to focus on something in particular and if the evidence is small enough to put below the camera, I can enlarge what I care about and focus the jury's (or a witness's) attention there.

Learn to Use the Document Camera in Your Courtroom

Document cameras come in different makes and models. They work differently and have different capabilities. The switches and buttons are in different places, and they have different sensitivities. You don't want to waste time or interrupt your own flow by having to figure out how to use the machine in the middle of your witness examination or argument. Get permission to visit the courtroom in advance of trial or take some time during a break in the proceedings to make sure you know how to turn the camera on, adjust focus, zoom in and out, and adjust the projector's brightness.

Write Legibly

If you're going to handwrite something, make sure everyone can read it. It's that simple. Whether you're making a list, drawing something, writing people's names on a map, or writing anything else, write neatly. If the jury can't read it, then when you come back to that document with another witness or in closing argument, its utility will be greatly diminished.

Write Enough to Make Sense Later

What makes sense during a witness examination today might not make sense in three days or three weeks or three months when the jury retires to deliberate. That doesn't mean you need to write in full paragraphs. But make sure the visual you're creating will be able to stand on its own later in trial.

Make Precise Markings

If you're marking a spot on a map, make sure it's in the right spot and only that spot. If you're circling key data, make sure your circle (or highlight, etc.) is capturing the right data point and only that point. If you're marking something near or on top of other text but you still want the underlying text to be legible, think about that before you start writing and then make your markings accordingly.

Enlargements (Foam-Core Boards)

Any static image can be reproduced and enlarged on a sturdy foam-core board to use with a witness or to show the jury directly. The foam-core allows for a lightweight but still rigid display that one person can lift without difficulty. I've displayed these boards multiple ways. I've set them on easels during closing argument, I've rested them on the witness box during examination, and I've held the board as I've walked along the jury box, making sure each juror was able to get a good view of the image I was displaying.

In one case, a security video from bank ATMs was key evidence. The prosecutor introduced the video on a DVD in her case in chief to establish my client's identity. (I'm not sure why, since that wasn't in dispute, but whatever.) She showed the video on a television positioned at the end of the jury box. The image was bright and clear, but the TV screen was too small. The four jurors closest to the monitor could see the video, but the rest of the jurors really couldn't.

Meanwhile, I loved the video. It was the best defense evidence in the case. Detail mattered, and I needed the jurors to be able to see it. So, for cross-examination, I loaded the DVD into a laptop and projected the image onto a very large screen. The video was now large enough for all jurors to see it, but a new problem emerged. By projecting light onto a screen rather than showing it directly from a monitor, the light had to travel too far and the video was too dark to be effective.

So, for closing argument, I enlarged screen captures from the video onto foam-core boards. I laid out the images sequentially, and included the time markers for the jurors. The video was in evidence, and if the jurors wanted to view it during deliberation, they could. I made sure to identify the key portions that mattered for my case so jurors could find them easily.

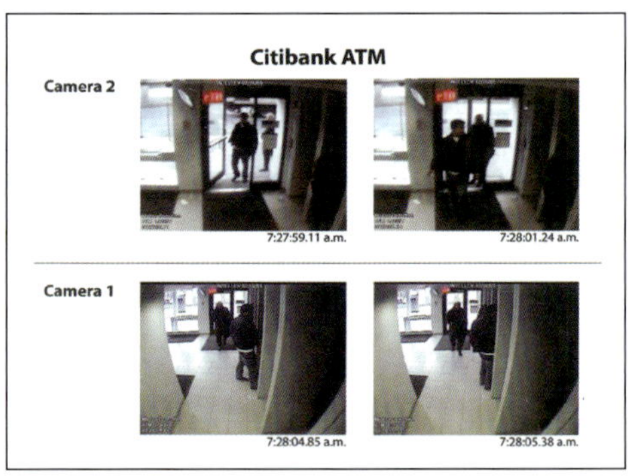

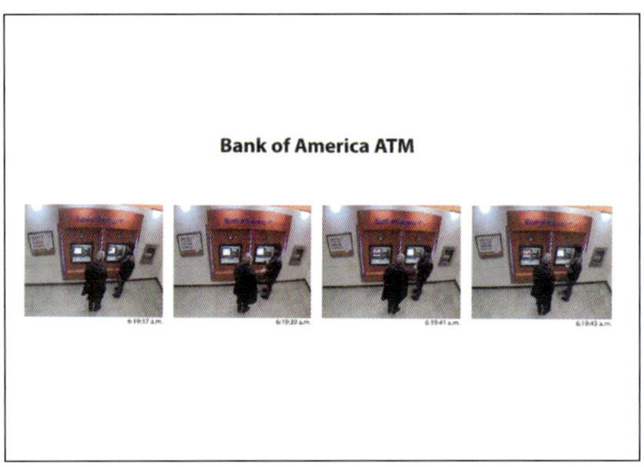

During my closing, I walked along the jury box slowly and deliberately, holding up these boards and pointing directly at what mattered. I called the jurors' attention to the time stamps, which most of the jurors wrote down in their notes. The boards displayed the important evidence more clearly than the too-small television or the too-dark projected image, and I was able to interact more closely with the jury when I used them. (Following a two-week trial, the jury acquitted my client of all fourteen charges after one day of deliberation.)

Carefully Consider the Size of the Board

Foam boards are printed in custom and standard sizes. Standard sizes include 15" × 20", 20" × 30", and 30" × 60". Think carefully about the size you need. Although a large foam board is light enough to lift, if it's too big it might be unwieldy in the courtroom. I learned this the hard way years ago when I enlarged a photo of a crime scene and printed it on a 30" × 60" foam board. The photo looked great, but I'm only 5'1" myself, so maneuvering with this board at trial was more of a challenge than it needed to be. Fortunately, it was a source of humor, and the witness was able to show a personal side by helping me hold the board while I balanced it on the witness stand. If I had thought through the sizing a bit more, I would have used a smaller board and asked the judge for permission to walk it along the jury box after the witness marked key locations on the image.

Use a Dry-Erase Coating if Markings Might Change

Foam-core boards can be printed with a dry-erase coating, just like a whiteboard. This allows you to easily erase and change markings if you make a mistake, something particularly useful if you're using the board with a witness.

Consider a "Reveal" Design

Just as you can build a slide created in PowerPoint or other software programs, you can build a preprinted enlargement by revealing one portion of the visual at a time. For example, if your case involves a complicated verdict form and you want to walk the jury through it, you can print the form onto an enlarged board and cover each question with a strip of poster board held on with magnets, clips, or Velcro. As you remove each piece, you reveal another question. Then you can write in the answer after you discuss the question. (Alternatively, if the court is still deciding on the substance or format of the verdict form so that you can't get it printed onto a foam-core board in time, consider displaying a copy of the finalized form on a document camera and using another piece of paper as a cover to achieve the same effect.)

Consider a Fill-in-the-Blank Design

A verdict sheet is a quintessential fill-in-the-blank form. But you can design other visuals to use this way, whether with witnesses or during argument. You could use a chart and fill in damages figures with an expert witness. You could list the elements of a claim during your opening statement with a "yes" and "no" check box at the end of each one, and then reuse the visual in closing, filling in the boxes as you discuss the evidence (or lack thereof) presented in the case. If you know several witnesses will testify about their observations of a crime or a car accident—answering questions such as "what color was the car?" or "how many people were in the store?"—you could list key questions down the left side of a chart and witness names across the top, writing in their testimony by hand as you use the visual with each witness.

To ensure this approach doesn't violate a Rule on Witnesses (where witnesses who have not yet testified are excluded from the courtroom and cannot be told what other witnesses have said), simply adjust what's shown to each witness. If you use a testimony chart, for example, you could cover the rows for the other witnesses and reveal only the row for the presently testifying witness. By the end of the trial, you'll have a complete demonstrative to use with the jury, but you won't have tipped off one witness to what others have already said.

The same considerations hold true when you use a map or diagram that multiple witnesses will mark. To avoid a Rule on Witnesses problem, you might take a photograph of the diagram after each witness testifies and then erase the markings before the next witness sees it. In the end, you'll be able to compare the photos side by side on a single slide, or alternatively move from one photo to the next where the map or diagram remains static and the only change is in each witness's markings.

You could also consider raising the issue with the court before you use the exhibit with multiple witnesses. If you strongly prefer to leave each witness's markings as they've written them and then build the visual as trial proceeds, it might be worth asking whether the trial judge will allow it. Where the witness testimony is unlikely to be influenced by what other witnesses say, you have a better chance of getting such a request granted.[2] Of course, if you'd prefer not to tip your hand to opposing witnesses, the safer course is to avoid revealing other witnesses' testimony (or markings or diagrams) to that witness.

Dry-Erase Boards/Flip Charts

Other options for the real-time creation of visuals are to use a dry-erase board or a flip chart. Dry-erase boards, also known as whiteboards, give you a large platform to write on in different colors and quickly erase to start a new visual or to make changes to an existing one.

Flip charts, which you'll typically display on an easel, have the advantage (and disadvantage) of permanence. It's harder to fix a mistake, but the visual is immediately preserved for later use with other witnesses or to display in closing argument.

Don't Block the Jurors More Than You Have To

When you're using a document camera, you're typically standing away from where the image is being projected so you're not blocking the jury's view. But with dry-erase boards and flip charts, you'll have to block the board while you're writing on it. Make sure you step aside when you aren't marking the board so that each juror can see what you wrote, drew, or circled. Likewise, be cognizant of where you're standing while a witness is writing on the board. If the room layout virtually guarantees that someone's view of your chart will be restricted at all times, and if you still want to use a dry-erase board or flip chart, then consider asking the court for permission to hold the board or chart up to the jury to make sure they can all see it.

Be Mindful of Talking While Writing

Your back is to the jury while you're writing. Either don't talk and write, or turn to the jury when you speak. If you must speak with your back to the jury, at least do so loudly.

Use Dark Ink and Write Neatly

Yellow ink on your white dry-erase board won't be legible for the jury. Neither will terrible handwriting. Dark markers and careful writing will go a long way.

Consider Having the Witness Do the Writing

Generally, I prefer to handle the writing. I can control what I write, leave room for other text, write legibly, and make sure my markings are precise. I don't leave anything to chance if I'm the one writing it. But sometimes, in the right case and context, it can be effective to have the witness mark a spot, draw a diagram, or write a few words or numbers. I've used this approach with experts more than fact witnesses, but as long as you can trust what the witness is writing (and hopefully you've discussed it in advance!), or if you have the means to impeach an adverse witness if they play games with their markings, it can be an engaging strategy.

Preserve It

If you use a dry-erase board to create a visual in trial, try to preserve it before you erase it. Some dry-erase boards are pretty high tech. They're capable of scanning and printing whatever is written on them. But those boards tend to be quite large and rather expensive. Instead, you can preserve the visual by simply taking a cell phone photo of the board. That allows you to use the same visual later in trial, either with a different witness or in closing argument. By uploading the photograph to your computer, you can paste the photograph onto a slide and display it as you would any other slide, even adding a heading, text, or other elements. Alternatively, you could print the photo and display it on a document camera. Or, you could enlarge the image onto a foam-core board.

I also recommend taking a picture of visuals created with flip charts. Although technically the image is captured, it's not very user-friendly. If you take a photo of the page, you'll have more flexibility in how you display it later.

Consider the Size

As with foam-core boards, be careful that you aren't using a dry-erase board or flip chart that's so large as to be unwieldy for use in court.

Bring Liquid Cleaner and a Cloth

Sometimes, the soft eraser we use with dry-erase boards doesn't completely remove all of our markings. Keep some cleaning solution and a cloth or paper towels on hand so you can get rid of old markings completely before you start a new visual.

There are only so many ways to display a visual in court. The method might be dictated by space constraints, budgetary concerns, or courtroom capabilities. As you think about which medium will work best for your message, factor in whether witness interaction would be helpful, as well. You can enhance the credibility of your visuals by having fact and expert witnesses create the visuals with you. This approach can also help an expert get into "teacher mode" at the outset of the examination. Witnesses (fact or expert) tend to be more comfortable when they're explaining something they're already familiar with, and the jury is usually more receptive to a witness who is genuinely trying to help them understand something (i.e., teach them)—often a necessary part of an expert's testimony. Work with your expert to think through visuals you can create or complete during the examination. They could draw something on a whiteboard, fill in numbers on a preprinted chart that's been enlarged on a foam board, or circle or mark something on a diagram. A visual might also help them explain a process they used in reaching their opinions in the case.

When it comes to the medium for displaying your visuals, don't be afraid to mix it up. You could use slides for most of your visuals but switch to an enlarged board for something you want to keep referring back to with witnesses or even during closing argument. For example, if a timeline in your case is significant, you could display it on a foam-core board resting on an easel next to you during closing argument. As you gradually reveal and discuss each event, you could display its evidentiary proof using computer-generated visuals on a monitor or projection screen.

Another option is to introduce a theme with vibrant slides projected onto a large screen, and then use a flip chart to list basic text points or draw a simple diagram. Not only does a mixed approach allow you to use whichever medium works best for particular content, it also keeps the jury interested and engaged, which will aid understanding and recall.

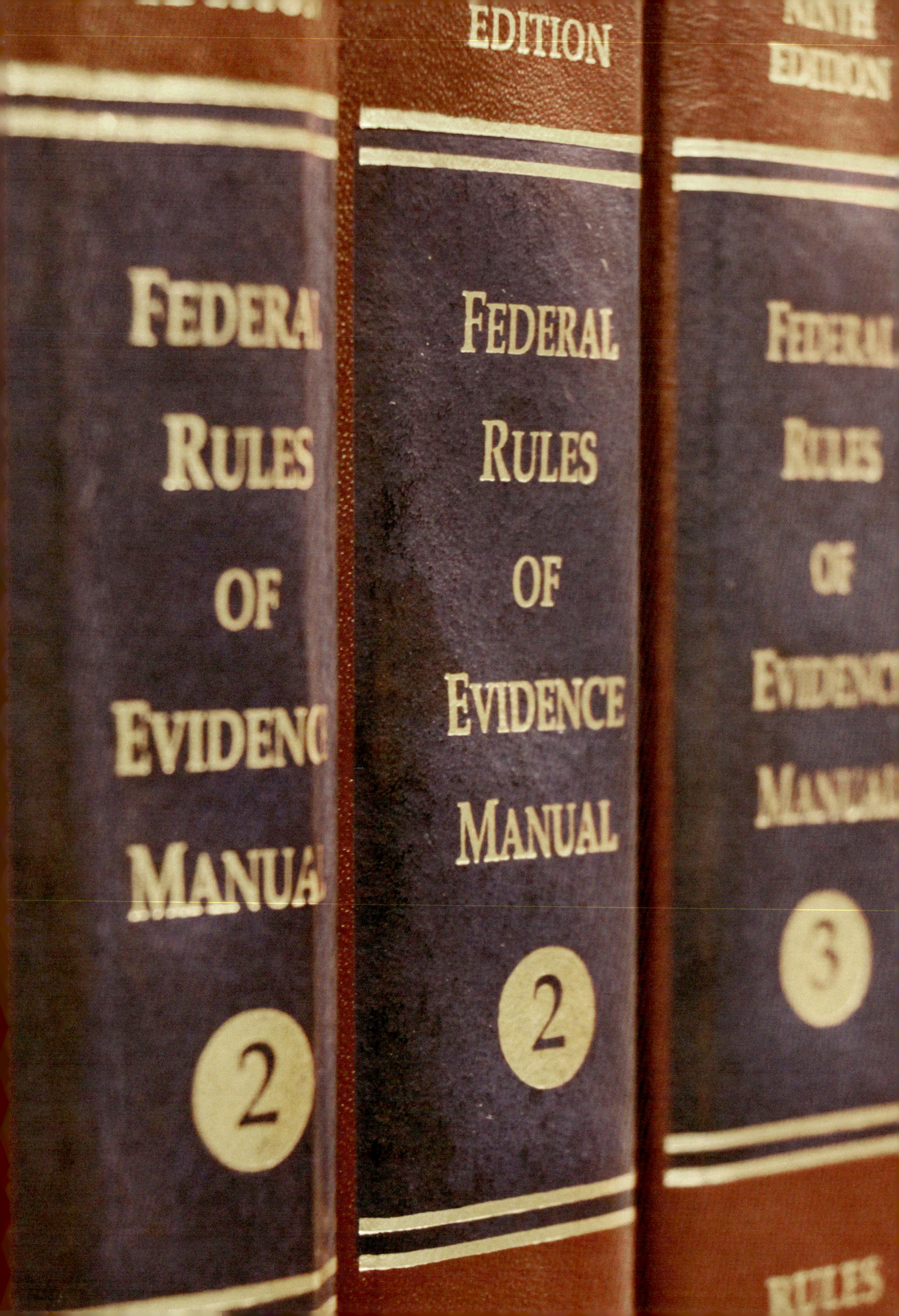
EDITION
FEDERAL
RULES
OF
EVIDENCE
MANUAL
2

24

Legal Considerations

Throughout this book, I've been discussing the design and use of jury visuals. There are a lot of names for these visuals: "demonstrative evidence," "demonstrative aids," "demonstratives," "pedagogical aids," and "illustrations" are some of the most common. Whatever they're called, these are typically exhibits with no independent evidentiary value. Rather, they're used to explain, illustrate, or summarize other evidence, testimony, or lawyers' arguments.

Photos, charts, graphs, and videos all can be either substantive evidence or demonstratives, depending on what they feature and how they're used in trial.[1] Perhaps predictably, then, courts are inconsistent in their determinations of what is demonstrative and what is substantive. In fact, a party might intend to use something only for illustrative purposes, but the court may find that its use or effect goes beyond that purpose and constitutes substantive evidence, holding it to that standard for use and admissibility.

With no federal evidentiary rules and only a few state rules[2] that directly define or govern demonstratives, courts analyze the use of jury visuals in various ways. Some allow lawyers tremendous latitude; others do not allow visuals at all. The propriety of any particular visual will be assessed on a case-by-case basis. This includes courts' assessment of physical objects as demonstrative aids. Scale models, for instance, can do wonders to help jurors visualize and understand something unfamiliar or complicated and are often used for illustrative purposes in court. Some of the cases cited in this chapter involve the use of physical objects as demonstratives, as the reasoning in those cases is largely transferrable to other jury visuals.[3]

Despite the confusion and inconsistency, there are some recurring considerations that arise when demonstrative evidence is at issue. This chapter provides an overview of how state and federal courts analyze jury visuals, and particularly what facts and factors courts consider when deciding whether to permit their use during trial and whether to send them back to the jury room during deliberations. An awareness of these issues allows you to plan for them in the design and use of your own visuals and arms you with arguments for defending your demonstratives or seeking to exclude your opponent's. In that vein, I've also included citations to state and federal cases from around the country, which are set forth with explanatory parentheticals in the back of this book.

Significance of Demonstratives vs. Rule 1006 Summaries

Federal Rule of Evidence 1006 and its state counterparts permit "the contents of voluminous writings . . . which cannot conveniently be examined in court [to] be presented in the form of a chart, summary or calculation." Often, these exhibits summarize documents that have not themselves been admitted into evidence, and thus the summaries are considered substantive evidence and are sent back with the jury.[4]

Demonstratives, on the other hand, help illustrate or clarify testimony or evidence and sometimes summarize witness testimony or documents already in evidence. Demonstratives often include express or implied suggestions as to how the jury should weigh or interpret evidence. Courts have mixed views on whether demonstratives themselves are evidence or are merely used to aid the jury in its understanding of evidence that itself has been admitted.[5] The Eastern District of New York, in 2004, discussed the issue in some depth in *Verizon Directories Corp. v. Yellow Book USA, Inc.*[6] The court disagreed with the then-prevailing view that pedagogical aids are not themselves evidence.[7] Instead, the court reviewed the various uses for such aids, explained their utility (and increasing use) in complex cases, and concluded that "[s]ubject to Rule 403, with somewhat more stringent control in jury trials, pedagogical aids should generally be admitted as evidence. They can be helpful to the court's understanding of the complex and voluminous amount of evidence presented[.]"[8] The court further explained its view that a district court's "normal discretion can be utilized to mitigate situations in which the parties have vastly different resources, creating an uneven technological playing field."[9]

The distinction between Rule 1006 summaries and demonstrative aids can be blurred in a particular jurisdiction or a particular case. As the First Circuit has held (relying on the Sixth Circuit), "in some cases, . . . pedagogic devices may be sufficiently accurate and reliable that they, too, are admissible in evidence, even though they do not meet the specific requirements of Rule 1006."[10] Not surprisingly, pairing argumentative language with an otherwise neutral summary that would satisfy Rule 1006 can turn that summary into a pedagogical aid.[11]

Some jurisdictions have expressly set forth considerations for the use of demonstrative aids. The Fifth Circuit, for example, has identified four requirements: (1) the aid must be based on competent evidence that is before the jury; (2) the primary evidence used to construct the aid must be available to the other side for comparison; (3) the person who prepared the aid must be available for cross-examination; and (4) the jury must be properly instructed concerning their consideration of the charts.[12]

The Sixth Circuit has identified a third category of exhibit—a so-called secondary-evidence summary—that doesn't meet the requirements of Rule 1006 but is "so accurate and reliable a summary illustration or extrapolation of testimonial or other evidence in the case as to reliably assist the factfinder in understanding the evidence."[13] These secondary-evidence summaries are admitted into evidence in addition to the evidence they summarize, and the jury "should be instructed that the summary is not independent evidence of its subject matter, and is only as valid and reliable as the underlying evidence it summarizes."[14]

Ultimately, "[t]here is some diversity of judicial opinion concerning [demonstrative evidence's] precise evidentiary status. Some jurisdictions treat such items as admissible exhibits which may be reviewed on appeal and sometimes viewed by the jury during deliberations. Other courts treat them differently, either admitting them for 'demonstrative purposes' only or refusing to admit them at all as exhibits."[15] In the 2013 case *Baugh v. Cuprum*, the Seventh Circuit, acknowledging that the Tenth and Fifth Circuits had taken positions contrary to its own, reversed a trial court's judgment to send to the jury room a physical demonstrative exhibit (a ladder) that had not been admitted into evidence, noting: "the general rule is that [demonstrative exhibits] not admitted into evidence simply should not be sent to the jury for use in its deliberations" absent consent of all parties.[16] The court dismissed the contrary cases as departures "from longstanding practice in this and other circuits . . . with only the most tenuous support."[17]

At bottom, whether demonstratives are treated as admissible evidence and whether they're sent back to the jury room for deliberations (even if not admissible) differs by jurisdiction and even by individual judge.[18] Courts have wide discretion in deciding whether to send demonstrative aids back with the jury, with or without consent of the parties, and courts have not taken a uniform approach in deciding the issue.[19]

As discussed in Chapter 2, whether the jury can examine your demonstratives in the jury room matters. Do what you can to find out, as early as possible, how your judge treats demonstratives. These considerations might influence your design and substantive choices, and even which display medium you use for a particular visual, so the earlier you know, the better.

Notice

There are no federal rules governing when or whether we must exchange demonstratives with our opponents, though there are such local rules in some jurisdictions.[20] At least four federal jurisdictions have applied the pretrial disclosure requirements of Federal Rule of Civil Procedure 26 to demonstratives used with expert witnesses, with varying outcomes.[21]

In *Roy v. St. Lukes Medical Center,* the defendant first disclosed two computer animations depicting a medical procedure on the fifth day of an eight-day trial, which was after the plaintiff's expert had testified.[22] The trial court allowed the defendant to use the animations, stating "[i]t certainly would have been better if this could have been provided earlier, but it's closer to just having a witness draw something in court or come in with a diagram to help illustrate testimony. And in that sense, I'm going to allow it."[23] The appellate court found no prejudice or undue surprise due to the late disclosure, emphasizing the plaintiff's lack of action upon learning of the animations.[24] In particular, the plaintiff did not request a continuance, present testimony in rebuttal, or indicate how the previous witness testimony would have been altered by an earlier disclosure of the animations.[25]

Often, courts are willing to defer to the parties' agreement on the timing of any demonstrative exhibit exchange. When that's the case, I try to think through the practical realities. When will I likely finish my demonstratives for any particular stage of the case? When do I really need to see the other side's visuals? How late can I delay giving my opponent my slides, especially if they'll provide a road map to my witness examination or arguments?

I've found that exchanging slides for opening statements and closing arguments the night before provides plenty of time to review them. In several cases, I've done the exchange only hours before argument. I actually prefer the latter, but it's sometimes proven difficult to get my opponent and the judge to agree to such a late disclosure. In contrast, I usually treat witness demonstratives the way I treat any exhibits I expect to use with witnesses. If the court requires the parties to provide exhibits in advance, then I typically agree with my opponent to exchange demonstratives at the same time. Likewise, if there is no requirement to provide witness exhibits in advance of the examination, then we don't exchange visuals, either.

Ultimately, when and whether the parties must exchange demonstratives before trial is largely left to the trial court's discretion.[26] In many instances, the court simply sets a deadline for the exchange in a pretrial order, and those deadlines can range from weeks to mere hours before the demonstrative will be used.[27] And, of course, courts have a great deal of discretion on whether to preclude the use of late-disclosed demonstratives.[28]

Relevance

Most courts define demonstratives as having no independent evidentiary value. But if that's the case, it should mean the demonstratives are irrelevant and should therefore be excluded. As it turns out, courts often overlook this conundrum. There aren't many cases excluding demonstratives purely on grounds of irrelevance.[29] Instead, when relevance is mentioned or implied as a reason for exclusion, it's usually paired with other grounds, such as Rule 403.[30]

Foundation

Laying a foundation for a demonstrative exhibit is generally straightforward. If there's a foundation for the underlying evidence the visual is illustrating, there is usually a foundation for the explanatory visual. What's more, courts tend to require less of a foundation for an illustrative visual than they require for admitting the underlying evidence. But overall, the admissibility—or even use—of a demonstrative in many cases has hinged on whether the proponent of the evidence establishes that it is a true and accurate representation of what it purports to represent.[31]

In that vein, the court in *Roy v. St. Lukes Medical Center*, discussed previously, allowed the defendant to use two video animations because they were "sufficiently similar" to the actual events.[32] The animations purported to depict the defendant's theory and the plaintiff's theory of what transpired during a medical procedure. The plaintiff objected to both animations as not fairly representing the actual events and as unfairly prejudicial in comparison to their probative value.[33] Finding the animations "substantially similar" and thus permissible as demonstratives, the court further noted that any prejudice could be cured on cross-examination.[34]

The level of foundation required is not always equal between types of demonstratives. In *Rodd v. Raritan Radiological Associates, P.A.*,[35] the appeals court reversed the trial court's decision to permit a defendant-doctor to use computer-produced "super-magnified" images of the plaintiff-patient's mammograms.[36] The basis for the appellate court's decision was primarily the potential for the demonstratives to confuse the jury, but the court also expressed concern about the lack of a complete foundation for the images.[37] As to the latter issue, the court noted "reliability problems" in creating computer-generated images, and said such exhibits require a more detailed foundation than was required for photographs or photo enlargements.[38] In particular, the court said that testimony from "a person with some degree of computer expertise" was required so they could be cross-examined about the functioning of the computer used to generate the images.[39]

Rule 403

Whether or not demonstratives are admitted into evidence, they are subject to Rule 403 and its state equivalents. Under the rule, the court may prohibit the use of a demonstrative if its probative value is substantially outweighed by the danger of unfair prejudice, confusion of the issues, misleading the jury, undue delay, waste of time, or the needless presentation of cumulative evidence. The Rule 403 factors are the most common challenges parties raise to exclude demonstrative aids.

Just as it is with substantive evidence, the Rule 403 analysis when applied to demonstratives is a subjective one. Whether the court excludes a demonstrative[40] or permits its use[41] typically comes down to case facts and how the jury is likely to perceive the demonstrative in the larger case context.

Photographs are ripe for Rule 403 challenges in light of their natural tendency to appeal to emotion. And a demonstrative using an emotional but otherwise admissible evidentiary photograph can violate Rule 403 when it is paired with unfairly prejudicial text. In *Spence v. State*, for instance, the government in closing argument displayed a slide depicting the victim's body "splayed and bloodied"—itself a photo that was already in evidence—with superimposed text stating that the defendant's "actions led to . . . Terror . . . Fear . . . And to the ultimate crime . . . MURDER[,]" with the word "MURDER" in large, red lettering.[42] The court held that the prosecutor's use of this slide was improper because it "served no purpose other than to attempt to inflame the jury," and the slide should have been excluded.[43]

Courts have broad discretion to exclude demonstratives on Rule 403 grounds or to fashion conditions for their use.[44] An example of the latter is *United States v. Johnson*,[45] wherein a district court in Iowa imposed multiple conditions on the use of witness photographs by both parties in closing argument.

Johnson was a death penalty case in which the defendant was charged with having murdered five witnesses in her now-former boyfriend's drug-trafficking trial.[46] For its closing argument in the murder trial, the government sought to mount 8.5" × 11" photos of all 75-plus testifying trial witnesses, as they appeared while testifying, on 5' × 5' boards. The government planned to detach the photographs one by one as that witness's testimony would be discussed in closing. In seeking this permission (pretrial), the government explained that because the trial would last over three months and the parties would call over 75 witnesses, the photographs would help jurors recall the witnesses' testimony and would be a persuasive way of demonstrating the amount of evidence the government had against the defendant.[47] The defendant objected, arguing that "trial of a defendant is not a numbers or pictures game," and that such a display would be inappropriate.[48] The defense further contended that if the government were allowed to use such photographs, the defense should be afforded the same privilege.[49]

In deciding the motion, the court noted that the photographs were demonstrative rather than summary exhibits, "intended and likely to assist the jury in remembering the names and testimony of the witnesses."[50] However, the court concluded that the potential for unfair prejudice substantially outweighed the legitimate purposes for displaying the photos in the manner the government proposed.[51] Recognizing the powerful impact of the visual display, the court explained:

> The court concludes that the potential for unfair prejudice of displaying *all* of the photographs continuously during what is likely to be a very lengthy closing argument . . . substantially outweighs the legitimate purposes for doing so. This is so, because the impact of *seeing* the photographs of all of the witnesses in a single display is more substantial than the impact of recalling that there were numerous witnesses. *Cf.* [*United States v.*] *Gaskell*, 985 F.2d [1056,] 1061 n. 2 [11th Cir. 1993] (noting that "[s]everal circuits have recognized that demonstrative exhibits tend to leave a particularly potent image in the jurors' minds") (citations omitted). Again owing to the potency of such a visual display, the court also finds that this potential for unfair prejudice could persist, even if the jury is properly instructed on the issue of the "number" of witnesses. Therefore, the court will not permit the government to display all of the witnesses' photographs in a single display for any significant period of time — certainly not for the full duration of a closing argument.[52]

To further illustrate its point, the court in *Johnson* added a footnote that included two photographs side by side. One was of the composite photo display proffered by the government in the drug-trafficking trial of Johnson's then-boyfriend, which involved 54 witnesses.[53] The second photograph showed how the 54 witness photos in the composite were mounted with Velcro for easy removal and use during the government's closing argument.

Ultimately, the *Johnson* court imposed a hybrid approach. The court allowed the government to use witness photographs but imposed six conditions: (1) a court employee would photograph the witness as he/she appeared at trial; (2) the photos would be printed and compiled in a notebook; (3) either party could use the photographs during closing argument to refresh the jurors' memories about the testimony of any witness; (4) neither party would be permitted to display more than one witness's photograph at a time without the court's permission, and the display must be shown to opposing counsel; (5) if more than one photo was shown in a single display (with the court's permission), the length of time for the display must be determined during a conference prior to closing arguments; and (6) the notebook would be sent to the jury room during deliberations unless a sufficient contrary showing was made after the conclusion of evidence.[54]

The Fifth Circuit explained the significance of Rule 403 as applied to demonstrative aids in *Muth v. Ford Motor Company*.[55] *Muth* was an automobile accident case involving a design defect. At trial, the defendant's expert testified about the results of two crash tests. He also intended to use, as demonstrative aids, video footage and photographs to assist the jury in understanding the general dynamic of rollover accidents.[56] The plaintiff objected to the video and photographs, arguing that there were several differences between the conditions in the test and the accident at issue.[57] The district court excluded the demonstratives but allowed the defendant's expert to discuss the data and conclusions drawn from the tests.[58]

On appeal, the Fifth Circuit agreed with the trial court on the facts of the case and explained the larger implications of Rule 403 and demonstrative evidence. "[W]hen the demonstrative evidence is offered only as an illustration of general scientific principles, not as a reenactment of disputed events, it need not pass the substantial similarity test. Such demonstrative aids, however, must not be misleading, in and of themselves, and one such way that a demonstration might mislead is when, as here, the demonstration resembles the disputed accident."[59] The court went on to explain that the most troublesome cases involving demonstrative evidence are those in which general principles may be demonstrated in a fashion that looks like a re-creation of the event at issue—but isn't.[60] The court concluded that the similarities between the defendant's theory of the accident conditions and the conditions of the tests had a prejudicial effect sufficient to justify the district court's decision to exclude the demonstrative aids.[61]

In the end, a Rule 403 decision about proffered visuals may come down to your own credibility with the court. Indeed, as with so many of the court's subjective judgment calls, your reputation and credibility matter. If the court doesn't think you're trying to improperly appeal to jurors' emotions with a particular photograph, a chosen color scheme, or the phrasing of a heading, a close call may be decided in your favor.

Hearsay

Not surprisingly, if the substance displayed on a demonstrative is itself inadmissible, the evidentiary problem isn't solved by typing the statement on a colorful slide or enlarging it on a foam-core board with an art-deco border. If something's hearsay on its own, it will still be hearsay in your visuals. The contrary is also true: if the visual is just displaying information already in evidence, then the visual itself is generally deemed permissible without violating hearsay rules.[62]

A more nuanced question arises when a demonstrative illustrates information that is not itself in evidence. The answer, not surprisingly, is typically case-specific. In *Diaz v. State*, for instance, an expert Spanish-language interpreter sought to testify in a post-conviction proceeding using a three-column chart to illustrate her conclusions about translation errors made during the defendant's plea hearing.[63] The trial court excluded the chart, sustaining the State's objection that the chart was hearsay.[64] On appeal, the court reversed and remanded for a new post-conviction hearing, explaining: "We see the chart not as hearsay but as a demonstrative exhibit prepared to facilitate a complete and accurate summary of the conclusions [the expert] reached after reviewing the recording of [the defendant's] guilty plea hearing. 'Demonstrative evidence is evidence offered for purposes of illustration and clarification.'"[65] In deeming exclusion of the chart reversible error, the appeals court noted that "the true benefit of [the expert's] expertise was hindered by the exclusion of her chart. When the question at issue is the accuracy of the interpreting at a plea hearing, we see the use of the chart or a similar demonstrative as being nearly inevitable."[66]

Similarly, the court in *Hinlicky v. Dreyfuss* found that a demonstrative flowchart was nonhearsay in light of how it was offered (and used) in trial.[67] The defendant, a treating physician, testified that he used a flowchart algorithm to make treatment decisions for the plaintiff-patient and that other physicians in the industry rely on this algorithm.[68] Defense counsel offered the algorithm into evidence.[69] The trial court allowed the defense to use the exhibit to explain the doctor's evaluation procedure, noting testimony that the procedure is reasonably relied upon by other physicians under the "professional reliability exception to the rule against hearsay."[70] The appeals court found that the algorithm was properly admitted, stating that "[w]hile it is true that the algorithm is an extrajudicial statement, it would only be 'classic' hearsay if offered to prove the truth of the matter asserted therein. . . . [Here], counsel offered the algorithm as a demonstrative aid for the jury in understanding the process his client had followed."[71]

The demonstrative-as-hearsay issue was particularly nuanced in *Baker v. State*, a criminal case in Texas.[72] Under Texas evidentiary rules, records and reports of matters observed by police officers are inadmissible hearsay in criminal cases.[73] During trial, the prosecutor used an enlarged copy of a blank police report form with a testifying officer.[74] As the officer testified about what he observed, the prosecutor filled in the blanks in the enlarged form.[75] The completed enlargement was essentially identical to the police report, which itself would have been inadmissible hearsay.[76] The defendant objected to the enlargement as hearsay, both as first introduced and after the prosecutor filled in the blanks.[77] The trial court admitted the exhibit solely as demonstrative evidence, and the appeals court affirmed that decision.[78] The court explained, "As initially offered by the State, the chart falls under the category of demonstrative evidence used as a visual aid or illustration. [The blank chart] contained no assertions of any kind," and thus could not have been hearsay.[79] The court further found that the chart remained nonhearsay even after the prosecutor filled it in with the officer's testimony, because "[b]y definition, the information offered by the officer as he testified was not an 'out of court statement' offered to prove the truth of the matter asserted."[80]

Whether you are defending against or asserting a hearsay objection, don't forget to consider seeking a limiting instruction if the court doesn't appear to be going your way.[81] Like everything else, this, too, is a strategic decision, as it calls attention to the problematic testimony. But if you don't request the instruction, just be aware that that decision could cut against you on appeal even if the objection is otherwise preserved.

Limits on Demonstratives at Various Points in Trial

Sometimes, a challenge to a demonstrative aid is based not on its content, but on the timing of its use. For example, because a demonstrative often explains, illustrates, or clarifies other evidence—evidence that might not be admitted at the time of opening statements—some parties have argued that demonstratives are not permissible during openings. Predictably, courts' rulings on these objections have differed and are fact-dependent.[82]

Similarly, to the extent a visual aid highlights an attorney's argument or is itself argumentative, that visual may draw an objection if used during an opening statement.[83] In *Watters v. State*, a prosecutor displayed a slide during opening statement that featured the defendant's "booking photo with the word 'GUILTY' written across his battered face."[84] This use of a visual was very similar to the prosecutor's visual in *State v. Walter*, discussed in Chapter 9, in which a booking photo of the defendant labeled "GUILTY" was used in closing argument.

In *Watters*, however, it was the use of this visual in opening statement that proved dispositive. The appellate court noted that the photo "declared Watters guilty before the first witness was called and should not have been allowed."[85] The court explained that opening statements outline evidence that will be presented but are not occasions for argument.[86] Thus, the court held that "a PowerPoint may not be used to make an argument visually that would be improper if made orally."[87] Because the prosecutor could not orally declare the defendant guilty in opening statement, the slide was also impermissible; the appeals court reversed Watters's conviction and remanded for a new trial.[88]

At the other end of the spectrum, demonstratives that might otherwise be objectionable under Rule 403 might be allowed during closing arguments, where counsel is generally given more latitude than at other stages of trial.[89] That said, if it appears counsel is going beyond mere argument and effectively introducing new evidence in closing that does not accurately reflect any admitted exhibits or testimony, the visual could be precluded even in closing argument (or the case could be reversed if its use was erroneously permitted).[90]

Trial Court's Discretion

As is clear from the cases referenced in this chapter, trial courts have broad discretion to control the presentation of evidence.[91] That includes the use of demonstratives.[92] Indeed, a judge has the latitude to permit or exclude a demonstrative, often without citing any rules or providing any legal basis, and appellate courts largely will defer to that discretion.[93]

So, your ability to use a specific visual in a particular case often comes down to the trial judge's subjective judgment. Here, too, your reputation and credibility could be the deciding factor in close calls. Take your judge's proclivities and temperament into account when it comes to demonstrative aids. If your judge generally is not a fan of demonstratives, err on the side of caution. Consider using illustrations instead of photos and making your headings matter-of-fact instead of argumentative. And, be prepared as best you can with a backup plan if your visual is excluded—either tone it down or swap it out.

Costs

Federal courts have permitted the taxation of costs for the production of demonstrative aids under 28 U.S.C. § 1920(4).[94] That said, courts still look to see whether the demonstratives were "necessarily obtained" for use in the case, as the statute requires, and whether the costs were reasonable.[95] As the District of Colorado put it, the question is "whether the manner in which the evidence was presented was vital to its effectiveness, or whether it was simply a convenience or extravagance."[96] So, the costs of a demonstrative aid that is deemed redundant, or which does little to aid the fact-finder's understanding of the evidence, or which presents evidence through an expensive means that could have effectively been presented in a less costly way, might not be recoverable.

Courts also disagree on whether the taxable costs associated with demonstratives are limited to the physical creation of the exhibit or include the costs associated with the intellectual efforts to design it. Several district and circuit courts have held that "design services" are akin to expert fees and therefore are not recoverable as "exemplification" under 28 U.S.C. §1920(4).[97] And, some courts that contrast physical preparation of demonstratives with the intellectual effort to create them go a step further, even denying costs of technical support and equipment rental.[98] Other courts disagree, recognizing that the means of presenting the visual is "key to the function of the exhibit."[99]

As with other considerations regarding demonstrative aids, the taxable cost analysis comes down to a case-by-case, and sometimes a visual-by-visual, assessment by the trial court. Most courts recognize, as the Southern District of New York noted, that "computers, computer graphics, digitized documents, and other technological advancements have become important tools of the modern-day trial lawyer. As long as the cost is reasonable and the devices aid in the efficient and effective presentation of evidence, a prevailing party should be allowed to recover their expense."[100]

In an unfamiliar court, some basic research and intelligence-gathering before you dive into your demonstratives is time well spent. Determine how your jurisdiction (and more importantly, your judge) treats demonstrative evidence, and plan accordingly. The most creative, well-designed, and persuasive jury visuals do you no good if you never get to present them. But when the pieces come together, you'll do wonders to help your jurors understand, believe and remember your message—all thanks to using images with impact.

Image Credits

All images throughout this book that are not listed below were designed or photographed by Kerri L. Ruttenberg.

Chapter 1

page 2: Image from Everett Collection/Shutterstock.com

page 3: Concept by Kerri L. Ruttenberg; image designed by Chicago Winter: Dan Winter and Carly Winter

page 5 (bottom): Design concept by Kerri L. Ruttenberg; image designed by Chicago Winter: Dan Winter and Carly Winter

page 10: Concept by Kerri L. Ruttenberg; image designed by Barnes & Roberts LLC: Jason Barnes and Sully Ridout

Chapter 2

page 12: Image from JeremyRichards/Shutterstock.com; image used under license from Shutterstock.com

page 20 (bottom set, top right): Design by Kerri L. Ruttenberg, using image from iStock .com/Pajomend (calculator and pen)

page 20 (bottom row): Designs by Kerri L. Ruttenberg, using images from iStock.com/ Creativeye99 (scales) and iStock.com/saijithsaam (gavel)

Chapter 3

page 22: Image from iStock.com/exdez; icons modified by Kerri L. Ruttenberg with assistance from Greg Wing

page 24 (left): Page capture from Bloomberg Law, *Brady v. Maryland*, 373 U.S. 83 (1963); Annotated design by Kerri L. Ruttenberg

page 24 (right): Page capture of False Claims Act of 1986; Annotated design by Kerri L. Ruttenberg

page 27 (bottom): Concept by Kerri L. Ruttenberg; image designed by RLM | Trial-Graphix: Tim Schelin

page 28 (top row): Concept by Kerri L. Ruttenberg; image designed by RLM | Trial-Graphix: Tim Schelin

page 29 (line graphs at bottom): Designed by Chicago Winter: Dan Winter

page 30 (bar graph, left): Designed by Kerri L. Ruttenberg with assistance from Greg Wing

page 30 (bar graph, right): Designed by Chicago Winter: Carly Winter

page 30 (pie graphs): Designed by Chicago Winter: Dan Winter and Michael Thomas

page 30 (bottom): Designed by Core Legal Concepts: Jeff Chabot

page 31 (top): Designed by Kerri L. Ruttenberg with assistance from Christine Panchur using map image from Google Maps and images from iStock.com/NirdalArt

page 31 (bottom): Designed by Kerri L. Ruttenberg with assistance from Christine Panchur using map image from Google Maps and images from iStock.com/mattjeacock

page 33: Concept by Kerri L. Ruttenberg; image designed by Chicago Winter: Dan Winter and Carly Winter

page 34 (top): Designed by Chicago Winter: Dan Winter and Robert Hodson

page 34 (bottom): Designed by Chicago Winter: Dan Winter and Kolin Pope with sampled SEM for texture

page 35 (right): Designed by Kerri L. Ruttenberg using images from iStock.com: iStock.com/Diane Labombarbe (stethoscope), iStock.com/tenmami (doctor), iStock.com/ryan burke (pills and container)

Chapter 4

page 38: Photograph from iStock.com/kmaassrock

page 41 (top): Designed by Edward A. Gold and reprinted herein with permission

page 41 (middle and bottom): Images designed by Kerri L. Ruttenberg using spreadsheet designed by Edward A. Gold

page 49 (top left): Text substance and design by Kerri L. Ruttenberg with assistance for text placement by Greg Wing using image from iStock.com/Ravennka

page 49 (top right): Text substance and design by Kerri L. Ruttenberg with assistance for text placement and icon selection by Greg Wing using image from iStock.com/theseamuss

page 49 (bottom left): Text substance and design by Kerri L. Ruttenberg with assistance for text placement by Greg Wing using image from iStock.com/TarapongS

page 49 (bottom right): Text substance and design by Kerri L. Ruttenberg using image from iStock.com/Vjom

Chapter 5

page 52: Photograph by nattanan726/Shutterstock.com; image used under license from Shutterstock.com

page 60 (top): Designed by RLM | TrialGraphix: Dave Johnson

page 60 (fists breaking chains build): Designed by Barnes & Roberts LLC: Jason Barnes

page 60 (climbing out of hole build): Designed by Barnes & Roberts LLC: Jason Barnes

page 61 (full build): Designed by Barnes & Roberts LLC: Jason Barnes; Photograph reprinted courtesy of Barnes & Roberts LLC

page 65 (bottom): Concept by Kerri L. Ruttenberg; image designed by Core Legal Concepts: Barbara Lucente

page 66 (top): Concept by Kerri L. Ruttenberg; image designed by Core Legal Concepts: Barbara Lucente

page 66 (bottom): Concept by Kerri L. Ruttenberg; image designed by Core Legal Concepts: Kim Levine, using images from depositphotos.com, 5752871, 3245280

page 68 (full flowchart): Designed by Core Legal Concepts: Kim Levine

Chapter 6

page 70: iStock.com/adamkaz

page 72 (top): Concept and text by Kerri L. Ruttenberg; image designed by Core Legal Concepts: Jessica Fowler

page 72 (middle): Designed by Barnes & Roberts LLC: Jason Barnes

page 73 (all images): Concept and replacement text by Kerri L. Ruttenberg; designed by TrialGraphix, Inc.

page 74 (top left and right): Designed by Core Legal Concepts: Kim Levine

page 74 (crime tape and guns): Designed by Core Legal Concepts: Derrick Sample

page 74 (smoke stacks): Designed by Core Legal Concepts: April Tishler

page 74 (crushed cars): Concept by Kerri L. Ruttenberg; image designed by RLM | TrialGraphix: Jason Young

page 75 (top): Designed by Core Legal Concepts: Derrick Sample, using image from depositphotos.com, 55025257

page 75 (middle): Designed by Core Legal Concepts: Katie MacInnes

page 75 (bottom): Designed by Core Legal Concepts: Kim Levine

page 76 (bottom left and bottom right): Designed by Kerri L. Ruttenberg with assistance from RLM | TrialGraphix

page 77 (bar graph and pie graph): Designed by Kerri L. Ruttenberg with assistance from RLM | TrialGraphix

page 78 (both line graphs): Designed by Kerri L. Ruttenberg with assistance from RLM | TrialGraphix

page 78 (bottom): Designed by Kerri L. Ruttenberg with assistance from Greg Wing

page 79: Designed by Kerri L. Ruttenberg, using image from iStock.com/vasabii

page 80 (both bar graphs): Concept by Kerri L. Ruttenberg; image designed by RLM | TrialGraphix

page 81 (top row, bar graphs): Designed by Kerri L. Ruttenberg, with assistance from Greg Wing

page 82 (both images): Designed by Kerri L. Ruttenberg using images from iStock.com: iStock.com/ET-ARTWORKS (cell phone "B"), iStock.com/ET-ARTWORKS (cell phone "D"), iStock.com/Ivcandy (cell phone "A"), iStock.com/VLADGRIN (cell phone "E"), iStock.com/vasabii (cell phone "C")

page 84: Design concept by Kerri L. Ruttenberg with assistance from Greg Wing

Chapter 7

page 86: Photograph from iStock.com/Ira Peters

page 89: Design concept and text by Kerri L. Ruttenberg; image design updated by Barnes & Roberts LLC: Jason Barnes

page 90: Design concept and text by Kerri L. Ruttenberg; image designed by RLM | TrialGraphix

page 92: Design concept, text and exhibits by Kerri L. Ruttenberg; image designed by Barnes & Roberts LLC: Jason Barnes, using photographs reprinted courtesy of Barnes & Roberts, LLC

page 93 (full build at the bottom): Design concept and text by Kerri L. Ruttenberg; image designed by RLM | TrialGraphix

page 94 (left image only): Design concept by Kerri L. Ruttenberg; image designed by RLM | TrialGraphix

page 95 (both images): Designed by Barnes & Roberts LLC: Jason Barnes

page 96: Text by Kerri L. Ruttenberg with assistance by Greg Wing to modify image from iStock.com/JDawnInk.

page 97 (top): Concept by Kerri L. Ruttenberg; image designed by Core Legal Concepts: Barbara Lucente

page 97 (middle): Designed by Core Legal Concepts: Jeff Chabot

page 97 (bottom): Designed by Core Legal Concepts: Jeff Chabot

page 98 (top): Designed by Core Legal Concepts: Kim Levine

page 98 (middle): Designed by Core Legal Concepts: Kim Levine, using image from depositphotos.com, 53266367

Chapter 8

page 100: Image from iStock.com/caracterdesign

page 102 (top): Authored by the National Nuclear Security Administration; work is in the public domain in the United States because it was prepared by an officer or employee of the United States Government as part of that person's official duties under the terms of Title 17, Chapter 1, Section 105 of the U.S. Code; available on Wikimedia Commons

page 102 (bottom): Designed by RLM | TrialGraphix: Jason Young, using image from Google Earth

page 103 (top; bottom set, top and bottom left): Designed by Chicago Winter: Dan Winter

page 103 (bottom set, right): Designed by RLM | TrialGraphix: Jared Schneidman

page 104: Screen captures by Kerri L. Ruttenberg, using images from Google Maps

page 105 (top images): Screen captures by Kerri L. Ruttenberg, using images from Google Maps

page 105 (top and bottom route maps): Designed by Chicago Winter: Dan Winter and Hui Feng, using images from Google Maps

page 106 (top): Designed by Core Legal Concepts: Bain Zietlow, data source: http://www.economist.com/content/big-mac-index

page 106 (bottom): Designed by Core Legal Concepts: Pamela Franz, data source: http://www.census.gov/censusexplorer/censusexplorer-retail.html

page 107: Designed by Core Legal Concepts: Kim Levine, using image from depositphotos.com, 926138

page 108 (top left U.S. map): Image from iStock.com/bamlou

page 108 (top right U.S. map): Image from iStock.com/HS3RUS

page 108 (bottom left U.S. map): Image from iStock.com/Stacey Lynn Brown

page 108 (bottom right U.S. map): Image from iStock.com/ziggymaj

page 108 (top route map): Design concept by Kerri L. Ruttenberg; image designed by Core Legal Concepts: Pamela Franz

page 108 (bottom route map): Design concept by Kerri L. Ruttenberg; image designed by Barnes & Roberts LLC: Jason Barnes

page 109 (top): Designed by Core Legal Concepts: Pamela Franz

page 109 (bottom): Concept by Kerri L. Ruttenberg; image designed by RLM | TrialGraphix: Jason Young

page 110: Replacement text and locations for confidentiality by Kerri L. Ruttenberg; confidentiality modifications implemented by RLM | TrialGraphix

page 111: Designed by Kerri L. Ruttenberg using image from Bardocz Peter/Shutterstock.com

page 112: Design concept by Kerri L. Ruttenberg; image designed by RLM | TrialGraphix: Guy Joubert

page 113 (left): Replacement text and locations for confidentiality by Kerri L. Ruttenberg; confidentiality modifications implemented by RLM | TrialGraphix

page 113 (right): Design concept by Kerri L. Ruttenberg; image designed by RLM | TrialGraphix: Guy Joubert

Chapter 9

page 114: Photograph by iravgustin/Shutterstock.com; image used under license from Shutterstock.com

page 116 (top): Design concept by Kerri L. Ruttenberg; image designed by Core Legal Concepts: Derrick Sample, using image from depositphotos.com, 13830322

page 116 (bottom): Photograph by Sergey Edentod/Shutterstock.com; image used under license from Shutterstock.com

page 118 (top): Image from iStock.com/adventtr

page 118 (bottom): Image from iStock.com/Maxim Chupashkin

page 120: Design concept and text by Kerri L. Ruttenberg using images from Ostancov Vladislav/Shutterstock.com (sushi) and MaraZe/Shutterstock.com (burger); images used under license from Shutterstock.com

page 121 (left): Design concept and text by Kerri L. Ruttenberg with assistance from Julianna Kovach-Zingale using photo from iStock.com/monainshanghai

page 121 (right): Design concept and text by Kerri L. Ruttenberg using photograph by XiXinXing/Shutterstock.com; image used under license from Shutterstock.com

page 122 (top row): Image captures from Google Maps

page 122 (bottom): Design and photograph by Kerri L. Ruttenberg; truck image from iStock.com/misterelements

page 124: Design concepts by Kerri L. Ruttenberg; images designed by RLM | TrialGraphix: Devin Price, using photograph by Dennis Schroeder, National Renewable Energy Lab, U.S. Department of Energy

page 128 (top): Designed by Kerri L. Ruttenberg, using image from iStock.com/AleksandarNakic

page 128 (left side): Designed by Kerri L. Ruttenberg, using image from iStock.com/minemero

page 128 (right side): Designed by Kerri L. Ruttenberg, using image from iStock.com/Adam Petto

page 128 (bottom): Designed by Kerri L. Ruttenberg, using image from iStock.com/Cerchi

page 130: Photograph obtained from public file in *State v. Walter*, No. WD76655, 2014 BL 281489 (Mo. App. W.D. Oct. 7, 2014), available through Missouri court Case.net system

Chapter 10

page 134: Image from Janaka Dharmasena/Shutterstock.com; images used under license from Shutterstock.com

page 136 (top left): Designed by RLM | TrialGraphix: Devin Price

page 136 (top right): Designed by Chicago Winter: Dan Winter with sampled SEM for texture

page 136 (bottom left): Designed by Chicago Winter: Dan Winter using NASA photo

page 136 (bottom right): Designed by Chicago Winter: Dan Winter and Carly Winter

page 137 (top): Image from iStock.com/CSA-Images

page 137 (middle): Designed by RLM | TrialGraphix: Devin Price

page 137 (bottom): Design and concept by Kerri L. Ruttenberg, with assistance from RLM | TrialGraphix

page 138 (top): Design and concept by Kerri L. Ruttenberg, with assistance from RLM | TrialGraphix

page 138 (bottom): Design and concept by Kerri L. Ruttenberg and Chicago Winter: Dan Winter and Carly Winter; image designed by Chicago Winter: Dan Winter and Carly Winter

page 139 (top): Designed by Chicago Winter: Dan Winter

page 139 (bottom): Designed by Core Legal Concepts: Derrick Sample

page 140: Image by Charles Joseph Minard (1781–1870), published 1869; work is in the public domain in the United States and available on Wikimedia Commons

page 141: Image authored by U.S. Department of Transportation, Federal Highway Administration; work is in the public domain and available on Wikimedia Commons, source: http://www.ops.fhwa.dot.gov/freight/freight_analysis/nat_freight_stats/images/truck_traffic_1998.pdf

page 142: Image authored by the National Oceanic and Atmospheric Administration and available at http://response.restoration.noaa.gov/oil-and-chemical-spills/significant-incidents/exxon-valdez-oil-spill/timeline-ecological-recovery-infographic.html; work is in the public domain and available through Creative Commons (license at https://creativecommons.org/licenses/by/2.0/legalcode)

page 143: Copyright Tokyo Metro Co., Ltd. and Transportation Bureau of the Tokyo Metropolitan Government, reprinted with permission and upon payment of fee to Metro Ad Agency Co., Ltd.

page 143 (bottom): Designed by Core Legal Concepts: Alex Miller

page 144 (top): Image from iStock.com/artvea

page 144 (middle left): Image from iStock.com/pop_jop

page 144 (middle right): Image from iStock.com/Askold Romanov

page 144 (bottom): Image from iStock.com/Bitter

page 145 (top): Image authored by U.S. Department of Justice; work is in the public domain in the United States because it was prepared by an officer or employee of the United States Government as part of that person's official duties under the terms of Title 17, Chapter 1, Section 105 of the U.S. Code; image reprinted in only available resolution

page 145 (bottom): Design concept by Kerri L. Ruttenberg; image designed by Barnes & Roberts LLC: Jason Barnes, incorporating images from iStock.com/Sieto

page 146: Design concept by Kerri L. Ruttenberg; image designed by Chicago Winter: Dan Winter and Carly Winter

page 147 (top): Design concept by Kerri L. Ruttenberg; image designed by RLM | TrialGraphix: Guy Joubert

page 148 (top): Concept by Kerri L. Ruttenberg; image designed by RLM | TrialGraphix: Dave Johnson

page 148 (bottom): Concept by Kerri L. Ruttenberg; image designed by Barnes & Roberts LLC: Jason Barnes and Sully Ridout

page 150: Design concept by Kerri L. Ruttenberg; images designed by TrialGraphix, Inc.

page 151 (top, Empire State Building): Designed by Chicago Winter: Dan Winter

page 151 (middle left, sporting venues): Designed by Chicago Winter: Dan Winter and Carly Winter

page 151 (middle right, pool): Designed by Chicago Winter: Dan Winter

page 151 (bottom, red dots): Designed by Chicago Winter: Dan Winter and Michael Thomas

page 152 (top left): Concept by Kerri L. Ruttenberg; Image designed by Core Legal Concepts: Kim Levine, using image from depositphotos.com, 6148050

page 152 (top right): Core Legal Concepts: Kim Levine, using image from depositphotos.com, 6148050

page 152 (bottom): Design concept by Kerri L. Ruttenberg; image designed by Chicago Winter: Dan Winter and Carly Winter

page 153: Concept by Kerri L. Ruttenberg; images designed by Barnes & Roberts LLC: Jason Barnes

page 154: Images designed by Core Legal Concepts: Kim Levine

page 155: Image designed by Core Legal Concepts: Derrick Sample, using image from depositphotos.com, 1964668

Chapter 11

page 158: Designed by Core Legal Concepts: Bain Zietlow, using image from depositphotos.com, 6639824

page 160 (top): Designed by Kerri L. Ruttenberg using image by Edward A. Gold and reprinted with permission

page 161 (top spreadsheet and bottom spreadsheet with graph): Designed by Chicago Winter: Dan Winter and Carly Winter

page 162 (top): Design concept by Kerri L. Ruttenberg with assistance from Christine Panchur, using image from iStock.com/sorendls

Chapter 12

page 164: Image from Fer Gregory/Shutterstock.com; image used under license from Shutterstock.com

page 165 (full crane animation): Designed by RLM | TrialGraphix: Devin Price

page 166 (top): Designed by RLM | TrialGraphix: Devin Price

page 166 (bottom, map animation): Designed by Core Legal Concepts: Chris Huffman

page 167 (top row, artery animation): Designed by Chicago Winter: Dan Winter and Robert Hodson

page 167 (middle, energy animation; bottom, brain animation): Designed by Chicago Winter: Dan Winter and Kolin Pope

page 168 (full conveyor belt animation): Designed by Core Legal Concepts: Chris Huffman

page 169 (full dot animation): Designed by Chicago Winter: Dan Winter and Michael Thomas

page 170 (full animation of contaminant seeping): Designed by RLM | TrialGraphix: Devin Price

page 170 (bottom): Designed by Chicago Winter: Dan Winter, with sampled textures and details

page 171: Designed by Chicago Winter: Dan Winter and Kolin Pope

pages 172–175 (all screen captures): Design concept and screen captures by Kerri L. Ruttenberg; underlying graph by RLM | TrialGraphix

Chapter 13

page 178: Image from iStock.com/esolla

page 181 (bottom overtime image): Designed by Kerri L. Ruttenberg with assistance from Greg Wing

page 183: Designed by Kerri L. Ruttenberg, using screen captures from Microsoft Word

page 185 (all images): Designed by Kerri L. Ruttenberg, using image from iStock.com/CHUYN

page 188: Image is Ishihara Plate 9 in color blindness test; image is in the public domain because it consists entirely of information that is common property and contains no original authorship; image available on Wikimedia Commons

Chapter 14

page 190: Hinochika/Shutterstock.com; image used under license from Shutterstock.com

Chapter 15

page 196: Images from joingate/Shutterstock.com; image used under license from Shutterstock.com

Chapter 16

page 204: Blue Vista Design/Shutterstock.com; image used under license from Shutterstock.com

page 206 (top): Design concept and text by Kerri L. Ruttenberg; Original design by TrialGraphix, Inc.; image updated by Barnes & Roberts LLC: Jason Barnes

page 208 (bottom right, bar graph): Design concept and text by Kerri L. Ruttenberg; image designed by RLM | TrialGraphix

page 209 (bottom): Design concept by Kerri L. Ruttenberg; image designed by Core Legal Concepts: Kim Levine, using images from depositphotos.com, 5752871, 3245280

page 210 (top): Images from depositphotos.com, 5483446, 12768932

page 210 (bottom): Design concept by Kerri L. Ruttenberg; image designed by Core Legal Concepts: Kim Levine, using images from depositphotos.com, 5483446, 12768932

page 211: Design concept by Kerri L. Ruttenberg; images designed by Core Legal Concepts: Kim Levine, using images from depositphotos.com, 5483446, 12768932

Chapter 17

page 214 (bottom): Designed by Kerri L. Ruttenberg using images from iStock.com/sajithsaam (gavel) and iStock.com/vasabii (money)

page 215 (top row): Designed by Kerri L. Ruttenberg using photograph by Kerri L. Ruttenberg and image from iStock.com/misterelements (truck)

page 217 (bottom): Designed by Barnes & Roberts LLC: Jason Barnes

Chapter 18

page 224 (all graphs): Design concept and text by Kerri L. Ruttenberg; image designed by RLM | TrialGraphix

Chapter 19

page 232: Designed and created by Eric Berlin with assistance from Julianna Kovach Zingale; reprinted with permission from Eric Berlin

page 233: Screen captures from https://color.adobe.com, using photograph by Kerri L. Ruttenberg

page 235: Screen capture from https://color.adobe.com

page 236: Screen captures from https://color.adobe.com

page 237 (top): Screen capture https://color.adobe.com

page 238 (bottom): iStock.com/PeterHermesFurian

page 239: Screen capture from https://color.adobe.com

page 240 (bottom): Screen capture from https://color.adobe.com

page 241: Screen captures from https://color.adobe.com

page 242: Screen capture from https://color.adobe.com

page 244 (middle): Designed by Kerri L. Ruttenberg, using image from iStock.com/fpm (chain)

page 244 (bottom): Image from iStock.com/

Chapter 20

page 250: Image from Gray Wall Studio/Shutterstock.com; image used under license from Shutterstock.com

page 252 (top and middle): Designed by Kerri L. Ruttenberg using PowerPoint template

page 253 (bottom): Designed by Kerri L. Ruttenberg, using image by Edward A. Gold

page 255 (bottom row): Designed by Kerri L. Ruttenberg, using image by Edward A. Gold

page 256 (top and middle right): Designed by Kerri L. Ruttenberg, using image by Edward A. Gold

Chapter 21

page 260: Image from iStock.com/Inok

page 264: Concept by Kerri L. Ruttenberg, with assistance from RLM | TrialGraphix

page 265 (bottom): Design concept by Kerri L. Ruttenberg; image designed by RLM | TrialGraphix

page 266 (top): Design concept by Kerri L. Ruttenberg; image designed by RLM | TrialGraphix

pages 266–268 (patent application graphics): Designed by Kerri L. Ruttenberg with assistance from RLM | TrialGraphix, using statistics from the U.S. Patent and Trademark Office, available at http://www.uspto.gov/web/offices/ac/ido/oeip/taf/us_stat.htm, and image by FatCow Web Hosting (http://www.fatcow.com/free-icons/), available at https://commons.wikimedia.org/wiki/File:Farm-Fresh_lightbulb.png

page 269: Authored by U.S. Department of Justice; work is in the public domain in the United States because it was prepared by an officer or employee of the United States Government as part of that person's official duties under the terms of Title 17, Chapter 1, Section 105 of the U.S. Code; image printed at only available resolution

page 270: Design concept adapted by Kerri L. Ruttenberg with assistance from Christine Panchur, using image from iStock.com/Kaan Ates (scales)

pages 273–274: Images used in public trial

page 275: Image modifications designed by Kerri L. Ruttenberg and implemented by TrialGraphix, Inc.

page 276: Original modifications designed by Kerri L. Ruttenberg and implemented by TrialGraphix, Inc.; further modifications made with assistance from Christine Panchur to replace original photographs, using images from iStock.com/Cameron Whitman; iStock .com/FredFroese; iStock.com/Juanmonino

Chapter 22

page 278: Image from iStock.com/Geber86

Chapter 23

page 288: Image from Corbis/Fotosearch.com

page 290: Photograph by Rawpixel.com/Shutterstock.com; image used under license from Shutterstock.com

page 293: Image from iStock.com/berya113

page 295 (top): Design concept by Kerri L. Ruttenberg with assistance from Christine Panchur, using photograph from iStock.com/SelectStock

page 295 (bottom left): Designed by Kerri L. Ruttenberg using photograph by wavebreakmedia/Shutterstock.com; image used under license from Shutterstock.com.

page 298: Image courtesy of ELMO USA Corp.

page 300: Designs by Kerri L. Ruttenberg using surveillance images shown in public trial

page 303: Image from iStock.com/klikk (whiteboard)

page 303: Image from iStock.com/Greeek (flip chart)

Chapter 24

page 313: Photographs from *United States v. Johnson*, 362 F. Supp. 2d 1043, n.6 (N.D. Iowa 2005); image printed at only available resolution

General Copyright Notices

References

Chapter 1

1. Harold Pashler, Mark McDaniel, Doug Rohrer & Robert Bjork, *Learning Styles: Concepts and Evidence,* 9 Psychological Science in the Public Interest, 105–19 (2009).

2. Jeffery R. Boyll, *Enhancing Juror Comprehension and Memory Retention,* 12 Trial Diplomacy J. 194–99 (1989).

3. Tor Norretranders, The User Illusion: Cutting Consciousness Down to Size 124–27 (1998). (Noting that the eye receives 10,000,000 bits of information every second, but our brains process only 40 bits (.0004%). At the same time, we hear 100,000 bits of information every second, but we process only 30 bits (.03%).)

4. John Medina, Brain Rules 42–47 (2d ed. 2014).

5. *See, e.g.*, Boyll, *supra* note 2, at 195; Medina, *supra* note 4, at 107–09.

6. Medina, *supra* note 4, at 115.

7. Boyll, *supra* note 2, at 197 (emphasis added).

8. Douglas R. Vogel, *Persuasion and the Role of Visual Presentation Support: The UM/3M Study,* Working Paper Series, June 1986.

9. *Id*. at 3.

10. *Id*. at 4–5.

11. *Id*. at 19.

12. Joline Morrison, *The impacts of presentation visuals on persuasion,* 33 Information & Management, 125–35 (1998).

13. Boyll, *supra* note 2, at 197.

14. John Medina, *Brain Rules*, www.brainrules.net/vision (last visited October 14, 2016).

15. Medina, *supra* note 4, at 181.

16. *Id.* at 191.

17. Brad E. Bell & Elizabeth F. Loftus, *Vivid Persuasion in the Courtroom,* 49 J. Personality Assessment 659 (1985); Dana Binder, The relationship between need for cognition, argument strength, and the persuasiveness of courtroom technology (2006) (unpublished Ph.D. dissertation, University of Wyoming–Laramie); Veronica Blas Dahir, The effect of presentation mode and argument quality on memory, comprehension, and decision-making: Implications for computer display usage and evidence strength in the courtroom (2005) (unpublished Ph.D. dissertation, University of Nevada–Reno); Linda C. Morell, *New technology: Experimental research on the influence of computer-animated displays on jurors,* 28 Sw. U. L. Rev. 411 (1999).

18. Ken Broda-Bahm, *Show, Don't Just Tell: Part 1, Continuity* (Persuasion Strategies Visual Persuasion Study), Persuasive Litigator (July 14, 2011), http://www.persuasivelitigator.com/2011/07/show-dont-just-tell-continuity.html.

19. *Id.*

20. Shelly Chaiken, *Heuristic Versus Systematic Information Processing and the Use of Source Versus Message Cues in Persuasion,* 39 J. Personality & Soc. Psychol. 752–66 (1980).

21. Jaihyun Park & Neal Feigenson, *Effects of a Visual Technology on Mock Juror Decision Making,* 27 Applied Cognitive Psychol. 235–46 (2012).

22. Binder, *supra* note 17.

Chapter 2

1. *See, e.g.*, Nancy Duarte, Slide:ology: The Art and Science of Creating Great Presentations (2008); Garr Reynolds, Presentation Zen Design (2010).

Chapter 3

1. Edward Tufte, Envisioning Information 67 (2d ed. 2001).

2. *Id.*

3. Robin Williams, The Non-Designer's Presentation Book 135 (2010).

Chapter 5

1. Edward Tufte, Cognitive Style of PowerPoint: Pitching Out Corrupts Within 15 (2d ed. 2011); John Medina, Brain Rules 197 (2d ed. 2014).

2. *See* Federal Rule of Evidence 1006 (allowing the use of a "summary, chart or calculation to prove the content of voluminous writings, recordings or photographs that cannot be conveniently examined in court").

Chapter 6

1. Edward Tufte, Envisioning Information 34 (2d ed. 2001).

Chapter 9

1. John Medina, Brain Rules 183–97 (2d ed. 2014).

2. *State v. Walter*, 479 S.W.3d 118 (Mo. 2016) (en banc) (photograph reprinted in court opinion).

3. *State v. Walter*, No. WD76655, 2014 WL 4976913 at *17 (Mo. App. W.D. 2014).

4. *Id.* at 17–18.

5. *Walter*, 479 S.W.3d at 127.

6. *Id.*

7. *Id.* at 122.

8. *Id.* at 127.

9. *Id.* (quoting Lucille A. Jewel, *Through a Glass Darkly: Using Brain Science and Visual Rhetoric to Gain a Professional Perspective on Visual Advocacy*, 19 S. Cal. Interdisc. L.J. 237, 289 (2010)).

10. *State v. Walker*, 341 P.3d 976, 985 (Wash. 2015).

11. *Id.*

12. *Id.*

13. *Id.* at 983, 985.

14. *Id.* at 985.

15. *See also Spence v. State*, 129 A.3d 212 (Del. 2015) (prosecutor showed photo depicting victim's body "splayed and bloodied" with superimposed text stating that the defendant's "actions led to . . . Terror . . . Fear . . . And to the ultimate crime . . . MURDER[,]" with the word "MURDER" in large, red lettering; court held this was improper, as it attempted to inflame the jury); *In re Glasmann*, 286 P.3d 673 (Wash. 2012) (The court determined that the word "GUILTY," displayed in red font across the booking photograph of the defendant, was an impermissible appeal to the jury's emotions. The court granted a new trial because the prosecution's slideshow presentation contained multiple assertions of the defendant's guilt, statements that the jurors could only acquit the defendant if they believed the defendant's trial testimony, and improperly modified exhibits.

In addition, the court found the misconduct to be so pervasive that it could not have been cured by an instruction.).

Chapter 10

1. EDWARD TUFTE, VISUAL EXPLANATIONS: IMAGES AND QUANTITIES, EVIDENCE AND NARRATIVE 73 (5th ed. 2002).

2. *Id.*

3. EDWARD TUFTE, THE VISUAL DISPLAY OF QUANTITATIVE INFORMATION 40–41 (2d ed. 2006).

4. The real informational graphic I used during that mock closing argument was translated from my cursory drawings very quickly by a generous graphic design firm that donated their services to the conference. For this book, I asked two other firms to redesign the slide into a style I would use in a real trial. (The firms are credited in the Image Credits section.) The core design concept and all of the inputs, however, are identical to what I used in the mock trial program.

Chapter 12

1. *See, e.g.*, *Verizon Directories Corp. v. Yellow Book USA, Inc.*, 331 F. Supp. 2d 136, 137–38 (E.D.N.Y. 2004) (reviewing relevant literature on pedagogical aids that categorizes computer-generated exhibits as static images, animations, simulations, and computer models; the court added a fifth category of enhanced images, and a sixth for writings and diagrams created in court).

Chapter 17

1. EDWARD R. TUFTE, ENVISIONING INFORMATION 53, 60–65 (2d ed. 2001).

Chapter 18

1. EDWARD TUFTE, THE VISUAL DISPLAY OF QUANTITATIVE INFORMATION 42 (2d ed. 2006).

2. JOHN MEDINA, BRAIN RULES 125–59 (2d ed. 2014).

Chapter 19

1. *See, e.g.*, Felix A. Wichmann et al., *The Contributions of Color to Recognition Memory for Natural Scenes*, 28 J. EXPERIMENTAL PSYCHOL.: LEARNING, MEMORY, AND COGNITION 509–20 (2002) (citing Donald Homa & Cynthia Viera, *Long-term memory for pictures under conditions of thematically related foils*, 16 MEMORY & COGNITION 411–21 (1988); Raymond S. Nickerson, *Short-Term Memory for Complex Meaningful Visual Configurations: A Demonstration of Capacity*, 19 CAN. J. PSYCHOL. 155–60 (1965); Roger N. Shepard, *Recognition Memory for Words, Sentences and Pictures*, 6 J. VERBAL LEARNING & VERBAL BEHAV. 156–63 (1967);

Lionel Standing, *Learning 10,000 pictures*, 25 Q.J. Experimental Psychol. 207–22 (1973); Kotaro Suzuki & Rika Takahashi, *Effectiveness of Color in Picture Recognition Memory*, 39 Japanese Psychol. Res. 25–32 (1997)).

2. *See, e.g.*, Jan V. White, Color for Impact (1997).

3. *See id.* at 4 (further noting that in a study of 25,000 magazines, ads had 52% higher readership when color was added).

4. Margaret Livingstone, Vision and Art: The Biology of Seeing 78–81 (2014).

5. You may notice when working with computers (or any digital media) that the basis for color creation is the RBG model—red, blue, and green. Color is created by mixing beams of red, blue, and green light in different amounts. In contrast, when you're working with print (such as your desktop color inkjet at home), the color model is CMYK—cyan (in the blue family), magenta (in the red family), yellow, and a "key" color, usually black. With those four colors, we can print thousands upon thousands of colors, shades, and tints. The CMYK model works like the traditional color wheel, with blue and yellow making green, etc. But with RBG, things are a little different. Red and green make yellow, blue and red make hot pink, and blue and green make cyan. Colors you see on a monitor in RBG can look different from colors printed in CMYK. If jurors will get hard copies of your slides to take into the jury room, keep this in mind. At bottom, however, although the color creation process differs between print and digital media, the ultimate color relationships discussed in this book are the same when selecting a color palette for your slides.

6. For additional reading on color models and color theory, *see* Tom Fraser & Adam Banks, Designer's Color Manual (2004); Aaris Sherin, Design Elements: Color Fundamentals (2012); Tony Seddon & Jane Waterhouse, Graphic Design for Non-Designers: The Ultimate Primer for the Design Rookie (2009); Robin Williams, The Non-Designer's Design Book (4th ed. 2015); Jan V. White, Color for Impact (1997).

7. Nancy Duarte, Slide:ology: The Art and Science of Creating Great Presentations 136 (2008).

Chapter 20

1. Robin Williams, The Non-Designer's Presentation Book 134 (2010).

Chapter 21

1. Edward Tufte, The Visual Display of Quantitative Information 55 (2d ed. 2006).

Chapter 23

1. Ken Broda-Bahm, *Show, Don't Just Tell: Part 1, Continuity* (Persuasion Strategies Visual Persuasion Study), PERSUASIVE LITIGATOR (July 14, 2011), http://www.persuasivelitigator.com/2011/07/show-dont-just-tell-continuity.html.

2. *See, e.g., Brown v. Cain*, No. 14-3538, slip op. at 10 (W.D. La. July 14, 2015) (The same photograph was shown to multiple witnesses, and each had the opportunity to place a sticker on the photo to show where the shooting occurred. The stickers were not removed between witnesses, but the court determined the stickers did not provide subsequent witnesses with enough information to fabricate their entire story of the shooting. The court determined that the witnesses could not come to their own conclusions about the sequence of events in the shooting merely by viewing the photograph with other stickers.).

Chapter 24

1. *See, e.g., Clark v. Cantrell*, 529 S.E.2d 528, 535–38 (S.C. 2000).

2. *See, e.g.*, Me. R. Evid. 616 (allows demonstratives—defined as otherwise inadmissible exhibits that illustrate witness testimony or counsel's arguments—to be used during jury deliberations if both parties consent or if the court finds good cause); Fla. R. Crim. P. 3.400 (demonstrative aids not admitted into evidence are not allowed in the jury room, *Douglas v. State*, 141 So. 3d 107, 128–29 (Fla. 2012)).

3. *See, e.g., State v. Butler*, No. A14-1073, 2015 BL 230331 at *4 (Minn. Ct. App. July 20, 2015) (allowing use of soccer ball to demonstrate how fluid travels when it comes off of a round surface impacted by force because it likely assisted the jury in understanding the witness's testimony; court noted that "appellate courts have admitted visual aids for illustrative purposes to allow a witness to explain injuries 'from a three-dimensional perspective.'") (quoting *State v. Rhodes*, 627 N.W.2d 74, 84 (Minn. 2001)).

4. *See, e.g., United States v. Janati*, 374 F.3d 263, 272–73 (4th Cir. 2004) (noting that because the underlying documents need be admissible but not actually introduced into evidence, Rule 1006 summary charts themselves are admitted as evidence "in order to give the jury evidence of the underlying documents"); *but see United States v. Taylor*, 210 F.3d 311, 315 (5th Cir. 2000) (stating "Rule 1006 applies to summary charts based on evidence previously admitted but which is so voluminous that in-court review by the jury would be inconvenient.").

5. *See, e.g., Uniroyal Goodrich Tire Co. v. Martinez*, 977 S.W.2d 328, 342 (Tex. 1998) ("Charts and diagrams that summarize, or perhaps emphasize, testimony are admissible if the underlying information has been admitted into evidence, or is subsequently admitted into evidence."). *See, e.g., Safety Nat'l Cas. Corp. v.*

U.S. Dep't of Homeland Sec., No. 4:5-cv-2159, 2007 WL 7131004, at *1 (S.D. Tex. Oct. 22, 2007) (a pedagogical summary is itself not considered evidence, but is "'used merely to aid the jury in its understanding of the evidence that has already been admitted'") (quoting *Janati*, 374 F.3d at 273); *United States v. Milkiewicz*, 470 F.3d 390, 397 (1st Cir. 2006) (pedagogical summary "must be linked to evidence previously admitted," and "the jury should be instructed that it is not to be considered as evidence but only as an aid in evaluating the evidence") (quoting *Janati*, 374 F.3d at 273); *United States v. Buck*, 324 F.3d 786, 790–91 (5th Cir. 2004) (government used summary diagram with witness to show connection between defendant and alleged misapplied federal funds; court stated "it was proper for the diagram to be shown to the jury to assist in its understanding of testimony and documents that had been produced, but the diagram should not have been admitted as an exhibit or taken to the jury room" because it was "plainly a pedagogical aid."); *United States v. Bray*, 139 F.3d 1104, 1111 (6th Cir. 1998) (demonstratives "may reflect to some extent, through captions or other organizational devices or descriptions, the inferences and conclusions drawn from the underlying evidence by the summary's proponent" and may be argumentative, unlike Rule 1006 summaries, which summarize voluminous documents without argument); *State v. Stewart*, 643 N.W.2d 281, 295 (Minn. 2002) (court held that admissibility of demonstrative evidence depends on relevance, accuracy and assistance to the jury in understanding witness testimony; court further held that computer animation of a shooting to aid medical examiner's testimony was erroneously admitted at trial because it included "facial expressions and movements" that depicted deliberate, intentional actions by the shooter, and thus the content exceeded what was in the record from witness testimony, created impressions about intent that the state needed to prove, and exceeded the purpose for which it was admitted); *Kinn v. HCR ManorCare*, 998 N.E.2d 852, 870–71 (Ohio Ct. App. 2013) (finding that timeline of events was a demonstrative exhibit, not a Rule 1006 summary, and "the better practice" is to use the timeline to illustrate witness testimony but not allow it to go to the jury room); *Dunkle v. State*, 139 P.3d 228, 247 (Okla. Crim. App. 2006) (stating that video and computer-generated reenactments should be considered demonstrative aids with no independent evidentiary value and therefore should not be available to the jury during deliberations).

6. 331 F. Supp. 2d 136 (E.D.N.Y. 2004).

7. *Id.* at 139–40 (citing cases and secondary source materials stating that demonstratives are not evidence and then departing from those cases and admitting into evidence all pedagogical aids used by the parties in the case before it).

8. *Id.* at 142.

9. *Id.*

10. *Milkiewicz*, 470 F.3d at 398 (citing *Bray*, 139 F.3d at 1112); *see also* Kenneth S. Broun, 2 McCormick on Evidence § 214 (7th ed. 2013) ("A major issue in recent case law is the evidentiary status of summaries and charts that present voluminous documentary evidence and testimony that have been admitted at trial in a mode "more akin to argument than evidence . . . [which] may reflect to some extent, through captions or other organizational devices or descriptions, the inferences and conclusions drawn . . . by the summary's proponent.") (quoting *Milkiewicz*, 470 F.3d at 397–98).

11. *See, e.g.*, *Murray v. Just In Case Bus. Lighthouse, LLC*, No. 13SC722, 2016 WL 3390765, at *11 (Colo. Jun. 20, 2016) (The court explained that under Colorado Rule of Evidence 1006, which tracks the federal rule, "trial courts abuse their discretion when they admit summary charts that characterize evidence in an argumentative fashion rather than simply organize it in a manner helpful to the trier of fact." A summary exhibit that organized relevant facts chronologically was properly admitted, and some bold text on the exhibit did not render it misleading, inaccurate, or prejudicial. However, the trial court abused its discretion in admitting a summary chart that included the titles "'Things Mahoney Knew' and 'Things Mahoney Did NOT Know.' These titles characterized the evidence in an argumentative fashion, rendering [the exhibit] a demonstrative device that should not have been admitted as evidence. The chart's headings attempted to persuade the jury to assign more weight to certain evidence and reach particular conclusions." The summary was not offered "merely to aid the jury in understanding the events leading up to the case, but to persuade the jury of an ultimate issue—that Mahoney was unaware" of key facts in the case during key time periods.).

12. *United States v. Palazzo*, 372 F. App'x 445, 453 (5th Cir. 2010) (affirming trial court's decision to allow government's expert to use a chart displaying the number of hours per day the defendant claimed to have spent providing services billed to Medicare because these requirements were met); *see also Sharbono v. Hilborn*, 12 N.E.3d 530, 543 (Ill. App. Ct. 2014) (holding that the three limits on demonstrative evidence are relevance, fairness, and a proper foundation).

13. *Bray*, 139 F.3d at 1112.

14. *Id.*; *see also United States v. Kerley*, 784 F.3d 327, 341 (6th Cir. 2015) (holding that the trial court did not abuse its discretion in allowing the government to admit secondary-evidence summaries, which accurately summarized thousands of pages of previously admitted exhibits, into evidence, and noting that the district court properly instructed the jury that the summaries themselves were not evidence and were only as valid and reliable as the underlying documents); *Stafford v. United States*, No. 3:12-cv-0909, 2013 WL 140605, at *11–12 (M.D. Tenn. Jan. 11, 2013) (summaries including both admitted and nonadmitted doc-

uments would likely be classified as "secondary-evidence summaries" because they were not prepared entirely in compliance with Rule 1006, were more than pedagogical aids designed to simplify and clarify other evidence in the case, and were admissible in addition to the evidence they summarized because they so accurately and reliably summarized complex or difficult evidence and materially assisted the jury in better understanding the evidence).

15. Broun, *supra* note 10, § 212; *see Peeler v. KVH Indus., Inc.*, 13 F. Supp. 3d 1241, 1254 (M.D. Fla. 2014) (court allowed sketch drawn by testifying witness to go to jury room over objection, noting that jurors "had the benefit of observing the source of the sketch, its purpose, and the circumstances under which it was prepared"); *Intrastate Gas Gathering Co. v. Dow Chem. Co.*, No. 99-20603, 2001 WL 85920, at *2 (5th Cir. Jan. 26, 2001) (district court sent demonstrative charts to jury room although they were not admitted into evidence; court instructed the jury that they were "not additional evidence," but rather were "like arguments" and were "just an illustration"; appeals court found no abuse of discretion, stating that whether or not demonstratives are admitted into evidence, there is no error if the district court instructs the jury on the proper use of the materials); *United States v. Downen*, 496 F.2d 314, 319–21 (10th Cir. 1974) (court allowed a blackboard chart the government used in its opening statement to remain before the jury during trial and go to the jury room during deliberations; defendants argued on appeal that allowing the chart to go to the jury room was improper because it had not been admitted into evidence and was "extremely prejudicial"; appellate court disagreed, noting that whether demonstratives are sent to the jury room is within the trial court's discretion, and demonstrative aids, whether or not admitted into evidence, may be sent to the jury if accompanied by careful cautionary instructions as to their use and limited significance, as the trial judge did here); *Big John, B.V. v. Indian Head Grain Co.*, 718 F.2d 143, 149 (5th Cir. 1983) (holding that submission of demonstrative aids to the jury during deliberations is within the trial court's discretion); *Shane v. Warner Mfg. Corp.*, 229 F.2d 207, 210 (3d Cir. 1956) (holding that district court has discretion to submit a written computation of damages proposed by the plaintiff's counsel with careful instructions as to its use and limited significance); *United States v. Capers*, 61 F.3d 1100, 1107 (4th Cir. 1995) (holding trial court has discretion to send transcripts not admitted into evidence back to the jury).

16. *Baugh* ex rel. *Baugh v. Cuprum S.A. de C.V.*, 730 F.3d 701, 703, 705–06 (7th Cir. 2013).

17. *Id.* at 710 (referring to *Downen* and *Big John*).

18. *See, e.g., State v. Lord*, 822 P.2d 177, 194 (Wash. 1991) (en banc) (court held that when a chart is used for illustrative purposes, even if admitted into evidence, the jury should be instructed that the chart is not evidence and it should not go

to the jury room); *United States v. Perez*, No. 01 CR. 848 (SWK), 2003 WL 721568, at *14 (S.D.N.Y. Feb. 28, 2003) (district court did not allow defendant to use enlarged transcript of witness testimony during summation because the transcript had not been formally entered into evidence); *Glossip v. State*, 157 P.3d 143, 155 (Okla. Crim. App. 2007) (during witness testimony, prosecutor made notes on large sheets of paper in view of the jury and were left visible for the duration of trial; defense counsel requested they be preserved for appellate review, but trial court denied the request; appellate court found error, stating that if demonstratives are allowed at trial, then the trial court, upon request from a party, must ensure that the demonstratives are made part of the record as court exhibits); *State v. Burbank*, 297 S.E.2d 602, 603 (N.C. Ct. App. 1982) (on cross-examination, attorney showed his own identification card to the witness to demonstrate that the card's reflective surface creates glare; appellate court held that the trial court erred in allowing this demonstration because "[g]enerally, documents must be admitted into evidence before they can be used to illustrate or clarify testimony"); *State v. Rich*, 185 S.E.2d 288, 291 (N.C. Ct. App. 1971) (defendant attempted to use photographs in cross-examination that were neither offered nor introduced into evidence; appellate court upheld trial court's exclusion of the photos, holding that there is no "right" to use photographs not admitted into evidence, and that "[p]hotographs must be introduced in evidence before they may be used to illustrate testimony.").

19. *See, e.g.*, *United States v. Harms*, 442 F.3d 367, 375 (5th Cir. 2006) (stating that pedagogical charts should "not [be] admitted into evidence and should not go to the jury room absent consent of the parties"); *In re Woods*, 114 P.3d 607, 621 (Wash. 2005) (en banc) (in criminal case involving the use of autoradiograms to illustrate testimony about DNA, the court stated that "when an exhibit is used for illustrative purposes only and the jurors are instructed that the exhibit is not evidence, than [sic] the exhibit should not go to the jury room"); *Fuller v. State*, No. AP-73106, 2000 WL 35432767, *8 (Tex. Crim. App. Dec. 20, 2000) (affirming trial court's refusal to send charts used during expert testimony to the jury during deliberations because the charts were a demonstrative exhibit not entered into evidence); *see also* 2 Federal Evidence Practice Guide § 5.01[4] (Matthew Bender 2015) ("Demonstrative exhibits that are not admitted into evidence should not go to the jury during deliberation, at least not without consent of all parties."); *United States v. Poschwatta*, 829 F.2d 1477, 1481 (9th Cir. 1987) (district court admitted into evidence a pedagogical chart portraying defendant's income; appeals court found no error, explaining "although the better practice may have been for the court to allow the charts to be used as testimonial aids only, the district court did not abuse its discretion" because (1) the figures in the chart were already in evidence, (2) the defendant did not challenge the figures

and had the opportunity to cross-examine the witness who used the chart, (3) the charts assisted the jury in understanding the evidence, and (4) the chart was a reasonable method of presenting the evidence).

20. *See, e.g., Metcalf v. Bochco*, 200 F. App'x 635, 639 (9th Cir. 2006) (In a copyright infringement action, the court denied the plaintiffs' request made the day of closing arguments to present a chart to the jury demonstrating the similarities between the parties' work. The court relied on Local Rule 16-2.10 for the Central District of California, which required parties to exchange pedagogical aids at least ten days before trial. Without a showing of good cause for the late notice, the court denied the plaintiffs' request. The court of appeals held that the trial court did not abuse its discretion.); *see also* Me. R. Evid. 616 (In Maine, an illustrative aid may be excluded if opposing counsel is not given a "reasonable opportunity to object"; advisers' note explains that "reasonable opportunity" will vary with the circumstances, as a simple illustrative aid may not need to be disclosed until immediately prior to use, while a complex illustrative aid, such as a computer simulation, should be disclosed far enough in advance to allow opposing counsel to understand and appraise it.).

21. *Dahlberg v. MCT Transp., LLC*, 571 F. App'x 641, 646–47 (10th Cir. 2014) (in upholding trial court's exclusion of computer animations of automobile accident that plaintiff disclosed just before trial, appellate court relied on Rule 26 and noted that "'*any exhibits* that will be used to summarize or support' an expert opinion must be included in a timely expert report" (quoting Fed. R. Civ. P. 26(a)(2)(B)(iii))); *Lekkas v. Mitsubishi Motors Corp.*, No. 97 C 6070, 2005 WL 2989899, at *1 (N.D. Ill. Nov. 3, 2005) (court held that illustrative exhibits "summarize[] or support[]" an expert's opinion under Rule 26 and so must be contained in the expert's report and disclosed with other pretrial disclosures); *Bradshaw v. FFE Transp. Servs., Inc.*, 715 F.3d 1104, 1108–10 (8th Cir. 2013) (expert's anatomical illustrations were disclosed the evening before trial; on appeal, defendant argued the district court should not have allowed plaintiff's expert to use them during his testimony due to the lack of notice; appellate court declined to decide whether Rule 26 applied because the objection was not timely raised but said its application would be unclear because the expert did not file a report); *Estate of Thompson v. Kawasaki Heavy Indus., Ltd.*, 291 F.R.D. 297, 313–15 (N.D. Iowa 2013) (defendants produced over 10,000 photographs, one hour of video footage and dozens of illustrations after the deadline for expert disclosures but six weeks before trial. The plaintiffs sought to exclude the demonstratives due to the late disclosure. The court found that the defendant was required to disclose these aids in his expert's report under Rule 26 but allowed the defendant to use the visuals regardless. The court found no bad faith on the part of the defendants, noting that despite the plain meaning of

the rule, there was no controlling authority on the issue. The court further noted that the defendants made the experts available for depositions well after expert discovery closed, allowing the plaintiffs to question the experts on the issues relating to the demonstratives.).

22. 741 N.W.2d 256, 259 (Wis. Ct. App. 2007).

23. *Id.* at 260.

24. *Id.* at 262–63.

25. *Id.*

26. *See Tull v. Fed. Express Corp.*, 197 P.3d 495, 496–97, 501 (Okla. Civ. App. 2008) (On the date set by the trial court to exchange exhibits, the defendants gave the plaintiffs a computer animation they intended to use with an expert witness, although the defendants maintained the animation was a demonstrative and not an ordinary exhibit. Plaintiffs sought to exclude the animation, asserting they had insufficient time to review it before trial. The appeals court upheld the trial court's decision to allow the animation, finding plaintiffs were not prejudiced by the timing of the exchange. The court noted that the defendants disclosed, a month before trial, that their expert would use "charts, graphs, reports, and other materials during his testimony," and the defendants provided the animation six days before trial, on the deadline for other exhibits.); *VIP Customs Brokerage Servs., Inc. v. ADESA Importation Servs., Inc.*, 2006 WL 2482904, *9–10 (Mich. Ct. App. 2006) (plaintiff used a chart depicting financial information in closing argument and did not provide a copy to the defense until after trial; appeals court found no error in the plaintiff's use of the charts without providing notice because the charts were demonstrative aids and thus "were no different than the use of an easel or chalk board").

27. *See, e.g., Goodwine v. Nat'l R.R. Passenger Corp.*, No. 12-cv-3882 (TLM), 2014 WL 1010928, at *1 (E.D.N.Y. Mar. 17, 2014) (court ordered parties to exchange demonstratives no later than sixty days before trial, along with all other exhibits); *Dynetix Design Sols., Inc.*, No. C11-5973 PSG, 2013 WL 4537838, at *7 (N.D. Cal. Aug. 22, 2013) (on plaintiff's motion to exclude demonstratives exchanged later than six days before trial, court ordered that demonstratives for opening statements be disclosed by the close of business the day before trial, and all other demonstratives be disclosed twelve hours before their expected use); *Carnegie Mellon Univ. v. Marvell Tech. Grp., Ltd.*, No. 09-290, 2012 WL 6578412, at *2 & n.4 (W.D. Pa. Dec. 17, 2012) (in ruling on defendant's motion to strike plaintiff's PowerPoint slide for lack of notice, court noted that it had allowed counsel to agree on when such slides would be exchanged; parties had agreed to exchange slides and objections over email the night before use, and the court took no issue with this agreement); *In re Welding Fume Prod. Liab. Litig.*,

No. 1:03-CV-1700, 2010 WL 7699456, at *276 (N.D. Ohio Jun. 4, 2010) (court ordered disclosure of demonstratives one day prior to expected use); *Exime v. E.W. Ventures, Inc.*, No. 08-60099-CIV, 2009 WL 454278, at *4 (S.D. Fla. Feb. 11, 2009) (in a pretrial order, court required disclosure of demonstratives no later than five days before trial); *Christopher v. Tulsa Ambassador Hotel, L.L.C.*, No. 05-CV-500-JHP-SAJ, 2006 WL 3628038, at *4 (N.D. Okla. Dec. 11, 2006) (on a motion to reopen discovery, court ordered counsel to exchange demonstratives, along with all other exhibits, 34 days before trial); *United States v. First Data & Concord EFS, Inc.*, 287 F. Supp. 2d 69, 71 (D.D.C. 2003) (In scheduling and case management order, court required parties to serve demonstratives on all counsel at least 48 hours before their expected use at trial, unless otherwise agreed or ordered.).

28. *See, e.g.*, *Branch v. Cleveland Clinic Found.*, 980 N.E.2d 970, 972–73 (Ohio 2012) (trial court permitted use of a computer simulation of "brain mapping" based on data from surgeon's notes regarding the procedure despite minimal notice; intermediate appeals court reversed, but state supreme court reversed again, noting that the patient had access to the underlying data used to create the simulation and had the opportunity to cross-examine the clinic doctors regarding the simulation).

29. *Highland Cap. Mgmt., L.P. v. Schneider*, 551 F. Supp. 2d 173, 190 (S.D.N.Y. 2008) (excluding indices of phone conversations admitted into evidence because they were no more helpful to the jury than the CDs from which the recordings came and the transcripts of the conversations); *Contract Mgmt., Inc. v. Babcock & Wilcox Tech. Servs. Y-12, LLC*, No. 3:10-CV-110, 2012 WL 2529214, at *2 (E.D. Tenn. Jun. 29, 2012) (court allowed plaintiff to use two illustrative charts as long as they were accurate and relevant); *State v. Godley*, 535 S.E.2d 566, 573–74 (N.C. Ct. App. 2000) (in questioning the defendant about operation of gun used in crime, court precluded prosecutor's use of investigating officer's gun to "illustrate [the d]efendant's testimony"; defendant objected that the officer's gun was "entirely prejudicial and inflammatory," but the court precluded its use as irrelevant under Rule 401 because the prosecutor did not "establish any relationship" between the officer's gun and the gun used in the crime, other than relative size).

30. *United States v. Laplatney*, 157 F. App'x 93, 95 (10th Cir. 2005) (trial court excluded defense counsel's effort to cross-examine witness with federal sentencing guidelines because they were neither relevant nor probative, and could lead the jury to consider how the defendant might be sentenced if found guilty; appellate court agreed, and said even if they were relevant, the defendant failed to show they were material to guilt or innocence); *Hartsock v. State*, 322 S.W.3d 775, 778 (Tex. Crim. App. 2010) (in drunk-driving case involving images of a person's eyes

with and without nystagmus, court held that the three limits on "visual aid[s]" or "illustration[s]" are relevance, materiality, and Rule 403); *Schwamb v. Delta Air Lines, Inc.*, 516 So. 2d 452, 464 (La. Ct. App. 1987) (use of demonstrative aids during closing argument is within the discretion of the trial court as long as they are relevant and not unduly inflammatory, misleading, or prejudicial); *Fowler v. State Farm Fire & Cas. Co.*, No. 1:06CV489-HSO-RHW, 2008 WL 3050421, at *2 (S.D. Miss. July 25, 2008) (defendants sought to show jurors video footage of events that occurred fifteen to twenty-seven miles from plaintiffs' property during Hurricane Katrina; court excluded videos as irrelevant and unfairly prejudicial, noting with respect to relevance that the defendant had failed to make "a sufficient showing of similarity between the events depicted in the videos and what occurred at [p]laintiffs' property").

31. **Charts and diagrams:** *Bradshaw*, 715 F.3d at 1109–10 (anatomical illustrations permissible as long as they were not misleading; because expert was using them as pedagogical aids and not representations of the plaintiff's actual injury, the illustrations need not be "substantially similar" to the injury); *Young v. Oury*, 827 N.W.2d 561, 565–66 (S.D. 2013) (defendant-doctor used an illustrative chart showing the "type" of information he provides to patients; plaintiff-patient objected that the chart was prejudicial because the doctor had not presented that information to patient and argued the chart lacked the requisite foundation; court ultimately excluded the chart finding it lacked any probative value, lacked the necessary foundation, and was vague; appellate court affirmed). **Physical objects:** *State v. Ehrlick*, 354 P.3d 462, 475 (Idaho 2015) (FBI forensic artist made clay model of victim's head to show where victim sustained injuries, relative size and significance of injuries, and to determine whether the victim's head created a hole found in apartment wall; although model was slightly smaller than actual victim's head, court allowed the exhibit and appeals court affirmed, citing the "small differences in the measurements and the jury's awareness of those discrepancies"); *People v. Langley*, 649 N.Y.S.2d 21, 22 (N.Y. App. Div. 1996) (permitting use of a baseball bat as a demonstrative aid "after receiving testimony that the model bat was similar in appearance, size and weight to the one used by the defendant in the commission of th[e] crime"); *Flanagan v. Redondo*, 595 N.E.2d 1077, 1084 (Ill. App. Ct. 1991) (stating that models of human skeletons may be inadmissible without a proper foundation, but model in the present case was properly used with a witness who testified that the model was "a true and accurate and fair representation of the skeletal anatomy"); *State Farm Fire & Cas. Co. v. Sawyer*, 522 So. 2d 248, 252–53 (Ala. 1988) (trial court permitted expert to use a duplicate stove as a demonstrative; appellate court found that proper foundation had been laid because a witness testified that the duplicate was "a true and fair representation" of the actual stove). **Photographs, videos,**

and computer animations: *Dahlberg v. MCT Transp., LLC*, 571 F. App'x 641, 647 (10th Cir. 2014) (trial court excluded computer animations depicting the accident because they did not fairly and accurately depict the underlying evidence; appellate court affirmed, noting that "demonstrative aids may be effective in illustrating relevant information to a jury, assuming a proper foundation is laid," and that "[i]n assessing foundation in this context, courts consider (among other things) whether the proffered demonstrative exhibit 'fairly and accurately summarize[s] previously admitted competent evidence.'"); *Riley v. Ford Motor Co.*, No. 2:09-CV-148-KS-MTP, 2011 WL 3236109, at *4 (S.D. Miss. July 27, 2011) (in design defect case, plaintiffs sought to use videos and photos of a study with dummies in car accidents; court held that if the videos and photos were being used to illustrate general scientific principles, their use as demonstrative aids was permissible as long as they were not misleading by too closely resembling the accident at issue; if, however, the study was intended to illustrate the conditions of the disputed accident, it must pass the substantial similarity test); *Stumbaugh v. Am. Com. Lines LLC*, No. 08-1669, 2009 WL 2922312, at *6 (E.D. La. Sept. 9, 2009) (demonstrative photos did not have to be exact replicas, but if they bore no resemblance to what they purported to represent, they would not be "effective for the ascertainment of the truth"; court held that the defendant's use of photographs as demonstratives would "require a foundation of fairness and accuracy," the plaintiff "would have the opportunity to attack this foundation at trial," and if "the photos are permitted for demonstrative purposes, the Court will provide the jury with 'appropriate limiting instructions.'"); *State v. Williams*, 324 P.3d 1078, 1114 (Kan. 2014) (holding that the two general limits on photographs used as demonstrative evidence are relevance and foundation, and a proper foundation establishes that the scene in the photograph is "the same or substantially similar" to the conditions of the actual event); *State v. Perea*, 322 P.3d 624, 635–37 (Utah 2013) (The trial court precluded the defendant from using computer animations depicting the shooting "to visually represent [expert witness's] testimony" because the expert did not know who created the animations or how they were created. The state supreme court disagreed, noting that to be used as a demonstrative, a computer animation need only accurately reflect witness testimony. Here, the animation had a proper foundation because the expert confirmed that it accurately represented his testimony. Ultimately, the error was deemed harmless in light of other evidence in the case.); *Pitcock v. B & W Inc.*, 476 S.W.2d 83, 95 (Tex. App. 1971) (allowing photographs of a staged airplane flight, re-creating the actual flight at issue in the case, because photographs are "admissible as illustrative testimony" provided that a proper foundation has been laid through witness testimony that "the objects and situations portrayed are faithfully represented").

32. 741 N.W.2d at 265.

33. *Id.* at 264.

34. *Id.* at 265; *see also People v. Douglas*, No. 14CA0012, 2016 WL 1593891, at *1 (Colo. App. Apr. 21, 2016) (prosecution permitted to introduce animation depicting collision in hit-and-run case because it was substantially similar to the collision it depicted; video correctly incorporated details the trooper entered into the computer program, such as distances, surrounding terrain, relative speeds of the car and bicycle, and their paths of travel); *People v. Buckner*, No. B247411, 2015 WL 1577772, at *15 (Cal. Ct. App. Apr. 8, 2015) (upholding trial court's admission of video showing demonstration of sobriety tests because video was an accurate representation of sobriety tests performed on defendant); *Ryan v. Blakey*, 389 N.E.2d 604, 614 (Ill. App. Ct. 1979) (affirming the trial court's exclusion of an in-court demonstration, appeals court held that a reconstruction experiment must be "substantially similar" to the circumstances surrounding the actual event, and here there was no evidence establishing that the materials the expert would use in his in-court demonstration resembled the car's impacted fuel system, "nor was any evidence introduced showing that the experiment recreated the collision of the two vehicles.").

35. 860 A.2d 1003 (N.J. Super. Ct. App. Div. 2004).

36. *Id.* at 1006.

37. *Id.* at 1011–12.

38. *Id.* at 1011–12.

39. *Id.* at 1012.

40. *See, e.g.*, *Hartin v. State*, No. 09-07-00547-CR, 2009 WL 1076799, at *3-4 (Tex. App. Apr. 22, 2009) (excluding chart defendant sought to use in closing argument explaining "beyond a reasonable doubt" with a colored column featuring gradations of proof; appellate court affirmed exclusion because the chart could have misled or confused the jury about the standard of proof); *Fowler*, 2008 WL 3050421, at *2-3 (defendants sought to show jurors video footage of events that occurred fifteen to twenty-seven miles from plaintiffs' property during Hurricane Katrina; court excluded videos as irrelevant and unfairly prejudicial, noting the videos would "likely mislead and confuse a jury, and could improperly suggest that what happened in the videos necessarily took place at [p]laintiffs' property"); *Raritan Radiological*, 860 A.2d at 1011–12 (The trial court's decision to allow the use of "super-magnified" medical images was reversed on appeal because the large size "had the clear potential to confuse the jurors and distract them from assessing defendant's actions under the correct standard of care." The appeals court found the images "unduly influential, potentially confusing,

susceptible of being accepted as substantive evidence, and clearly capable of producing an unjust result.").

41. *See, e.g.*, *Johnson v. United States*, 118 A.3d 199, 206–07 (D.C. 2015) (The trial court allowed the government's expert to testify with slides explaining the characteristics of DNA, how it is tested, and how the results are analyzed. The defense had objected that the slides were misleading because they did not discuss false positives, lacked information on error rates for DNA testing, and did not explain why the accused individual's DNA was found only on certain parts of the gun. In allowing use of the slides, the court determined they would be helpful to the jury and were not misleading but gave the jury a limiting instruction that trial evidence was to be given more weight than the demonstrative slide presentation if the two were contradictory. The appeals court upheld the trial court's determinations.); *Sheffield v. United States*, 111 A.3d 611, 625 (D.C. 2015) (During witness testimony, the government had a male witness put on a black ski mask and stand next to a photo of another man wearing a black ski mask to demonstrate that an eyewitness to the shooting at issue could have mistaken the two men. The trial court found that the demonstration was relevant to the eyewitness's testimony and that the demonstration was more probative than prejudicial. The appellate court found that the demonstration was not an abuse of discretion, holding that a demonstrative aid is permissible if it is relevant and the probative value of the demonstrative is not substantially outweighed by the danger of unfair prejudice.); *Colgan Air, Inc. v. Raytheon Aircraft Co.*, 535 F. Supp. 2d 580, 585–86 (E.D. Va. 2008) (allowing expert to use a mock-up of a portion of an aircraft to explain how the mechanics work even though its size did not reflect the actual size and position of the parts; court found the mock-up would assist jurors in assessing causation, and that differences between the mock-up and actual aircraft could be addressed in cross-examination); *United States v. Gardner*, 611 F.2d 770, 776 (9th Cir. 1980) (In this tax evasion case, the defendant argued that he was unduly prejudiced by the government's use of a chart summarizing his assets, liabilities, and expenditures as a testimonial aid for a government witness. The witness who presented the chart was examined and cross-examined extensively regarding how the figures on the chart were determined and the sources from which the information was derived. All of the facts and calculations that the chart summarized were admitted as evidence. The circuit court found that it was well within the discretion of the trial court to allow the chart's use because the defendant had the full opportunity to "challenge the facts, figures, calculations, and underlying documents upon which the chart was based," and because the chart "contributed to the clarity of the presentation to the jury, avoided needless consumption of time and was a reasonable method of presenting the evidence."); *State v. Gutierrez*, 726 N.W.2d 542, 563–64 (Neb. 2007) (abrogated on different

grounds by *State v. Thorpe*, 783 N.W.2d 749 (Neb. 2010)) (trial court permitted prosecution to display a chart depicting the personal and business relationships of the many people involved in the case over defense objection; appellate court affirmed the trial court's exercise of discretion, finding clear support in the record for the information in the chart and noting that the chart helped the appellate court during its own review of the trial record); *Martin v. Nabors Offshore Corp.*, No. 00-3284, 2002 WL 34360292, at *4 (E.D. La. Apr. 2, 2002) (in personal injury suit with causation at issue, trial court permitted defendant's expert to use a chart showing plaintiff's five-year medical history, giving an appropriate limiting instruction to explain that the chart is not evidence but rather is a tool to assist the defense in presenting its theory of the case); *Commonwealth v. Rickabaugh*, 706 A.2d 826, 837 (Pa. Super. Ct. 1997) (in closing argument, government used chart titled "Rickabaugh Cocaine Organization," which was based on the testimony and evidence produced over a month-long trial supporting the government's argument that the defendant controlled a cocaine distribution network; appeals court held that the trial court did not abuse its discretion by allowing the chart upon finding it could assist the jury in understanding the evidence); *Brads v. First Baptist Church of Germantown*, 624 N.E.2d 737, 747–48 (Ohio Ct. App. 1993) (in breach of contract case, the plaintiff used "cartoonish caricatures concerning [his] termination with the [defendant] Church" during closing argument; appeals court upheld use of the drawings because they were not inflammatory; rather they were "simply used to illustrate the arguments of [the employee], much the same as writing on a blackboard"); *People v. Burrows*, 592 N.E.2d 997, 1022 (Ill. 1992) (During closing argument, the government displayed a chart with an arrow connecting the name of the defendant's lawyer to the name of another indicted individual to help the jury understand "how the many names in the evidence fit together." The state supreme court affirmed the trial court's decision to allow the chart because the evidence at trial established that the two individuals listed on the chart had, in fact, communicated. Therefore, the chart was not clearly irrelevant or unfair.).

42. *Spence v. State*, 129 A.3d 212, 220 (Del. 2015).

43. *Id.* at 223.

44. *See, e.g.*, *Hinton v. Outboard Marine Corp.*, No. 1:09-cv-00554-JAW, 2012 WL 243210, at *2-3 (D. Me. Jan. 25, 2012) (During a trial involving a boating accident, the plaintiff requested that the court exclude various demonstrative aids that were to be discussed by an accident reconstruction expert. The demonstratives included (a) a diagram of the boat's path, illustrating witness testimony; (b) diagrams of where people were positioned; (c) photographs showing how the plaintiff could have avoided injury, with text explanations; (d) a chart describing propeller-related fatalities; (e) a comparative chart of the relative risks of various

activities; (f) photographs of the boat accompanied by text stating, "boat NOT defective or unreasonably dangerous" and "11 years later, the ladder still does what it was designed to do" in bold font; and (g) a textual slide regarding facts not in dispute. The court found that under Rule 403, the photographs depicting how the plaintiff could have remained uninjured were appropriate, but the comments must be removed; the chart describing propeller-related fatalities was excluded because fatality rates were not relevant in a case where no one was killed and only served to emphasize how dangerous propellers are; and the photographs accompanied by boldface text could not be used during the expert's testimony but could be used during closing arguments.).

45. 362 F. Supp. 2d 1043 (N.D. Iowa 2005).

46. *Id.* at 1049.

47. *Id.* at 1056–57.

48. *Id.* at 1057.

49. *Id.*

50. *Id.* at 1059.

51. *Id.* at 1060–61.

52. *Id.* at 1060–62 (emphasis in original; internal citations omitted).

53. *Id.* at 1113 n.6, displaying images from the drug-trafficking trial of Johnson's boyfriend, Dustin Honken. The court explained that in Honken's trial, the court did not permit the government to use the full display of prosecution witness photos "because the issue of its use arose at the eleventh hour, immediately before final arguments, neither the defense nor the court had previously been shown the display, the defense strenuously objected to use of the full display on the grounds of surprise and prejudice, and there was little time for the court to reflect on the matter. The court did, however, permit the government to use individual photographs of witnesses during its closing argument. In the present case, the government has taken the precaution of raising prior to trial the issue of proper use of photographs of witnesses during trial and arguments. Therefore, after a fuller opportunity to consider the question, the court will allow the government to make limited use of the full display, as explained in the body of this order." *Id.*

54. *Id.* at 1063.

55. 461 F.3d 557 (5th Cir. 2006).

56. *Id.* at 561, 566.

57. *Id.* at 566.

58. *Id.* at 561.

59. *Id.* at 566; *see also Bradshaw*, 715 F.3d at 1109 (in vehicle accident case involving a neck injury, expert's use of anatomical illustrations was proper because the illustrations were merely pedagogical aids; as long as they were not unfair or misleading, they could be used as demonstratives).

60. *Muth*, 461 F.3d at 566.

61. *Id.* at 567.

62. *See, e.g.*, *Uniroyal*, 977 S.W.2d at 342 (holding that a timeline used by an expert was not hearsay because all of its content was already in evidence; court explained, "Charts and diagrams that summarize, or perhaps emphasize, testimony are admissible if the underlying information has been admitted into evidence, or is subsequently admitted into evidence.").

63. 934 N.W.2d 1089, 1092–94 (Ind. 2010).

64. *Id.* at 1093.

65. *Id.* at 1094 (quoting *Wise v. State*, 719 N.E.2d 1192, 1196 (Ind. 1999)).

66. *Id.*

67. 848 N.E.2d 1285, 1290 (N.Y. 2006).

68. *Id.* at 1287.

69. *Id.*

70. *Id.* at 1287–88.

71. *Id.* at 1290.

72. 177 S.W.3d 113 (Tex. 2005).

73. *Id.* at 122.

74. *Id.* at 120–21.

75. *Id.* at 121.

76. *Id.* at 122.

77. *Id.* at 121.

78. *Id.* at 121, 123–24.

79. *Id.* at 123–24.

80. *Id.* at 124; *see also State v. Daly*, 775 N.W.2d 47, 66–67 (Neb. 2009) (PowerPoint slides with diagrams, photos and videos explaining the effect of drugs on movement of the eyes in DUI case were not hearsay when used with testifying expert witness because they were not out-of-court statements offered to prove the truth of the matter asserted; rather, they were illustrative of the expert's in-court testimony, which was subject to cross-examination.).

81. *See Hinlicky*, 848 N.E.2d at 1291 (noting that the plaintiff did not request a limiting instruction); *cf. United States v. Mendez*, 2016 WL 1459194, at *4-5 (5th Cir. Apr. 13, 2016) (government projected pictures of the defendants on a screen while playing a recorded conversation and highlighted the speaker's photograph; Fifth Circuit upheld the trial court's approach of "explicitly and repeatedly advis[ing] the jury that the photographs represented only the government's contention" about each speaker's identity).

82. *See, e.g.*, *Stoker v. Stemco, L.P.*, 571 F. App'x 326, 327–28 (5th Cir. 2014) (In a Title VII race discrimination case, the defendant used a demonstrative chart in opening statement summarizing nine previous disciplinary actions taken against the plaintiff. The chart was given to plaintiff's counsel before trial, the court determined at that time it was a demonstrative aid, and the court said any objections must be made before the chart was presented to the jury. The plaintiff did not object to its use. Upon its use, the court instructed jurors that the chart was not evidence but merely summarized documents that would later be admitted as evidence. The Fifth Circuit upheld the trial judge's decision to allow the chart. The court reasoned that the plaintiff did not object before the demonstrative was used, the district court has "wide latitude to allow counsel to use a demonstrative exhibit that was later supported by evidence," and the district court gave an appropriate limiting instruction.); *United States v. De Peri*, 778 F.2d 963, 978–79 (3d Cir. 1985) (A group of police officers from the Philadelphia Police Department were charged with violating the Racketeer Influenced and Corrupt Organizations Act and the Hobbs Act, obstructing justice, and conspiring to extort gambling money. In its opening statement, the government used a chart with the defendants' names, service dates, and divisions. On appeal, one defendant argued that the chart deprived him of his right to a fair trial because it linked him to the conspiracy before evidence regarding the conspiracy had been introduced. The appeals court found no error in allowing such a demonstrative aid during opening statements because it avoided inadmissible evidence and reference to matters that could not be proven. The court noted that "such charts are often employed in complex conspiracy cases to provide the jury with an outline of what the government will attempt to prove."); *State v. Fairbanks*, 842 N.W.2d 297, 305–06 (Minn. 2014) (In a murder trial, the government used "several 'graphic' and 'disturbing' autopsy photographs" of the victim during opening statement. The defendant objected on the grounds that the use of the photographs during opening statement deprived the defendant of a fair trial. The appellate court held that, within the trial court's discretion, "photographs, documents, charts, and the like" may be used on opening statement provided that either (a) they have been preliminarily admitted into evidence or (b) "the court otherwise grants leave." Here, both options were satisfied: the trial court denied the defendant's motion

in limine to exclude the photos, and the trial court granted "leave of court" by overruling the defendant's objection at trial.).

83. *But see Riverside Hosp., Inc. v. Johnson*, 636 S.E.2d 416, 419 (Va. 2006) (state supreme court upheld trial court's decision to allow plaintiff's counsel to use bar graphs in opening statement over defendant's objection that they were not evidence; supreme court explained that "opening statement is argument of counsel and does not involve admission of evidence.").

84. 313 P.3d 243, 245 (Nev. 2013).

85. *Id.* at 247.

86. *Id.*

87. *Id.* at 245.

88. *Id.* at 247–48.

89. *See, e.g.*, *Master-Halco, Inc. v. Scillia, Dowling & Natarelli, LLC*, No. 3:09-cv-1546 (MRK), 2010 WL 1553784 (D. Conn. Apr. 19, 2010) (In responding to several objections to demonstrative aids that the plaintiffs intended to use during expert testimony, the court noted that while the parties "are free to use argumentative charts and summaries in their closing arguments, it would be improper to introduce argument through charts used by their experts." Therefore, the court stated that the permissible tone of a demonstrative may vary based on the point of trial in which it is used.); *United* States *v. Crockett*, 49 F.3d 1357, 1361-62 (8th Cir. 1995) (circuit court concluded the prosecutor's use of argumentative transparencies was not unfairly prejudicial because they were being used in closing argument and the judge had properly cautioned the jury; the court noted, however, that it "do[es] not encourage the use of such devices in the future" and that it "will necessarily be more inclined to reverse in a close case if the testimony has been unfairly summarized or the summary comes wrapped in improper argument.").

90. *See, e.g.*, *Friend v. Yokohama Tire Corp.*, 904 S.W.2d 575, 578–79 (Mo. Ct. App. 1995) (In an action regarding damage to property, the defendant created four illustrations that showed calculations of the amount of soil removed from the property. For example, one exhibit showed a picture of a dump truck followed by "x 122." The trial court excluded these during witness testimony but allowed them to be shown during closing argument because they were used as "illustrations of an argument." The appellate court found the use of the exhibits during closing argument to be improper, as they effectively presented new evidence in closing, and there was no indication that the exhibits accurately reflected any witness testimony.).

91. *See, e.g.*, Federal Rule of Evidence 611(a) ("The court should exercise reasonable control over the mode and order of examining witnesses and presenting evidence so as to: (1) make those procedures effective for determining the truth; (2) avoid wasting time; and (3) protect witnesses from harassment or undue embarrassment.").

92. *See, e.g.*, *Castaldi v. Land Rover N. Am., Inc.*, 363 F. App'x 761, 762 (2d Cir. 2009) (defendant sought to use a chart summarizing expert testimony that emphasized inadmissible facts relied upon by the expert; trial court allowed the chart, and appeals court found the trial court did not abuse its "broad discretion to determine the mode by which evidence is presented[,]" which "generally encompasses the authority to allow the use of demonstrative aids," where the court instructed the jury that the chart at issue was merely a demonstrative and not the proper basis from which to evaluate the quality of the expert's testimony); *Miller v. Hometown Propane Gas, Inc.*, 167 S.W.3d 172, 178 (Ark. Ct. App. 2004) (allowing attorney to "flick[] a Bic cigarette lighter on and off" in opening statement based on trial court's "wide discretion in determining whether to allow the use of a demonstrative aid").

93. *Poff v. Elkins*, 449 S.W.3d 315, 321 (Ark. Ct. App. 2014) (upholding trial court's exclusion of demonstratives during opening statement, even if such exhibits are allowed during trial); *B&B Med. Servs., Inc. v. United States*, No. 11-73C, 2011 WL 1882993, at *1 (Fed. Cl. May 17, 2011) (holding plaintiff could not bring a piece of equipment into the courtroom during oral argument because he was already being permitted to use photographs of the equipment and "there is no added benefit of having one present in the courtroom"); *S. Energy Homes, Inc. v. Washington*, 774 So. 2d 505, 515 (Ala. 2000) (upholding trial court's decision to allow counsel to "list the dates of the alleged telephone calls on a placard for the jury to see" because "this Court has consistently upheld the use of visual aids to illustrate testimony"); *Raney v. Suffolk Obstetrical & Gynecological Assocs., P.C.*, 606 N.Y.S.2d 729, 730 (N.Y. App. Div. 1994) (stating that "[i]t was within the trial court's discretion to refuse permission for the plaintiff's attorney to display a chart [contents unknown] to the jury during summation"); *Spence v. S. Pine Elec. Co-op*, 643 So. 2d 970, 972 (Ala. 1994) (permitting placards that displayed enlarged deposition testimony excerpts because "[t]he time, manner and character of . . . opening statement[s] . . . are within the trial court's discretion"); *Brown v. G&M Distribs., Inc.*, 461 N.E.2d 95, 100 (Ill. App. Ct. 1984) (upholding exclusion of a flip chart during closing argument because "the use of a flip chart during closing argument [is] within the sound discretion of the trial court"); *Schwamb v. Delta Air Lines, Inc.*, 516 So. 2d 452, 463–64 (La. Ct. App. 1987) (in closing argument, plaintiff's counsel showed the jury a cartoon of a suitcase falling from an overhead luggage bin onto a passenger and used it to argue "how

easily [the airline] could have warned its passengers of the danger" of overstuffed bins; appellate court affirmed trial court's decision to allow the exhibit, noting that the use of demonstratives during closing argument is within the discretion of the trial court provided they are relevant and not unduly inflammatory, misleading or prejudicial); *United States v. Posada-Rios*, 158 F.3d 832, 869 (5th Cir. 1998) (upholding trial court's decision allowing government to use summary and organizational charts throughout trial, noting it was "satisfied that Fed. R. Evid. 611(a) afforded the district court discretion to allow the government to use summary charts and organization charts"); *State v. Battle*, No. 8499, 1985 WL 7850, *2 (Ohio Ct. App. Mar. 7, 1985) (upholding trial court's decision to use a chart [undescribed] because "[b]lackboards or other visual aids can be used for illustrative purposes subject to the court's discretion").

94. 28 U.S.C. § 1920(4) provides: "A judge or clerk of any court of the United States may tax as costs the following: . . . (4) Fees for exemplification and the costs of making copies of any materials where the copies are necessarily obtained for use in the case[.]" *See also DiBella v. Hopkins*, 407 F. Supp. 2d 537, 539 (S.D.N.Y. 2005) (holding that the cost of producing demonstrative aids falls under section 1920(4)).

95. *See, e.g., Crandall v. City and Cty. of Denver, Colo.*, 594 F. Supp. 2d 1245, 1251 (D. Colo. 2009) (holding "such costs are still subject to the requirements that they be 'necessarily obtained' for use in the case and that the costs incurred be reasonable"); *Fresenius Med. Care Holdings, Inc. v. Baxter Intern., Inc.*, No. C 03-1431 SBA, 2008 WL 2020533, at *5 (N.D. Cal. May 8, 2008) (denying defendant's request for costs for "preparation of graphics, animation and illustrative materials" because he failed to demonstrate that the costs were necessary to the presentation of his case, even if the aids were helpful and simplified issues).

96. *Crandall*, 594 F. Supp. 2d at 1251 (citing *Leggett & Platt, Inc. v. Hickory Springs Mfg. Co.*, 149 F. Supp. 2d 394 (N.D. Ill. 2001)).

97. *See, e.g., Warner Chilcott Labs. Ireland Ltd. v. Impax Labs., Inc.*, Nos. 08-6304(WJM), 09-2073(WJM), 09-1233(WJM), 2013 WL 1876441, at *13 (D.N.J. Apr. 18, 2013); *Race Tires Am., Inc. v. Hoosier Racing Tire Corp.*, 674 F.3d 158, 169–70 (3d Cir. 2012) (in assessing whether an electronic discovery vendor's charges qualified as fees for "exemplification" under §1920(4), court distinguished between intellectual effort required to produce documents and the physical preparation thereof; held that services leading up to the production of electronic copies did not constitute "making copies," and thus only the costs of scanning and file format conversion were recoverable as the costs of making copies under the statute); *Romero v. City of Pomona*, 883 F.2d 1418, 1428 (9th Cir. 1989) ("Section 1920(4) speaks narrowly of '[f]ees for exemplification and copies of papers,' suggesting that fees are permitted only for the physical

preparation and duplication of documents, not the intellectual effort involved in their production."); *IMRA Am., Inc. v. IPG Photonics Corp.*, No. 06-15139, 2012 WL 6553523, at *5 (E.D. Mich. Dec. 14, 2012) (noting that demonstratives are especially necessary to the understanding of intellectual property cases and may be necessarily obtained for use in such cases, but court limited the costs to those resulting from the physical preparation of the demonstrative); *Pinasco v. California*, No. CIV S 09-0777, 2012 WL 6589801, at *2 (E.D. Cal. Dec. 17, 2012) (denying cost of animation, which was itemized on invoice as a "retainer" or "fees for preparation," because "[r]etainers and fees are the very 'intellectual efforts' the [9th circuit in *Romero*] found to be outside the scope of exemplification costs permitted by 28 U.S.C. § 1920.").

98. *See, e.g., Plantronics, Inc. v. Aliph, Inc.*, No. C 09-01714, 2012 WL 6761576, at *9-10 (N.D. Cal. Oct. 23, 2012) (disallowing cost of technical support and equipment rental to present visual aids during Markman hearing); *but see infra* note 100.

99. *Cefalu v. Village of Elk Grove*, 211 F.3d 416, 428 (7th Cir. 2000) (taxed as costs a computerized multimedia system used to present exhibits to the jury, rejecting the district court's distinction between physical preparation of the exhibits and the means of presenting them; circuit court stated, "Allowing fees for the cost of preparing the transparency but not for renting the projector would in this sense be a highly formalistic distinction, as each is key to the illustrative function of the exhibit." It further held, "So long as the means of presentation furthers the illustrative purpose of an exhibit, we believe it is potentially compensable as an exemplification."); *see also Alfonso v. SCC Pueblo Belmont Operating Co.*, No. 11-cv-01186-PAB-KLM, 2013 WL 1704294 (D. Colo. Apr. 18, 2013) (clerk allowed taxation of $800 that the defendant paid for a special-effects system to present evidence at trial, disagreeing with plaintiff's argument that the cost was not "reasonably necessary to the litigation" because the defendant's evidence could have been shown on the court's ELMO system; the court held that the information the defendant presented using the special-effects system was not redundant and that it aided the court and jury in understanding the evidence; court further held that it was not unreasonable for the defendant to assume that the jury might expect a visual presentation of the evidence, and $800 seemed reasonable for the service).

100. *DiBella*, 407 F. Supp. 2d at 540.

Index

M

N

O